Mummies
and
Mortuary
Monuments

# MUMMIES and MORTUARY MONUMENTS

A
Postprocessual Prehistory
of
Central Andean Social Organization

William H. Isbell

University of Texas Press
Austin

Copyright © 1997 by the University of Texas Press
All rights reserved
Printed in the United States of America

First edition, 1997

Requests for permission to reproduce material from this work should be sent to Permissions, University of Texas Press, Box 7819, Austin, TX 78713-7819.

♾ The paper used in this publication meets the minimum requirements of American National Standard for Information Sciences—Permanence of Paper for Printed Library Materials, ANSI Z39.48-1984.

Library of Congress Cataloging-in-Publication Data
Isbell, William Harris, 1943–
   Mummies and mortuary monuments : a postprocessual prehistory of central Andean social organization / William H. Isbell. — 1st ed.
     p.   cm.
   Includes bibliographical references (p.   ) and index.
   ISBN: 978-0-292-71799-2
   1. Incas—Funeral customs and rites.  2. Indians of South America—Andes Region—Funeral customs and rites.  3. Incas—Antiquities.  4. Indians of South America—Andes Region—Antiquities.  5. Sepulchral Monuments—Andes Region—History.  6. Social structure—Andes Region—History.  7. Andes Region—Antiquities.
I. Title.
F3429.I83   1997
306.9′0985—dc21                                      96-51237

for Judy
with my love
and
appreciation

●

CONTENTS

Acknowledgments
xiii

I
On Knowing the Past
1

II
Royal Mummies of Inca Cuzco
38

III
Ancestor Mummies in Huarochirí
69

IV
Competing Theories of *Ayllu* Origins
101

V
The Open Sepulcher
136

VI
Distribution of Open Sepulcher Monuments
158

VII
The Open Sepulchers of Chota-Cutervo
214

VIII
Origin of the *Ayllu* and the Andean Past
284

Bibliography
317

Indexes
359

# ILLUSTRATIONS

## Maps

| | |
|---|---|
| 1.1. The Central Andes | 17 |
| 2.1. The Inca Empire | 39 |
| 3.1. Huarochirí and Early Colonial Locations | 73 |
| 5.1. Open Sepulchers and *Huaca* Cemeteries | 145 |
| 6.1. Open Sepulcher Sites in the South-Central Andes | 164 |
| 6.2. Open Sepulcher Sites in the Mid-Central Andes | 178 |
| 6.3. Open Sepulcher Sites in the North-Central Andes | 206 |
| 7.1. Location of the Chota-Cutervo Region | 216 |
| 7.2. Chota-Cutervo Area | 217 |

## Figures

| | |
|---|---|
| 1.1. Central Andean Chronology | 19 |
| 2.1. Inca Burial | 42 |
| 2.2. Burial in Chinchaysuyu | 43 |
| 2.3. Celebrating the Dead in Chinchaysuyu | 44 |
| 2.4. Burial in Collasuyu | 44 |
| 2.5. Burial in Condesuyu | 45 |
| 2.6. Burial in Antisuyu | 45 |
| 2.7. Inca Royal Dynasty | 59 |
| 5.1. Huallanay Open Sepulcher | 151 |
| 5.2. Quebrada de la Vaca Open Sepulcher Mortuary Monument | 154 |
| 5.3. Orientations of Open Sepulcher Entrances, Toconce Site | 155 |
| 6.1. Open Sepulcher from Sillustani, Puno | 165 |
| 6.2. Open Sepulcher from Paucartambo, Cuzco | 179 |
| 6.3. Open Sepulcher from Kachiqhata, Ollantaytambo, Cuzco | 180 |
| 6.4. Rock Shelter with Open Sepulcher, Chicha-Soras Valley | 183 |
| 6.5. Open Sepulchers of the Huarochirí Area | 193 |
| 6.6. *Kullpi* House-Tomb from Canta, Lima | 194 |
| 6.7. Callejón de Huaylas Open Sepulcher, Tornapampa Site | 197 |
| 6.8. Callejón de Huaylas Open Sepulcher from Honcopampa | 202 |
| 6.9. Cerro Amaru Mausoleum, Huamachuco | 207 |
| 6.10. Burial Towers at Marcahuamachuco, Huamachuco | 208 |
| 6.11. Niched Hall in Late Style, Early Intermediate Period, Marcahuamachuco | 209 |
| 6.12. Utcubamba Open Sepulcher | 212 |

| | |
|---|---|
| 7.1. Ideal Chota-Cutervo *Chullpa* | 220 |
| 7.2. Condorcaga Sculptural Detail | 223 |
| 7.3. Wire Frame Perspective of *Chullpa* Types | 228 |
| 7.4. Platform and *Chullpa* at Condorcaga | 230 |
| 7.5. Condorcaga Tower 1 | 232 |
| 7.6. Condorcaga Relief Sculptures | 233 |
| 7.7. Negropampa *Chullpa* | 238 |
| 7.8. Negropampa Relief Sculptures | 241 |
| 7.9. Chetilla Tower 1 | 244 |
| 7.10. La Torre Tower 1 | 249 |
| 7.11. La Torre Tower 1 Relief Sculptures | 252 |
| 7.12. La Torre Tower 2 | 256 |
| 7.13. La Torre Tower 2 Relief Sculptures | 259 |
| 7.14. La Torre Sculptures | 264 |
| 7.15. La Torre Decorated Ceramics | 266 |
| 7.16. La Torre Plainware Ceramics | 267 |
| 7.17. Pérez Bocanegra Diagram of Inca Kinship | 274 |
| 7.18. Four-Generation *Ayllu* Marriage Cycle | 277 |
| 7.19. Four-Generational *Ayllu* Kinship Structure | 278 |
| 7.20. *Ayllu* Kinship and Chota-Cutervo *Chullpa* Types | 280 |

## Photographs

| | |
|---|---|
| 6.1. Altiplano Phase *Chullpa* at Malcoamayo, Puno | 167 |
| 6.2. Chuquito-Inca Phase *Chullpa* | 167 |
| 6.3. Sillustani *Chullpas* | 168 |
| 6.4. Cutimbo *Chullpas* | 170 |
| 6.5. Excellent Masonry of *Chullpa* at Cutimbo | 171 |
| 6.6. *Chullpa* of Adobe near Coro Coro, Bolivia | 172 |
| 6.7. *Chullpa* at Chiar Jakke, La Paz | 172 |
| 6.8. Rough Stone *Chullpa* near Sandia | 174 |
| 6.9. *Chullpa* at ColoColo, near Patanbuco, Sandia | 175 |
| 6.10. "Village" of *Chullpas* above the Site of ColoColo | 176 |
| 6.11. *Chullpa* with Human Remains | 177 |
| 6.12. Mummy from a Cave near Saqsamarca, Ayacucho | 184 |
| 6.13. Megalithic Chamber in Cheqo Wasi Sector of Huari | 185 |
| 6.14. Cheqo Wasi Megalithic Chamber | 186 |
| 6.15. Overview of Megalithic Chambers at Cheqo Wasi, Huari | 186 |
| 6.16. Wilkawain "Temple," the South Face | 199 |

| | |
|---|---|
| 6.17. Wilkawain "Temple," the North Face | 199 |
| 6.18. Wilkawain "Temple," the West End | 200 |
| 6.19. Interior of the Wilkawain "Temple" | 200 |
| 6.20. Group of Multistoried "Temples" at Honcopampa | 203 |
| 6.21. Largest *Chullpa* at Honcopampa | 203 |
| 6.22. Niche Tombs, Ventanillas de Otusco, Cajamarca | 210 |
| 6.23. Entrance to a Chambered Shaft Grave at Kolketín | 211 |
| 6.24. Interior of Chambered Shaft Grave at Kolketín | 211 |
| 7.1. Chetilla Tower 1, Masonry of the East Face | 221 |
| 7.2. Unfinished Sculpture from Condorcaga *Chullpa* | 224 |
| 7.3. Chetilla Tower 1, Original Form of Chota-Cutervo *Chullpa*s | 225 |
| 7.4. Condorcaga *Chullpa* Showing Aligned Doorways | 231 |
| 7.5. Condorcaga *Chullpa*, East Side, Sculptures B, C, and D | 235 |
| 7.6. Condorcaga *Chullpa*, West Side, Sculptures E and F | 236 |
| 7.7. Condorcaga *Chullpa*, North Side, Unfinished Sculpture | 237 |
| 7.8. Negropampa *Chullpa*, East Side, Sculptures A and B | 239 |
| 7.9. Negropampa *Chullpa*, North Side, Sculptures C and D | 240 |
| 7.10. Chetilla Tower 1, West Side, Second Floor Doorway | 245 |
| 7.11. Chetilla Tower 1, South Side | 246 |
| 7.12. Chetilla Tower 1, Interior of First Floor, South End | 247 |
| 7.13. La Torre Tower 1, Southeast Face | 248 |
| 7.14. La Torre Tower 1, West Side | 250 |
| 7.15. La Torre Tower 1, Sculpture B | 251 |
| 7.16. La Torre Tower 1, Sculpture A | 253 |
| 7.17. Moche Ceramic Feline Sculpture (from Lothrop 1964: 165) | 254 |
| 7.18. La Torre Tower 1, Sculpture C | 255 |
| 7.19. La Torre Tower 2, West Wall, Sculptures A, B, and C | 257 |
| 7.20. La Torre Tower 2, West Wall, Profile Feline | 258 |
| 7.21. La Torre Tower 2, West Wall Sculptural Group | 260 |
| 7.22. La Torre Tower 2, Northwest Corner, Sculptures C and D | 261 |
| 7.23. La Torre Sculptures in Modern Buildings | 262 |
| 7.24. La Torre Sculpture in Modern Chapel Facade | 263 |
| 7.25. La Torre Stelelike Sculpture | 265 |

# Acknowledgments

I want to thank my wife Judy for convincing me that this study of mortuary monuments, ancestor mummies, and the *ayllu* should be a book rather than several articles. Judy encouragingly read drafts of the text. Her sense of logic, penetrating questions, and many ideas helped me sharpen my thoughts and improve the presentation. Her encouragement was unfaltering and much appreciated. My dear friends Alberto and Scarlet Carbajal and their family contributed immeasurably. Their home in Lima has been my home. Alberto is very knowledgeable about Andean archaeology, and we have shared many experiences since we excavated together at Garagay in 1973–1974.

I greatly appreciate Theresa May's efforts to get the manuscript to publication. Best has been the opportunity to work with two outstanding referees who read the draft for the University of Texas Press. Tom Dillehay and Clark Erickson were both willing to identify themselves and to correspond with me as I revised the work for publication. I learned a great deal from them, and they helped me improve the final manuscript.

The information presented in this book was collected over a generation. In 1966 Don Lathrap encouraged me to undertake an archaeological survey in Sandia, east of Lake Titicaca, where I first discovered *chullpa* burial monuments. I also visited Sillustani and other great mortuary monument sites on the *altiplano* for the first time during that year. My research in Ayacucho did not focus on mortuary monuments, but I had many occasions to photograph them and make observations. Under Tom Zuidema's direction in 1967, and with my first wife, Billie Jean Isbell, I conducted ethnography in Chuschi, but I also visited mountaintop sites in the Río Pampas Valley that included caves containing mummies, as well as a few *chullpa* buildings. I will never forget the month-long walking trip with Salvador Palomino, Ulpiano Quispe, and Tom Zuidema, when we visited and photographed modern villages, colonial documents, prehistoric ruins, and local collections of artifacts in the hands of community schoolteachers. Our trip took us from Chuschi, across the Pampas River suspension bridge to Sarhua, and on to San José de Huarcaya, Saqsamarca, Huanca Sancos, and other communities.

In the remote *puna* of Huanca Sancos we attended a week-long *herranza de ganado* of the *cofradía* herds that numbered nearly a thousand sheep. This event reconstructs the collective identity of the entire settlement. Over subsequent months in Chuschi I attended the *herranzas* of extended families, revealing to me the nested structure of the village and its reconstitution in annual rituals. I suspect that in Peru's central highlands today symbolic meanings once created in *ayllu* ancestor worship have transformed into rituals of protection and multiplication for herd animals and their mountain deity patrons—the *wamani*.

In 1969 I excavated Jargampata in the San Miguel Valley, and on my days off I visited key sites that included *chullpa*s, often with my host, Alvino Añaños. I thank the National Science Foundation and Fulbright-Hayes Foundation for financial sponsorship.

From 1973 to 1981 I focused on investigating Huari. My colleague Mario Benavides shared with me many of his thoughts regarding his excavations of the stone chambers at Cheqo Wasi. Other archaeologists who had spent years at the Universidad Nacional San Cristóbal de Huamanga, and especially Enrique González Carré, Duccio Bonavia, and Luis Lumbreras, informed me about mountaintop sites throughout Ayacucho, where *chullpa*s occur. With my Peruvian students from San Cristóbal, and my North American students from the State University of New York's Binghamton University, we traveled throughout the highlands visiting many of these sites. Chief among these students and collaborators were Katharina Schreiber, Patricia Knobloch, Anita Cook, Abelardo Sandoval, Sabino Arroyo, Pablo de la Vera Cruz, Raúl Mancilla, and Apolonio Flores. My work in Ayacucho was made possible by grants from the National Science Foundation, the National Geographic

Society, the Fulbright Foundation, and Binghamton University, as well as cooperation from San Cristóbal de Huamanga.

In 1987 I cleared and excavated at Honcopampa in the Callejón de Huaylas. César Aguirre, director of the Museo Nacional de Ancash, was profoundly helpful and became a good friend. I was accompanied in the research by Sabino Arroyo, Pablo de la Vera Cruz, and Hartmut Tschauner, while Alberto Carbajal provided logistical support. Steve Wegner and Joan Gero offered stimulating discussion about the area, as did John Topic with his Huamachuco perspective. The Heinz Foundation sponsored the program, in which we excavated one mortuary monument and photographed and recorded many others in the course of our work.

In 1991 I recorded *chullpa* sites in Chota-Cutervo, sponsored by Binghamton University. Alberto Carbajal accompanied me, as did archaeologist Daniel Morales, whose knowledge of the region was invaluable. Penny Vavura of Binghamton University's Anthropology Department wrote a bachelor's thesis on Chota-Cutervo iconography, working with me to create many of the computer drawings reproduced in this book.

During the 1990s I have worked in the Bolivian *altiplano*. Thanks are due to Oswaldo Rivera, Clark Erickson, Carlos Ponce Sanginés, Johan Reinhard, Amy Oakland, Alan Kolata, Christine Hastorf, Marc Bermann, and the Tiwanaku crew for important contacts and aid. I particularly recognize my current co-investigator, Juan Albarracin-Jordan, with whom I have had exciting discussions about *chullpa*s and *ayllu*s. Dwight Wallace first convinced me of the inadequacy of the Tiwanaku ceramic chronology, and his influence figured prominently in my new choice of the Tiwanaku problem. Karen Mohr Chávez and Sergio Chávez have taught me a great deal, and I have enjoyed visiting their field projects over the years. Eduardo Pareja accompanied me in 1992 on an excursion to identify sites that might yield a new Tiwanaku ceramic sequence. But we also visited several *chullpa* remains that I was anxious to explore because of interests promoted by long conversations with John Hyslop, Catherine Julien, and Susan Niles. David Browman has been a source of inspiration and a colleague with whom I love to test controversial ideas.

Special recognition is due to Tom Dillehay and his conference "Tombs for the Living" that I attended at Dumbarton Oaks in October 1991. My thinking was especially stimulated by Frank Salomon's paper, and subsequent discussion contributed by Dorothy Menzel, John Rowe, and Patricia Lyon. Dr. Menzel's comments alerted me to the Quebrada de la Vaca data, and I thank Fritz Riddell for lending me unpublished material from his and Menzel's original excavations as well as later research he and his co-workers conducted at the south coastal site. John Verano's work revealed new directions, as did that of Jane Buikstra and Joseph Bastien.

In 1993 I organized a symposium at the Society for American Archaeology meetings in St. Louis to present the argument that ancestor mummies and open sepulchers were the material cultural components of *ayllu* organization. In addition to my position statement, papers were presented by Charles Stanish, Lisbet Bengtsson, Juan Albarracin-Jordan, Tom Zuidema, Daniel Sandweiss, and John Topic. I am grateful to them and to everyone who participated in the heated discussion that followed.

While I have never met Mary Doyle, her doctoral dissertation contributed greatly to my recognition of the essential links among the *ayllu*, the ancestor mummy, and the open sepulcher. I hope she publishes her historical study for everyone to enjoy. Finally, I want to state that many colleagues have contributed to my thinking, such as John and Theresa Topic, John Hyslop, Ramiro Matos, Mike Moseley, Charles Stanish, Richard Burger, Shelia and Tom Pozorski, Jeff Quilter, Charles Hastings, Craig Morris, Patricia Netherly, Chris Donnan, Mario Rivera, John Rowe, Alana Cordy-Collins, Jim Richardson, Tamara Bray, Richard Schaedel, Irene Silverblatt, Gray Graffam, Catherine Allen, Enrique Mayer, Richard Daggett, Tom Patterson, Hernán Amat, Gordon McEwan, Rogger Ravines, Izumi Shimada, John Murra, Jeff Parsons, Scott Raymond, Bill and Barbara Conklin, Dorothy Menzel, Katharina Schreiber, Duccio Bonavia, Helaine Silverman, Tom Zuidema, Gary Urton, Luis Lumbreras, Tony Aveni, Elizabeth Benson, Brian Bauer, Patricia Lyon, Lucy Salazar Burger, Ruth Shady, Paul Goldstein, Robert Feldman, and others.

Of course, I profoundly appreciate my stimulating colleagues in the Department of Anthropology at SUNY's Binghamton University, especially those with whom I have taught jointly. Ann Stahl is developing exciting ideas about evolution and history in culture change. Randy McGuire's Marxist thinking challenges me. Charles Cobb has helped me deal more clearly with political economy. Peter Stahl is my area colleague, who never lets me forget about site formation processes, ecology, and rigorous laboratory methods. Susan Pollock has stimulated my methodological focus and ideas about gender. Carmen Ferradás, with whom I teach Concepts in Anthropology, and Richard Antoun, with whom I have taught Symbolic Anthropology and Archaeology, contribute continually to my theoretical understandings. Jane Collins, a former departmental colleague, and Michael Painter, formerly of Binghamton's Institute of Development Anthropology, deserve credit for promoting my critical thinking about "Andean culture" and recent processes of change in the Andes. My current students read the book, in draft form, for my seminar on Andean prehistory. I thank them—especially JoEllen Burkholder, Emily Stovel, Tom Besom, Catherine Bencic, and Tyler O'Brien—for stimulating discussion, penetrating questions, and careful proofreading.

I have many debts of gratitude, but most of all I thank my colleagues and students for helping to make anthropology and the Andean past such fascinating topics. Of course, I accept responsibility for the way the archaeological and historical information has been interpreted.

Mummies
and
Mortuary
Monuments

CHAPTER

I

On
Knowing
the Past

We live in the twentieth century. Obviously this imposes limitations on what we can know about the past, but can we nonetheless understand how people lived in prehistoric times? Can we know how humans acted or apprehend why cultures of the remote past changed the way they did? The job of archaeologists is to construct human prehistory, but how do we inform ourselves about peoples and cultures long dead, who left no written accounts? How reliable are our methods and our results? Native South Americans of the central Andes—most of what today is Peru and Bolivia, as well as northern Chile, northwestern Argentina, and a part of Ecuador—did not use writing, and their digital, knotted string records called quipus may never be deciphered. Are archaeological understandings of the pasts of these ancient men and women nonetheless accurate and reliable?

In this book I propose a new vision of the Andean past, arguing that the currently popular narrative, based on the theory of processual cultural evolutionism, is inadequate. I plan to show that these inadequacies result from depending too much on theories and assumptions about the past and not enough on material remains provided by the archaeological record. Consequently, much of this book is a discussion of archaeological remains that support my vision of the Andean past, but I must also consider the theoretical and methodological sources of error in the popular representation of the Andean past and at the same time show that my approach to knowing the past is philosophically sound. Consequently, my discussion of what happened in the Andean past is accompanied by discussion and critique of how we know what happened.

My examination of the Andean past seeks to determine the origin, history, and nature of the *ayllu*. This lineagelike social grouping appears to have been the virtually universal unit of Andean social organization, above the level of the household, when Spanish invaders seized the Inca Empire early in the sixteenth century. Today many indigenous Andean peoples are still organized into *ayllu* groups, and a popular conviction among anthropologists and archaeologists is that *ayllu* organization is an ancient and fundamental—even an essential—feature of Andean culture. As we will see, archaeologists affirm the origin of *ayllu* organization thousands of years ago, and many believe that its unique and unchanging structure provided both the context and constraints within which inequality and hierarchy developed, shaping a singularly Andean kind of economy, state, and social system (cf. Moseley 1992: 42–72).

Questioning this representation of the *ayllu* in the Andean past involves looking beyond archaeological remains to the methods and theories archaeologists use to know when the *ayllu* originated and its development through time. I must show you that *what* archaeologists know about the past is a function of *how* we know the past. Our theories and assumptions about the past influence what and how we investigate, the way we study artifacts and other material remains, and how we think about prehistoric lives and social relations. Consequently, representations of the Andean past are not objectively constructed from "facts" that are free of bias. Facts are constituted in terms of what we observers consider to be relevant, so our investigations and visions of the past express our convictions about the nature of culture as well as culture change. This means that to adequately critique current ideas about *ayllu* antiquity and evolution, and to offer an alternative hypothesis, I must examine and critique the way of knowing—the theories and assumptions in terms of which the past of *ayllu* organization has been constructed. This is not an easy task, for most assertions about early *ayllu* origins do not include discussion of material remains or even explicit arguments. Claims are simply stated, making it necessary for me to infer the logical processes behind them, deconstructing the thinking and presenting it as a set of statements that articulate a general theory for knowing the past. Only then may I look for inconsistencies and inadequacies in the approach, to determine what a superior theory and approach should include. My procedure is similar to that of feminist anthropologists and archaeologists who are combating androgynous theories of culture that construct pasts without women by first revealing the logic and assumptions of a popular theory so its inadequacies can be exposed and amended (Conkey and Gero 1991; Conkey and Spector 1984; di Leonardo 1991; Spector 1993; Wylie 1991).

Exposing the inadequacies in processual evolutionary interpretations of *ayllu* antiquity is my point of departure for an alternative theory and approach to the past that is based on postprocessual archaeological thinking. It makes different assumptions and suggests a much later origin for the *ayllu*. I can then ask which of the two representations of the past better accounts for the archaeological record and determine this by an examination of the archaeological remains, much as scientists test competing hypotheses.

We will track the *ayllu* through Andean time and space using architectural remains from a distinctive kind of mortuary monument that housed the mummy of each *ayllu* founder. The history implied by this archaeological record will be used to test the processual "ancient *ayllu* hypothesis" of the Andean past, as well as my postprocessual alternative, "the recent *ayllu* hypothesis." I hope that determining which representation of the past best corresponds with the archaeological record will also indicate which theoretical approach, processual or postprocessual, performs better. Review of the archaeological remains then constitutes a test of culture historical hypotheses as well as the theoretical approaches responsible for generating them, providing a basis for preferring one kind of theory for knowing the past over the other. If archaeological facts are not "objective," if their collection and interpretation are not free of theory, our problem, of course, is whether testing competing accounts in terms of the "data," to determine which is superior, is a valid procedure or is simply an example of vicious, circular thinking.

Archaeologists inform themselves about the prehistoric past using three sources of information. The first and principal source, and indeed the only direct information about prehistoric people, is the archaeological record. It consists of the material remains as well as the relationships and associations among these remains left by the prehistoric peoples as a result of their daily activities. Many things are manufactured by humans to create and communicate social information. Landscapes and monuments such as palaces and tombs are especially good examples, but less grandiose objects like the pins with which Andean women fastened their wrap-around clothing or the ear spools worn by elite Inca men communicated gender, status, ethnicity, and other information about social relations. In the words of Clifford Geertz (1973: 452), rather than being data, these cultural material remains are like an "ensemble of texts" that may be "read" by archaeologists (Conkey 1990: 10–12; Moore 1988; Tilley 1989: 111–112, 1994: 29–34). Other remains from the past may not have been intended to communicate information. For example, while a family's trash may never have been intended to signal anything, family trash nonetheless contains information about gender, status, and ethnicity, as well as diet, demography, work organization, and much more. In fact modern people consider their trash extremely private, and celebrities must sometimes go to extremes to protect it from news reporters. Thus the trash of prehistoric peoples is also a text to be read by prehistorians.

However, a meaning for a prehistoric text is constructed by the reader, from information the reader brings to the reading and from relationships among the objects that constitute the text. Assumptions about universals of human symbolic communication—use of metaphor, synecdoche, and other tropes to construct meaning—play an important role, but the more the prehistorian knows about the people and the culture responsible for the archaeological record, the more s/he can read in the texts of prehistoric refuse. As Geertz (1973: 453) explained, ". . . societies, like lives, contain their own interpretations. One has only to learn how to gain access to them."

Since reading and interpreting the remains of the prehistoric past depends on knowledge that archaeologists have as much as it depends on the archaeological record, the second basis for archaeologists' knowing the prehistoric past is information about people and cultural activity. This information comes from studies of recent and modern cultures that have been observed and from comparative generalizations about how humans think and act. Especially valuable is information from modern or recent cultures that belong to the same tradition as the prehistoric societies under study or cultures judged to be similar for other reasons—for example, the people lived in the same sort of natural or social environment. Archaeologists refer to this approach to the past as analogical reasoning. It is based on the conviction that human culture is systemic in nature, so if some observable similarities exist between a source culture (a modern or historic people whose culture has been described) and a subject culture (a prehistoric group whose artifacts and remains are known from archaeological studies) then other similarities are also likely to have existed that cannot be observed directly in the archaeological remains (Ascher 1961; Binford 1967; Strong 1936). For example, if some artifacts from a prehistoric subject culture are similar to those used by shamans in a recent source culture, analogical reasoning would suggest the existence of shamanistic beliefs among the people of the prehistoric culture, even though beliefs leave no direct physical record for archaeologists to recover. Similarly, if a prehistoric village plan closely resembles the plans of recent Amazonian communities characterized by moiety organization, moiety division could be inferred in the past. Of course, the security of an analogical inference of this sort depends on the strength of the relationship between the observable material remains and the unobservable activities and beliefs (Wylie 1985, 1988).

Archaeologists bring another kind of knowledge to the material texts of prehistory—the third source for knowing the prehistoric past. This is anthropological theory about the nature of culture as well as the way cultures are organized and change through time. For example, processual archaeology is founded on Lewis Binford's (1962, 1964) assertions that culture is the means by which humans adapt to natural and social environments. Culture change is understood as the functional response of institutions to adaptive pressures. This theory of cultural evolutionism goes on to indicate that egalitarian societies precede rank societies, and they are associated with simpler material cultures as well as little or no surplus food production. Similarly, state government is associated with economic classes and private property, while chiefly organization relates to economic redistribution (Sanderson 1990; Stocking 1968, 1974). These examples should show that while there is a real difference between analogical inferences about individual past cultures and theoretically based assumptions about the nature of culture, in practice the two ways of knowing the past virtually merge at the point of cultural generalization accepted as theoretically correct. For example, many rituals observed by anthropologists enhance and legitimize the prestige and power of a political office, and the centralization of power in a leadership office is a key feature of state formation processes. When archaeologists infer that evidence for prehistoric rituals documents the concentration of power in leadership offices, is that an interpretation based on evolutionary theory or analogical reasoning? Clearly, both contribute. I take the position that such inferences are based on theoretical expectations.

Returning to anthropological and archaeological theory as a means of knowing the past, we must recognize that theory influences the way archaeologists make observations of the past, the questions they ask of the material texts, their structures for organizing information, and the relationships that they privilege. Does this mean that archaeologists can never be sure that an interpretation is correct?

In recent years anthropology and archaeology have become deeply concerned about this question of validation, as positivist assumptions about the ability to make objective observation have been discredited. Clifford Geertz (1973) promoted the study of culture as texts, launching a school of literary anthropologists who have gone beyond his original realist orientation. Taking a more constructionist position, they argue that culture is interpreted and that this process is not objective or scientific and cannot lead to explanation. Rather, the task of the ethnographer is to interpret meaning and write the experience of cultural "otherness" without reducing it to the reader's knowledge (Clifford 1988; Clifford and Marcus 1986; Crapanzano 1992; Geertz 1973, 1983, 1984; Marcus and Fischer 1986; Rabinow 1977; Rosaldo 1989; Tyler 1986). The goal is value-free understanding, recognizing that facts are theory-laden and theories are socially constituted. Since science and objectivity must be rejected there is no basis for judging one interpretation of a culture truer than another.

Literary anthropology's epistemological relativity and denial of scientific goals is under attack (D'Andrade and Scheper-Hughes 1995; Kuper 1994; Roscoe 1995), and Stephen Reyna (1994) argues that a postpositivist approach to explaining and validating the experience of reality, employing "relative correspondence," does allow anthropologists to differentiate superior propositions from less satisfactory accounts.

> ... validation is never that of a single theory and always that of alternative explanations of the same realities. This means that theories are always judged against other theories. It is a question therefore of relative validation. A theory which accounts for more observations while encountering fewer counterfactual observations than its alternatives is of greater approximate truth than its rivals. (Reyna 1994: 557)

Archaeological theorizing has followed a course similar to anthropology but perhaps even more acrimonious. Insistence on a scientific archaeology based on a logical positivist search for the laws of culture, using a hypothetico-deductive method (Binford 1962, 1964; Fritz and Plog 1970; Watson, LeBlanc, and Redman 1971), characterized processual archaeology during the 1960s and 1970s. The contradictions and inconsistencies of positivism and the hypothetico-deductive methods of this archaeology were pointed out by philosopher Alison Wylie (1981) at about the same time that postprocessual archaeology was born in Britain as a response to such naive scientism (Hodder 1982a, 1983, 1985, 1986, 1989, 1991; Shanks and Tilley 1982, 1987a, 1987b). Internalizing the knowledge that "facts" are not free of theory and that interpretations of the past can never be completely objective was an important step toward a mature discipline of archaeology. It has resulted in new insights, such as critical archaeology (cf. Leone 1995). Literary archaeology emphasized the analogy between material remains of the past and an "ensemble of texts," promoting constructive discussion of meanings in archaeological remains. Rather than focusing almost exclusively on quantitative description and adaptive explanations of institutions, postprocessual archaeology put people as human actors into the past.

But the literary approach to archaeology is also promoting a relativism about knowing the past that threatens to merge archaeology with entertainment and political propaganda. In its extreme form, all interpretations—or experiences—of the past must be equally valid, and the only criterion for selecting alternative representations, other than internal consistency of the argument, is relevance in the present. And, of course, relevance usually turns out to be defined by the author's political agenda. Current debate does not make it completely clear whether any of the literary archaeologists actually advocate such an extreme position, but Michael Shanks (1994) argues that the role of archaeology is to produce "heritage," communicating emotive experiences of the past that resonate with local presents. Experience of the past may be based on selected remains, perhaps a single pot, and it requires that the archaeologist "us[e] the present to reconstruct the past" (Shanks 1994: 40). But make no mistake; this is not analogical reasoning as described above, which involves systematic arguments from observed similarities between source and subject cultures. Shanks's use of the present means that the past should be interpreted in terms of the social tensions of the author's society, such as contemporary issues of nationalism, gender identity, racial ideology, ethnicity, and class conflict.

Critical validating procedures are not discussed, so I conclude that "anything goes" just so long as an interpretation is relevant to present interests—interests of constituencies the author wants to entertain, inspire, or promote. But many postprocessual archaeologists, in spite of their rejection of positivism, *are* expressing concern about verifying their representations of the past, as well as critiquing theories on which they are based (cf. Hodder 1991: 10; Shanks and Tilley 1989: 43–44). Peter Kosso (1991) has shown that the hermeneutic practices of many literary archaeologists share the same fundamental concerns of verification through testing propositions that characterize processual research. Alison Wylie (1992b; see also 1989) shows that accounts of the past by processual and by postprocessual archaeologists frequently turn out differently than expected, so outcomes must not be completely determined by theory. Furthermore, both approaches critically evaluate the security of the arguments relating remains to interpretations and consider the independence of different parts of an argument (Wylie 1992b: 278–281). Wylie refers to this validation procedure as "mitigated objectivity."

While "mitigated objectivity" is certainly not the scientistic objectivity assumed by positivist archaeologists during the 1960s, it nonetheless provides an acceptable basis for evaluating alternative proposals about the past. Several postprocessual literary archaeologists have begun to redefine their project, renaming it "interpretative archaeology" (Hodder 1991; Tilley 1993), and I suggest that interpretative archaeology recognize "mitigated objectivity" and "relative correspondence" as its validating tools. This, I believe, is the archaeology of the future. Mitigated objectivity furnishes a meaningful way to evaluate data and interpretations in terms of the theories and methods by which they were constituted. Relative correspondence allows us to compare alternative interpretations against data—data already validated by the mitigated objectivity approach—determining which "accounts for more observations while encountering fewer counterfactual observations" (Reyna 1994: 557).

To know the past, the archaeologist may proceed by constructing a mental vision and narrative description of the past, employing many theories and collecting as much archaeological information as possible. What is important is that theories used to define data are independent of the theories used to interpret them. For instance, the archaeologist's theories about site formation processes and about style and communication will certainly determine the "data" from a stratigraphic excavation and a ceramic classification. But if these theories are independent of interpretive theories—demographic theory of state formation or the Friedrich Engels/Eleanor Leacock (Engels 1972) theory of gender inequality and private property—archaeological argument is not becoming viciously circular. Even when the same theory contributes to the construction of data and their interpretation, security can be evaluated by critiquing the reliability of the theory.

The archaeologist may go on to explore the implications of the vision and narrative, using theory and analogy to develop its logical entailments and conceptualize relationships that should follow—relationships that should be observable in the prehistoric remains. Eventually the archaeologist returns to independently constituted archaeological description. Can the anticipated relationships be identified? Do details resonate with broad patterns, or are there inconsistencies? What is inconsistent? In what ways? Might inconsistencies disappear in light of different initial theories? If inconsistent data do not reshape under questioning, what revisions of the initial vision would be more consistent with the remains? Do such revisions ring true in terms of what anthropologists know about later descendants of the culture and believe about human cultural behavior generally? What new information would support or negate the interpretation, and can this information be collected? Once the vision is revised, has independence been maintained, and what are the implications of this new representation? Finally, competing visions or accounts are compared. Which offers a better fit with the archaeological data? Of course, this will probably require evaluation of competing constructions of the archaeological record. But such evaluations are not arbitrary, for they employ the same criteria of independence and security.

What I am describing is a hermeneutic circle—not a logically vicious circle—in which the archaeologist works back and forth between a representation of the past and the texts of the archaeological record, theories and assumptions, generalizations about culture, analogical arguments, details and general patterns, always conscious of the security and strength of the theories, as well as the independence of their applications. Interpretations can improve as inconsistencies and contradictions are worked out, and the security of supporting arguments is increased. Competing interpretations can be judged in terms of performance against data. In this way the archaeological record does not speak for itself; it speaks with voices given it by archaeologists, but those voices need not succumb to naively circular positivism or to extreme epistemological relativism. We can determine that some representations are superior, for they fit the archaeological record better than others. In this fashion I will evaluate the "ancient *ayllu* hypothesis" against my "recent *ayllu*" alternative. The competing hypotheses' relative correspondence will be evaluated with archaeological information collected and presented in terms of a mitigated objective approach.

Now that we have identified the epistemological grounding for this study, let us consider the question of where the archaeologist enters the interpretative circle of learning about the prehistoric past. In addition to the archaeological record, the basis for anthropological knowledge has been a spectacular corpus of information about human societies, cultures, and behavior—the ethnographic record. Hunters and gatherers from southern Africa, the Arctic, Australia, the American Great Basin, the Amazon, and elsewhere have been described in detail. Farmers from the Americas, New Guinea, eastern Asia, and elsewhere, as well as pastoral and agropastoral societies of northern Asia, Africa, and the Middle East, are part of the record. Chiefdoms and rank societies have been described in Oceania, Central America, and other world regions. Kingdoms and preindustrial cities from Africa, Mesoamerica, Asia, and the Andes have been subjects of anthropological study. These descriptions cannot contain all the variation possible in human culture, but they contain a great deal from which archaeologists may draw to understand the prehistoric past. Assuming cultural uniformitarianism—that the processes at work in cultures of the present were at work among cultures of the past—the ethnographic record prepares archaeologists to read the texts of the past. However, not all modern or historically described cultures are similar to the prehistoric peoples under investigation, so archaeologists must decide which descriptions to employ and which to ignore. How does the archaeologist judge what cultural descriptions are most likely to resemble the particular cultures of the past s/he is investigating?

It is generally agreed that if a historical or modern people belong to the same cultural tradition as the producers of some archaeological remains, cultural similarity is more likely (Ascher 1961; Strong 1933, 1935). Continuity with the past will almost certainly be assumed if the customs of the contemporary survivors are primitive by contrast with those of the modern intruders (for a critical discussion of these issues see Stahl 1993). Cultural comparisons may also be made with unrelated modern cultures, especially if they occupy a similar environment and the means of production appear to resemble those of the prehistoric culture. In such cases other things like family organization or status differentiation may also be similar. But we are now moving from the domain of cultural description to that of theory about how cultures work.

As we resolved above, theoretical ideas about the nature of culture determine to a large extent the way we extract and read the texts of the past, and they shape the visions of the past that we construct. For example, what is the relevant unit for description and analysis? Why and how does culture change? What are actual sources of information about change and the past? Regarding the unit of analysis, the theory of processual cultural evolutionism asserts that human behavior is shaped by cultural institutions. If so, individual humans may be more or less irrelevant to the study of culture and the past. It is the institution that adapts. Culture change is adaptation to the physical and social environment by natural selection favoring behavior routines that produce more energy or manage resources more effectively. Because of their powerful norms and adaptive advantages successful old institutions (marriage, patrilineal kin groupings, etc.) remain virtually unaltered. If not extremely impacted by foreign cultures in modern times, deep cultural patterns remain unchanged for hundreds and perhaps even thousands of years. Jacqueline Solway and Richard Lee (1990) argue that San-speaking Bushmen of Dobe have resisted such pressures, retaining an ancient and traditional hunting and gathering lifestyle. Finally, implicit in the theories of many evolutionists is the conviction that adaptive behavior arises by adding new and usually more complex institutions better able to meet environmental challenges (cf. Carneiro 1962; Steward 1955). Complex cultures must therefore be collections of institutions that appeared at different times in their histories. In a sense, then, surviving cultures are time capsules, containing the institutional building blocks that were added one by one over millennia.

This evolutionary perspective represents one way of thinking about the prehistoric past. Alternatively, some anthropologists believe that people make informed choices about action (Barrett 1988; Giddens 1979, 1981, 1984). Intentional meanings and significance given to objects and practices inform the strategies of individual actors, who construct and reconstruct culture in the recurrence of their daily activities. If this is so, people, not institutions, are the units that must be studied by archaeologists (Hodder 1991). Furthermore, culture must be quite plastic in its constant reproduction under the pressures shaping informed action. Traditional cultures of the contemporary world could not possibly encapsulate their own developmental sequence (Hanson 1989; Hobsbaum and Ranger 1983; MacGaffey 1986; Thomas 1992). Rather, the past and its cultural changes must be understood in terms of contingent histories. For example, the San Bushmen have reinvented hunting and gathering in a complex and heterogeneous history of peoples' responses to pressures and opportunities of European colonialism (cf. Schrire 1980, 1984; Wilmsen and Denbow 1990).

We may begin informing ourselves about the Andean past with culture theory, with modern or recent cultural descriptions that may be uniform with the past, and with the archaeological record. But whatever avenue provides the entry, continued study requires all three. In the to and fro circle the archaeologist works from text to inference using cultural theory and description to frame questions and make data meaningful. A narrative vision of the past is tested by rereading the material texts in terms of new insights provided by that vision. Inconsistencies and inadequacies must be dealt with, often stimulating field research to search for additional archaeological remains and theoretical discussion to improve thinking about culture, time, and change. A new synthesis or vision of the past must emerge, and then another reevaluation. Many archaeologists believe that through this process of back and forth reevaluations the vision comes more and more to represent the real past (Trigger 1989; Watson 1986), while other scholars describe the evaluations as revealing some visions to be more plausible than others (Wylie 1985, 1988).

## AYLLU, *BUILT ENVIRONMENT,* AND THE ARCHAEOLOGICAL RECORD

The subject of our study is the *ayllu* in Andean prehistory. What was the *ayllu*? Determining its essence has been the goal of many authors, and even whole conferences (Casenelli et al. 1981). There are numerous descriptions of *ayllu* organization from modern and recent Andean communities (Albó 1972; Allen 1988; Bastien 1978; Gillet 1992; Harris 1978, 1982; B. J. Isbell 1974, 1978; Klein 1993; Molinié-Fioravanti

1986; Platt 1982a, 1982b; Rasnake 1988; Rowe 1946; Urton 1984, 1988, 1992) as well as from historical documents (Espinoza Soriano 1981; Marcus and Silva 1988; Murra 1975a, 1980; Rostworowski 1978, 1981a, 1988; Rowe 1946, 1985a, 1985b; Salomon 1991, 1995; Sherbondy 1982, 1992; Spaulding 1984; Valcárcel 1925; Zuidema 1990c). What is clear is that when the Spanish arrived Andean peoples were grouped into *ayllu*s that shared certain features with the family and lineage, the ethnic group, and even the kingdom. They ranged from quite small in size to tens of thousands of members, and at least some may have been hierarchically nested, with minimal *ayllu*s combined into *ayllu*s, and *ayllu*s combined into maximal *ayllu*s, albeit all simply and confusingly called *ayllu*s.

The Incas used *ayllu*s as administrative units within their empire, creating a confusion between *ayllu* and *pachaca*, the Inca number 100 that was used to designate a unit of that many taxpayers. Later, the Spanish Viceroyalty also used *ayllu*s as administrative units. Most scholars are convinced that both empires appropriated the *ayllu*s from older traditions, bending them only slightly to their own use. But today the features of *ayllu* organization are highly variable. Many local communities divide into constituent *ayllu*s that organize the labor of their members for communal tasks, from seasonal rituals to constructing roads and managing irrigation works. Obligations are shared out among the *ayllu*s by tradition or by agreements among *ayllu* leaders so that obligation corresponds with the current size or wealth of the membership, which rarely exceeds 100 persons (cf. Urton 1984, 1988). In other areas an *ayllu* may include thousands of people and participate in a complex regional structure governing access to land, multicommunity political organization, or periodic ceremonies (cf. Platt 1982a, 1982b; Rasnake 1988). In some places *ayllu* members recognize one another as kin, but elsewhere they may simply live next to one another. In other communities they occupy a territory; in still other places members are identified by last names (cf. Allen 1988; B. J. Isbell 1978).

Some scholars argue that the ancient essence of the *ayllu* was communal holding of lands, in which all members received usufruct rights for their family's subsistence (Espinoza Soriano 1981; Rowe 1946). Other scholars focus on the existence of a leader. But for every generalization about the *ayllu* there seem to be examples that are contrary. However, the point to be realized from this long search for a definition capturing the essence of *ayllu* organization is that it is based on an assumption of long-term uniformity in Andean culture. A defining essence of the *ayllu* can only be discovered if the *ayllu* is characterized by unchanging institutions with resolutely established norms. In fact, a search for the essence of the *ayllu* precludes a theory of culture that recognizes heterogeneity of informed action by individuals or, more simply stated, the contingency of history.

Like the much debated Bushmen, we cannot be sure that the *ayllu* has retained an unchanged essence into modern times. Consequently, I plan to virtually ignore modern and recent descriptions of the *ayllu*. To discover prehispanic properties of the *ayllu* I will focus on the earliest descriptions, hoping to minimize the effects of profound changes imposed by Spanish colonization. Readers will have to wait until the end of Chapter 3 for my definition of the *ayllu*. First we must examine the earliest historical descriptions—those from early-sixteenth-century Cuzco (Chapter 2) and the information from late-sixteenth- and seventeenth-century Huarochirí (Chapter 3). On the basis of these ethnohistorical descriptions, along with the political, religious, and economic pressures that were affecting *ayllu* organization, I will define the *ayllu*. But my definition describes the *ayllu* in the historically specific context of the sixteenth and early seventeenth centuries. And it is this *ayllu*, of sixteenth-century Cuzco and seventeenth-century Huarochirí, that I trace into the archaeological past. I make no claims to archaeologically track some other kind of *ayllu*, the hypothetical "essential *ayllu*" or archaic *ayllu*-like ur-institution.

Our review of Andean ethnohistory will show that European invaders' earliest descriptions of Andean societies establish a firm link between *ayllu* organization and mortuary monuments of a particular kind. This relationship has not been recognized and employed previously for interpreting the archaeological past of *ayllu* organization. However, this approach to *ayllu* prehistory that uses the built environment offers exceptional possibilities for a whole new vision and understanding. Mortuary monuments are durable material remains and excellent texts from the past. Formal transformations of the built environment are created by humans to channel social activities, to establish categories, and to promote emotions and meanings (Agnew and Duncan 1989; Appaduri 1988; Gupta and Ferguson 1992; King 1980). Formal organization of space established with buildings of various types—among them mortuary monuments—creates durable contexts for periodic activities that construct and reconstruct culture. Changes in the form, organization, and use of built environments are key parts of strategies to construct, enhance, or contest power (Duncan 1990; Feld 1982; Gad and Holdsworth 1987; Gupta and Ferguson 1992; Karp and Lavine 1991; Markus 1993; Rodman 1992). Human experience is spatial and temporal, and knowledge seems to be organized in terms of experiences linked to sequencing an individual's activities in places (Gell 1992; Relph 1976; Rodman 1985). People construct space in terms of meaningful "place," in which the built environment plays a structuring role. In fact, Peter Wilson (1988) asserts that the space and the built environment provide the geometry and tropes in terms of which we understand human relations. One's family members are usually said to be "close," while friends are only a little more distant, authority is high or low, politics is right or left. Power is narrow or broad, and sometimes overarching. Command may be pyramidal, linear, or branching, and it may be strong or flimsy.

The dead also play important roles in modeling human relations (Dillehay 1995b). The dead represent the past, and as such they are the authority of tradition. When combined with the built environment and the activities it channels, bodies of the dead become powerful symbols presencing certain meanings. This may be less apparent in our modern societies accustomed to a tradition of municipally administered public cemeteries where the dead from different parts of the society are brought together and almost completely separated from the living. Today it is even common to speak of the "disposal of the dead." This approach to the dead can probably be traced to crowded cities of thirteenth-century Italy, with subsequent spread though Europe to replace the thousand-year-old pattern that linked the living with the dead in the saint's church and churchyard cemetery, while equally segregating living and dead residents of a city on the basis of these patronal affiliations (Colvin 1991: 364–374). The public cemetery reached more or less its current form in the urban environment of nineteenth-century capitalism, which emphasizes secularism and egalitarianism, relegating the dead to a status having little significance for the living. After all, today's dead no longer control capital.

But this has not been the human condition throughout the past. Resourceful actors have not missed the opportunity to construct power and authority by manipulating space, the built environment, and bodies of the dead—even bodies not yet dead. In 28 B.C. Caius Julius Caesar Octavianus, who was soon to become Augustus, was building himself a monumental mausoleum in the Campus Martius of Rome. This was among the city's most prestigious public spaces, and only one or two of Rome's most famous men had been buried there before. For Caesar, constructing a mausoleum for his body was more than an assertion of his importance and power, for these were already confirmed. Caesar was reconstructing social space, with new actions and relations that would promote his imperial dynasty at the center of what had been a republic (Colvin 1991: 43).

Like Caesar and the Romans, Andean peoples used mortuary monuments and bodies of the dead to create new social space as well as new social and political relations. However, as I will argue, they used the bodies not just to promote centralized state authority, but to contest it and to defend kin group interests. Many of the monuments involved in this construction of social behavior survive into the modern archaeological record. They are the texts from the past that we will read. They are also the physical structures and organizing geometries created by builders and repetitively used by actors to promote new meanings, to create and contest power, and to construct new social and political relations. As archaeologists we enjoy the unparalleled opportunity to construct a new vision of the past on the basis of the same buildings that prehistoric peoples fabricated to create the new social relations we seek to understand. This approach offers spectacular insights and understandings.

## THE SPACE-TIME CONTEXT FOR AYLLU PREHISTORY

An Andean culture area was firmly identified by Julian Steward when, as editor of the *Handbook of South American Indians*, he devoted one volume to "The Andean Civilizations" located in the region of western South America that is dominated by the Andes mountains. According to Steward (1946: xxv), Andean peoples were responsible for indigenous civilization, for the evolution of complex societies had begun before the beginning of the Christian era. The greatest social development was in the central Andes of Peru, western Bolivia and northern Chile, and the northwest corner of Argentina (see Map 1.1), an area that culminated in the Inca Empire. Significantly, it was also in this area that native peoples most successfully survived European invasion and colonial extinction. Today large populations of indigenous peoples exercise strong cultural influence on the modern nation states of the central

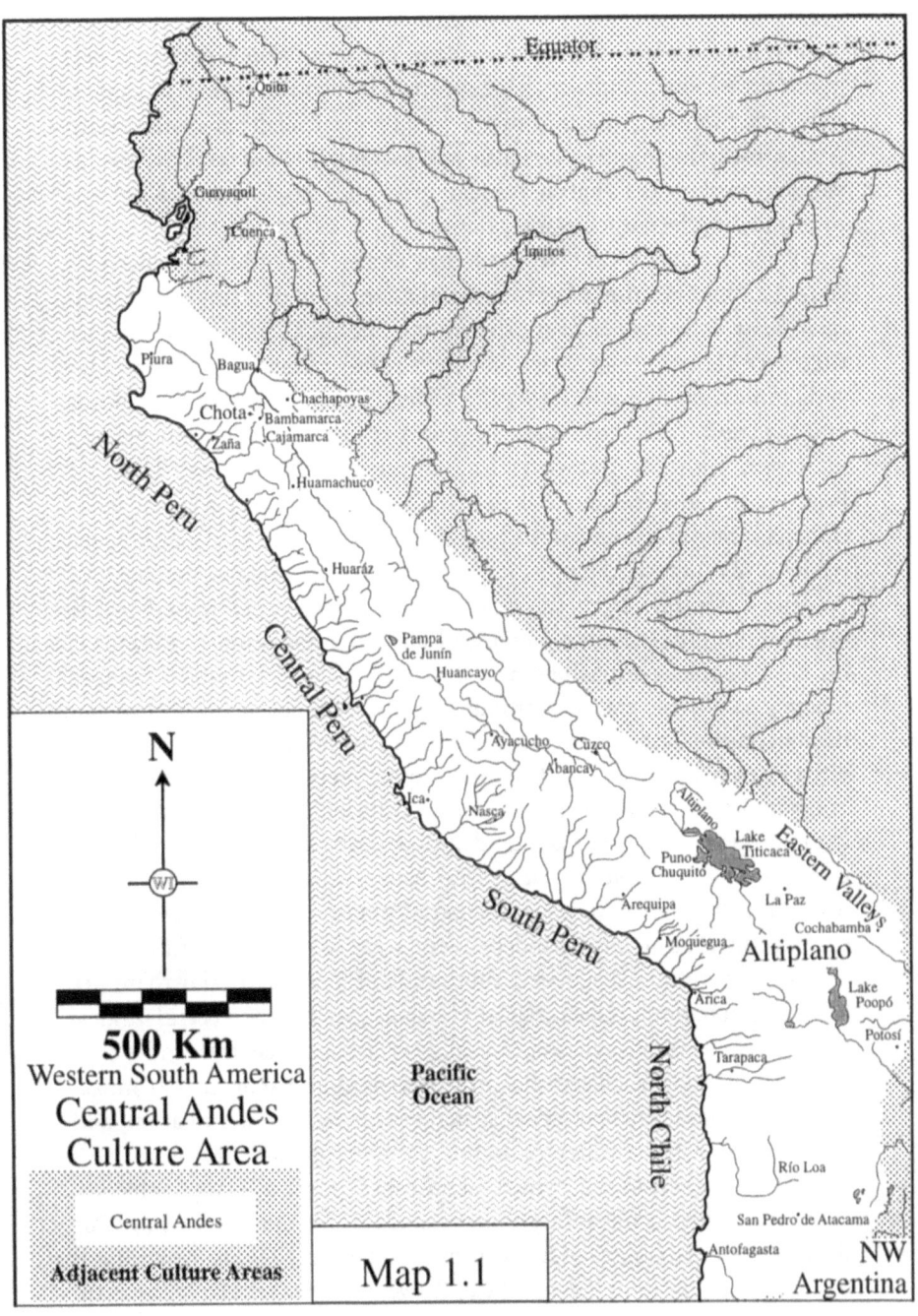

Map 1.1. The Central Andes

Andes. In the south Andes of central Chile and adjacent Argentina there were somewhat less developed Andean cultures, whose prehistory remains little known and who have survived into modern times in smaller numbers. Similarly, the impressive prehistoric kingdoms of the north Andes, including modern Ecuador and Colombia, have received less investigation than the central Andean past, and native peoples are less prominent in the contemporary nations.

Since Steward's time research has shown that the central Andes shared a long tradition of agropastoral adaptation to a similar environment as well as a great deal of economic, political, and social interaction over thousands of years (Bennett 1946; Lumbreras 1974b; Masuda, Shimada, and Morris 1985; Willey 1971). Peoples of the north and the south Andes adapted to somewhat different environments and interacted with the central Andean cultures less intensively. They are best recognized as related, but more or less independent, cultural traditions, at least until the Incas conquered much of the north and south Andes a few decades before the Spanish invasion. At that time central Andean colonizers from the heart of the empire were settled in the north and south Andean regions, and Inca administration was imposed on local people, establishing a thin veneer of central Andean culture. Coming to us from this Stewardian construct, the culture of central Andean peoples—or more correctly a normative and ideal construct somewhat resembling culture in the ethnographic present, as created by early anthropologists—is known as "Andean culture." Contrary to the seeming implication, the name is intended to describe the long cultural tradition of only the peoples of the central Andes. Cultural traditions of the north and the south Andes participated only modestly and should be seen as constituting largely independent areas of cultural tradition.

Andean culture originated thousands of years ago, and there are long and complex archaeological chronologies for the central Andes. Unfortunately, the conviction that all peoples of the central Andes participated in Andean culture has not prevented archaeologists from establishing unique chronological structures for each modern nation, and sometimes for every valley or basin. To avoid undue confusion I will employ only one scheme, which I find most universally applicable because it is based on absolute time periods, not evolutionary stages or the distinctive attributes of local cultural sequences. This is the chronology proposed by John Rowe (1962; Rowe and Menzel 1967) for Peru, in which dates that begin and end periods refer to critical events in one single locality, the Ica Valley (see Fig. 1.1).

| Chronological Periods | | North Peru | Central Peru | South Peru | Bolivian Altiplano | Bolivian Eastern Valleys | North Chile | NW Argentina |
|---|---|---|---|---|---|---|---|---|
| Late Horizon | 1430 | Salsipuedes Chupachu *chullpas* Chachapoyas Cists Pirka Pirka Rapayan Tinyash Tornapampa Tantamayo | *kullpi* Wanka Queca Huarochirí *chullpas* Apcara Andamarca Cinco Cerros Jatun Malka Huallanay | Cuzco Quebrada Chuquito-Inca *chullpas* de la Vaca Sillustani Ollantaytambo Paucartambo Altiplano Phase *chullpas* | Anantoko Chuquito-Inca *chullpas* Salla Chiar Jakke Altiplano Phase *chullpas* | adobe *chullpas* | Toconce *chullpas* | |
| Late Intermediate Period | 900 | Honcopampa Wilkawain | *machay* interments Jargampata Huari | | | Tiwanaku Urn Burials | | |
| Middle Horizon | 500 | Cerro Amaru Ventanillas Chota-Cutervo Huamachuco de Otusco *chullpas* Niched Halls Coyor Moche Culture Pashash | | Nasca Culture | Tiwanaku | | | |
| Early Intermediate Period | 0 | | | | | | | |
| Early Horizon | 500 B.C. | Kuntur Wasi Chavín | | | | | | |
| | 1000 B.C. | | | | | | | |
| Initial Period | 1500 B.C. | | Kotosh Shillacoto | | | | | |
| | 2000 B.C. | | | | | | | |
| Preceramic | 5000 B.C. | | Paloma | | | | Chinchorro | |
| Paleoindian | 14000 B.C. | | | | | | | |

Figure 1.1. Central Andean Chronology

In John Rowe's scheme, prehistoric time is divided into two great units, all the time before the invention of pottery and all the time after the appearance of ceramics. In the Ica Valley ceramics appeared shortly after 2000 B.C. The Preceramic Period has many subdivisions, but they have little importance for our study. Mortuary monuments diagnostic of *ayllu*s were absent, so it is sufficient to know that the peoples and cultures of the central Andes before 2000 B.C. may all be assigned to Preceramic periods, even the first migrants to reach the central Andes more than ten thousand years ago.

The invention of pottery, or its arrival in the Ica Valley, began the Initial Period, probably about 1800 B.C. (see Fig. 1.1). After almost a thousand years a distinctive art style named Chavín—for a spectacular archaeological site in the north highlands (Burger 1992) where the style is well represented in stone sculpture—reached the Ica Valley. Because Chavín art is very widespread during a relatively short period, it constitutes a horizon style, and this period in central Andean prehistory is called the Early Horizon. It should be remembered that the Early Horizon Period from 1000 to 200 B.C. synchronizes cultures from Bolivia and Chile even though they lie outside the sphere of Chavín artistic influence. When the last evidence of the Chavín style disappears in Ica about 200 B.C., the Early Horizon ends and the Early Intermediate Period begins. The term "Intermediate" was chosen to indicate that it lies between two horizon styles, although some of Peru's best-known regional cultures and art styles come from the Early Intermediate Period—Nasca, Moche, and Recuay, for example.

The Early Intermediate Period ended with the spread of Tiwanaku-Huari art, which constitutes a second great horizon style. Consequently, this period is known as the Middle Horizon. It began about A.D. 500 and lasted until about A.D. 900. The transition from Early Intermediate Period to Middle Horizon is dated by the arrival of the diagnostic art in the Ica Valley. Even though the city of Tiwanaku in the Bolivian highlands may have enjoyed a Tiwanaku ceramic style by the third or fourth century, the Middle Horizon does not begin until A.D. 500, or perhaps a little later.

There can be little doubt that the spread of closely related Tiwanaku and Huari art and iconography was promoted by political expansionism, and the Ica Valley probably became a provincial colony of the highland city of Huari. But Huari collapsed within a few centuries, and in spite of the fact that Tiwanaku continued to produce characteristic art for several centuries, the Ica Valley embarked on a road of artistic and cultural independence, giving the name Late Intermediate Period to this next time unit.

The time from about A.D. 900 till the Inca expansion that reached the Ica Valley about A.D. 1470 belongs to the Late Intermediate Period. Central Andean polities experienced a great deal of demographic growth and apparently also a great deal of warfare. Probably no more than a hundred years before the Spanish invasion the Incas of Cuzco perfected a military and administrative machine capable of overcoming all opposition. Incas spread their control along with distinctive Cuzco art to create a third horizon style in the central Andes, the Late Horizon. In 1532 the Spanish invaders initiated the Colonial Period, although it was several years before this political and cultural change became apparent in the archaeological record of the Ica Valley (Menzel 1959).

Archaeologists divide the central Andes into a number of zones (see Map 1.1). In part these divisions reflect the distribution of artifact styles that define prehistoric cultures. In part they recognize the realities of the Andean environment. And in part they result from the history of political change and academic research. Beginning in the north, Ecuador belongs to the northern, not the central Andes. North Peru is divided into the north highlands and the north coast. Central Peru includes the central highlands and the central coast, while southern Peru also consists of a south highlands and a south coast region. In adjacent Bolivia there is a large *altiplano* region from the south shores of Lake Titicaca to Lake Poopó and farther south. To the east are the mesothermal valleys that constitute a cultural zone below the *altiplano*, but above the lowlands of the Beni, Mojos, and Chaco. Cochabamba is the largest of the mesothermal valleys. The people of the far northern portion of Chile are also assigned to central Andean culture, as are those of northwestern Argentina. Because they figure only modestly in this study, I will not discuss their regional chronologies.

## WRITING AYLLU PREHISTORY

Reading archaeological texts of past cultures, and interpreting their meanings, requires that the archaeologist know as much as possible about the peoples who created the texts, about archaeological methods, and about culture as well as culture theory. But the individual archaeologist always brings personal experience to the reading as well. What has contributed to my vision of the Andean past? This short discussion of how I came to write this book may help the reader to know more about what I bring to this study. It results from the intersection of two topics that I have been interested in for a long time, but that have always been secondary to my research with other archaeological problems, especially Huari and Tiwanaku. One is the concept Andean culture, and the way archaeologists use it to construct the past. The other involves architecture and mortuary monuments.

I first became involved with Andean culture in 1967 when, as graduate students, Billie Jean Isbell and I spent most of a year doing ethnography in the remote central highland village of Chuschi, under the supervision of our professor, Tom Zuidema. This was the time when Andean culture was being "discovered," and I feel that I had a hand in the process. At the time, older scholars emphasized the tremendous changes that Andean societies suffered throughout the Spanish invasion, the colonial centuries, and republican times. There had been great depopulation. Most of the native languages disappeared. People were resettled, reorganized, and Christianized. Traditional chiefs and kings were replaced by Spanish administrators and Indian collaborators appointed by them. Many traditional customs were prohibited by law. New economic relations were imposed. Indians were forced to work in the mines. They were obliged to buy European goods and pay taxes in money. In short, Andean culture of Inca times had been destroyed. But Tom Zuidema brought a Lévi-Straussian, structuralist vision of "cold" societies that resisted history to Andean research (cf. Fabian 1983; Gell 1992: 23–29). He was not alone.

In 1967 John Murra was investigating provincial Inca economics and administration in the highlands of Huánuco. The program included ethnohistory and archaeology, but also ethnographic studies in remote villages where the descendants of the precolumbian Chupachu, Wamali, and other *ayllu* or ethnic kingdoms lived. Most of these people still spoke the Quechua language. Murra and his colleagues and students were finding that the economic theories of Karl Marx, Karl Polanyi, and others did not adequately explain observable Andean economic behavior, so it became necessary to discover uniquely Andean economics. The research led to the formulation of an important economic model for Andean culture that was called vertical ecological complementarity (Murra 1972, 1985a, 1985b). (Initially Murra used the name "verticality" but later changed to "ecological complementarity." To avoid confusion I have combined the names.) Significantly, vertical ecological complementarity as a model was constructed on the basis of economic strategies described for prehistoric Andeans and for modern indigenous peoples (Alberti and Mayer 1974a, 1974b; Brush 1977; Fonseca 1974; Fonseca and Mayer 1978; Mayer 1974, 1977, 1985; Muñoz Ovalle 1993; Orlove 1977b; Wachtel 1973). Consequently, it seemed apparent that Andean culture could still be observed, having endured through the centuries.

Tom Zuidema and his students and colleagues were investigating Inca social structure, combining studies of ethnohistory and ethnography. They were finding that elementary systems of kinship (Lévi-Strauss 1969), and particularly asymmetric alliance, did not explain Andean social organization. Uniquely Incaic models of kinship and social organization were required, and these studies resulted in a parallel descent model of Inca kinship (Zuidema 1977, 1989b), a dual moiety kingship model for Inca rule (Zuidema 1964, 1973, 1989b, 1990b, 1990c), and other insights into Andean social and political organization (Zuidema 1992). These were important and valuable achievements. But the investigation of Inca culture was hampered because of its destruction by Spanish colonialism. Investigation had to be reconstructive, gleaning information from whatever sources were available. Ethnographic research in remote villages quickly revealed rich traditions and beliefs that were not Spanish. Neither were they Catholic or capitalist. It seemed that they must be "Andean," representing tradition coming from the Inca past. The ethnographic information was compared with what was known about the culture of the Incas. What seemed consistent with descriptions from colonial contexts or with expectations about Inca culture was ascribed to Andean culture and to a general Andean past (Allen 1982; B. J. Isbell 1978; W. H. Isbell 1978a; Sherbondy 1982; Urton 1981).

Were students of Andean culture discovering it or creating it? At any rate, we established the survival of Inca or Andean culture in remote villages. Contrary to the conclusions of our predecessors, we found Inca structures and ideologies, as well as traditional Andean myths, astronomies, economic institutions, and social practices, coexisting beside, and resisting, the influence of Hispanic, national, and capitalistic culture. A new concept was being constructed. "Andean" and "Inca" were becoming virtually synonymous as descriptions from different times and places were conflated. This disparate information was modeled into a single, normative ideal conceptualized as a deep essence—

"Andean culture," in Spanish, "lo Andino"—that was highly resistant to external influence or change.

As this construction of Andean culture continued I was enthusiastically using it to construct Andean prehistory. Vertical ecological complementarity, dual organization, *ayllu* kin groupings, rotating cargo systems, and economic institutions like ethnographically known *ayni* and *minka* were all inferred for the Andean past by my generation of archaeologists. For me, the Río Pampas villages where I worked in 1967 and again in 1969–1970 were living examples of Andean culture.

Paradoxically, during the years that I was participating in the construction of homogeneous and continuitous Andean culture, I was witnessing heterogeneity and change in the Andes all around me. From my archaeological workmen at Huari (1973–1981) I learned that migration was essential for most peasant households—usually periodic trips to the coast to work on big plantations for wages. When my excavations offered enough work some men of the community could remain at home with their families for several years in a row. These workmen were delighted, and they were as anxious for good reviews of our National Science Foundation and National Geographic proposals as I was. I failed to see the capitalist economic forces shaping peasant strategies and imagined that migration was an ancient Andean cultural pattern, part of vertical ecological complementarity, and perhaps an adaptive response to environmental constraints on highland agriculture. I considered modern migration from Ayacucho as a possible model for Middle Horizon Huari cultural influences on the Peruvian coast.

Consistent with my archaeological specialization, it was material culture—pottery, of course—that first shook my faith in immutable Andean culture. Quinua is a famous pottery-producing village about 35 km from the provincial city of Ayacucho. Its lovely ceramic craft may have come to the village with Acos Indian settlers from Cuzco, brought by the Incas long before the Spanish invasion (Arnold 1993: 44–45). Thus, Quinua pottery must be quintessentially traditional. But between 1967 and 1981 I saw the inventory of Quinua vessel shapes transform radically. The pottery was changing in response to market opportunities, especially rising tourism and the collecting of "folk art." At first I rejected the new figurines, teapots, and ashtrays as inauthentic bastardizations of Andean tradition, and I rejected changes in the way the craft was organized as "acculturation." For me, Quinua tradition was the utilitarian jars, pitchers, and cups, as well as the modeled bulls and churches that I first saw in 1967. I had seen these shapes in local native rituals, so they must be authentic. And Quinua's potters were peasants, living on the edges of the village, where they practiced agriculture and potted part-time in their modest huts. In 1967 only a few potters had moved to houses on the plaza or streets of the village, where hardy tourists visited occasionally to buy the quaint wares. But during the late 1960s their success was causing potters to give up agriculture and become full-time ceramicists, and foreign development programs were offering training to "improve" the quality of ceramic production.

By the late 1970s the plaza of Quinua was dominated by little ceramic workshops, each with its sales display. Few potters were farming anymore or living among their fields. And change was intensifying. Ceramics manufactured by the better potters were being contracted by big stores in Lima and elsewhere. In fact, by 1981 you could visit Quinua and hardly find any good-quality pottery for sale. Everything was packed and shipped to higher-paying "folk art" markets. And the Quinua potters were moving away to the cities, some to Ayacucho, others to Lima. During the next decade and a half I believe that Quinua pottery became a craft practiced by enclaves of migrants located in Lima and Ayacucho. Old potters trained youths in the art, which had lost all utilitarian vessel forms in favor of highly marketable figurines playing quaint musical instruments and similar things. The little sculptures were appearing in franchised "folk art" stores like Pier 1 in the United States and elsewhere through the world. Master potters made occasional trips "home" to dig "traditional" clay and pigments, but I suspect that new raw materials were replacing those of the past. In no small measure, changes in Quinua pottery were promoted by the social and economic conditions fostered by Sendero Luminoso (the Shining Path guerrilla movement) and the war against capitalism.

It became apparent to me that if I had first witnessed the Quinua ceramic tradition in 1990 I might have imagined an "Andean cultural craft" consisting of full-time specialists who lived in distant urban enclaves, returning on pilgrimages to the homeland for materials and to recruit kin into the trade. In the distant enclaves apprentices produced under the instruction of a master potter until they took over the shop or moved to another location to found a shop of their own. It also became apparent that the condition I witnessed in 1967 must also have been a "snapshot" in time, part of a continuous process of change. It seemed ridiculous to imagine that Quinua pottery production had remained unchanged since the arrival of Acos resettlers in Ayacucho in about 1475, only to disintegrate before my eyes between 1967 and the 1990s. Something I had learned while doing ethnography in Chuschi kept coming back to me.

One morning in 1967 I had found one of my informants, a man, weaving a woman's shawl on a backstrap loom. I was surprised, for I believed that by tradition this was woman's work. So I asked about the norms associated with weaving, including the gendering of activities, and other questions that might help me understand how craft production was organized and how the rules of tradition were being preserved. The informant, however, replied that weavers were poor. If a man did not have enough land to support his family, he had to migrate in search of work or produce craft goods for trade or sale. He assured me that many men were weaving, and while saddle blankets were viewed as "right" items for men to make, most were weaving whatever they could sell. What I learned provoked me to think that the explanation of Quinua pottery might not be in a precolumbian origin and organizational structure. What we needed to understand were the pressures on production over the last century that obliged Quinua peasants to supplement agricultural cultivation with income from ceramic manufacture. Certainly tradition and resources played some role, but not as much as the rise in tourism and "folk art" collecting that quickly transformed the craft as demand and value increased.

Early in the 1980s Ayacucho was plunged into civil war. My research became impossible, but I kept hearing from my friends and former workmen about profound cultural changes provoked by isolation from the cash economy and by the impacts of violence and depopulation. I began a new project in the north of Peru. In Atoccpampa, where I lived while excavating Honcopampa in the Callejón de Huaylas (1987), I witnessed community organization that was unlike that of the villages I knew in Ayacucho. I could not account for such profound differences in terms of a single continuum of acculturation from Andean culture to Hispanicized peasant culture. During these years I was also discussing Andean political economy with Jane Collins (cf. 1988) and Michael Painter (cf. 1991). I realized that local history of the Callejón de Huaylas, where big haciendas had predominated in the nineteenth and early twentieth centuries, had promoted an Andean culture that was really quite different from what I knew in Ayacucho and the Río Pampas villages, where *reducción* villages survived into recent history. It was also becoming clear that the peasant economies I knew were not simply pieces of Andean vertical agriculture mixed with pieces of European capitalist production. They represented creative new adaptations to scarce land, labor shortage, poor market opportunities, and low wages. Farming sparse and exhausted lands was inadequate to meet family needs, but sale of products and working for wages were insecure and very poorly paid. The response was simultaneous participation in two economies, one of subsistence and one of wages, but the two belonged to a single economic and historical context. I was not witnessing a survival of ancient Andean culture resisting a European economy (cf. Herzfeld 1987).

In the Bolivian *altiplano* where I lived while excavating Iwawi (1993) I witnessed *ayllu* organization that was vastly beyond the scale of anything in Peru. These *ayllu*s spread over hundreds of kilometers, linking multiple communities into complex relationships (Albó 1972; Harris 1978; Rasnake 1988). Bolivian *ayllu*s had not experienced reorganization into local, indigenous communities, created by law in early-twentieth-century Peru. But they were no more the "true Andean *ayllu*" than the Peruvian examples, for their histories all participated in complex political and economic processes that involved change and innovation.

I did not conclude that Andean culture and tradition from the past were without any influence on human action. But I did decide that my old view of culture greatly overdetermined human behavior. Equally seriously, I realized that anthropologists, historians, and archaeologists like myself might be constructing Andean culture and an image of cultural immutability and essentialism through the methods we were using for knowing the past. By inferring institutions from modern ethnography and recent history into the prehistoric past because they fit our expectations, we created the cultural continuity we expected. Was the past an artifact of our ideas about it? I became convinced that it would be necessary to seriously reevaluate what I thought I knew about Andean prehistory.

During the years I was formulating and reformulating my thoughts about Andean culture I was also accumulating observations on mortuary monuments. The great *chullpa* burial towers around the city of Puno profoundly impressed me when I first visited them in 1964. They conditioned my reaction to numerous tiny *chullpa*s, many full of human remains, that I found in the *montaña* of the eastern part of the Department of Puno in 1966. Later, in Ayacucho, I saw other *chullpa*s, although rarely so well preserved as those in Puno. These mortuary buildings seemed never to be more than four or five centuries older than the Spanish invasion, and I began to wonder whether their origin was in the megalithic chamber tombs I knew from Huari. Of course, all the megalithic chambers of Huari were looted long ago, so it was only through indirect evidence from Mario Benavides's (1991) excavations in the Cheqo Wasi sector, as well as our exposures in the Moraduchayuq sector (Isbell, Brewster-Wray, and Spickard 1991), that I could infer a mortuary function for the stone boxes.

In 1987, when I excavated at Honcopampa in the Callejón de Huaylas, I was impressed by spectacular *chullpa*s and mortuary buildings. Of course, I was inclined to infer that they were a Huari form introduced to the north early in the Middle Horizon. Other buildings at Honcopampa were certainly influenced by Huari architecture (W. H. Isbell 1989, 1991a). I enjoyed discussing these ideas with my north highland colleagues, especially Theresa and John Topic (1984), who insisted that they had dates from a similar mortuary building in Huamachuco, showing that it was full of mummies during the Early Intermediate Period. I was incredulous and felt such early dates must be in error. The problem for me was that Ruth Shady and Hermilio Rosas (1976) claimed that *chullpa*s farther north in the Chota-Cutervo region also belonged to the Early Intermediate Period, though their dating seemed poorly substantiated.

In 1991 I set out to Chota-Cutervo hoping to show that the *chullpa*s were actually Middle Horizon or later. I expected to continue developing my argument for Huari origins of megalithic tombs above the ground and their development into mortuary houses and towers as part of the diffusion of a Huari-based funerary cult during the Middle Horizon. But instead I corroborated the Early Intermediate Period date for the Chota-Cutervo *chullpa*s, recording impressive relief sculptures on large stone building blocks that related to Moche, Vicús, Recuay, and other Early Intermediate Period styles.

My ideas about mortuary monuments and *chullpa*s were wrong, and this sent me to the literature to learn more about mummies and ancestor worship, especially from Peru's earliest colonial documents (cf. Salomon 1995). Very salient in these descriptions is the involvement that the living had with the dead, activities that struck Spanish observers as macabre exaltations of desiccated corpses. Of profound importance was the attachment early Andean informants had to their ancestor mummy and the role of the ancestor's body in the production and reproduction of *ayllu* culture, ideology, and space-time. In fact, it was these ancestor bodies that were targeted for destruction by Spanish missionaries who wanted to break *ayllu* religious ideology. And earlier, Inca factions that wanted to break the power of a rival *ayllu* had also destroyed the ancestor mummy.

I realized that, for the central Andes, *ayllu* history was ancestor mummy history, and ancestor mummy history was the history of *chullpa*s and similar mortuary monuments where ancestor bodies could be safely curated. I had discovered a way to track the *ayllu* in prehistoric times, without written records. I also had a tool for reevaluating an important part of what my colleagues and I thought we knew about Andean culture in the prehistoric past. A paper on mummies and *ayllu* prehistory at the American Anthropological Association meetings in 1992 and a symposium at the Society for American Archaeology meetings of 1993 contributed to the development of these ideas, presented in this book.

## PREVIEW OF THE CONTENTS

In writing this book I had to decide where to begin. As we have discussed, constructing knowledge is not a linear process, but a back and forth circle involving the prehistoric archaeological record, ethnographic and ethnohistorical descriptions, anthropological theories of culture, and the emerging vision of the past. I considered beginning with a discussion of the theories that motivate and inform interpretation, but I have held that discussion for Chapter 4. I also considered beginning with discussions of the archaeological record, but I have placed the material remains in Chapters 5, 6, and 7. I chose instead to begin with independent descriptions of Andean cultures, ethnohistorical accounts that provide information in terms of which we may read the archaeological texts of material culture from the past. Each avenue of entry is equally valid and also equally inadequate without the others. The advantage of beginning with the final moments of Inca civilization and the opening decades of colonial culture is that it allows us to immerse ourselves in the specifics of Andean life before taking on discussion of culture theory and the contrasting Andean pasts visualized by different theories. Saving the archaeological remains till last means that readers will be prepared to make their own readings of the prehistoric texts, to better evaluate my test of two theoretically motivated and competitive interpretations of the past.

The book contains eight chapters. This introduction explains the need for and epistemology of the study. Chapters 2 and 3 contain independent descriptions of two early postconquest Andean societies, the best-documented sixteenth- and seventeenth-century cases. In Chapter 2 we inspect the Incas of Cuzco and in Chapter 3 the Yauyos of Huarochirí. These discussions firmly link *ayllu* organization with an ancestor mummy and the mummies with open sepulchers of the *chullpa* variety. It is from these early colonial descriptions of two distinct Andean peoples that I develop a definition for the *ayllu*, as it existed in the sixteenth century, at the end of Chapter 3. Finally, these two chapters help to show *ayllu* organization, not as a stable institution, but as changing sets of relationships.

Chapter 4 discusses and contrasts two theoretical approaches for knowing the past. It outlines the different visions of the Andean past that each approach constructs, focusing on the history of the *ayllu*. I will cite influential Andean prehistorians' claims for *ayllu* organization thousands of years ago and show that these claims are unsupported proclamations that must be understood by deconstructing them and articulating the underlying ideas about culture and knowing the past. Two pasts are offered, the "ancient *ayllu* hypothesis" and the "recent *ayllu* hypothesis," to be tested by studying the prehistory of the *ayllu* as revealed by mortuary monuments.

The goal of Chapter 5 is to establish criteria for identifying mortuary monuments in which *ayllu* ancestor mummies were kept. As our epistemological discussion has shown, we must have independent and secure criteria to apply if we are to avoid vicious circularity in our argument. Perhaps most importantly, I evaluate the conviction that to be identified as a mortuary building archaeological architecture must contain human remains.

Chapters 6 and 7 trace the spatial and temporal distribution of identifiable mortuary monuments. Chapter 8 concludes the study, showing that the most popular vision of the Andean past, the "ancient *ayllu* hypothesis," is inconsistent with the archaeological record. The study of mortuary monuments reveals a much more recent origin for the *ayllu* and supports an approach to the Andean past that emphasizes contingent histories produced by human actors employing innovative strategies to create and contest power rather than following age-old norms subject only to the processes of adaptive evolutionism.

I am anxious for readers to experience Cuzco of the Incas through the only descriptions of an Andean culture that are early enough to permit us to discount culture change due to pressures from Spanish influence and control. While I argue in favor of culture as a contingent process of production and reproduction I have no desire to deny the profound "otherness" of the Incas and their contemporary Andean societies. I do not want to show Andean culture as homogeneous, but I hope that each reader develops an interpretive experience of Cuzco and the Inca Empire by reading Chapter 2. I want you to witness the omnipresence of ancestor mummies in daily life. I also want you to appreciate the prominence dead bodies were given in everything from family affairs to the great rituals of imperialism. Lacking written accounts of prehistoric Cuzco, we begin our study with the arrival of Spanish invaders in the capital, descriptions that highlight ancestor mummies. We follow the efforts of Inca nobles to protect their ancestor mummies, probably the most valuable demonstrations of how these cadavers related to the organization and power of Inca society. Of course, our goal is to learn about the Andean *ayllu*, its associations with ancestor mummies, and the relationships *ayllu*s and mummies had with mortuary monuments that leave durable archaeological remains. To do so we must also understand the contexts within which Andean culture was described by Spanish conquerors. For example, it is important to realize that the earliest accounts are limited to Inca nobles in the capital city. Little or nothing was written about lower-status provincial peoples for many years. The social unit that the invaders witnessed in Cuzco was the *panaca*, a royal Inca version of the *ayllu*.

Political, economic, and ceremonial life in Cuzco publicly featured mummies, especially the mummies of former emperors whose bodies were brought out into the great ceremonial plaza of Haucaypata perhaps daily, but certainly for all important occasions. In relation to these mummies, the noble Incas of Cuzco were divided into kin groups, real or fictional, each one descended from one of the dead kings. These groups, or *panaca*s, were organized into a hierarchy that determined rights and privileges, including relations with the living king, and political opportunities within the imperial administrative machine. Ancestor kings' mummies were consulted by their descendants, given rich offerings, and beseeched for abundance and well-being. These ancestor mummies were never buried, but seated in special buildings where they could be viewed, approached, and venerated by their descendant worshipers. The sumptuous offerings that accompanied them attracted Spanish looters faster than the dead bodies attracted flies, as vividly related by the first Spaniard to describe Cuzco's great Sun Temple.

Inca religion seems bewilderingly complicated, but Father Bernabé Cobo's seventeenth-century analysis of its hierarchical organization reveals the structural position of ancestor mummies within the greater cosmos. In order to understand how mummies participated in the production of the *ayllu* as well as the entire social and political organization of Cuzco we explore the complexities of Inca ceremonialism, calendrics, kinship, and spatial organization. This takes us into the shadows of two competing explanations of Cuzco and the royal Inca dead. First I summarize John Rowe's historiographic model. Next I offer an interpretive synthesis of Tom Zuidema's structural model. The two models give different interpretations of the meanings that royal mummy ancestors had for the Incas and civic life in their capital. However, both agree on the crucial role these mummies had for *panaca*, or royal *ayllu*, organization.

We must be aware that there are omissions in these early accounts, and there are obvious biases. Perhaps the greatest bias is that of gender. We have very little information about mummies of women. Women, when mentioned, usually appear only as mourners, not as *ayllu* or *panaca* founders. Virtually everything written by colonial witnesses expresses a male perspective (cf. Silverblatt 1987). One might infer that only males were revered as descent-group founders, but occasionally female mummies are listed or illustrated, such as among the ancestors captured at Vitcos, the Inca capital in exile established after the fall of Cuzco. If female mummies were valuable enough to be sneaked out of Cuzco and taken to the provisional capital in the jungle, they must have been more important than the Spanish descriptions admit. But I have no more data upon which to draw, so in spite of my conviction that gender bias is represented, I do not know how to correct the problem.

Having determined the dependence that *panaca* or royal *ayllu* organization among the Incas had on ancestor mummies and temple-mausoleums, we must ask whether similar relationships characterized other Andean peoples. Chapter 3 examines the role of mummy ancestors and mortuary monuments among the Yauyos peoples of Huarochirí. It is also necessary to evaluate the colonial context of these descriptions, which come from the end of the sixteenth and the seventeenth centuries. The Huarochirí mummy documents come from the Catholic Church's inquisition of native religion, which was intended to stamp out or extirpate idolatrous practices. The beginning of the extirpation inquests followed a great religious rebellion among the Indians and the massive resettlement of Indians by the Spanish Viceroyalty to facilitate taxation. But in a curious way, these very events may have contributed to cultural conservatism in Indian protest religion. Father Pablo José de Arriaga's description of the Yauyos cosmos at the end of the sixteenth century shows that it was significantly similar to Inca cosmological thinking and that ancestor mummies occupied a similar position in both cultures. Significantly, Arriaga provided profound information about family religious practice and the use of divination that may have been overlooked by witnesses of spectacular state spectacles in Cuzco.

Extirpation testimonies about mummy worship are fascinating, but often confusing. The mortuary monuments were no longer the centers of Indian life, but located in the old towns forcibly abandoned as a result of viceroyal resettlement policies. Descriptions of the mummies are not eyewitness accounts of rituals but transcriptions of confessions extracted during compulsory interviews and torture. When Indians confessed to mummy worship they were punished and their ancestors' remains were sought out and burned. I infer that the testimonies were frequently meant to admit and inform as little as possible. I also suggest to readers that the recurrence of some mummy names does not indicate a unified pantheon. Rather, these names were descriptive and for that reason they recur in many communities.

In the midst of the terminal sixteenth-century conflicts over mummies and idolatry native peoples of Huarochirí transcribed a corpus of myths. This history or title of one of the Yauyos *ayllu*s is invaluable, for it shows how one microethnic group articulated itself with the past, its land and water resources, its neighbors, and the inequality on which social relations were based. This and shorter testimonies show that in the ideal past ancestors had founded *ayllu*s of descendants and endowed them with resources through heroic deeds. Founders were organized into flexible, dynamic structures of inequality modeled on descent and using the idiom of kinship. Around these mummies and idols, and in the built environment that spatially organized them, social life was constructed and reconstructed in the rituals of veneration. Much remains to be learned, but relations among *ayllu* organization, ancestor mummies, and open mausoleums are confirmed for both Cuzco and Yauyos. I am convinced that these relations inform us about the broader Andean past.

In Chapter 4 we discuss the most popular approach to the Andean past, based on processual cultural evolution, which assumes culture change as a result of adaptive addition of new institutions. Examples of several authors' processual evolutionism are presented that place the *ayllu* at the beginning of "Andean culture," usually centuries or millennia before the Christian era. I show how this conclusion is promoted by assumptions about the nature of culture and the way culture changes. It proceeds with methods for constructing the past out of the present or, more appropriately, out of an idealized ethnographic present that conflates ethnohistory and ethnography.

An especially influential and current example of processual evolutionism is Michael Moseley's book *The Incas and Their Ancestors: The Archaeology of Peru*, published in 1992. Since it is probably today's most frequently read text on Andean prehistory, and it lays out many premises of processual evolutionism quite explicitly, I have paraphrased material from it, having been denied permission to use direct quotes. I provide page references to the 1992 text so readers may consult the original to confirm the unity in processual evolutionary thinking.

In Chapter 4 I contrast the processual approach to the Andean past with a view of history that assumes the contingency of culture change as well as informed human action. This is a postprocessual approach that makes different assumptions about the nature of culture and cultural change and in this offers a critique of the processual vision of Andean prehistory. It suggests a much more recent origin for the *ayllu*.

The processual and postprocessual visions of the Andean past, and the role played by the *ayllu*, are set up as broad hypotheses to be tested by the study of mortuary monuments. If the processual vision tests better in regard to its ideas about the prehistory of the *ayllu*, then its assumptions and methods would be supported, as would its general account of the Andean past. If the postprocessual vision corresponds more with findings revealed by mortuary monuments, then its assumptions and methods would seem to provide the better understandings of culture and culture change, to say nothing of the prehistory of the *ayllu* in the Andean past.

In Chapter 5 I undertake the task of determining how to identify mortuary monuments associated with *ayllu* ancestor mummies in the

Andean archaeological record. Colonial descriptions of Indian tombs are examined. They are very helpful, but a great deal must be inferred. As I show, policies of the Spanish government and church were hostile to the worship of ancestor mummies. They assured that Indian chroniclers avoided this topic, and Spanish writers were often kept ignorant or misinformed. Nonetheless, a broad dichotomy between burial above ground in open buildings and burial below ground in less accessible graves was noted by early Spanish observers. This typology serves as a point of departure for my investigation.

The archaeological record is rich in information about burial below ground in inaccessible graves, especially in the fill of platform temples. I call this the *huaca* cemetery pattern of burial and describe it from some of the best-known examples, especially Moche burial practices described so brilliantly by Christopher Donnan (Alva and Donnan 1993; Donnan 1995; Donnan and Castillo 1992; Donnan and Mackey 1978; Donnan and McClelland 1979).

*Huaca* cemetery burial contrasts with above-ground placement of the dead in accessible buildings that I call open sepulchers. In the archaeological record we must be able to identify open sepulchers on the basis of their form, for it is unrealistic to expect that mummies, or their bones, will still be present in many of these buildings. But well-preserved open sepulchers from the site of Quebrada de la Vaca that are still full of human remains show that criteria mentioned by Spanish chroniclers, such as an east-facing doorway and small-sized entrances, were popular, but not necessary, characteristics of the above-ground tomb. A constellation of features does help identify open sepulchers, but in the final analysis they will have to be understood in terms of local and regional traditions whose specific changes must be tracked in time and space.

Chapter 6 begins my survey of the spatial and temporal distribution of open sepulchers in the Andean highlands. Since the preservation of human bodies on the Peruvian and Chilean coastal deserts may not depend on open sepulcher buildings, coastal history of ancestor mummies will require independent studies not undertaken here. The central Andean southern highlands have long been recognized as the home of open sepulcher burial towers called *chullpas*. While the Andean term *chullpa* can be used interchangeably with my name "open sepulcher," *chullpa* does not seem to be an old Andean term for the open sepulcher.

*Chullpas* of the south appear rather late in Andean prehistory, certainly not before the Late Intermediate Period. Survey to the north indicates progressively earlier examples of open sepulchers as we examine

Cuzco, Ayacucho, the Mantaro Valley, and surrounding mountains of Junín as well as Huarochirí. At least some examples seem to belong to the Middle Horizon, but the record is confusing and research is scarce. Furthermore, *chullpa* monuments are often assumed to be diagnostic of the Late Intermediate Period and are used to date the sites in which they occur. This circular thinking makes dating the monuments difficult and shows why we must seek independent means to determine the antiquity of open sepulchers.

The Upper Marañón River Valley has a wealth of little-studied, but spectacular, mortuary buildings. At least some seem to date as early as the Middle Horizon. In fact, along the Marañón River there is such diversity in mortuary buildings that seem to have been open sepulchers that a long and ancient tradition is implied. In the northwestern tributaries of the Marañón, such as Huamachuco, and in the Callejón de Huaylas, we find evidence for open sepulchers during the Early Intermediate Period.

Chapter 7 takes a detailed look at the most northerly examples of open sepulchers, in the Chota-Cutervo region. Based on field reconnaissance I conducted in 1991, I describe the buildings and their sculptural decorations. I feel secure dating them to the Early Intermediate Period, confirming dates from the Huamachuco Valley and implied dates from the Callejón de Huaylas. Furthermore, the ideal forms of these burial monuments are consistent with a kinship model appropriate for *ayllu* organization.

Chapter 8 concludes that mortuary monuments of the open-sepulcher type have a continuous distribution in space and time. They originated in the northwest highlands of Peru during the Early Intermediate Period. They spread south, reaching the *altiplano* of far southern Peru, Bolivia, and Chile in the Late Intermediate Period, and perhaps the most remote regions even later. At the time of the Spanish invasion open sepulchers were associated with *ayllu*s that were social groups organized in terms of kinship idiom, whose members shared the administration and proceeds of a set of resources bequeathed them by an ancestor. The ancestor's mummy embodied the group, was its principal cult object, and focused kin-structured inequality within the *ayllu*. While we cannot examine every mortuary monument in this study for all these criteria of *ayllu* organization, the earliest *chullpa*s of Chota-Cutervo indicate a social group, common or corporate interests, a kinship model for organization, and a venerated ancestor mummy. If we can show these features of *ayllu* organization to be associated with open sepulchers during the invasion and early colonial period, and during the initial appearance of the open tombs in the Early Intermediate Period of the Chota-Cutervo Valley, it is not a leap of faith to infer that all four features of *ayllu* organization were associated with the *chullpa*s temporally (and spatially) in between.

This study does not support the processual evolutionary account of adaptive addition of institutions that proposes very early appearance of the *ayllu* in Andean prehistory. The *ayllu* was not the primordial and essential element of Andean culture. Contingent history influenced by informed action, a postprocessual approach to the Andean past, suggests that *ayllu* organization was a late means of resisting the processes of state building and defending kin organization. And this study of mortuary monuments indicates that the *ayllu* originated relatively late in Andean prehistory. The implications are profound, suggesting urgent need for a complete reevaluation of Andean prehistory.

CHAPTER

II

# Royal Mummies of Inca Cuzco

On November 15, 1533, a small army of Spanish invaders marched into Cuzco, the sacred capital of the Inca Empire (see Map 2.1). Among them was Pedro Pizarro, first cousin of leader Francisco Pizarro. The young Christian had agreed to represent an Inca captain in his request for a noblewoman's hand in marriage. Pizarro later wrote how he was taken to the great plaza of Haucaypata to address the master whom the woman served.

> Well, I expected to speak with a living Indian but they took me before the bundle of one of those corpses, where it was placed in a litter, in the manner that they were kept, with the Indian designated to speak for him on one side and the woman in question on the other, seated next to the mummy. Once we went before the corpse the translator repeated the message, and while we remained somewhat suspenseful and silent, the Indian looked at the woman (which I assume was to understand her will); well having done as I said the two answered together that her dead lord declared that it should be so, that the woman should be taken to the captain as the *apo* (referring to the Marqués, Francisco Pizarro) wished. (Pizarro [1571] 1978: 53–54)

Among the Incas, bodies of dead leaders were not disposed of by burial, but kept where they could be visited, adored, consulted, and

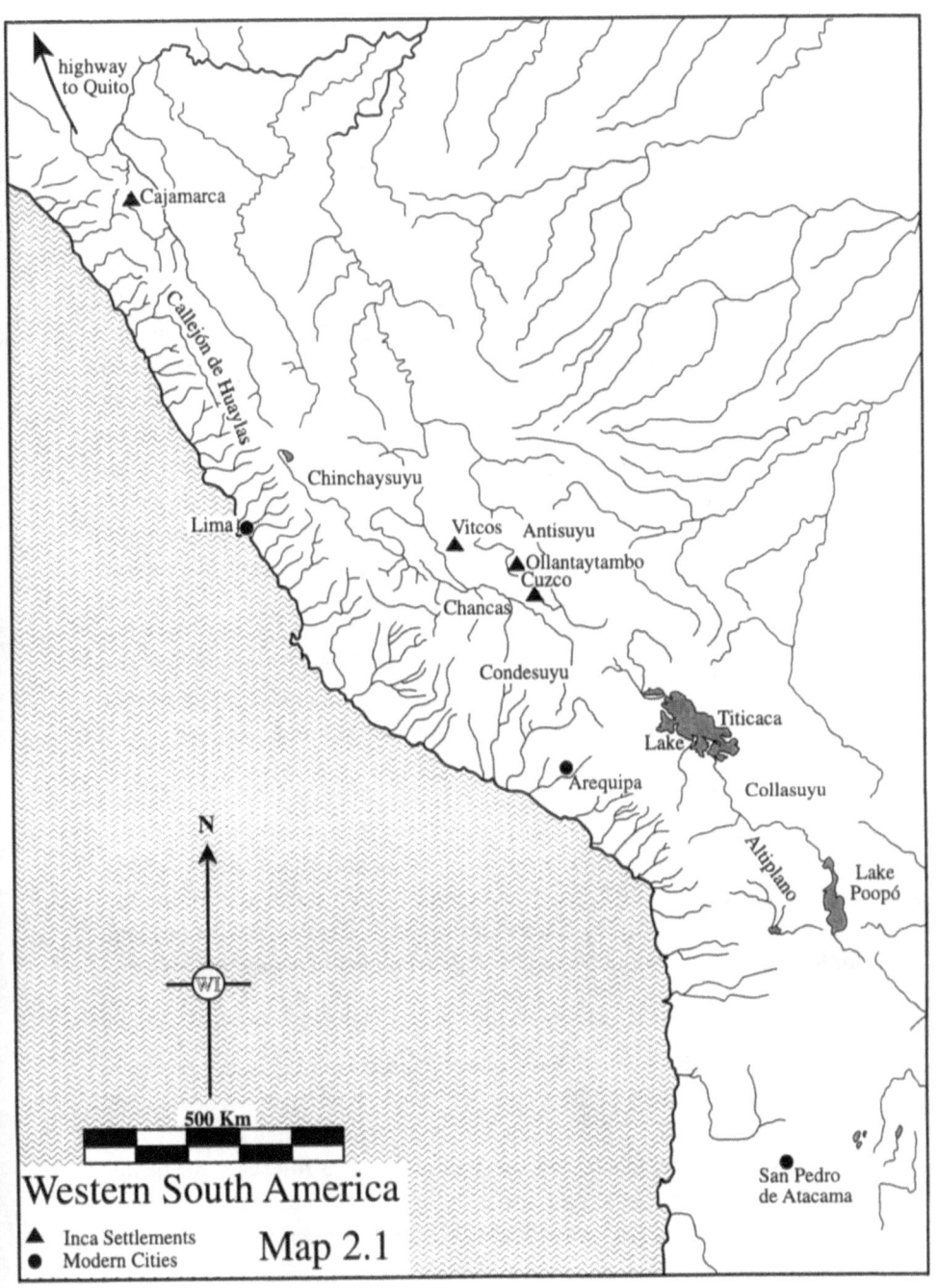

Map 2.1. The Inca Empire

feted. Mummies of former kings were certainly the most prominent, as the anonymous Sevillano Cristóbal de Mena ([1534] 1967) reported. His account described looting the Coricancha, Cuzco's Sun Temple, in March 1533, while the bulk of the Christian army was holding Inca Atahualpa prisoner in the provincial capital of Cajamarca.

> In another house [within the Sun Temple] they entered they found a bench of gold where sacrifices were made. This bench was so big that it weighed nineteen thousand pesos, and two men did not fill it. In another very big house [part of the same temple compound] they found many clay vessels covered with heavy gold leaf. They did not want to break them to avoid angering the Indians. In that house were many women. Also there were two corpses of male Indians as if embalmed. Next to them was a live woman with a gold mask on her face, whisking away the dust and the flies with a fan. The mummies had very rich staffs of gold in their hands. The woman would not let anyone come in until their shoes were removed; taking off their shoes [the Christian looters] went to see these dried-out bundles. They took many valuable objects from them but did not take all for the lord [Inca emperor in captivity] Atahualpa had begged them not to because [one of the mummies] was his father [Huayna Capac], so they did not dare take more. (Mena [1534] 1967: 93–94)

From resting places in the Sun Temple and their palaces (Rowe 1995: 30) surrounding Cuzco's sacred plaza the dead bodies of the former emperors were brought into Haucaypata plaza to receive offerings and to consult with the living, as Pedro Pizarro had seen on his entry into the city.

> It was the sight of the soldiery who were in this city of Cuzco that caused wonderment. . . . most of who served these dead folk whom I have mentioned, for each day they took them all out into the plaza and sat them down in a row, each according to his antiquity, and there the men and women servitors ate and drank. And for the dead they made fires before them with a piece of very dry wood which they worked into a very even shape. Having set this piece of wood on fire, they burned here

everything which they had placed before the dead in order that he might eat of the things which they eat, and here in this fire they consumed it. Likewise before these dead people they had certain large pitchers, which they call verquis, made of gold, silver or pottery, each according to his wish, and into [these vessels] they poured the chicha [corn beer] which they gave to the dead man with much display, and the dead pledged one another as well as the living, as the living pledged the dead. When verquis were filled, they emptied them into a round stone in the middle of the plaza, and which they held to be an idol, and it was made around a small opening by which it [the chicha] drained itself off through some pipes which they made under the ground. (Pizarro [1571] 1921: 251–252)

Keeping bodies of the dead where they could participate in activities of the living was, among Andean peoples, not limited to the Incas. Offerings of gold, silver, and coca leaf were typically placed in the mouths of the deceased, they were dressed in the finest textiles, and excellent serving vessels were dedicated to them, as were food and drink on a regular basis. A person's prized possessions, such as the big metal shawl pins worn by women, accompanied her in death. Then the bodies were placed where they could be visited and venerated. Felipe Guaman Poma de Ayala ([1615] 1980, Poma [1615] 1978), a native Andean who between 1567 and 1615 wrote a 1,200-page letter to the king of Spain, described these customs region by region. Unfortunately his account is limited to men, so we see women only as mourners rather than venerated ancestors in their own right. This represents a problematic bias, for the list of sacred Inca mummies expropriated by chief magistrate Juan Polo de Ondegardo in 1559 included both kings and queens. Furthermore, Guaman Poma's normative descriptions also make it hard to tell when he is discussing royalty, nobles, or simple commoners.

According to Guaman Poma ([1615] 1980: 262–263; Poma [1615] 1978: 81), the Incas placed the bodies of their dead in specially prepared vaults called *pucullo*s, although Pizarro and others made it clear that emperors and high nobles were kept in temples and palaces. Poma illustrates a *pucullo*, a stone building with an entrance through which a skull and long bone may be seen (see Fig. 2.1). He wrote that dead Inca emperors were called *yllapa* (lightning), while all others were *aya* (dead, mummy). At death, the length of the wake, the extravagance of the

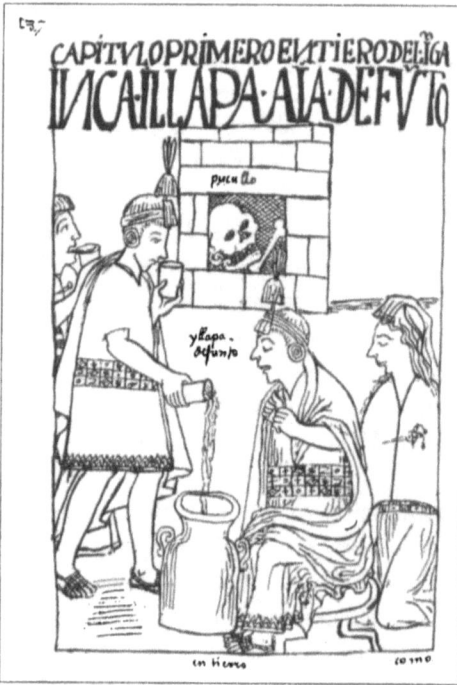

Figure 2.1. Inca Burial (from Guaman Poma [1615] 1936: 287)

feasts, and the richness of the offerings varied with the rank of the deceased. Emperors and highest nobles were embalmed carefully so that they would look as they had in life. Their bodies were dressed in fine clothing, placed on a stool, and accompanied by wives and servants as well as rich offerings of gold and silver, especially large serving vessels for giving food and drink to the mummy. In his illustration Poma shows the body of an Inca emperor, accompanied by his dead wife immediately behind him, both seated in the foreground of the drawing. Before the monarch is the large offering vessel, clearly what Pizarro referred to as *verquis*. A living Inca emperor pours a cup of liquid, almost certainly corn beer called *chicha*, into the *verquis* as he and a companion drink from similar cups. Apparently these bodies appeared much as they had in life.

> This king's body [Pachacuti Inca] was entombed by those of his tribal group [*ayllu*] in Patallacta, from where it was moved later to Totocache, and there it was found by Licentiate Polo; the body was kept with great care, and it was so well preserved with certain bitumen and concoctions that it appeared to be alive. Its eyes were made of a thin golden cloth; its hair was gray, and it was entirely preserved, as if he had died that same day. The body was very well dressed with five or six magnificent mantles, the royal fringe, and some well made *llautos*. (Cobo [1653] 1979: 141)

The Chinchaysuyu peoples of the northern province of the Inca Empire practiced similar rites, although Guaman Poma ([1615] 1980: 264–265) wrote that there was some difference from one *ayllu* ethnicity to the next (see Fig. 2.2). The dead were placed in the open *pucullo* after the body was washed, dressed in its finest clothing, and escorted about the lands for five days. In another part of his discussion Guaman Poma ([1615] 1980: 230–231) makes it clear that at least the important mummies of Chinchaysuyu peoples were brought out of their *pucullo* for feasts and dances given in their honor. He says that much was expended in these rituals and offerings, and he illustrates a mummy, seated on its litter, as it was carried from house to house and through the streets and plaza. Poma places this ritual in November (see Fig. 2.3), perhaps to sanitize such rites by associating them with the Christian Day of the Dead, for the practice appears to be consistent with the Incas, who, according to most descriptions, brought out their dead emperors on many occasions throughout the year.

Figure 2.2. Burial in Chinchaysuyu (from Guaman Poma [1615] 1936: 289).

The people of Collasuyu, the southern quarter of the empire, built open burial vaults similar to those of the Incas and Chinchaysuyus (Guaman Poma [1615] 1980: 268–269). At the time of death offerings were made for five days, and then again at ten days, six months, and a year, but it was important not to let the dead remain alone, hungry and thirsty (see Fig. 2.4). Poma tells us that, unlike the Chinchaysuyu, Collasuyu peoples built their *pucullo*s away from their residences and did not remove the dead to parade them about at the time of special cele-

 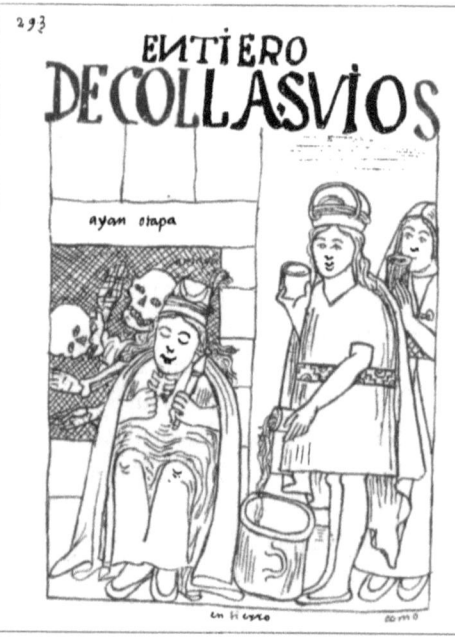

Figure 2.3. Celebrating the Dead in Chinchaysuyu (from Guaman Poma [1615] 1936: 256)

Figure 2.4. Burial in Collasuyu (from Guaman Poma [1615] 1936: 293)

brations for the dead. Rather, the living came to the *pucullos*, which were referred to as the "village of the dead," for festivals and offerings.

In the southwestern quarter of the Inca Empire, Condesuyu, peoples of the remote past placed their dead in caves, cliffs, and crags. More recently, but beginning before the time of the Incas, stone mortuary vaults were constructed (see Fig. 2.5; Guaman Poma [1615] 1980: 270–271). Mortuary buildings were arranged in groups, often brightly painted, and called *ayap llactan* (village of the dead), much as in Collasuyu.

Only the Indians of Antisuyu, the east, failed to preserve and revere the bodies of their dead, for according to Guaman Poma (see Fig. 2.6; [1615] 1980: 266–267), these Indians of the eastern jungles did not put offerings into the mouths of their deceased, or place them in vaults with possessions, or visit and adore their ancestors after death. Rather, at death the bodies were dressed specially for the great wake, but later the flesh was stripped and eaten until only bones remained. These bones were placed into a hole in a tree, sealed up, and never again visited.

ROYAL MUMMIES OF INCA CUZCO • 45

Figure 2.5. Burial in Condesuyu (from Guaman Poma [1615] 1936: 295)

Figure 2.6. Burial in Antisuyu (from Guaman Poma [1615] 1936: 291)

Guaman Poma's dismay and disgust at the disposal of the dead by Antisuyu Indians, biased as it is, is an obvious clue to the importance that the bodies of dead ancestors played in the lives of Andean peoples. Another clue is the aversion Andeans had to Christian burial in the ground, a practice that accelerated decay of the body and also removed it from direct contact with the living. For more than a century after the Spanish invasion, Indians continued to be punished by ecclesiastical judges for excavating dead relatives in churchyard cemeteries and slipping their bodies away to caves and *pucullo*s. To understand the significance of these mummified bodies we begin with an examination of the Inca emperors and other royal bodies that confronted the Spanish upon their arrival in Cuzco.

Pedro Pizarro and the other Spanish invaders had many opportunities to observe the mummified bodies of the former Inca emperors, their queens, and other high-ranking nobles in their palaces and temples, as well as in the streets and plazas of Cuzco between March 1533 and December 1535. Cuzco was a great ceremonial center with hundreds of shrines and a ritual calendar that constructed the year through daily celebrations.

Following the execution of Inca Atahualpa in Cajamarca, and the death of an heir, Tupac Huallpa, during the Spaniards' march from Cajamarca to Cuzco, the Incas were without an emperor. The new conquerors supported a young son of Huayna Capac whom they thought they could control as a puppet. At the beginning of 1534 he was crowned Manco Inca Yupanqui and the Spaniards witnessed one of the Incas' greatest rituals, an emperor's inauguration in Haucaypata plaza. At sunrise Manco entered the plaza in his litter, with the litter and mummy of Huayna Capac at his side. All the deceased Incas, with their retainers, followed. Once in the plaza each mummy was placed on his own seat, and the feasting began. At regular intervals activities were interrupted so all could listen to songs extolling the victories, accomplishments, and valor of each former king. At other moments there were prayers to the Sun, the creator and protector of the Inca dynasty. At dusk the spectacularly costumed mummies were escorted back to their palaces by their entourages of attendants, so the festivities could be renewed the following day. In this way the celebration lasted for more than a month: each king, back to the founder Manco Capac, gave his approval and authority to the new sovereign. And the priest of the Sun reminded the new Inca that he must imitate his forbears in their accomplishments (MacCormack 1991: 71).

In April 1535 cleric Bartolomé de Segovia described the last celebration of Inti Raimi by Incas in their capital of Cuzco (MacCormack 1991: 74–75). After the new maize was ripe the people brought out all the mummies and idols from their shrines and *pucullo*s to the plain that faces the rising Sun at the edge of the city. The most important bodies were placed under feather awnings that formed two lines with more than three hundred mummies each, leaving an avenue thirty paces wide between them. The royal Incas could be recognized by their golden ear spools, fine cloaks and tunics, bracelets, and head ornaments of gold, as well as many elegantly dressed attendants, both men and women. Silently they all waited for the Sun to rise, and as it did, but before it had cleared the horizon, they began a chant, slowly, quietly, with great order, and moving forward. As the Sun rose the chant intensified.

The living Inca sat under his own awning a short distance from the lines and rose to his feet to begin the chant. With great elegance and authority he started the song at the head of all. So they sang as the Sun rose. Until noon they heightened their voices, always in accord with the movement of the Sun, and once it passed zenith, they lowered their voices until it set. Throughout the day sacrifices were made; in one place meat was burned in a flame. Elsewhere llamas were set loose for distribution among the residents of the city, and two hundred young women, walking in files of five, brought jars of *chicha* beer and baskets of coca leaf to be offered to the Sun. Many other celebrations and sacrifices were made. After beginning the song the Inca king returned to his seat, where he conversed with worshipers that approached, and at regular intervals he went to his own group of singers to accompany them for a while.

As the Sun approached the western horizon they all showed great sorrow for its impending departure, dulling their voices. When it disappeared completely they clasped their hands, expressing adoration, shock, and profound humility. Soon they carried the mummies back to their respective abodes, also packing all the fine things so they could be brought out again the next day. And in this fashion the Inti Raimi celebration of the Sun lasted eight or nine days in succession. This celebrated the maize harvest, and when it was over the Inca initiated plowing of the land for the next planting (MacCormack 1991: 75–76).

This described what Guaman Poma called Inca Raymi Quilla, when the Inca emperor invited people of all ranks to eat and drink in celebration of the new harvest (Poma [1615] 1978: 26). On this occasion the Inca performed a special song that "began with an imitation of the bleat of the llama, a rhythmical repetition of the animal sound 'yn' on low and high notes, and continued with the song of the rivers, which was a more melodious representation of the sound of running water."

Father Bernabé Cobo's authoritative description of Cuzco and Inca religion was not completed until the middle of the seventeenth century, but it can be treated as a synthesis of sixteenth-century accounts, for he based it on descriptions written in the first decades after the invasion, many of which were subsequently lost. He studiously wrote about Inca religion in past tense, revealing his desire to represent conditions as they existed at the time of the invasion (see Rowe 1979). Cobo ([1653] 1990: 47) placed the royal mummies in a hierarchy of supernaturals, or *huaca*s, indicating that *huaca* (or *guaca*) was a term used "for all of the sacred places designated for prayers and sacrifices, as well as for all of the gods and idols that were worshipped in these places."

At the top of Cobo's Inca pantheon was a nameless creator god metaphorically referred to as Viracocha, Ticci Viracocha, or Pachayachachic—of divine origin or Creator of the World (Cobo [1653] 1990:

22–24). Viracocha had been recently promoted, being recognized as superior to the Sun during the reign of one of the former Incas. There was a statue to him/her of solid gold the size of a ten-year-old boy and a temple, the Quishuarcancha, that faced on the Haucaypata plaza. But s/he had no estates to produce offerings since goods produced for the other gods were offered to Viracocha and these lesser deities should intercede with Viracocha in favor of their human supplicants. Perhaps Cobo was accommodating Inca religion to Catholicism and its saints in this interpretation.

Second in Cobo's pantheon was the Sun, patron and father of the Incas, emperors and otherwise. Throughout the land every town had a Sun temple with attendants, landed estates, and income, but the most magnificent one was the Coricancha of Cuzco, which was also the primary temple of the capital city. There were several idols of the Sun, one a human figure of gold with a cavity where the ashes of the hearts of deceased Inca emperors were placed. A representation of the Sun as a human face from which rays emanated, said to have been on a wall of the Coricancha where it caught the first rays of the rising Sun, may never have existed (Duviols 1976). Other images of the Sun, its brother, and its son were made of cloth and dressed in special costumes that included the weapons of the Sun, long shafts with gold axe heads. Cobo also identified these three images as the Sun itself, the day, and the growing power of the Sun. For certain rituals the figures were removed from the Coricancha by priests in special costumes, and the "statue of the Sun was seated in the center of the square on a small bench which was completely covered with mantles made of fine, colorful feather cloth. The other two statues were stationed on each side with their shafts held up" (Cobo [1653] 1990: 25–28). I infer that the Sun and its images were considered to have been the founding ancestor of the Inca ethnic group.

In addition to the Coricancha, fourteen other solar shrines called *sucancas* marked the movements of the Sun on the western horizon, determining the start of each month. "After the sacrifices were taken to the other *huacas* [shrines] in the order in which they were located on the *ceques* [lines], as will be explained in the proper place, what was left over was offered to these markers [*sucancas*]. This was because the markers were not located in the same order as the other shrines but were distributed according to the course of the Sun, and each one came with a sacrifice to the marker-shrine located nearest to his *ceque*" (Cobo [1653] 1990: 27–28).

Cobo ([1653] 1990: 29–34) next discussed the Moon and Stars. However, he stated that in "authority and honor" Thunder ranked second after the Sun. The Moon was a woman and wife of the Sun. Her statue in the Coricancha was cared for by an order of priestesses, and when the idol went forth to ceremonies it was carried on the shoulders of these women. The lunar cult had estates managed by the priestesses so that the income would support their order and furnish many of the offerings made to their deity. Influential arguments have been made that the Moon headed an entire religious and political structure of women that more or less paralleled that of Inca men, but that was largely overlooked by gender-biased reporting (Silverblatt 1987).

The Stars were believed to include a patron or creator for each species of living thing. This expresses consistent ontological and cosmogenic principles: the Incas with their ancestor the Sun, and the Stars as ancestral founders of animal and plant species. All sprang from the constellation known as Collca, the Pleiades, which was especially revered.

Thunder was imagined as a man who lived in the sky, with a war club in his left hand and a sling in his right (Cobo [1653] 1990: 32–33). His flashing garments gave off lightning when he whirled his sling, and the crack of the sling made the thunder. Drawing water from the river of the sky, the Milky Way, he let it fall as rain to the earth. Thus the Thunder God was responsible for rain, hail, lightning, thunder, rainbows, storms, whirlwinds, and even clouds. His idol was made of fine cloth and he had a son and a brother, as did the Sun. There was also a special temple to Thunder, in the Totocache district of Cuzco, and in it was a gold statue of Thunder placed in a gold litter. This statue was made by Inca Pachacuti and was taken by this Inca to be his "brother."

There were temples to Thunder thoughout the land, and many sacrifices were made to request rain for crops. Any object that was found to hold water when it rained was said to have been sent by Thunder to be worshiped.

The Sea was called Mamacocha or mother of water and lakes. It was revered by all, but especially by the coastal peoples and most by fisherfolk. The Earth, Pachamama, was also sacred and offerings were made to her. She was asked for fertility of the fields.

This set of natural phenomena that heads Cobo's discussion actually seems rather difficult to rank within itself. Significantly, all these supernaturals seem to have been shared with other Andean peoples. Subsequently Cobo listed only shrines that related specifically to Inca history and mythology. First were the *pururauca*s, stones that had temporarily turned into warriors to assist the Incas in repelling a military attack by the rival Chancas. To commemorate this victory that inaugurated their empire, Inca Pachacuti had some of the stones brought to the Coricancha and others placed at important locations. All were assigned people responsible for making offerings to them, and hence these stones became idols.

Next in the discussion were the idols called *guaugue*s or brothers (Cobo [1653] 1990: 37–38). These were statues taken by living kings and other high nobles as patrons or "brothers." It was thought that as long as the figures endured they had the same power as the living humans. Their presence could inspire a contingent of troops while the emperor and generals remained safely in council.

Third, Cobo discusses mummies of the dead:

> No matter how important and esteemed a person may have been while his vigor and strength lasted, when he grew old, they paid very little attention to him for the rest of his life. However, when he died, they took great care in respecting his dead body, so much so that they worshipped it like a god, and as such they made sacrifices to it. For this purpose, as soon as the soul had left the body, the members of the deceased's *ayllo* [*ayllu*] and family unit would take the dead body, and if the deceased was a king or great lord, the body would be embalmed with great skill. As a result, it would be preserved intact for many years, and it would not deteriorate or give off foul odor. All of their personal property would be taken, including dishes of gold and silver. None of this was given to the heirs. Part of it was placed with the deceased, and part of it was buried in places where the deceased customarily spent his leisure time when alive.
>
> The relatives of the deceased would look after these dead bodies, and they kept them adorned and carefully preserved. The bodies were wrapped in a large amount of cotton with the face covered. The bodies were not brought out except for major festivals. No ordinary people saw the bodies except for those responsible for dressing them, watching over them, and caring for their preservation. These attendants sustained themselves on the farmland that the descendants of the deceased had

designated for this purpose. The embalmed bodies were greatly venerated and sacrifices were made to each one according to their resources. Some kept the bodies of their relatives in their own houses, but the bodies of the Inca kings were placed at first in the Temple of the Sun, each one in its own chapel with its own altar. Later it was determined that in order to preserve these bodies with more decorum, the members of their family unit should be put in charge of them, and so it was done. Each body was placed along with its *guaugue* in a house of its own, with an adequate number of attendants and servants, befitting the rank of the deceased. However, the lords and chiefs of their family units always looked after them, and the whole family devoted itself to paying tribute to their deceased. The bodies were brought out with a large retinue for all solemn festivals, and for less solemn occasions, in place of the bodies, their *guaugues* were brought out. In the square they were seated in a row according to their seniority, and there the servants and guardians ate and drank. A flame was kindled before the deceased of a certain firewood that was carved and cut all the same length. The food set before the dead bodies for them to eat was burned in this flame. (Cobo [1653] 1990: 39–40)

Cobo's description goes on to ceremonial drinking and mutual toasting between living and dead, as observed by the first European invaders. But in addition to offerings, prayers were made to the dead, in some cases asking the deceased ancestor to intercede on the behalf of the descendant with Viracocha or some other powerful deity. This suggests that in addition to any supernatural power the dead themselves had, they were able to mediate with higher authorities. This is an aspect of divination even more apparent among the Yauyos, discussed in the next chapter.

Cobo notes that not all the living worshiped all the dead, nor even all their dead relatives. Rather, they worshiped the dead from whom they were direct descendants, so father, grandfather, and great-grandfather were venerated, but not a father's brother. However, there seems to have been another principle at work, that of fictional ancestor of a social group, for Cobo notes that important lords were venerated for a long time. "For everyone else it discontinued when the deceased's children or grandchildren died, and after that the deceased was forgotten" (Cobo [1653] 1990: 42).

Following the discussion of ancestor mummies, Cobo ([1653] 1990: 44–46) lists *huaca*s that were natural objects but unusual or somehow marked as special. They included especially large fruits or potatoes, unusually shaped ears of corn, very high mountain peaks, oddly formed lakes or rivers, strange stones, and people of extraordinary birth. Recognition of such *huaca*s, as well as images made expressly to imitate something, does not seem to be specific to the Incas and their history. Similar *huaca*s existed in households all across the central Andes.

Having listed the hierarchy of supernaturals recognized by the Incas, Cobo ([1653] 1990: 47–84; see also Rowe 1979) turned his attention to the actual shrines in Cuzco and then to the calendar of rituals carried out through the year, month by month (Cobo [1653] 1990: 126–151; see also Zuidema 1964, 1974–1976, 1990a, 1990c, 1992). The Coricancha temple of Cuzco lay at the center of forty-one constellations of *huaca*s that defined the empire's capital. Each constellation was a line that extended out from this center so that each *huaca* could be numbered consecutively in terms of its order from the Coricancha. These lines, or *ceque*s, were organized into four groups according to compass quarters—the same division that gave its name, Tawantinsuyu, the four quarters, to the Inca Empire. Cobo listed the *huaca*s quarter by quarter. Each quarter had three groups of three lines, except for Condesuyu, which had fourteen lines, and there was a total of 328 *huaca*s on the lines. "On each one of those *ceque*s were arranged in order the *huaca*s and shrines which were in Cuzco and its region like stations of holy places, the veneration of which was common to all" (Cobo [1653] 1990: 51). Each *ceque* was the responsibility of the kinship units and families of the city of Cuzco, from which came the attendants and servants who cared for the *huaca*s of their *ceque* and saw to offering the established sacrifices at the proper times.

Tom Zuidema (1964, 1974–1976, 1990a, 1990c, 1992) infers that the Incas employed a ritual agricultural calendar with ten months totaling 328 days that began with planting and ended with harvest, to which was added two months totaling 37 or 38 days outside the farming season to complete the solar year. John Rowe (1979) has argued that Cobo's list of *huaca*s was not complete and that the total should have been greater. Furthermore, there is reason to believe that the Incas employed a calendar of twelve months of thirty or thirty-one days to constitute the solar year. Be that as it may, each day of the year in Cuzco a specific kin group sponsored a particular ceremony, at a special location. This system established an integrated map of calendrical time, geographic space, social organization, ritual practice, and mythical history—for each *huaca* participated in Cuzco's past.

Discussion of the 328 *huacas* listed by Cobo is beyond the scope of this work, but four examples suffice to reveal the relevance of these sacred shrines for Inca mythical history and organization.

1. The third *huaca* on the second line of Chinchaysuyu was "an idol of solid gold named *Inti Illapa*, which means 'Thunder of the Sun,' which was set on a rich litter of gold. Inca [Pachacuti] Yupanqui made it and took it for his *guauque* or brother. It had a house in the district of Totocache, and they did it great veneration. In the same house was the body of the said Inca Yupanqui" (Cobo [1653] 1990: 54).
2. The third *huaca* on the third line of Chinchaysuyu was a "fountain [that] belonged to the *coya* or [first] queen Mama Ocllo. In it were made very great and ordinary sacrifices, especially when they wanted to ask something of the said Mama Ocllo, who was the most venerated woman there was among these Indians" (Cobo [1653] 1990: 55).
3. *Huaca* seven on line five of Chinchaysuyu was called Chacaguanacauri, and young noblemen visited the site during initiation activities (Cobo [1653] 1990: 58). Zuidema (1986: 192–193) points out that this is probably the "Chaca" where, when the sixth king Inca Roca had his ears pierced (part of the nobleman's initiation ritual), he lay down and placed his left ear to the ground. He could hear water running inside the earth so he plunged his arm into the ground and opened access to the water that fed the most important irrigation canal in upper Cuzco.
4. *Huaca* five on the second line of Antisuyu was the place where, before he ascended the throne, Inca Pachacuti saw the Sun God in a vision (Zuidema 1974–1976). Subsequently he defeated the Chanca warriors and became the ninth Inca emperor.

Clearly the *ceques* and *huacas* of Cuzco referred to the events and the individuals of Inca history. They accounted for rights to water, rights to lands, the existence of political and religious power, and perhaps even the shape of the land itself. The *ceques* and *huacas* provided the Incas what maps, land titles, and family histories furnish in modern societies.

Each day had its own social group and religious observation, but each of the twelve months also had a special focus, with characteristic rites and sacrifices. During the first month at the time of the December solstice the Incas conducted elaborate rituals for the initiation of young noblemen. I have already described parts of Inti Raymi or Inca Raymi Quilla of the fourth month. The tenth month, the beginning of the rainy season called Coya Raymi, focused on cleansing the city of sickness and misfortune. All people who were deformed were removed from Cuzco. Following many offerings and observations of the moon, evil was driven out by relays of armed warriors who ran along the four highways till they reached the first great river, where they bathed and washed their weapons. So each month and each day had its observances, its social groups, and its specific goals that were necessary for the well-being of all the inhabitants. Inca culture was woven on a great web of space-time practices, channeled by landscape and the built environment, that structured kinship, community, and politics into cosmic order.

By 1536 the Spanish occupation of Cuzco was becoming extremely oppressive, and early in that year the Incas secretly withdrew the royal ancestor mummies from the ceremonial city, to the safety of Inca military headquarters at Ollantaytambo. In April the puppet emperor Manco Inca escaped Spanish control and began a rebellion. Soon it became clear that his reconquest was not succeeding, so a court in exile was established at Vitcos, in the forested Vilcabamba Valley north of Cuzco and Ollantaytambo. Manco Inca had the bodies of former Incas, both men and women, brought to Vitcos, where houses were established for the veneration of each.

In July 1537 Vitcos was sacked in a raid led by Rodrigo Orgóñez. According to Manco Inca's son, Titu Cusi Yupanqui ([1570] 1973: 100), who was taken captive, the bodies of Huanacauri, Viracocha Inca, Pachacuti Inca, Topa Inca Yupanqui, and Huayna Capac, along with many bodies of women as well as jewels and riches, were captured by Orgóñez and returned to Cuzco. In fact, it may have been the great wealth associated with these mummies that distracted the Christian raiders long enough for Manco Inca to escape. At any rate, in 1541 Luis de Morales testified that the replacement puppet Inca Paullu (brother of Manco Inca) was in control of the body of his father, Huayna Capac, and many of his other ancestors, in Cuzco. Under Morales's supervision they were supposed to have been buried in a secret place known to only a few persons (Guillén 1983: 32). But these mummies were too important to disappear so quietly.

In 1559 the chief magistrate of Cuzco, Juan Polo de Ondegardo, was ordered by the Spanish viceroy to confiscate the remaining mummies of the dead Inca emperors. Not only were the mummies objects of pagan religion that impeded Christianization, but they promoted support for Inca reconquest. Official historian Pedro Sarmiento de Gamboa ([1572] 1965: 223; Guillén 1983: 32–35) wrote of Polo's success, albeit not without considerable insistence and force, for the Indians in charge of the bodies hid them and skillfully moved them from place to place to avoid capture. Eventually Polo succeeded in recovering most of the royal bodies, who according to consensus history should have included five kings of the lower moiety followed by five kings of the upper moiety, and then Huayna Capac, also of the upper moiety, whose sudden death precipitated the civil war preceding the Spanish invasion.

Following the viceroy's orders, chief magistrate Polo recovered the following Inca mummies.

*Upper Moiety*

> The body of Inca Huayna Capac, eleventh and final Inca before the Spanish Invasion. Huayna Capac was the father of Huascar, Atahualpa, Manco Inca, and Inca Paullu.
> The idol "brother" or *guaugue* of the tenth king, Topa Inca Yupanqui, but not his body.
> The body of Pachacuti Inca Yupanqui, ninth Inca emperor.
> The ashes of the body and the idol of Inca Viracocha, eighth emperor. (The body of Inca Viracocha had been burned by Gonzalo Pizarro some years earlier.)
> Neither the body nor the idol of Yawar Huaca, seventh king, was found.
> The body and idol of the sixth king, Inca Roca, were both recovered.

*Lower Moiety*

> The body and idol of Capac Yupanqui, fifth king.
> The body and idol of Mayta Capac, fourth king.
> The idol of Lloque Yupanqui, third king, but not his body.

The body and idol of Sinchi Roca, second king.

The idol but not the body of Manco Capac. Manco Capac was the reputed founder of the Inca dynasty, and its first king, who had emerged from the underworld at Tambotoco.

Also recovered were many bodies of past Inca queens. Polo hid the royal mummies in his Cuzco home. Later he sent several to Lima, including Pachacuti Inca and Huayna Capac (ninth and eleventh kings), where they were supposedly buried on the grounds of the hospital of San Andrés.

While it would seem that Polo should have achieved a sweeping victory with the confiscation of nearly all the Inca mummies, as late as 1570 Viceroy Francisco Toledo continued to lament the power of royal mummies being venerated in Vitcos (Guillén 1983: 33). Scholars have questioned who these mummies actually were. If they were the real emperors' bodies then perhaps the mummy guardians had fooled Polo with look-alike cadavers. A popular but unfounded argument asserts that the real Incas' bodies still lie hidden somewhere in the jungles of the Vilcabamba River Valley. No one can resolve this question, but the difficulty in disposing of the ancestor mummies vividly demonstrates how important these bodies were for the *panaca* and *ayllu*, at the core of Inca social organization and political identity. The struggle shows also that the Incas could be flexible and innovative in the apparent preservation of key mummies as well as manipulating them as political symbols.

A likely explanation for the destruction and reappearance of royal mummies lies in their apparent ability to be duplicated, as we know from the *guaugue* or "brother" images described by Cobo ([1653] 1990: 37–38) and other chroniclers. While Andean ancestor worship focused on the body of the deceased, alternatives—or perhaps secondary figures—were made for the same purpose. For example, Polo's search for royal mummies also netted a number of "brother" or *guaugue* idols. Cobo made it clear that these idols could represent the living king during his life, and after death they were more or less equivalent to the mummy. I suspect that these figures of the kings made the long journeys, ventured out in bad weather, and went into battle in place of the actual mummy, for the deterioration or loss of the body itself was vastly more serious. I also believe that the secondary ancestor figures, or idols, included a part of the original body, which might be ashes of the burned viscera or bodily exuvia such as a lock of hair or fingernail trimmings, incorporated into the clay or wood figure. In fact, early observers of the royal mummies in Cuzco noted that a box was kept with each mummy that contained all the nail cuttings and hair trimmed from the body during life. Consequently there was a large supply of basic material from which a new *guaugue* idol could be made upon demand. While it was never stated that the power of the idol depended on its containing some actual part of the original body, this certainly seems to have been desired. Perhaps even stone and gold idols contained a compartment for body remains. The gold idol of the Sun God discussed above (Duviols 1976: 171) was said to contain the ashes of the hearts of former Incas. Perhaps it represented the living Inca king's father in a fashion much more literal than we generally imagine.

Idols could also represent mythical ancestors who probably never lived in flesh and blood. Titu Cusi ([1570] 1973), son of exiled Inca Manco and heir to the neo-Inca throne in Vitcos, dictated an account of the resistance. In his description of the successful raid on Vitcos in 1537, when he was captured and returned to Cuzco with the royal mummies, he wrote that Huanacauri was among them. Huanacauri was a brother of Inca dynasty founder Manco Capac, whose body was never found by Polo. According to the myths, Huanacauri had turned to stone on the mountaintop that bears his name at the edge of the Cuzco Valley before Manco Capac and his sisters entered the valley to found their kingdom. It seems unlikely that he was ever flesh and blood; he was probably a mythical ancestor who symbolically mediated the relationship between the Incas in Cuzco and outsiders beyond the border of the valley where his shrine was established. He must have been represented by an idol alone, as seems to have been the case for Manco Capac, his brother. The relationship between an ancestor mummy, a "brother" or *guaugue* idol, and an idol *per se* must have been something of a continuum, but functionally they probably all fulfilled the same role. What this proliferation of mummies and idols suggests is that descent as a prerequisite for membership could be fictionalized for the sake of political goals as long as the fiction was validated with an appropriate ancestral figure who was treated as the founder of the group.

To expand our understanding of Inca ancestor mummies and their significance for the kinship and organization of Cuzco we need to review two interpretations of the Inca history and royal mummies, one historiographic and the other structural. First, we need to realize that

Inca status was not limited to the emperor (who was called the Sapa Inca or Unique Inca) but included all who were recognized as descendants of an Inca emperor, as far back as Manco Capac, who emerged from the underworld to found the nation. Incas were an ethnic group organized in terms of kinship categories that had farmed the Valley of Cuzco for centuries. They became a class of privileged elite as a result of military conquests and incorporation politics. Within the group there were tremendous differences in rank, power, and wealth.

John Rowe (1945, 1946, 1967) has proposed a historical, descent-based and dynastic explanation of the Inca ancestral mummies. The Incas and other Andean peoples had no system of writing, so descriptions of their empire and culture are limited to accounts written by Spanish invaders, except for a few Indian chroniclers in later colonial times. The invaders' accounts agree that the mummies were the bodies of former rulers who succeeded one another in kingship over the Incas, usually from father to son. In fact, the Spanish viceroy Francisco Toledo had Inca history investigated very intensively, especially by Pedro Sarmiento de Gamboa ([1572] 1907, [1572] 1965). The goal was to discover the basis of Inca claim to legitimate rule over their empire of Tawantinsuyu. The viceroy was delighted to discover that the Inca dynasty had only very recently become conquerors, creating their state by forcibly taking power from earlier kings, chiefs, and councils. Sarmiento's history was sent to the king of Spain, but Viceroy Toledo was so pleased with it that in January of 1572 he had the history read to an obligatory assembly of all the descendants of Huayna Capac, placing them on notice that the Incas were not true kings, but usurpers (Hemming 1970: 415).

It is hard to know how much the Spanish investigators cast Inca culture into a European mold and how much their desire to prove the illegitimacy of Inca rule may have influenced the outcome of their investigation. However, Rowe observes that in spite of the Incas' lack of writing, official accounts of royal accomplishments were memorized by specialists and recited in narrative poems at special occasions, such as the coronation of Manco Inca witnessed by the Spaniards in 1534. Furthermore, events were recorded in paintings. The Spanish chroniclers, and especially the official historian Sarmiento, had access to these accounts. While they may have been embellished and modified, the importance of kinship and descent in social organization demanded at least basic historiographical truth. Furthermore, Sarmiento and the other historians of the time were able to cross-check accounts by different Inca factions and compare these with the reports of non-Incas.

Evaluating each chronicler's sources of information and comparing the accounts with one another, Rowe reached the conclusion that the Incas officially recognized a royal dynasty consisting of twelve or thirteen kings, depending on whether Huascar and Atahualpa were both counted as legitimate rulers (see Fig. 2.7).

Each of these kings was represented by a mummy or an idol that was venerated by his descendants who lived in Cuzco. However, a reliable history of events only began in the reign of Viracocha Inca or Pachacuti Inca, as demonstrated by greater consistency among

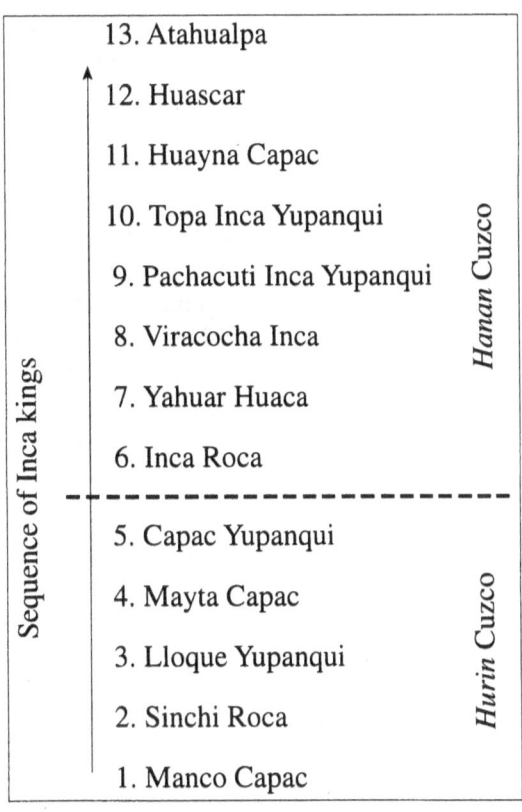

Figure 2.7. Inca Royal Dynasty

the chroniclers' accounts of events. Furthermore, durations given for the reigns of the subsequent Incas are realistic in light of human lifespans, and one chronicler, Miguel Cabello de Balboa ([1586] 1951), integrated events into a very reasonable sequence correlated with Christian calendar dates. Rowe's historical interpretation proposes the following account (Rowe 1945, 1946, 1967).

The Incas had been living in the Cuzco Valley, probably for a couple of centuries, farming the land and raising llamas. Led by war chiefs, they engaged in mutual raiding until the ascension of Viracocha Inca early in the fifteenth century. This militarily successful Inca initiated policies of control over defeated groups rather than simply taking booty after a successful raid. He consolidated Inca occupation in the Valley of Cuzco as well as control over the neighboring Valley of Anta, the Urubamba from Quiquijana to Calca, a hilly district southwest of Cuzco, and perhaps somewhat more, but nothing significant beyond some 75 km from their original farmsteads.

About 1438 the Chancas, a similar group of newly successful combatants from the valleys to the west, attacked Cuzco. The elderly Viracocha retreated to a mountain fortress with his son and heir, while a secondary son organized a defense of the valley. Following a religious vision in which he saw the Sun God (at a place that was to become *huaca* five on the second line of Antisuyu) this youth gained a stunning upset victory, usurped the crown, and named himself Pachacuti Inca—cataclysm and reformer of the world. Pachacuti seized the initiative, expanding Inca control down the Urubamba and pursuing the Chancas to defeat. Many more military campaigns were conducted, and most were followed by the imposition of provincial organization. As his armies of citizens and allies swelled, the Incas became virtually invincible and conquests more sweeping.

Emperor Pachacuti was blessed with a long life and a militarily brilliant son, Topa Inca. He also had an equally able but less ambitious son, Amaru Inca, who directed the Cuzco government during Topa's absences for conquests. In old age Pachacuti turned the armies over to Topa (around 1463) and devoted himself full-time to organizing his state administrative apparatus, rebuilding Cuzco, and putting Inca "history" in order. His goal was to create a regal capital city and an illustrious dynasty of privileged emperors from a dusty village and a succession of grizzly war chiefs.

The new city included a magnificent and centrally located palace for Pachacuti and another for his son, Topa. In the process of rebuilding Pachacuti also had palaces constructed for each of the royal ancestors, who lacked an appropriately impressive abode. The mummies of these ancestral rulers who figured prominently in oral history were in the Sun Temple, called the Coricancha, although some were probably only idols that represented mythical ancestors, such as Manco Capac, the dynasty founder and link with the Sun God.

Pachacuti appropriated land outside Cuzco as a personal estate, and so did Topa. As with the palaces, Pachacuti went on to create estates for each royal ancestor. Inca custom denied a king the inheritance of personal property from his predecessor, so these estates became eternal trusts of each mummy, its income supporting the ancestor's descendants in their adoration of the body. This made it possible for Incas of

Cuzco to make rich offerings to their past kings and ancestors, creating an affluent and impressive ceremonial life in their capital. Furthermore, by treating deceased kings of past generations to the luxuries and privileges Pachacuti Inca was creating for himself and his son, he appropriated the past and the ancestor mummies to legitimize new class differences.

Official oral history recognized eight Incas before Pachacuti, so, in addition to the palaces and estates of Pachacuti and Topa, eight others were created. Direct descendants of each Inca constituted his *panaca* or descent group, which was responsible for rituals and offerings to the mummy, as well as stewardship of the mummy, the palace, and the estate. All Incas were recognized as descended from at least one of these ancestors, although there actually may have been considerable freedom of choice regarding the *panaca* with which one affiliated. For ceremonial and perhaps administrative purposes, the ten Inca *panacas* (divided into an upper and a lower moiety in which the first five kings and their descendants belonged to the lower moiety) were paired with ten larger kin groups or *ayllus* of local Cuzco region peoples of lesser status.

Topa Inca ascended the throne in about 1471 and ruled until about 1493. By the end of his reign the Incas controlled western South America from Quito to central Chile. Topa continued the policies of his father, including the construction of Cuzco as a monumental capital devoted to impressive ceremonies.

When Huayna Capac became the eleventh emperor about 1493 his major task was the consolidation of the vast conquests of Topa. He also had to build his own palace, create an estate, and establish his *panaca*. During his reign Huayna Capac received reports of Spaniards reconnoitering the edge of his empire. But before he could complete the conquests in which he was engaged along the northern frontier a devastating plague swept the empire. Most likely the plague was a smallpox epidemic, introduced to the South American mainland by *conquistadores* in Colombia and Panama, or perhaps via the Río de la Plata and across the Bolivian Chaco. The disease spread through the dense Andean populations even faster than the Christian invaders' advance, and hundreds of thousands died. Huayna Capac's designated heir succumbed, and so did the emperor before a new successor was clearly named. In uncertainty, Huayna Capac's mummy was carried from Quito in the far north back to Cuzco and one of his sons, Huascar, was made Inca in 1527.

Soon conflict broke out between Huascar and half-brother Atahualpa, who also claimed the throne and backed his claim with the seasoned armies of Huayna Capac's northern campaigns. In the civil war that followed, Atahualpa's troops eventually took Cuzco by force, capturing Huascar, killing as many of his kin as they could lay hands on, and, according to some, destroying the mummy of Topa Inca, whose *panaca* descendants supported Huascar's claim to the throne.

As luck would have it, Francisco Pizarro and his invaders arrived at Atahualpa's camp in Cajamarca on November 15, 1532, as he was awaiting news of his general's assault on Cuzco. Learning of the victory may have contributed to Atahualpa's sense of invincibility, making him an easier victim for a Spanish ambush. At any rate, seized and imprisoned by Pizarro, Atahualpa ordered that Huascar should be killed on the road from Cuzco to Cajamarca, as he was being brought back in defeat. Atahualpa hoped to prevent the Spanish from siding with Huascar's faction—which of course they did, also casting themselves in the role of liberators rather than invaders—as soon as they extracted a great ransom and executed Atahualpa.

In John Rowe's historiographic interpretation, Viracocha Inca, Pachacuti Inca, Topa Inca, and Huayna Capac were real historical kings who succeeded one another, father to son. They founded their own *panaca*s, and at least the last two built their own palaces and estates. Viracocha Inca was officially descended from a line of seven earlier kings, some surely real persons and others surely mythical. But Pachacuti Inca made the dynasty magnificent by creating palaces and estates for each ancestor, formalizing his *panaca* of descendants, and guaranteeing his cult. When the Spanish arrived they found Cuzco organized in terms of ten mummies, ten *panaca*s, and ten *ayllu*s, divided into two moieties of five each. But this was a moment in history, for it would have changed to eleven with the integration of Huayna Capac's descendants once a new king was securely installed. With the death of Huayna Capac's legitimate successor, whether Huascar or Atahualpa, and the succession of one of his sons, the dynasty would have included twelve kings, and so on, if the invasion had not interrupted Inca history.

Tom Zuidema (1986, 1989a, 1989b, 1989c, 1990a, 1990b, 1990c, 1992) offers a structural alternative to Rowe's historical interpretation of the Inca mummies. He believes that two moieties with ten mummies, ten *panaca*s, and ten *ayllu*s represent an organizational structure, not a moment in the history of a royal dynasty. In his view the Inca narratives about royal ancestors were not really concerned with dynastic succession but with embodying social groups and defining relationships among them. In the construction of inequality within Inca society, privileges and responsibilities were based on the idiom of kinship, order provided by astronomy—solar, lunar, and astral calendars—and the irrigation cultivation of sections within the Cuzco Valley.

First, Cuzco was divided into two moieties. Like other central Andean kingdoms, each moiety had its own king. The two ruled simultaneously and were more or less equal in internal politics, but in regard to external affairs the upper moiety king was supreme. Based on their experience that was limited to a single king, the Spanish identified the king of the upper moiety as emperor. Thus, Zuidema disputes the foundation of Rowe's history asserting that the five kings of lower (*hurin*) Cuzco, and the five kings of upper (*hanan*) Cuzco were not sequential but simultaneous, providing a dual dynasty of five kings each.

Incas included all who traced their descent from one of the emperors, but among them they were differentiated by how closely they were related to the ruling emperor—or perhaps more precisely stated, what kin terms were used to express the relationship with the ruling emperor. This was not simple, because the emperor practiced polygynous marriage, and marriage was the chief means of formalizing alliances with foreign groups. Consequently, the status of the mother became key in defining the status of the Inca emperor's children. If the mother was of Inca origin the child was also Inca and belonged to the upper moiety. Within the upper moiety, if the wife was a full sister of the emperor, her male child was referred to by the emperor as son, and he called the emperor father. If the mother was a first cousin, her son was referred to by the emperor as grandson. If the mother was a second cousin, her son was referred to by the emperor as great-grandson, and so on, according to the distance of the mother. The son's status depended on the number of generations he was removed from the Inca emperor by the kin term of address.

From a patrilineal perspective, what became important was the implied distance of the common male ancestor linking the boy to the emperor. For the son of the Inca emperor by a full sister, the linking ancestor was in the first ascending generation. For the (parallel) first cousin's son the linking ancestor was in the second ascending generation. For the (parallel) second cousin's son the linking ancestor was in the third ascending generation; for the son of the next closest female relative the link was in the fourth ascending generation. For the son of an "unrelated" Inca woman (ultimately all Incas were recognized as descended from one of the emperors and therefore kin, but beyond four generations the relationship had no significance for marriage) the common male ancestor was apparently considered to lie in the fifth or sixth ascending generation. Consequently among the Inca emperor's sons by Inca women there was a whole array of different statuses, and some children referred to the emperor as great-great-great-grandfather even though it was impossible that in his lifetime any man would have such distant descendants.

Note that this entire system had to be reorganized each time a new Inca took office. The status of nobles' children would decline with each new succession, for the linking relative to the new emperor became generationally more distant. But there were rules for offsetting status decline that involved marrying close relatives, so not only were kin terms used between the emperor and his children social rather than biological categories, but the terms for all Inca "relatives" were reshaped by similar social rules that related to hierarchy and privilege.

The Inca emperor's children by non-Inca women were also Incas, but they belonged to the lower moiety. And they were not called sons, grandsons, great-grandsons, etc., but sister's son, niece's son, etc., depending on the status of the mother. Consequently, collaterality (focusing on the cross cousin relationship) and generational distance to the ascending male linking ancestor were both used to express relative status. The classes of kin established in this way were used to organize the rest of the lower moiety, and a term meaning sister's daughter's daughter's daughter's son, used for an actual son of the emperor by a non-Inca woman of little political importance, was also used with other lower moiety people of low status.

As we saw above, the Incas manipulated descent terms to create groupings that were politically expedient. What was required to legitimize the fiction was a founding ancestor for each descent group—a mummy, a *guaugue*, an idol, or, better yet, all three. As a member of a descent group one participated in the veneration of the founding ancestor, and the internal organization of the group could take place around these ritual activities rather than actual kinship relations, albeit employing the terms supplied by kin terminology. In Cuzco the royal descent groups were called *panacas*, a term related to the word *pana*, "sister," probably in recognition of the fundamental relationship brothers have with their sisters (Sherbondy 1982).

Cuzco's system of social statuses that were based on kin terms focused on the reigning Inca implied a succession of male ancestors of the emperor, who were the social ancestors of all the Incas. They need not be real biological ancestors, although in some cases they might be and in other cases they certainly were not. In Tom Zuidema's image of Cuzco social organization, the royal Inca mummies were implied ancestors attributed with founding the essential status groups into which Cuzco Inca society was divided. Thus they embodied the status categories of Cuzco, and concerns about real biological or indeed even real chronological relationships were never significant questions for Incas.

Each mummy was the "founder" of a group whose statuses related to a kin term and its reciprocal used by the Inca emperor and a member of Inca society, which required the mummy as the linking male ancestor. These people constituted the mummy's *panaca*, a group of socially determined "descendants" who expressed their unity in rituals for the founder and in the calendrically mandated ceremonies of Cuzco. Zuidema found that the depth of kinship recognized seemed to express an Andean preference for ten and twelve generations (an ego with four or five ascending ancestors and four or five descending descendants), a number based on the division of the solar calendar.

The Inca calendar for the solar year was divided into twelve months—an almost universally discovered solution for accommodating synodic lunar months to the length of the solar year. For Zuidema, two months lay outside the agricultural calendar and ten within it, creating ten periods for internal order and two expressive of external relations. The performance of rituals in the ceremonial capital and the distribution of labor obligations were organized in terms of rotational turns based on these twelve months.

The Huatanay River runs down the middle of the Cuzco Valley, creating a north and a south moiety called upper and lower, respectively. Each moiety was divided into two *suyu*s, so in the upper moiety were Chinchaysuyu and Antisuyu while in the lower were Collasuyu and Condesuyu. Each *suyu* contained three administrative districts or *chapa*s, probably based on irrigation waters and land, for a total of twelve.

One *chapa* was associated with each month of the solar year, and its peoples were responsible for certain rituals and duties in Cuzco during the appropriate month.

Two *chapa* districts were assigned to the pre-Inca peoples of the Cuzco Valley for their needs, and they represented the non-Inca outside world. The remaining ten *chapa*s were assigned to Inca peoples, one to each of the ten *panaca*s, five in the upper and five in the lower moiety. This structure probably furnished the Incas a model for administrative incorporation of the first peoples conquered around Cuzco, who were required to give labor service to the ceremonial city on a rotating basis. Each servile group was assigned to one *chapa*, receiving land where they could construct storehouses and residences and cultivate crops to maintain themselves during their periods of service. The period of service apparently corresponded with that *chapa*'s month, and its *panaca* members directed the labor of the servile group. These servile groups were the ten *ayllu*s of lesser Incas that were paired one each with the royal *panaca*s.

Zuidema speculates that the confusion experienced by Spanish chroniclers recording Inca "history" was due to several factors. One was Spanish inclination, and probably even explicit desire, to create the Inca past in terms of a dynasty of successive kings, like European ones, to which European criteria of legitimacy could be applied. Second was the complexity of the Inca system, with its use of terms of kinship and generation to designate social status. A third was the fact that Inca social history was designed as a dynamic system that reconstructed itself each generation with the ascension of a new emperor, who became the conceptual "founder" and center of the social system. For example, in Zuidema's vision, the kings of lower Cuzco and upper Cuzco were simultaneous kings. Spanish investigators became confused because the upper moiety was superior to the lower moiety, and kin terms expressing this rank relative to the Sapa Inca (the ruling emperor of the upper moiety) used generations of removal to indicate status. Thus the founders of the ranked *panaca*s of the upper moiety were father, grandfather, great-grandfather, etc., of the living king. Founders of lower moiety *panaca*s were probably great-great-great-great-grandfather and even more distantly removed from the king. These terms were understood as generations of history by Spaniards, not links of removal in a system of relative status. But by the time most of the Spanish accounts were written Inca social history had become frozen, for no Inca had reigned in

Cuzco for forty years. Not only was its conceptualization becoming progressively idealized, but also its implications were being manipulated by surviving Incas interested in improving their fortune within colonial society. (For a study of how Inca origin myths were manipulated in early colonial times to improve the lots of particular interest groups, see Urton 1990.)

The importance of the living Sapa Inca, and continuously reconstructing Inca society in the calendrical rituals of Cuzco that rewove the web of kinship, space, religious practice, and administrative organization around his person, cannot be underestimated. Franklin Pease (1965) has argued very convincingly that the war between Huascar and Atahualpa was a logical consequence of the Incas establishing a second ceremonial capital in the north at Tumibamba. During his prolonged military campaigns, emperor Huayna Capac's association with Tumebamba allowed it to become an independent center where the Inca society and cosmos were constructed independent of Cuzco. When Huascar was crowned emperor at Cuzco about 1527, Atahualpa's first claim was that on his deathbed Huayna Capac had divided the empire, ceding the north to Atahualpa and the south to Huascar. When Huascar responded with war Atahualpa set out to take the whole empire by force. Perhaps Atahualpa was right. Huayna Capac had divided the empire, albeit not by proclamation on his deathbed. By residing so long in Tumebamba the Sapa Inca created a social and ideological center competitive with Cuzco. The social order of each capital could only be reconstituted around its own Sapa Inca, so in effect Huayna Capac had divided the empire.

After the last Inca rituals in Cuzco in 1535, Inca society deconstructed or, perhaps more correctly, was no longer constructed and reconstructed. The integrated meanings that things like kinship terms, royal mummies, *huaca* rituals, geographical places, and mythical/historical events had once possessed were no longer present. When Spanish historians interviewed surviving members of the Inca nobility in the 1560s and 1570s we may suspect that words were inadequate to express what had formerly been constructed in lived experience, including dance, sacrifice, and ritual display.

Fortunately, we do not have to resolve the controversy between John Rowe's historiography and Tom Zuidema's structuralism, for they agree that ancestor mummies were key foci for the Inca social system of *panaca*s and *ayllu*s. On one hand, I feel that Cobo's description of the *ceque* system of Cuzco's sacred places is incomplete, and consequently Tom Zuidema's analysis may erroneously identify some accidental features such as the total of 328 *huacas*/days as structurally fundamental. This must demand some serious reevaluation of the structuralist assertions about Inca logic and order. On the other hand, John Rowe's historiography fails to account for the recent archaeological evidence obtained by Brian Bauer (1992) in Paruro, south of Cuzco.

Paruro is located immediately south of the Inca's Cuzco Valley so the historiographic theory would predict very late but transformational changes, occasioned by the imposition of Inca rule under Pachacuti Inca. This should have occurred no earlier than the 1450s. It should have been a sudden event, following an extended period of conflict and raiding among more or less equivalent polities ruled by war chiefs. But Bauer (1992) finds archaeological evidence for the expansion of Inca-style pottery out of Cuzco quite a bit earlier and only after a long period of interaction with local Paruro ceramics. Bauer argues that Cuzco was the singular center for the region soon after A.D. 1000. Subsequently changes were gradual, with increasing Cuzco influence and control until by about 1400 Paruro was integrated into an Inca state. So the story of Cuzco's modest dynasty of chiefs until Inca Pachacuti also seems to be in need of reevaluation.

In spite of contradictory conclusions from a historiographic and a structural approach, the Spanish chronicles do provide meaningful insights into Inca ancestor mummies. Each mummy was the symbol of a social unit in Cuzco. It was the founder and charter for the cohesion of its social group, with its land and other resources, its ritual and administrative obligations, its internal order, and its corporate interests. The mummies were foci for actions that created solidarity, hierarchy, and group identity for each *ayllu* or *panaca*. Furthermore, relations between mummies—biological or fictitious—described more inclusive social relations and were essential for political unity as well as for inequality and governance. Together the mummies embodied Inca society. Each group in Cuzco had its place, established by its founder, a venerated mummy, on which the descendants' claims to social status, to land, and to other rights—as well as their claims to participate in Cuzco's ceremonial constitution of society—depended. All Incas descended from a single founder, Manco Capac, whose descent line distinguished Incas from the rest of the world.

CHAPTER

# III

# Ancestor Mummies in Huarochirí

The Spanish invaders of Inca Tawantinsuyu immediately attacked the Sapa Inca, subverted the power of the high nobility, and seized control of government in Cuzco. In doing so they made themselves the only eyewitnesses of the Inca state and its capital city, for both were destroyed in the process of transforming them into a Spanish colony. Today we may wish there had been more scholars among these soldiers, but they did leave accounts and descriptions of Cuzco, its royalty, and its rituals that are invaluable. Forty years after the invasion the Spanish Viceroyalty in Lima ordered studies for a written history of Inca kingship. The result revealed the Incas as recent empire builders whose rule was based on force of arms. It fell short of European demands for legitimacy, associated as they were with millennia-old Rome and the beginnings of Christianity. Unfortunately, the Incas were not described in their own terms, but with European values and with the goal of judging their legitimacy in terms of European ideas about dynastic succession and right to rule. But these histories do preserve testimonies by the most knowledgeable survivors of the Inca court, and they are rich in detail about Inca life, social structure, and the organization of the capital and empire.

Both the invaders and the historians tell us that Inca social groups were inseparable from founding ancestors whose mummies were revered as supernaturals. The Inca ruling class consisted of ten kin groups, each tracing descent from a former emperor. The mummies of ten former emperors, each the founder of one of the groups, were carefully preserved. Not only were the mummies venerated by their descendants, but they were paraded about the city and across the lands. They continued to own, or to hold in trust for their descendants as a corporate group, valuable resources such as land and water whose exploitation and proceeds were administered by the living leader of the descent group for mutual benefit that included offerings and rites for the founder's mummy.

As we have seen in the preceding chapter, according to John Rowe's vision of Inca Cuzco the kin groups or *panaca*s contained the genealogical descendants of former emperors. The fact that there had been ten kings who founded ten *panaca*s was a historical moment that would have changed as soon as a successor to Huayna Capac, the eleventh emperor, was firmly enough established that Huayna Capac could become an ancestor with *panaca* and estates through customary rules of inheritance. In Tom Zuidema's vision of Cuzco ten *panaca*s of ten kings represented two moieties and dual kingship. Five and five was an organizational structure that would never change. The ruling king always had five ascending generations of ancestors and five descending generations of offspring—or more correctly, the king used kin terms to classify the Inca residents of Cuzco into groups in terms of five ascending and five descending generations to express their social status as genealogical distance from his royal self. In this way Inca society was reorganized each time a new Sapa Inca ascended the throne. While the Inca class did consist of descendants or at least relatives of all the kings, in Zuidema's vision, the royal mummies were symbolic founders of fictive kin groups whose members shared the same kin terms of address and the same social status relative to the ruling Inca king.

Whether we subscribe to Rowe's historical or to Zuidema's structural representation of Cuzco, it is clear that Inca organization was based on a special kind of group that required a founding mummy. Group membership and organization was based on kinship—real or fictive. It developed its unity, corporate interests, and internal differentiation around the cadaver of a real or symbolic founding ancestor. This founding ancestor embodied the group by providing it with—or legitimized its corporate control of—essential resources (see Sherbondy 1982). The founder's mummy mediated between the living group members and greater supernatural power. It was the most important source of well-being, fertility, wealth, and security. And to ensure these benefits the descendants venerated the mummy, making offerings that required direct access to the body.

Sixteenth-century descriptions of the royal Inca mummies occasionally mention other mummies, including queens and nobles. This provokes speculation that a link between the basic social group and a mummified ancestor founder was not unique to the organization of Inca kingship. Perhaps any illustrious person who accumulated sufficient wealth to endow a group of descendants, real and fictive, with resources for survival would establish a descent group, being remembered and venerated as its founding ancestor. By the same token, it seems probable that the basic social group, organized in terms of real or fictive bonds of kinship, was constituted around a founding ancestor, real or fictive, whose mummy was the focus of cult activities that constructed and reconstructed the group.

To explore this hypothesis we need to examine the organization of social groups among non-Inca and commoner peoples of the central Andes. Unfortunately, as I have pointed out, eyewitness accounts of the first invaders and the Viceroyalty's official histories are of little use, for they refer exclusively to the Inca nobility. To discover non-Inca cultural patterns we must study societies that did not capture the attention of the earliest invaders, and whose legitimacy was not investigated and recorded by court officials. The best information about the role of mummy founders in the constitution of non-Inca social groups comes from church documents collected at the end of the sixteenth and during the seventeenth centuries. So it is to these documents and their social context that we now turn.

As the number of priests among the Indians increased Spaniards began to realize that idols—in most cases the mummified bodies of ancestors—continued to be objects of religious veneration among the native Andeans. To eradicate this ideological menace knowledgeable clerics prepared detailed descriptions of traditional idolatrous practices, including specific instructions on how to discover and destroy the objects of native religious belief. Church archives were packed with transcriptions of testimonies from native "idolaters" who were interrogated, sometimes under torture, about the nature and location of their sacred objects. Natives were questioned about the rites they continued to conduct to traditional idols, the wealth still owned by these shrines and sacred objects, the priests and people who served them, and much more. Subsequently the "idolatrous" religious objects were to be sought out and destroyed, as their property was confiscated and their worshipers punished. This context shows clearly that the church testimonies do not describe preconquest religion, but native religious practices conducted in secrecy and in opposition to the authority of early Spanish colonialism. Consequently, we must familiarize ourselves more with the pressures on Andean natives during the early Viceroyalty if we are to be secure that information about mummy worship applies to precolumbian institutions.

The Spanish rulers' first hint of the lingering power of Andean religion came in the 1560s, with a religious rebellion independent of the Inca court in exile at Vitcos. It involved no military force and seems not to have emphasized ancestor mummies. According to the preachers of the new movement called the Taki Onqoy or dancing sickness (Castro-Klarén 1990; Millones 1971, 1990; Stern 1982; Varón 1990) the Christian God had created Europeans and all that came from Europe, but the Andean *huacas* had created Indians and all that was indigenous to their world. At the time of the Spanish invasion the Christian God had defeated the *huacas* one by one, but now the *huacas* were resurrected; they had joined forces and they were on the verge of defeating the Christian God. In the past the *huacas* had preferred to occupy idols, mountains, and lakes, but now they flew through the air and entered the bodies of their believers, making them tremble, shake, and dance uncontrollably. When victory over the Christian God was final all the Spaniards, all the things of their world, and all their collaborators would be destroyed. To be spared this destruction Indians must put aside all that was European—clothing, crops, religion—and return to venerating exclusively the *huacas*. Only Indians who purified themselves by rejecting all that came from the Christian world would participate in the new Andean paradise that was coming.

Apparently the Taki Onqoy began near the old region from which the Chancas had originated before their thwarted attack on Cuzco, the Pampas River Valley of Ayacucho and Andahuaylas (see Map 3.1). It spread quickly among the ethnicities of Huamanga and then northwest to Jauja, Cajatambo, Huarochirí, and Lima. To the east and south it reached Cuzco and Charcas. One can only conclude that the messages intoned by the dancing and trembling preachers, possessed as they were by the *huacas*, had strong appeal among Indians of many ethnicities.

As soon as the Taki Onqoy was discovered Catholic ecclesiastics began to put it down, questioning Indians in order to identify and punish

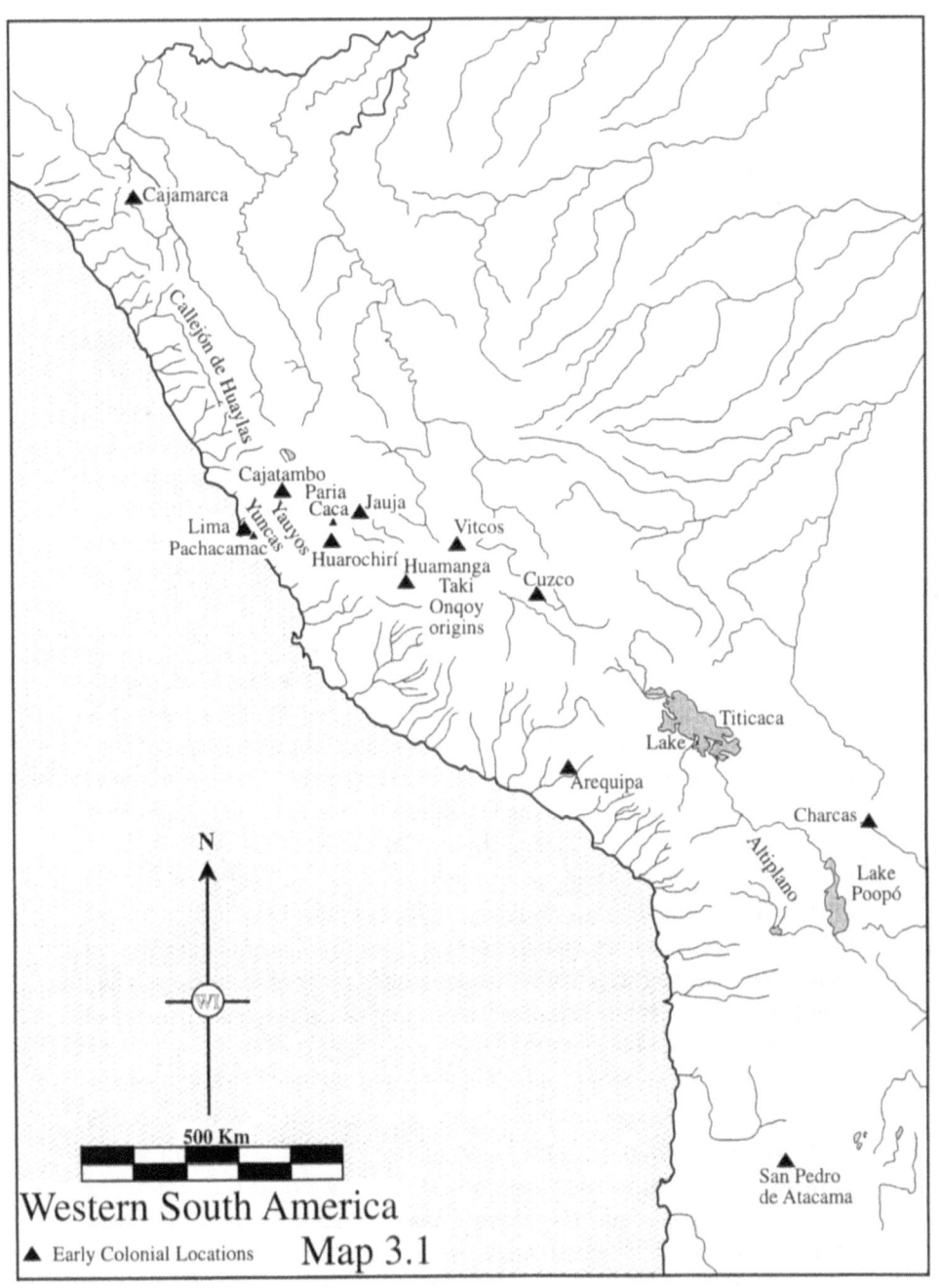

Map 3.1. Huarochirí and Early Colonial Locations

its promoters and believers. Testimonies of Taki Onqoy converts were recorded by church scribes. As the important *huaca*s of the new alliance they identified natural phenomena such as the high mountains Carhuarazo, Sara-Sara, Chimborazo, and Huanacauri, as well as Lake Titicaca, and important pre-Spanish temples or places of supernatural power, such as Pachacamac, Tiwanaku, Pacaritambo, and Cuzco's Coricancha. The list of lesser *huaca*s venerated by individual Taki Onqoy converts was much longer and may have included mummies, but mummies did not play the key role in this great Indian attempt at nationalistic unification. I suspect that the Taki Onqoy sought a universal coalition among Andeans, based on a unified identity that was inconsistent with the veneration of individual ancestor mummies. As we will see below, rites for ancestor founders established boundaries that excluded all but the social descendants of the mummy. Deemphasis of ancestor mummies by the Taki Onqoy, compared with their importance in later investigations of Andean religion, implies that ancestor veneration was about exclusion, group solidarity, ownership, and boundary formation much more than it was about building alliances, unifying great confederacies, and constructing a nationalistic racial identity.

On the other hand, the Taki Onqoy put great emphasis on the purity of Andean social and religious practice by condemning any native who mixed European with traditional practices. Since it occurred only thirty years after the conquest all senior adults remembered preconquest life, so they were experts in the qualities that would bring deliverance from colonialism. Surely during the decade of Taki Onqoy the generation of Indians born after the Spanish invasion renewed their knowledge and practice of precolumbian traditions under the instruction of elders. I believe that this is an important factor in the confidence we can have in the "authenticity" of native religious practices recorded in vivid detail at the onset of the seventeenth century, when personal memory of preconquest life was essentially dead.

The eradication of the Taki Onqoy brought a sense of victory to the teachers of Catholic doctrine that was only short-lived. Within another thirty years the church would be attacking indigenous religion again. Francisco de Avila, a priest assigned to Huarochirí in the mountains east of Lima (see Map 3.1), would make the startling announcement that the Indians of his parish were still addicted to *huaca* idols. Heresy continued to threaten Christendom, he argued, so religious inquisitors had to be sent to investigate the religious practices of natives, discover every idolatry, describe them so other priests would recognize similar practices in their own villages and hamlets, and destroy every last trace (Salomon and Urioste 1991; Salomon 1991). By the beginning of the seventeenth century Avila was authorized to begin a religious inquisition, the "extirpation of idolatries" that became the scourge of Andean natives for more than a century. However, before this campaign began, Peru's Indians were dealt what may have been the most devastating blow of colonialism against their native traditions from another quarter. They were forcibly resettled into Spanish-style communities away from their traditional religious monuments and under the immediate surveillance of Spanish political as well as ecclesiastical authorities. On the other hand, I believe that this created a unique environment for the clandestine continuation of traditional worship, creating the context that soon led to the "extirpation of idolatries."

When the fifth viceroy, Francisco Toledo, came to power around 1570 the Spanish were seeking means to increase Indian labor in the silver and mercury mines. Among the problems they faced was the Indians' preference for dispersed residence in many tiny hamlets rather than a few large villages. Not only were the people so spread out that they were very difficult to keep track of, but individual settlements were so tiny that removing even a few adult men could endanger the activities necessary for production (a situation exacerbated by the fact that most Indian groups had experienced dramatic population decline from Old World diseases). Toledo's solution was to resettle the Indians into a smaller number of large villages or towns. During the 1570s and 1580s the Indians were obliged to build new houses at designated village sites and then move with their families to occupy them. A traditional Spanish plan was employed for the new villages, called *reducciones*. They were laid out in a grid with a plaza in the center. Facing the plaza was the Christian church, the priest's residence, the municipal buildings, and the jail. Ideally, each village was to be a parish, with its resident priest to instruct the natives. Karen Spaulding (1984: 213–217) presents an excellent discussion of the impact of *reducciones* in the western Andean range around Huarochirí. She points out that more than one hundred hamlets were "reduced" into ten villages. While the size of the *reducción* villages is not known, census records from 1571 suggest an average of about 200 to 250 tributary households or some 1,000 to 1,700 inhabitants. Population surely varied from *reducción* village to village, but it seems that the ideal was to make them more or less similar in size, so at least for the western Andes above Lima this figure may have been fairly typical.

The *reducción* villages were administered to promote Spanish goals so there was a Spanish magistrate or *corregidor de Indios* (Spaniards were not subject to this government), as well as a priest to oversee all aspects of Indian life. The Indian community was directly governed by a council of Indians or *cabildo*. Within the *cabildo* the key figures were a pair of mayors or *alcaldes* (the two could not come from the same *ayllu*; as subsequently modified, towns with less than eighty households should have but one *alcalde*), appointed by Spanish authorities. Assisted by a scribe, one or two *regidores*, and several *aguaciles* (including an *aguacil mayor* who was responsible for such activities as patrolling the village after curfew and arresting lawbreakers), the *alcalde* was responsible for the collection of taxes and execution of orders from the provincial Spanish *corregidor*. He was also responsible for the lands of the Indian villagers and the conduct of their affairs. He was in charge of the maintenance of roads, bridges, and *tambos* (roadside inns for travelers) of the village as well as the hospital and market mandated by the Spanish Viceroyalty and the welfare of orphans and supervision of the *caja de comunidad* or community funds. Finally, the *alcalde* was "enjoined to inspect the homes of the Indians to make sure that they used the appurtenances of civilization prescribed for them, such as beds and tables, and he was expected to uphold the dictates of the Catholic religion and report any evidence of the practice of traditional ceremonies or rituals" (Spaulding 1984: 217).

Indians were assigned to *reducciones* according to their *ayllu* or traditional kin group. Each *ayllu* was to reside in its own section of the village. Each family was to build its own house, and every house was to have its own entrance to the public street, probably to discourage polygyny and perhaps other sexual customs considered illicit by ecclesiastical authorities. Since the idea was for the Indians of the *reducción* villages to farm so that their surplus production would support colonial society, each *ayllu* was to have fields within a league—about 5 km—of the village. This must have occasioned significant land redistributions, but since traditional patterns of land tenure were to be followed, *reducción* Indian lands were to be the property of each *ayllu*, with usufruct rights distributed to *ayllu* members by native authorities. In addition, documents proclaim that Indian *ayllus* were entitled to retain rights to the other lands they had traditionally "owned" and cultivated.

When the new villages were completed Indians were obliged to move, and their old homes were burned. The *reducción* policy was not really intended to reshape the *ayllu* or to force natives away from traditional mortuary monuments, ancestral mummies, and ceremonial buildings that had constituted the core of community life, but it did both. Many Indians attempted to return to their former hamlets, but Spanish administrators passed new laws making it illegal to leave. *Reducción* authorities were empowered to bring escapees back forcibly. In the new villages Andeans were under the scrutiny not only of the Spanish bureaucracy, but also of the church. Andean religion, social organization, spatial geography, and land tenure—for as we have seen in the Inca case, they were inseparable—experienced what was surely the most profound transformation of the colonial regime. But in creating *reducción* communities traditional Indian settlements were abandoned intact, even though they were often burned. Stone house foundations, plazas, tombs, and monuments retained their spatial associations and remembered meanings, isolated from new ideologies and behavioral routines being enforced in *reducción* towns.

Traditional religious observations and native rites were secretly continued in the "old towns," as they were called in the "extirpation of idolatries" documents of subsequent decades. Old hamlet sites far from the *reducción* towns were perfect places for the ministers of native religion to reassemble Indian believers, conduct periodic rites, and recreate precolumbian social relations. In fact, during the years following the creation of *reducción* towns, strong force was employed to prevent such practices. The priest could appoint as many Indian officials as he needed to enforce his bidding, from obliging attendance at mass to spying on clandestine indigenous ceremonies. Furthermore, Indians appointed to these church offices could receive temporary and sometimes even lifetime exemptions from tribute duties, including the mining *mita*, so they were enthusiastically received. But excessive appointments resulted in new laws setting limits. For each one hundred parishioners, one *sacristán* would be named to care for the church, two or three *cantores* to lead in singing, and one *fiscal* to enforce the priest's will. In addition, laws that called for a school to be built for each *repartimiento* were increased to each parish, and an Indian teacher who could speak Spanish was to be appointed and paid from community funds. As colonial life settled into *reducción* towns, abandoned hamlets of pre-*reducción* life became scenes for the preservation of precolumbian religion. Native priests employed the precolumbian built environment, including monuments and courts of "old towns," to continue Indian ideologies and practices, modified only to promote secrecy. Far from the eyes of Spanish priests they continued making offerings at shrines and sacrificing to ancestor mummies.

"Extirpation of idolatries" visits to *reducción* villages early in the seventeenth century exposed and recorded a great deal of information about the veneration of ancestor mummies. Investigative visits were carried out throughout Peru, but the archive of the archbishopric of Lima preserved an excellent and well-organized collection of these documents, attracting a great deal of scholarship in the late twentieth century. Among them are numerous reports from the province and town of Huarochirí in the western Andes above Lima. There is no reason to think that indigenous religious practices around Huarochirí were particularly noteworthy (the veneration of founder mummies by descendant kin groupings is reported elsewhere in colonial Peru: cf. Duviols 1966; Salomon 1987; Wightman 1981), but documents are especially abundant for Huarochirí because of the role this region played in the origin of the extirpation campaign, and they are well preserved in Lima's excellent archive. Consequently, it is to Huarochirí that we turn to study the role that ancestor mummies had in the formation and maintenance of social groups among non-Inca, commoner peoples of the Andes. It is important to remember that these are descriptions of native culture under Spanish control. The Taki Onqoy promoted ideological purity in Andean tradition, and shrines of abandoned "old towns" provided contexts for secrecy, but Andean peoples were under increasing compulsion to accommodate to colonial administrative demands and to convert to Christianity. Written descriptions of religious and social organization for non-Inca commoners are otherwise unavailable. Imperfect as they are, the extirpation of idolatries testimonies of seventeenth-century Huarochirí are the best we have.

With these cautions in mind we turn to Huarochirí (Map 3.1) and its extirpation documents, whose value and veracity are immeasurably enhanced by a treatise known as the "Huarochirí Manuscript" (Salomon and Urioste 1991). It is a unique collection of native myth-histories from the *reducción* town of Huarochirí, transcribed from oral narratives sometime between 1598 and 1608. Consequently, it dates to the moment that "extirpation of idolatries" investigations were to begin, so it describes Huarochirí religious beliefs that constituted the broad cosmological framework underlying specific practices confessed to in forced testimonies by accused Indians. However, we cannot assume that the Huarochirí Manuscript represents a naive and pure statement of native ideology. The fact of its recording at the moment that persecution of native religion was to be renewed makes this implausible. The remarkable Huarochirí Manuscript was preserved among the books and papers of Father Francisco de Avila, along with a paraphrased version that he was writing but never completed. We must inquire how such a unique document came into Avila's hands, why it was transcribed, and how he intended to use it.

Father Avila was born in Cuzco in 1573. He studied in Lima and was ordained a priest of the Jesuit order in 1596 (Salomon 1991: 24–26). The following year he was posted to San Damián de Checa, a *reducción* village and parish in the Huarochirí province. After several minor legal disputes with his Indian parishioners—apparently common at this time, for Indians were seeking legal recourse to curtail increasing demands for labor made on them by priests and magistrates—Avila was accused of serious infractions in 1607. Scholars of this period infer that many parish priests turned a blind eye to Indian religion as long as they received the same gifts of labor, harvests, and young women conferred on priests of the traditional idols. Avila may have enjoyed such privileges, but perhaps exceeded the limits of the informal bargain, for he was accused of fathering an illegitimate son with an Indian woman. At any rate, he turned the tables on his parish accusers by denouncing them for idolatrous practices and arguing that their accusations against him were actually motivated by his zeal for rooting out and destroying their idols. In 1608 he led ecclesiastical judges to important *huacas* in the local territory and supervised their destruction. Apparently during the preceding months he had been using Indian collaborators to collect specific information about native religion. It is probable that these confederates had the Huarochirí Manuscript transcribed from narrative testimonies by Indian elders who were unaware that this mythical history about the origins and founders of their *ayllu* might subsequently be used against them. The manuscript was written in Indian Quechua, but Avila had begun to write his own paraphrasing of the myths. He probably intended to offer it in his defense against improprieties, proving the Indians to be idolaters by their own accounts of their idols and ancestors.

Avila did not need all the evidence he was collecting to win his legal case. In 1609 a new archbishop of Lima was appointed who was much more favorably inclined to the persecution of Indian idolaters. Avila staged an anti-idolatries extravaganza, bringing a load of mummies and other *huaca*s to Lima's central plaza, where he burned them before thousands of aggrieved natives who were forced to watch. The event included music, sermons, the whipping of idolaters, and public sentencings. A few days later Avila was absolved of the accusations brought against him and was promoted to the office of "visiting judge of idolatries." From this post he launched the inquisition that destroyed thousands of mummies and idols, extracted confessions under torture, and meted out punishments that ranged from whippings and prison sentences to the appropriation of property and long terms in forced work houses.

It must be surmised that the narratives of the Huarochirí Manuscript were collected to support Avila's counterattack on his parishioners. Avila's collaborators were probably instructed to emphasize narrations with explicit discussions of idols and mummy ancestors. On the other hand, Indian narrators were surely too familiar with ecclesiastical persecution to allow anything being transcribed not to be reshaped at least a little for Christian consumption. But Salomon (1991) concludes that the Huarochirí myths recount traditions of precolombian origins, at least as these were understood three-quarters of a century after the invasion.

Idolatries visits by Avila and others (Avila [1611] 1966; Arriaga [1621] 1968; Hernández Príncipe 1923; for excellent general studies, see Doyle 1988 and Duviols 1988) revealed many religious practices that non-Inca Andean peoples shared with the Incas of Cuzco. Since many of these practices do not seem to have supported the ideology of state government, it seems unlikely that they were imposed during the years of Inca control.

As among Cuzco's Incas, it had not been the custom of Huarochirí Indians to bury the bodies of dead ancestors so they might return to dust. Rather, native testimonies indicated that the bodies, called *malqui*s or *aya*s, but frequently referred to by priests simply as idols, were kept in special mortuary buildings or in dry caves, usually called *machay*s. Here the desiccated bodies were visited, viewed, and adored. They were cared for, given offerings, venerated, consulted, and asked for favors that ranged from good crops and good weather to protection, health, and riches.

"Extirpation of idolatries" investigators learned that it was not just any mummy that was venerated, but one's recognized ancestors, especially the founders of one's kin group or *ayllu*. In a brief summary Avila ([1611] 1966: 255–259) placed ancestor mummies in a supernatural context by describing the full range of religious objects he had found in the Indian villages around Huarochirí, organizing them in terms of a hierarchy. He wrote that the Indians inherited their idols and that they were cared for by the principal male member of each family. In fact, this principal kinsman was executor of the goods and estate passed on by the ancestor.

The lowest status idols were called *chanca* and *cunchur*, small stones wrapped in fine cloth with offerings and other paraphernalia for divination. The *cunchur* mediated with the supernaturals, speaking with and for them. The *chanca* stone was used to obtain answers—responses to specific questions directed to the *cunchur*—by casting it like dice and watching how it fell. For example, if someone were ill, the principal family member would get out the *chanca* and *cunchur* and surround them with ritual items, including seashells, powders of various kinds and colors, gourds of *chicha* beer, special corn dough, guinea pigs, and other items. Then addressing the *cunchur* he would say, "Father of mine, *cunchur* ____ [speaking his name] my son is ill—or I must undertake such and such a task—and you are my lord over this family; I beg of you to intercede for us with the god causing this; I ask that you free me of it; and to know which supernatural is angered against me." And saying this he tossed the *chanca*, asking a specific question such as "Lord, *cunchur*, is the Sun angry?" By proceeding with specific questions one by one, and casting the *chanca*, responsible supernaturals were identified and appropriate offerings determined (Avila [1611] 1966: 255–259).

Father Arriaga ([1621] 1968: 22–32) listed a host of other household *huaca*s in his much longer treatise that instructs priests how to discover and eradicate Andean religion. Very common were *conopas* or house guardians, which were unusual stones such as crystals or rocks in the shape of animals, as well as exceptional ears of corn, fruits, or tubers. Some household heads had more than a dozen of these *conopas* to which offerings were made by the family. There was also the *zaramama* or cornhusk doll dressed like a woman, which was credited with the power to create abundant corn crops. *Curi* were twins, and if they died young their bodies were kept in the home as a sacred object. *Chacpa* was an infant born feet first and received the same treatment as the *curi*.

A higher level in the hierarchy of idols consisted of the mummies that Avila ([1611] 1966: 255–259) identified as the people's ancestors, but he insisted on the importance of the transfer of goods and rights as part of the ancestral relationship. Consequently these mummies were as much the benefactors as the biological founders, and they were given offerings during the new and waning moon. The dried bodies were kept in caves and special buildings and treated like gods, which suggests to me that Avila meant that they were among the supernaturals consulted using the *chanca* and *cunchur*. Avila went on to state that among the ancestor mummies were hanks of hair, nail cuttings, hands, heads, and other body parts also considered sacred. He briefly described masks consisting of human faces that had been cut from the dead bodies and mounted on leather, which were worn at certain festivals.

Avila made no comment about the ideology that underlay attitudes toward the dead in the mountains above Lima, but the Huarochirí Manuscript furnishes valuable information. Fernando Fuenzalida (1979) investigated the topic, focusing on the manuscript, but also employing other colonial and some recent materials. His conclusions are insightful. Andean highlanders recognized a reciprocal relationship between themselves and the earth as provider of sustenance. Immortality was the mythical original human condition, but it had caused overpopulation and scarcity of food. A covenant was made, offering mortality in exchange for fecundity and well-being. Simply stated, to ensure a reliable supply of food, abundance, and prosperity, Andean peoples' mythology recognized the necessity of death. By extension, living people sanctioned claims to land, resources, and their products by descent from the dead, who, by the act of dying, embodied the fulfillment of the reciprocal contract with the earth. Consequently, one's dead ancestor was more than the founder of one's *ayllu* and more even than the group's entitlement to land and water. The dead body announced ongoing fulfillment of the terms of the sacred contract of fecundity with the earth. Display and veneration of the ancestor mummy, or mummies, was a religious act rich in meaning and essential for continued well-being of the descendants. I might speculate that according to this ideology human sacrifice must have been a sort of conspicuous offering to the earth, virtually a way of coercing the earth to give forth its bounty in exchange for premature death.

Avila ([1611] 1966) continued his hierarchy of Andean supernaturals with the level above that of ancestor mummies. This was the idol of the entire *ayllu*. He described the *ayllu* as all the people of a common origin, like Smiths or Joneses. Typically this idol was a mountaintop or a cliff and had its own priest, fields, and annual ritual. Still higher was another idol or deity for the entire province. In the case of Huarochirí and its ethnic group known as Yauyos, this superior deity was the snow-covered peak of Paria Caca. Paria Caca was said to have been a person in the remote past and to have done many marvelous things.

At the highest level of Avila's ([1611] 1966) pantheon were the Sun, Moon, and certain stars that were worshiped, especially the Pleiades, for they were responsible for the fertility of herds. Each had its special sacrifices and an entire hierarchy of priests and ministers. In addition (and apparently somewhat outside Avila's hierarchy) the Indians worshiped animals, forests, hills, sticks, animal skins, stones, feathers, and idols made of stone and wood as well as the irrigation canals, the rivers, and the earth.

Avila ([1611] 1966) made it clear that Andean supernaturals were too complex and diverse to be understood in terms of a single principle or hierarchy. However, his brief presentation seems reasonably consistent with father Bernabé Cobo's ([1653] 1990, summarized in Chapter 2). At the top of the cosmic hierarchy are natural phenomena such as the Sun and Moon that were responsible for cosmic order. If we attribute Avila's omission of Thunder to the brevity of his account (and we will see that Thunder was an important religious figure in specific extirpation testimonies from the western Andes), the main difference was Cobo's insistence on Viracocha as universal creator and his location of the patron and creator of the Incas within the highest level of supernaturals in the form of the Sun God. Perhaps these relate to Inca restructuring of their pantheon to legitimize their superiority and state rule.

In Avila's account and the Huarochirí Manuscript the patron and creator of the Yauyos peoples belonged to the lower level of supernaturals, regional natural phenomena such as lakes and mountain peaks. From this supernatural patron of an ethnic group down through intermediate-level idols, and to the mummy founders of local *ayllu*s, kin terms were used to describe relationships. A supernatural genealogical network was implied that confirmed the relative status of deities and social segments. This ideology associated distant peoples, even though many genealogical links remained unspecified. The Huarochirí Yauyos *ayllu*s recognized specific ancestor mummies, some said to descend from specific idols, and all were the children of Paria Caca. Among the Incas a similar but more specific supernatural descent line is indicated by the hilltop deity of Huanacauri, Huanacauri's brother and founder of the Incas, Manco Capac, and Manco Capac's royal descendants.

Avila and Arriaga gave much more attention to household deities than did Cobo. This may reveal the loss of higher-level Andean religion when *reducciones* forced Indians out of their traditional communities. It is clear that their precolombian hamlets had focused around ceremonial centers with ritual calendars, even though they were very modest by comparison with Cuzco. The difference may also express the experiences of parish priests who were confronted by Andean household religion much more than with the great seasonal feasts of an imperial capital, witnessed among the Incas by early invaders.

I suspect that the *chanca* and *cunchur* represent an important feature of Andean religion with analogs from the ruling class down to the most humble peasant. Descriptions of Inca religion recount the casting of lots and use of similar devices of divination to determine the will of *huaca*s. While it seems that some *huaca*s spoke directly to their pilgrims, divining devices like the *chanca* and *cunchur* probably characterized most *huaca* worship.

Extirpation testimonies and the Huarochirí Manuscript confirm that mummies or *malqui*s were recognized as ancestors by their worshipers, but they were also viewed as the creators, or conquerors and embodiment, of the goods and estates which they entrusted to their descendants. Each ancestor had specific power over his creations, controlling their fates in the real world, from the health of their children's children to the fertility of the fields they had left to them and the abundance of irrigation waters they had created or appropriated. Rich offerings would bring benevolence from the *malqui*s, but allowing them to go hungry and cold could bring terrible disasters. *Ayllu* members consulted or, perhaps more appropriately, sought permission of their *malqui* regarding decisions, acts that were mediated by *huaca* priests. Pierre Duviols (1986: 142–143) cites testimony from one *huaca* priest who experienced a state of trance upon embracing the *malqui* and heard the ancestor speaking inside him in answer to questions posed. It seems reasonable to guess that in the case of forces beyond the direct control of the *malqui*, this mummy founder would intercede in favor of his descendants with more powerful supernaturals. Significantly, the Huarochirí Manuscript indicates that a high-order *huaca* would ask whether petitioners had properly consulted their low-order, hereditary *malqui* prior to a visit, and, if not, it instructed them to do so first (Salomon 1991: 17). Clearly, religious hierarchy was to be observed, even in the absence of a centralized political structure.

The supernatural hierarchy abstracted by Avila appears in native testimonies. One idolater stated that his own ancestors' mummies were the objects of greatest adoration; next were his idols, and last were the Sun and other elements (Huertas 1981a: 60). Mummies were unambiguously identified as ancestors by the idolaters. "[Asked] whose bones those were, he said they were the bones of his malquis, who are his progenitors" (quoted and translated by Doyle 1988: 81).

Testimonies also reveal that *malqui*s were ordered in terms of genealogical descent from higher-order idols and natural phenomena. "This malqui [the mummy Guaman Cama] was a nephew of the idols Caruatarqui Urau and Ticlla Urau, and the progenitor of this ayllo [*ayllu*] Chacas, and he was a son of Libiac [Lightning], and he nurtured people, multiplied them, guarded their fields, and gave them money and wealth" (quoted and translated by Salomon 1991: 20; for a transcription of the whole testimony, see Huertas 1981a: 104–119).

Not only did an *ayllu* have a *malqui* ancestor, and sometimes several, but the *ayllu* could consist of many branches or sub-*ayllu*s, each with a founder represented by a *malqui*. The same term, *ayllu*, was used for the smaller unit as well as the larger social group.

> And this ayllu Yanaqui used to have nine ayllus, and each ayllu had its malquis; Alcaguicamal is of the ayllu Julca; Collana ayllu, Allauca malqui, who is also of this ayllu; Cocha Auqui malqui is of the ayllu Yanaqui and Ancos Ambrari is of the ayllu Poma . . . Poma Tapra malqui, and this was malqui of the ayllu Poma; Raupoma malqui and Aparam malqui are malquis of the other ayllus [the names of] which he does not remember; and those of this ayllu revered and adored all of these malquis and this witness is minister of these idols and malquis, with the other people he named previously, and two times a year, at Pocoimita and Caruamita, they made sacrifices and offerings of guinea pigs, coca, and llamas to them in the old town of Yanaqui. (quoted and translated by Doyle 1988: 81)

The status of venerated ancestor seems to have required that the individual leave an estate to descendants. Testimonies suggest that deceased bodies only became venerated *malqui*s if they transferred significant rights or powers that could be enjoyed corporately by an aggregate of descendants. Such rights and powers included control of water and land, but perhaps also special knowledge and even social status. These resources might have been inherited by the mummy, but native testimonies more often reveal the mummy as creator of the new "estates," by conquest or by construction.

In the community of Ocros near Cajatambo, extirpator of idolatries Hernández Príncipe (1923; Zuidema 1973) found an important sepulcher with mummies that included a principal *ayllu* founder and *kuraka* (*ayllu* chief, principal kinsman, or king), Caque Poma. Caque Poma had been elevated to his status by one of the Inca kings for constructing an irrigation canal that required the cooperative work of several villages. His elevation required that he sacrifice his daughter as a *capac hucha*, after sending her to Cuzco, by burying her alive in a shaft tomb. The shaft tomb was located on a hilltop where the irrigation canal could be viewed as it emerged from a canyon. At the same site storehouses were built for goods from the newly irrigated land and a cult was dedicated to the girl, who became a local female deity. This account shows that *ayllu* unity could be forged around the sharing of a key resource, whose creator may not have been the biological progenitor of its users, but the symbolic or social progenitor.

In the Huarochirí Manuscript and extirpation testimonies from the western Andes, conquest was by far the most common motif explaining the origins and rights of *ayllu* founders and their descendants. In fact, the conquest motif also explained hierarchical relations among different *ayllu*s. The following section from a long testimony establishes the mythical charter for *ayllu*s of conquerors, *ayllu*s of conquered peoples, and the sepulchers of venerated *malqui*s. In fact, at the destruction of the community mummies by the extirpation judge, this testimony recounts a history of the ancestors as a highly compressed, and somewhat confusing, history of the settlement. It begins with the mythical ancestor's fall from the sky, continues with his children's wanderings in search of a promised land, their conquest and subordination of older *ayllu*s, and the disposition and adoration of mummy ancestors of the community reconstituted by conquest, and ends with the destruction of these mummy ancestors by order of the Christian extirpator. Some of the confusion results from the highly symbolic way conquest is described, and some results from terms that cannot be translated. But confusion also arises from the union of the mummies as actors in the past with their existence as objects of adoration and authority in the present.

> And the history of these malquis is the following: that as far as he remembers and has heard his forefathers say, that Apu Libia Cancharco fell from the sky like a lightning bolt, and he had many sons, and some he sent to some places and others to others, as for example Libiac Choquerunto, Libiac Carua Runtuy, the first progenitors of the ayllu Chaupis; Osirac Otuc and Libiac Raupoma and Ucchu Poma of the ayllu Xulca; and Libiac Ñauim Tupia and Libiac Guac Tupaic of the ayllu Allauca; all of these were Llaquaz conquerors to whom, when their father sent them, he gave them a little soil that they should carry in order to conquer lands where they would live; he told them that upon finding soil similar to that which they carried they should stay in that place, because there they would have their food and drink and possessions, and having arrived at Mangas, the Indians of the said town did not want to receive them, with which they went on to the town Guancos, the people of which received them with friendliness, and they were with them for one year, and upon comparing the soil and seeing that it did not match that of the said town of Guancos, they went on to the said town of Otuco, and when they were above it they sent a boy with a llama to the Indians who at that time lived there in this town, in their fields, and they were called the ayllu Guari Guachancho and the ayllu Taruco Chancho; they [the Llaquaz conquerors] sent [the boy and llama to the people of Otuco] requesting *mircapa* (travel provisions) and food from them, and the said Indians killed the said boy and skinned the llama alive, and in this way returned it to the above mentioned [Llaquaces], who seeing this went down to where those of the ayllu Chichos were, and finding them dancing the Guari Libiac with drums and *pincollos* (*quenas*), they first sent an Indian converted into a little bird they call a *chiuchu*, who came singing "chiuchu," and those of the ayllu Guari Guachico asked who those Llaquaces were who had so few *tulmas* [?]. Since they sent that chiuchu, and the above-mentioned [Llaquaces], as if put to shame, started a storm with dense fog and great hail stones the size of large eggs, and covered (equipped?) themselves with *rivas* [sling-

stones?] of gold and silver, *chaupis guaras* [?], and with *suintas* [?], which are large *rives*, they killed all of the Indians there were in those ayllus, possessors of the town, with which they conquered them and took away houses, fields, possessions, and food and they only left one alive, because he humbled himself before them, called Marca Cuipac, and his brother Paria Putacac, and for this reason and because they were the first conquerors, they kept them alive in three elaborately constructed underground vaults, up in the old towns called Marca Putacum, buried in them, and all of his family in the vault or machay Choqueruntu, and his brother Carua Runtuo was in another with his family, where there were 75 heads from the said ayllu of Conde Ricuy, and in the ayllu Chaupis Otuco and [in?] that of Xulca was Libiac Raupoma [and] Libiac Uchuppoma and their [or his] family, which were 42 heads, and Libiac Nauim Taupia and his brother Libiac Guayau Tupia is in the ayllu Allauca with 44 heads of his family who were shown and burned just now by the said [extirpation] *visitador*. . . . (quoted and translated by Doyle 1988: 79–80)

The most lengthy and detailed oral charter for an *ayllu* or collection of *ayllu*s that has survived into modern days is the Huarochirí Manuscript. It provides a window into one example of the rich tradition of narrative myths and histories upon which the very brief and simplified testimonies at idolatries trials must surely have been based. The Huarochirí Manuscript describes and accounts for the origins of several interrelated social groups who occupied a local area and relates them to neighboring groups (Salomon 1991: 4–12; Salomon and Urioste 1991). The narratives were probably told by informants who belonged to an *ayllu* known as Checa, who had been resettled into the *reducción* village of San Damián in the parish of Santa María Jesús de Huarochirí. Prior to Viceroy Toledo's instigation of *reducciones* the Checa lived in many hamlets focused around a ceremonial center called Llacsa Tambo (Salomon 1991: 4–12). The Checa were part of a larger ethnic unit called Yauyos, who shared a common origin as the children of Paria Caca, a great snowcapped peak to the east of Huarochirí. For many generations Yauyos had been expanding out of high pasturelands, pressing into warmer irrigated valleys across the continental divide, where they displaced groups collectively known as the Yunca (Rostworowski 1978: 31–147). The Huarochirí myths allegorize this epic Yauyos migration.

In colonial testimonies, claims were made that the ancestors of the Yauyos all recognized the "Ninavilca" lords from their core territory around the *reducción* parish of Huarochirí. This name suggests religious rather than political authority, and it is unlikely that before the Incas incorporated them the Yauyos ever had kings or political unity. Their ethnic identity was based on their common cult and mythical origin—reinforced by shared language, culture, and history. Each group had its own perspective on the past, with special interests in its local territories. Groups that figure prominently in the Huarochirí Manuscript are the Checa, the Mama, the Allauca, and the neighbors of the Checa, the Concha. But other Yauyos told the same stories, as María Rostworowski (1988: 54–57) has shown for the Chacalla, albeit always from their own point of view. Finally, the Huarochirí Manuscript contains some stories that do not relate to Paria Caca or his cult. They appear to have come from other peoples with whom the Checa and Yauyos intermarried, most likely Yunca groups.

Frank Salomon (1991: 5) believes that the intent of the original editor of the Huarochirí Manuscript was to arrange the stories into a chronological order so that archaic events would be told before more recent ones. However, the stories do not all follow from the same origin events, and they are full of references to times other than those that should be central to a historiographic account of the past. In addition the manuscript is riddled with second thoughts and tangents that express concerns that have little to do with temporal sequence.

The narrator of the Huarochirí Manuscript tells us that he will recount the achievements of the Indian peoples from the dawning age to the present, village by village. The myths begin by constructing order in the world using characteristically Andean concepts—converting chaotic difference into complementary, dualistic opposition. For example, deities who were strange and hostile to one another became husband and wife who embodied opposed ecological principles. Before the present human race appeared a tropical environment extended far up the mountains, providing much greater abundance than today. Humans lived forever, returning to life after five days of temporary death, but they had to sacrifice half of their children to a fierce fire god, Huallallo Caruincho. Stories attributed to this remote time include those of Cuny Raya as

Vira Cocha, who created nature in an empty universe, as well as a deluge story and a story in which the sun disappeared.

Paria Caca appeared as five eggs that became five falcons that became five men who founded the human groups around which the stories center. Paria Caca embodied the unity of his descendants and focused their organizational idiom of kinship. In different accounts Paria Caca defeated another deity, Huallallo, relegating him to another ethnic group, the Huancas of the Jauja region. Before the defeat the two did cosmic battle, volcanic fire against storm water. In the process the landscape was shaped and alien ethnic groups were conquered and subjected to the sons of Paria Caca. In another sequence Paria Caca gave power to a poor man to defeat a rich man, and in a third Paria Caca saved a Huallallo worshiper from having to sacrifice his child.

Chapter 12 records the conquests of Paria Caca's children, Choc Payco, Chancha Runa, Huari Runa, Utco Chuco, Tutay Quiri, Sasin Mari, and Pacha Chuyru. The brothers fought their enemies together, although Choc Payco was the eldest and traveled in a litter. Tutay Quiri was the strongest and led in conquests, planting his staff to make boundaries that vanquished the Yunca. Eventually he was beguiled by a woman; had this not been the case, "Huarochirí and Quinti fields would now reach as far as Lower Caranco and Chilca" (Salomon and Urioste 1991: 82–83). Tutay Quiri was the heroic ancestor of the Checa, and his venerated mummy was discovered and destroyed by idolatries extirpators (Spaulding 1984: 64). Chapter 24 of the manuscript (Salomon and Urioste 1991: 117–118) weaves Yunca ancestors into the Checa past, including Chupa Yacu, Yuir Naya, and Chauca Chimpita, who according to Francisco de Avila (Salomon and Urioste 1991: 117ff., 590) were the mummies identified as founders of three *ayllu*s around San Damián.

The Huarochirí Manuscript shows how *ayllu*s could be divided and subdivided into smaller and smaller groups or combined into larger and larger units, but without specifying rigid descent relationships that would have created formal segmentary lineages. Rather, space and myth seem to have been used to state relationships, for "related" ancestors were enshrined together and their descendants simply claimed common origins at greater generational removes. In 1657 an idolatries visitor to the *reducción* village of San Pedro de Acas in Cajatambo discovered little buildings resembling chapels where mummies were kept. His inventory suggests that each tomb contained the *malqui* bodies of a mini-

*ayllu* and that fields of such tombs constituted larger *ayllu*s (Huertas 1981a: 65–67). The cemetery of the entire community may have formed a still larger *ayllu*.

Ayllo Yanaqui

> Auquis Julca with the bodies of 45 family members
> Anco Sambrari with the bodies of 4 family members
> Allauca with the bodies of 35 family members
> Cochanqui with the bodies of 4 family members
> Atoclloclla with the bodies of 15 family members
> Aparan with the bodies of 45 family members
> Paquirachin with the bodies of 68 family members (this mummy was libiac ["lightning"])

Ayllo Carampa

> Puma Guaraca and his brother
> Chupis Guaraca with the bodies of 160 family members
> Julca Guaraca with the bodies of 6 family members
> Caratupaico with the bodies of 56 family members
> Tumas Libiac with the bodies of 84 family members
> Rica Guaraca with the bodies of 55 family members
> Chaupis Guaraca y Choque Runa with the bodies of 98 family members
> Hasto Malqui with the bodies of 227 family members
> Malqui Huari, who was given a special cult because he gave us our fields, with the bodies of 54 family members
> Chichi Cito, who brought us potatoes

An idolatries description of a ceremonial center shows another example of spatial relations communicating social order.

> They discovered a large simulacre and temple from pagan times that had a small plaza and many small rooms all around it, and in the middle three tombs enclosed by stone walls, and they opened and dug in the middle one and showed the idol called Auca Atama, which was a corpse of a pagan individual whom the Indians of this ayllu [Chamas] and those of Nanis

adored because he was their first progenitor and conqueror and founder of the town, and they opened and dug up the two tombs that were on both sides and showed four malqui idols called Poron Tambo, Cunquis, Xulcas, and Pariasca, who through the said interpreters they said were sons of the said malqui called Auca Atama, and at the sides of the said malquis, in some small windows like chapels, they showed four conopa idols. (quoted and translated by Doyle 1988: 130)

Sometimes the mummies were kept in dry caves. But whether caves or funeral buildings, the mortuary monuments included a flat, open space, often formed by terracing in front of the building or cave, that was called *cayan*. Here worshipers gathered to conduct rituals to the idols and *malqui*s. Father Arriaga ([1621] 1968) warned other priests what these rituals were like:

> ... they bring out all the accessories of the idolatry. They are grouped about the plaza by . . . [*ayllu*] and bring out the mummified bodies of their ancestors, called *munaos* in the lowlands and *malquis* in the sierra, together with the bodies taken from the church [colonial burials stolen for the churchyard cemetery] and it looks like the living and the dead come to judgment. They also bring out their personal huacas, and the more eminent ministers bring out the huacas that are worshipped in common. Offerings are prepared for them and they display the garments used in the festivals and the plumage in which they deck themselves; the pots, jugs, and tumblers used to make and drink *chicha* and offer it to the huacas; the trumpets, usually of copper although sometimes of silver, and the great horns and other instruments by which they are summoned to a festival. There are also a great many well-made drums of small size, for nearly every woman brings her own for the songs and dances. The towns of the lowlands have their elaborate cradles, their antlers and horns of mountain goats, their fox skins and lion pelts, and many other things of the sort, which have to be seen to be believed. (Arriaga [1621] 1968: 19)

Such descriptions allowed idolatries judges to detect these festivals, even from bare remains alone.

And at a small pampa [flat place] attached to the machay [cave], there was fresh and old corn, which had been burned, as was seen because it had turned to charcoal, and two guinea pig heads that weren't completely burned and appeared to be fairly recent; and [there was] a *callana* [large pottery sherd] where there was burnt lard, and straw, where the Indians sat when they went to revere the said corpses and went to make sacrifices to them, for which they took llama meat and offered blood to the machays along with other rituals and ceremonies. (quoted and translated by Doyle 1988: 131)

The Huarochirí Manuscript does not present a unified genealogy that precisely specifies every group's relations and rights in descent terms. Rather, it lays out a flexible kin-based structure in terms of which such relations and rights could be negotiated by the living descendants. For example, in Chapter 31 (Salomon and Urioste 1991: 136–137) we learn that the Concha *ayllu* was founded by five brothers. Three of the mythical brothers arrived together at the village of Concha, conquering its Yuncas. In the seventeenth century their land claims, almost surely embodied by ancestor mummies, referred to these myths. On the other hand, the other two mythical brothers were said to have gotten lost, and they only caught up with their senior brothers after the victories, when the spoils of war had been divided. These *ayllu*s were landless in the seventeenth century (Spaulding 1984: 29). I infer that stories and founders were recreated to correspond with changing reality—if, for example, a landless *ayllu* acquired significant resources and an influential set of descendants its status could be improved by making more conspicuous offerings to its founder mummy and sponsoring generous festivals to which dominant *ayllu* descendants would be invited. One idolatries testimony reports that the status of a kin group was enhanced by the fine architecture of their ancestor's sepulcher (Duviols 1986: 465–466).

*Ayllu* organization seems to have been very efficient in constructing strong identity and common interests within relatively small groups. It also provided powerful tools for ranking individuals within the *ayllu*, based on real or fictitious genealogical distances and seniority of lineage in relation to the founder. Finally, the same kin idiom facilitated the ranking of the *ayllu*s relative to one another. But the *ayllu* structure seems weak in constructing aggregates and large groups. As common origin and linking ancestor receded into the remote past, and as common property interests declined, relations became less important to their descendants and less able to support social and political obligations. Only joint participation in rituals of solidarity and mutual interests would bind such remote relations into a single unit. An example of this seems to be the loose relationship of diverse Yauyos people who only vaguely recognized common priest leaders, the Ninavilca, as opposed to the frequent rituals of group intensification focused on the mummy ancestors and Sun God among the Incas of Cuzco. Of course, the Incas shared common goals in the conquest and administration of an empire.

The Huarochirí Manuscript reveals important tensions associated with the construction of larger groups. One was a tension between peoples of different origins, the conquered and conquerors—Yuncas and Yauyos. Repeated in many forms, this relationship found expression not in descent but in affinal kin relations of marriage and in-laws. Another tension relates to new Yauyos migrants and their relationships with long-established Yauyos conquerors already well integrated into the enriched social, religious, and ecological world of the wealthy Yuncas. At least sometimes these tensions were dealt with in terms of honored senior kin and unwanted younger siblings. It is clear that in myths such as those composing the Huarochirí Manuscript Andean cultures sought to resolve ambiguous relationships by subordinating them to structures defined by the idiom of kinship (Salomon 1991: 6–8).

Flexible and atomizing tendencies of *ayllu* organization probably operated very well in the context of highly dispersed settlement patterns characteristic of the western Andes of Huarochirí, and perhaps much of the Andean highlands, before European contact. However, one must wonder how any economic and political unity could be maintained. When the Huarochirí Manuscript was transcribed Andean natives had been resettled into the European-style *reducción* villages. The settlement pattern of preinvasion times that probably survived relatively unaffected until the 1570s is poorly known but was clearly very different. The first European description for Huarochirí recorded some 200 tiny settlements, so there were more hamlets and homesteads than villages and towns (Spaulding 1984: 44). The archaeological site of Huachoc, a couple of valleys north of Huarochirí, may be more or less characteristic of Inca and immediately pre-Inca hamlets on the western slopes of the Andes. This site has ten to fifteen small, irregularly shaped buildings of stone, and it is unlikely that it ever housed more than twenty-five to fifty residents (Marcus and Silva 1988: 25). Rostworowski (1988: 59) reports that a pre-*reducción* description of the Canta, one of the northern Yauyos macro-*ayllu*s, listed a village and sixteen hamlets for every *ayllu*. Each of the hamlets was occupied for only a short time, during which special communal activities were carried out.

Descriptions from 1549 make it clear that the tasks associated with each hamlet were assigned to members of the *ayllu* in advance, on the basis of a carefully planned system of rotation. When the work conducted at a particular hamlet was completed, it was abandoned until the next rotation period. By far the most common work was farming, but herding, potting, weaving, sandal making, and hunting birds were other hamlet specializations. John Murra (1972, 1985a, 1985b) argues that there was an Andean cultural pattern underlying periodic moves from specialized hamlet to specialized hamlet, a logic based on production in the variable environments of the high Andes, where different temperature patterns, humidity regimes, and crops characterized different altitudes. Diversifying in this way the *ayllu* did not have to depend on trade with other social groups (see also Brush 1977; Fonseca and Mayer 1978; Mayer 1974, 1985; Orlove 1977b). This model implies that lands exploited by an *ayllu* were not a continuous unit, but a number of small pieces dispersed across the ecological diversity of the mountains, what Murra and other Andeanists have referred to as a complementary archipelago. Small wonder the Spanish government was so anxious to reorganize native residence patterns and land tenure!

If *ayllu* organization dealt very successfully with division into smaller and smaller units, and with ranking between and within these little social groups, there must have been a counterprinciple for constructing larger economies and bigger ethnic units. Certainly the demands of agropastoral production in the Andes, of political alliance, and of state building in opposition to competitive polities would require such unions. I believe that this centralizing force was manifest in *llacta* organization. While the nature of the *llacta* demands its own study, a few comments seem to be in order to balance the discussion of *ayllu*.

Completing his dictionary after the implementation of *reducción* villages, Diego G. Holguín ([1608] 1989: 207) translated *llacta* as *pueblo*—village or people—and *llactayoc* as a native or resident of a *llacta*. This suggests a simple territorial identity. But Salomon (1991:

23–24) recognizes a different, pre-*reducción* Andean meaning that was not really based on a residential relationship. Chapter 24 of the Huarochirí Manuscript mentions the division of llama herds among the *llacta*s, and a note in the margin of the text explains that this means the idols. If *llacta*s were idols, then *llactayoc*s were not village residents but worshipers (or descendants) of the idols (mummies). In fact, in the Andean reality co-residence may have been a poor bond, for *llactayoc*s may have resided in different hamlets, and some may have moved from hamlet to hamlet during the year. Instead, "community" or common identity was probably constructed around the recognition and veneration of the same idols, through participation in the same rituals. I infer that *llacta* religious observations were organized in terms of a calendric cycle and focused on a ceremonial center, but probably included key pilgrimage sites that linked the *llacta* communities of kin into larger ceremonial constellations. I think this *llacta* structure underlies Inca ceremonialism in Cuzco, with its mummy founders, whether or not royal mummies represented historical kings with fixed statuses. At a larger scale, interregional *llacta* organization was expressed in periodic pilgrimages to Titicaca, Apurímac, and other shrines equally sacred to non-Inca ethnicities. Presumably to express or promote unity, a common ancestor could be identified from whom all members, ancestor mummies, and idols of a potential group could be derived—like Paria Caca among the Yauyos or the Sun God of the Incas. Consistent with this notion, John Rowe (1960) argues that shortly before the Spanish invasion the Incas had begun to formalize Viracocha as a universal creator or ancestor for all Andean people. If Viracocha was universally recognized and celebrated, this would have established the entire empire as one super *ayllu*.

The *llacta* ceremonial centers of the Yauyos were among the "old towns" referred to in the extirpation of idolatries documents. They consisted of idols and *malqui*s in special houses or caves that were located in relation to a ceremonial plaza or *cayan* where rites were conducted in accordance with a ceremonial calendar. *Ayllu* members assembled for periodic rituals, in which subgroups surely sponsored celebrations that recognized their most immediate ancestors, but all participated and benefited from the entire ritual cycle, which was probably considered vital for the maintenance of world order. Close by the *cayan*, where the ancestors presided, *ayllu* members built houses, frequently just below the ceremonial center (Salomon 1991, 1995), but the result was certainly not a European-style village, like the *reducciones*.

I suspect that it was within the *llacta* that *ayllu*s worked out relations with one another. Over time new distributions of population, resources, and status came about. Myths and testimonies recognize conquest and construction as key processes, but less dramatic causes probably played important roles as well. The realities of these changes could be ceremonially expressed and, through practice, translated into the kin-based terminology of social structure and myth—in much the same way that Joanne Rappaport (1988, 1990, 1992, 1994) describes correcting the past among the modern Cumbe. The tools were ritual and ceremony. In Inca times Caque Poma's elevation to the status of *ayllu* founder and *curaca* or chief was not achieved by completing the new irrigation canal alone (Zuidema 1973). He also had to sacrifice his daughter so that she became a new cult figure. Her shrine probably became a focus for a larger *llacta* community, with Caque Poma—her father—the ancestor and founder.

How did *llacta* differ from *ayllu*? I infer that *llacta* constructed interdependence and inclusion while *ayllu* ranked and divided. The ceremonial center with its ritual calendar integrated various idols and *malqui*s of different origins—Yauyos and Yuncas, for example. I suspect that a successful ritual calendar had to make every idol and *malqui* celebration essential for the pleasure of a higher-order supernatural, so each social unit, even though its members specialized in the veneration of their own *ayllu* founder, was necessary for the well-being of the entire *llacta* community. In terms of function the *llacta* could cut across the fundamental feature of *ayllu* organization, which was based on a common founder, to include ethnically diverse peoples who recognized different founders but whose idols could all participate in one annual ceremonial calendar and an integrated myth-history. Like the *ayllu*, *llacta* organization also seems to have employed the idiom of kinship, but if the Huarochirí Manuscript provides meaningful insights, descent relations were complemented by analogies based on marriage and in-law obligations.

In literate societies power is vested in land titles, maps, contracts, birth certificates, and treaties. In Andean culture this kind of power was created in sacred landscapes, their integration into the myth-histories, and resonance of landscape and myth-history with the rituals and social organization of resident groups. Legitimacy was established, not by recourse to written documents, but by the consistent order of space, time, ritual, and kin organization. Interpretative control was not in the courts or treaty tables but in the society of the *llacta* ceremonial center, reconstructing itself yearly in rituals that sanctioned and naturalized transformations. Cuzco seems to have been functioning as this kind of ceremonial center when the Spanish invaded. Perhaps establishing the competitive ceremonial *llacta* at Tumebamba fostered the political rift that followed Huayna Capac's death, as Pease (1965) has argued.

In the western Andes above Lima numerous *ayllu*s worshiped a collection of idols and *malqui*s that participated in calendrically regulated rituals of their *llacta*. The Yauyos of Huarochirí, who contributed to the Huarochirí Manuscript, are good examples. These rituals continued until Indians were forced to abandon their "old towns" for *reducción* villages, and the mummified *ayllu* founders were searched out and destroyed by extirpation priests.

On the basis of the discussion in this and the previous chapter I now feel prepared to offer a definition of the Andean *ayllu* as it seems to have existed in the sixteenth century. Characteristically the Andean *ayllu* has been thought of as some sort of kin group with corporate interests in land (Brush 1977: 41; Espinosa 1981; Rowe 1946: 254–255). Recently, David Gillet (1992: 18) defined it as "a corporate descent group that collectively owned resources such as land and water and practiced endogamy." Herbert Klein (1993: 58) writes that basically "the *ayllu* is a group of families claiming a common identity through real and fictive kinship and using the claim to hold communal land rights." But María Lagos (1993: 181) correctly points out that a meaningful definition of the *ayllu* must be historically specific. So I emphasize that my definition refers to the moment of contact and immediately subsequent decades of the sixteenth century. My definition is, of course, based on the Incas and the Yauyos, but I suspect that it had wider application during that half-century. Soon, however, the *ayllu* was reshaped by *reducción* resettlement, when a contiguous communal territory was established for each *ayllu*, and its officials were appointed by Spaniards. It was further reshaped by the extirpation of idolatries, when mummy founders were systematically destroyed, and members who continued to recognize them were severely punished.

On the basis of the preceding chapters I suggest that for the early sixteenth century *ayllu* is best understood as a group of people who shared a resource attributed to a founder or ancestor and whose members could therefore be ranked in accord with the idiom of kinship when the founder was employed as a common ancestor. Four elements were essential. Three of these were a social group, a communal resource, and ranking according to kinship idiom. The fourth element held the other three together: a founder or ancestor.

The founding ancestor embodied the shared resource, providing a symbol of its unity and its potential productivity. The founding ancestor was imagined as the creator of the resource and therefore retained control over it and alone could assure its bountiful production. But the founding ancestor was equally necessary for the application of a kinship idiom to the social group. Imagined as his descendants, the social group was organized, and privileges were dispersed, in terms of genealogical distance and seniority of line from the perspective of the ancestor. Real genealogy probably characterized most *ayllu*s, but, as we have seen in the structural interpretation of Cuzco and elsewhere, actual biological descent was not the key issue underlying the *ayllu*. Hierarchical distinctions were ordered in terms of a kinship model, and appropriate behavior and obligations were regulated by reciprocal terms of kinship. It appears that as long as the mutual terms were accepted, and the behavior was appropriate, actual kinship relationships were secondary (Salomon 1995).

We need also consider whether the *ayllu* was linked to corporate landholding, as Waldemar Espinosa (1981) and some other Andeanists have argued. Jeanette E. Sherbondy's (1982) study of irrigation in Cuzco led her to argue that it was a shared source of irrigation water that established the *ayllu* and *panaca*. What seems to be essential is a shared resource acquired from the common ancestor that could be held corporately for the benefit of all the offspring. While it seems reasonable to suppose that this would usually have been land in an agropastoral society, I see no reason that it could not have been something else. Fishing rights or perhaps even a skill or profession may have been enough (Rostworowski 1981a). One of the earliest descriptions of the *ayllu*, written by Domingo de Santo Tomás in the 1560s, seems to support this thesis.

> Among them, if a gentleman is particularly known in some way his children take on his name; and not only the children, but all his descendants, and in that way are formed among them the

lineages that they call ayllu and pachaca. And so it goes in all of the rest of the provinces of Peru [where] particular lineages, which they call ayllus, take the name of their ancestors. (quoted in Spaulding 1984: 28)

In conclusion, I suggest that no feature of the *ayllu* was the quintessential one; all four were equally basic—social group, communal resource, ranking in terms of an idiom of kinship, and a founding ancestor. With this definition I believe we capture the essence of the *ayllu* in the central Andes before it was reconstructed by viceroyal decrees and Christian religious persecution. We capture the key features of Cuzco's royal *ayllu* or *panaca* as well. Furthermore, realizing that it was not simply biological descent, but behavior appropriate for a descendant (Salomon 1991: 22–23; Spaulding 1984: 28–30 and 48–52) in venerating the founder, in employing the resources he left, and in working cooperatively with other *ayllu* members to protect and improve those resources, we have the key for tracing *ayllu* organization—as it existed in the sixteenth century—backward into the prehistoric past.

CHAPTER

# IV

# Competing Theories of *Ayllu* Origins

Our two case studies of ancestor mummies, the royal Incas of Cuzco and non-Inca peoples of Huarochirí, show that the *ayllu*—and its royal equivalent the *panaca*—was inseparable from the body of its founder. The founding ancestor's cadaver was the primary object of religious veneration for all the *ayllu* members, who gave the mummy offerings in return for prosperity and abundance. It was also the focus of group organization, based as it was on the idiom of kinship. Dependence of *ayllu* organization on the venerated mummy of its founder offers an opportunity to trace the history—or prehistory—of the *ayllu* with archaeological methods. By identifying the kind of mortuary monuments that were required for the preservation and veneration of ancestor mummies, and by determining their spatial and temporal distribution, we will discover the past of the *ayllu*, as it was defined in Chapter 3. We should be able to show when and where ancestor mummy veneration originated, as well as a great deal about its development. But before turning to the archaeological record I want to examine two alternative hypotheses about the origin and prehistory of *ayllu* organization, to guide our investigation.

In this chapter I summarize and deconstruct the most popular vision of Andean prehistory. As I expose its hidden assumptions I also show why I am dissatisfied with many of them. Next I discuss a different approach to the Andean past, which does not depend on so many problematic assumptions and employs a different epistemology to reach a different vision of Andean prehistory. My goal is to present two ways of knowing the Andean past, each with its history of the *ayllu*. By establishing alternative accounts of the *ayllu*, based on different assumptions and approaches, we can compare each account with the implications of our archaeological study of mortuary monuments. In this way we will be able not only to illuminate the origins of the *ayllu*, but also to evaluate the competing ways of knowing the past.

Archaeologists construct different pasts not just because they disagree about the interpretation of archaeological remains—what is the date of a site, which is the correct stylistic affiliation for a potsherd, and whether artifacts *A* and *B* were really associated with one another. Archaeologists bring to the study of the past different assumptions about culture and human behavior. They also have different ideas about what constitutes valid information about the past. And they disagree about the role that human actors have had in culture change, as well as the ways the political and economic ideas of the present interact with our representations of the past. The first past to be discussed is the most popular and current vision of Andean prehistory and the role of the *ayllu*. It is promoted by many North American archaeologists and, as introduced in Chapter 1, characterizes processual cultural evolutionism. It is responsible for the "ancient *ayllu* hypothesis." The alternative vision is a postprocessual critique of this majority position. It produces the "recent *ayllu* hypothesis" about the Andean past. My goal in this chapter is to show that *what* we know depends on *how* we know. Questioning our assumptions and methods for knowing the past reveals alternative perspectives and reflexively creates alternative pasts that may be evaluated for "relative correspondence" against the archaeological remains.

It may come as a surprise, but our first approach to the Andean past actually constructs much of prehistory on the basis of the present. It produces the broad outlines of past cultural development with little or no direct information from the past—that is to say, without an archaeological record. Rather, general patterns of cultural evolution take priority. They are assumed first, and then archaeological remains are integrated into and interpreted in terms of this broad outline. Because cultural evolutionism assumes a succession of adaptive stages, with adaptation accounting for change from one stage to the next, it visualizes the past in terms of a story or narrative account. This makes it easy for archaeologists to write the past.

The second approach examined does not begin by assuming the outlines of a story about cultural adaptation. It is based on critiques of the assumptions underlying cultural evolutionism and on critiques of constructions of the past that rely on generalizations about culture in the present. It insists on historical contingency in each and every past, focusing on prehistoric people as actors within particular social contexts. Consequently, we cannot present this past as a grand narrative, but must identify points of difference between it and the processual past so the two can be reformulated as hypotheses to be tested with archaeological data.

First, I will describe processual evolutionism as a theory and approach to culture and culture change, showing how it allows prehistorians to construct an Andean past based in large part on modern and recent information. Second, I will point out the inadequacies of processualism in terms of a postprocessual approach and theory. Third, I will critically examine the application of the first approach to Andean prehistory, citing numerous authors and presenting their narrative as it relates to *ayllu* origins. Finally, I will critique this narrative past from a postprocessual perspective, pointing out essential differences in the way the *ayllu* is inferred to have originated and developed.

## PROCESSUAL EVOLUTIONISM

The current and popular approach to the Andean past is what may be described as processual evolutionism. Processual evolutionism is primarily a North American approach to archaeology, although it has many followers in Britain and elsewhere in the world. It is more or less the same thing that Elizabeth Brumfiel (1992: 551) calls the "ecosystem approach," stating that "ecosystem theorists propose that human populations adapt to their environments through culture-based behavioral systems."

Processual archaeology has produced an abundance of theoretical and methodological literature, but there is considerable variation in how it is applied. Consequently, to describe processual approaches to *ayllu* prehistory in the central Andes, I discuss its theoretical literature only very briefly, focusing more on current archaeological practice among Andeanists. In fact, much of what I write is based on self-analysis of the way I have thought about, and constructed, the Andean past throughout most of my career. In the third section of the chapter I have selected numerous quotations from recent publications by other Andean prehistorians to support my arguments about processual thinking, but my analysis of processualism began with my own realization that I was constructing the Andean past not primarily on the basis of archaeological information, but on the basis of ethnography and ethnohistory, reorganized in terms of a processual theory of cultural evolutionism. I found myself constructing pictures that corresponded with evolutionary expectations, modified to accommodate local archaeological remains. As I became increasingly doubtful about these visions I began to critically examine my bases for knowing the past.

Processual archaeologists view culture as humanity's nonbiological means of adaptation to the environment (Binford 1962). Each culture consists of adaptive behaviors learned and manipulated by its members. Every culture is a self-regulating and bounded entity governed by laws of evolution that are essentially independent of the people participating in it. Cultures consist of institutions organized into functional subsystems, and they change in response to adaptive pressures, usually conceptualized as environmental challenges. More adaptive institutions are selected for and less adaptive institutions are selected against, resulting in culture change. At a greater scale, more adaptive cultures replace less adaptive ones. However, it is typical for archaeologists to conceptualize change as the development of new institutions within a culture, establishing new levels of sociocultural integration (Steward 1955). Robert Carneiro (1962) used scale analysis to determine which institutions come early and which come later in cultural evolution, based on a sample of modern and recent cultures. Consequently, culture changes from primitive or simple to advanced and complex. Because of periodic challenges followed by successful adaptations at new levels of complexity, prehistoric cultures' evolutionary trajectories consist of steplike transformations consistent with the stages identified by cultural evolutionism (Sanderson 1990). Critics of these processual ideas argue that cultural evolutionism is based not on Darwinian theory but on Spencerian ideas and that it is really a social philosophy of progress (cf. Dunnell 1980; Stocking 1968).

The theory of cultural evolution was founded in the nineteenth century in an attempt to understand the diversity of human cultures, especially "primitive" cultures, discovered by Europeans during the age of exploration. It did not escape travelers that stone and bronze tools used by exotic natives were very similar to examples found in Europe, suggesting that in the remote past ancestors of Europeans had lived much as did the "primitive" people observed in remote places. The idea was born that "as they are, we once were, and as we are, they will become." In his book *Time and the Other*, Johannes Fabian (1983) shows how such thinking participated in the creation of a European identity that opposed itself to the "primitive," in which we Europeans exist in the present while "primitives" are distanced into the past. This doctrine, closely related to ideas about the psychic unity of humanity, implies that spatial difference is equivalent to temporal difference. It proposes a universal succession of progressive changes in all cultures (Sanderson 1990: 131–168), manifested by similar evolutionary stages passed through until "civilization" is achieved.

Cultural evolutionists have established a universal sequence of evolutionary stages. First they compiled descriptions of many contemporary and historic cultures. The second step was to compare the sample of recent cultures and classify them on the basis of similarities—creating a typology. Finally, the classes or types were arranged into logical order, usually based on the complexity of the cultures in each class, in terms of technology and/or the number of and degree of differentiation among each culture's institutions. This typological order was assumed to represent a sequence of change in time and to depict the general outline of cultural evolution experienced by all cultures. While late-nineteenth-century sequences were often rather complex and specific, those of the mid to late twentieth century became general, tending to converge around three or four stages often characterized as (1) egalitarian, band society or hunters and gatherers; (2) sedentary, agricultural, rank society or chiefdom; and (3) stratified state or urban society. Frequently, the last stage was divided into two, the initial stage considered to lack institutionalized use of force or in other schemes to be preindustrial and the subsequent stage based on control of force or by others to be capitalist or industrial (Carneiro 1962, 1981; Fried 1967; Polanyi 1944, 1957, 1959; Sahlins 1958, 1972; Service 1962, 1975).

Processual theorists consider all cultures to be functionally integrated wholes subject to the same general laws, but each culture also has its particular environment and its own worldview that imparts a unique structural logic. Throughout their evolutionary histories cultural institutions develop in terms of these laws, the constraints of their environments, and the logic of the cultural whole. The result is an internally consistent, bounded, and self-regulating system, making each culture an entity. Consequently, a culture is capable of confronting other cultures, of defending itself, of resisting external influence, and of replacing less adapted cultures.

But when anthropologists deal with the dynamics of change, cultures cannot be treated as the seamless, adaptive wholes of functional models. Within a single culture institutions confront and resist one another. Of course, each institution develops within the structural and functional constraints of the cultural whole, but institutions may operate with different structural principles. Marxist anthropologists are particularly interested in how ideology masks and mediates these inconsistencies (cf. Friedrich 1989; Thompson 1990). In Andean culture, it is generally accepted even by processualists that households relate to one another in terms of symmetrical reciprocity. But the Inca state related to local communities in terms of asymmetrical exchange. Maurice Godelier (1977b) argues that to avoid internal conflict around this structural discontinuity mediating or mystifying ritual was developed by the Incas. Institutions then, much like cultures, must be bounded entities resistant to the influences of other institutions as well as the logics of foreign cultures.

John Murra (1980) wrote on the economic organization of the Inca state. He argues that Inca statecraft was based on the use of older institutions of kinship and community organization. His construction of pre-Inca culture assumes that lower-order institutions are older than higher-order ones, expressing the logic of cultural evolutionism. The logic appears little changed in Michael Moseley's (1992) recent book on the Incas. Institutions within a culture represent adaptive responses to economic challenges. Major new economic challenges are usually met by the innovation of new institutions, increasing the level of sociocultural complexity, as in the origin of state government. Ideology and ritual mediate discontinuities between institutions so they remain little changed for centuries and even millennia. Consequently, in Andean culture the household must have appeared in response to challenges very early in prehistory. Community and local forms of organization arose in response to subsequent challenges. Andean state administration must represent a relatively recent response to different economic challenges that superimposed higher-order institutions on older household and community structures, with little or no change in these ancient and adaptive institutions. In effect, cultural institutions and their ideologies are like layers in an onion, each new one developing on top of the older ones, differentiated from them, and at least to some degree resistant to their influences. This kind of logic underlies the conviction that in remote Andean communities precolumbian organization and ideology survive today (cf. Bastien 1995), and Tom Dillehay (1995a: 20) speaks for most evolutionists when he asserts that "many [Andean] communities still cling to old religious rites."

Now we can follow the assumptions of processual evolutionism a step further. If culture consists of relatively resistant institutions that originated at different times in the past, to some degree each culture contains within itself a record of its temporal development. Stated oversimplistically, each institution represents the adaptive solution to a past environmental challenge. To construct the past we can unpack culture, teasing it apart into component institutions. Then the institutions can be ordered in terms of their temporal development. Of course, the problem that confronts processualists' attempts to temporally order the institutions of a modern or historic culture is that, unlike the onion, the relations among cultural institutions do not reveal the order of their addition. So it is necessary to consult another body of information to determine this order. The theory that provides an answer is cultural evolutionism, based as it is on the analogical projection of contemporary cultures into the prehistoric past (Ascher 1961). Cultural evolutionism provides a succession of culture types or stages, each characterized by certain kinds of institutions and relations. Unpacking a modern culture into its component institutions, the evolutionist can organize them in terms of formations more egalitarian, more chiefdomlike, and more preindustrial urban or statelike. The approach implicitly reverses Carneiro's (1962) scale analysis, using evolutionary generalizations to organize a sequence of change for each specific culture.

Among Andean practitioners of processual evolutionism there is another important aspect of this technique for reconstructing the past from the present, and this is Andean culture. Modern Andean peoples have one or more layers of European or Hispanic institutions imposed upon their culture, and before prehistorians set about reconstructing the past they must "peel off" the Hispanic layers. Unfortunately, this leaves only a partial culture. But since institutions are resistant and independent cultural layers, institutional layers from ethnographic descriptions can be supplemented by cultural layers from historic descriptions. According to this thinking, it ought to be possible to construct an essential Andean culture by evaluating the Andean credentials of individual institutions, and sometimes even individual beliefs and behaviors, and adding those that pass the test to composite Andean culture. In the process, institutions that are added to Andean culture often are not descriptions of observed behavior, but analytical constructs influenced by assumptions about precapitalist economics, the persistence of deep structure, core-periphery models of interaction, conceptualizing culture in terms of an opposition between modern and traditional behavior, and other theories (cf. Starn 1991, 1994). Consequently, Andean culture is not a real, observable culture but an ideal construct, normative and homogeneous, created by anthropologists and their theories. It includes information from modern and historical cultures of the Andes, heavily processed by theoretical convictions.

Processual evolutionists frequently employ ideal and essentialist Andean culture to construct the Andean past. Andean culture is the onion that is peeled into constituent institutions, which are isolated from one another and then reordered in terms of the expectations of processual evolutionism. This sequence is presented as temporal and evolutionary change in Andean prehistory. It is this intellectual process, essentially independent of archaeological information, that is responsible for the "ancient *ayllu* hypothesis" about Andean prehistory.

## POSTPROCESSUAL CONTINGENT HISTORY

Anthropologists who assume that culture is constructed and reconstructed in the informed action of individuals and interest groups must reject the conclusion that any institution, including the *ayllu*, can descend into modern times essentially unchanged since its origin millennia ago. William Roseberry and Jay O'Brien (1991; cf. Giddens 1984; Long 1992) argue that cultural institutions undergo significant change as a result of human action in the contexts of historically unique social processes. Consequently, cultures and institutions must not be conceptualized as entities with independent existences that resist other cultures and institutions and resist change. This perspective is fundamental to the postprocessual approach to prehistory (Barrett 1988; Brumfiel 1992; Hodder 1982a, 1991).

Since institutions are not entities insulated from one another, neither cultures nor institutions can resist change and retain forms characteristic of past stages of evolution. Certainly I do not wish to deny that there is continuity in culture, but cultural continuity results from individuals' recursive behavior in a structured material environment that includes the acts and expectations of other actors. There is no psychic unity, archetypal memory, or deep structure that determines human action. Culture change is not limited to the addition of new institutions, leaving old ones essentially intact. Change takes place subtly and throughout a culture. In fact, functional or systemic relations among institutions make it very unlikely that one institution can experience change without others being affected. A postprocessual approach to the past must reject the notion that state institutions can be imposed on the household without significantly altering social relations within it. To the contrary, significant change in any behavior is likely to put strains on behavior characteristic of other domains, obliging change in those activities as well. Old institutions are continually recreated in new ways by informed human actors subject to political and economic pressures brought to bear by particular historical circumstances. (For an example of this process at work on Andean myth, see Urton 1990.) Humans are creative innovators quick to experiment with behaviors that benefit them in their current situations, and institutions are constantly reshaped by new demands on time and scheduling, as well as new relations of power. Consequently, cultures and institutions of a given moment and place are created by the participating actors in accord with particular situations and current contexts. New behavior is always conditioned by former experience, but no institution is an archaic and resistant survival from the past.

For many years processual evolutionism has been a relatively unified field with numerous Andean practitioners. On the other hand, postprocessual prehistory is not unified and is quite recent. It shares a critique of scientistic objectivism and of cultural evolutionism, but it has not established a consensual vision of an alternative Andean past. To date, postpocessual Andean pasts are mostly local or regional case studies that emphasize actors, interest groups, and contingent history (cf. Gero 1991; Hastorf 1990a, 1992; Patterson 1987). But once the postprocessualist rejects the assumption that some cultural institutions remain virtually unchanged for thousands of years, then constructing the past on the basis of modern institutions judged to be archaic is revealed as constructing the past in terms of our expectations.

Roseberry and O'Brien (1991) show that many anthropologists and historians think of the increasingly homogeneous world of industrial urban life as "new"—created in the present—while the realm of cultural heterogeneity and ethnic difference belongs to "tradition." Tradition is assumed to be old and created in the past. But pasts constructed by projecting the traditional elements of culture back hundreds or thousands of years actually create an image that is nothing more than the opposite of what we assume to be modern. We have learned nothing about the actual past, but only about our concepts, categories, and prejudices regarding modernity and its opposite. Andean culture is being used in this way, and it is not a problem limited to South Americanists. Critiquing Africanist prehistorians, Ann Stahl (1993, 1994) identifies the use of ideal types and oppositional categories to create pasts that are not supported by rigorous research.

## PROCESSUAL EVOLUTIONISM AND THE ANCIENT AYLLU HYPOTHESIS

Now that we have outlined the theoretical assumptions of processual evolutionism we may examine the evolutionary vision of the *ayllu* in Andean prehistory. The goal is to determine when the *ayllu* is believed to have appeared, and the contexts of its appearance, so that the proposal can be restated as a hypothesis to be tested by the study of mortuary monuments that follows in Chapters 5, 6, and 7. As part of this exercise I want to show how Andean cultural evolution has been constructed, with assumptions about Andean culture, resistant institutions, the adaptive nature of culture change, and other expectations of evolutionism. I want readers to realize how little of this vision actually comes from the archaeological record.

Processual evolutionism assumes that cultures adapt to their natural and social environments. Normally adaptive change occurs because of some kind of challenge, such as population growth, that is most efficiently resolved by the addition of new institutions. Unless circumstances are unusually strained, new adaptive institutions follow patterns characteristic of the logic, economics, social relations, and worldview already established in the culture—the culture's deep structure. Andean culture is the product of the deep structure shared by the native peoples throughout the central Andes for many millennia, and economic patterns, logic, worldview, and other institutions conform to its patterns (for an archaeological study of deep structural continuity in Andean culture, see W. H. Isbell 1978a).

Now with these theoretical issues firmly in mind, let me describe what I call the temporal inversion of Andean culture, which relates to the way evolutionists construct this cultural ideal. The purest example of Andean culture for which we have any written information was witnessed by the early-sixteenth-century Spanish invaders when they marched into the Inca Empire. Unfortunately, these soldiers were less concerned with recording social customs than with plundering gold, and they left only sparse accounts of the fabulous civilization they were destroying. What they did record is almost limited to the culture and government of the elite Incas among whom they settled, and even these descriptions must be treated with caution, for there were different motives for writing—including profits in publishing sensationalized accounts of the New World.

The invasion period and earliest postconquest chronicles are supplemented by a wealth of administrative documents, mostly from later years. Many include transcriptions of native testimonies. There are also official histories collected by viceregal decree, a few discussions of Andean culture written by Indian elites in reply to the Spanish accounts, and the Huarochirí Manuscript. These contain vast amounts of information, but Andean culture must have been succumbing to European influences.

Colonial officials of the Spanish Viceroyalty collected a great deal of information during their organization of provincial administration. The first descriptions were collected so that the new masters from Spain could use information about the Inca Empire to facilitate their own rule. Indeed, much of the early Spanish colonial administration used Inca structure. There were also disputes to be resolved in Spanish colonial courts that stemmed from events in Inca times, and so Inca laws, including claims about the rights, privileges, and the organization of provincial kings and kingdoms, had to be recorded in detail. Consequently, collection of information about the organization of intermediate-level political institutions began with the first *visitas* about 1550 and continued into the 1700s.

Many late-eighteenth- and nineteenth-century documents from Andean communities exist, but the next most important sources for the description of Andean culture are ethnographic studies of modern indigenous communities, most conducted since the 1940s. These data must be evaluated for recent change and outside influence, but if one assumes that institutions confront external influences and resist change, in remote villages one may still find Andean institutions effectively insulated from the influences of national government and capitalist economics. However, what modern ethnography can collect about Andean culture is limited to household and community levels of organization, as well as information about symbolism, religion, and ritual. Higher-level institutions associated with multicommunity and state organization are no longer Andean, having become Hispanic and republican.

Here is the temporal inversion. Descriptions of the earliest, household evolutionary stage of Andean culture depend on information that comes primarily from modern ethnographic studies. Consequently, households and communities of the egalitarian stage of Andean culture tend to resemble those of modern peasant villages, described in the decades following 1950. Ideas about chiefs and kingdoms from the intermediate, rank stage in the evolution of Andean culture tend to be informed by reconstructions of provincial Inca organization by Spanish administrators between 1550 and the 1700s. State societies from the urban stage of Andean culture are based on descriptions of the Inca Empire observed by Spanish invaders between 1532 and the 1550s and collected from older Incas through 1570 or 1580. Father Cobo's ([1653] 1964) influential accounts from the subsequent century used descriptions from this time that were later lost.

The earlier the evolutionary stage is in the development of Andean culture, the more recent is the source of written information on which current discussions draw. It is as though evolutionists thought that deculturation of Andean peoples under Spanish colonialism and later national governments recapitulated their evolutionary experiences in reverse—although no one would admit this.

Evolutionary analyses of the Inca state identify its central institutions as those involved in revenue collection. Taxes were exacted in labor that included military service, construction, and other jobs, but the most important and ubiquitous citizen service was agricultural work. The Incas set themselves up as the stewards of all land and resources. Upon the incorporation of an area or polity into the Inca Empire, all resources passed to the Incas. Administrators inventoried, censused, and redivided everything. Part was allocated to the people of the incorporated polity, another part to the shrines of the empire, and a third part to the Inca king. Then the newly incorporated peoples were assessed labor obligations that included cultivating the lands of the Inca and the shrines; constructing state storehouses; reclaiming new lands; building new imperial infrastructure; producing craft goods, especially textiles; and doing other work (D'Altroy 1992; Morris 1982, 1992; Morris and

Thompson 1985; Moseley 1992; Murra 1975b, 1980; Patterson 1991). This required a full-time managerial class in command of military force, supervising resources and accounts, censusing and allocating human labor, and managing the products and goods created. The members of this class constituted a hierarchically and spatially organized bureaucracy that collected and processed information, made and communicated decisions, and used force of arms to ensure that its decisions were carried out. Religion and ideology supported these relations, and ritual, costume, conspicuous generosity, and feasting expressed relations of super- and subordination between the levels of the bureaucracy. At the pinnacle of the hierarchy was the Inca king or Qapacapu of Cuzco.

Proceeding to construct the past, processualists first attribute these features of the Inca state to idealized Andean culture. Once they enter ideal culture the descriptions apply equally to any time, even the origin of Andean states centuries before the Incas. Consequently evolutionary archaeologists often affirm the antiquity of such institutions without validating their inferences with actual archaeological remains.

Michael Moseley (1992: 65) simply states that the administrative institutions of the Inca Empire were based on principles of community organization that were much older than state government. Deflecting attention away from the question of how we know about the antiquity of ethnohistorically described institutions, such as the *ayllu*, Moseley focuses on the way taxes were collected. He indicates that the kind of relationship existing in Inca times between local chiefs and households was an unchanging essence of "Andean culture." Inca imposition of higher-level administrative institutions in new provinces is cited to create the sense that culture change is additive and historically sequential, inviting the reader to adopt the author's premise that levels in the Inca state administrative hierarchy represent a sequence of cultural additions in terms of which the Andean past may be reconstructed.

Alan Kolata (1993: 209) reveals the same approach for determining the nature and origins of the Tiwanaku state:

> The agricultural labor tax was not an invention of the Inca, but an ancient feature of the Andean social landscape. Throughout the Andes, local political leaders and ethnic lords had extracted surplus labor in community owned fields from their subjects for generations before the coming of the Inca. The Inca, operating within an idiom familiar to any pre-Columbian Andean peas-

ant in which work rather than money was the essential means of discharging economic and social debts, simply assessed additional labor obligations on the local communities.

Tom Patterson (1991: 33–34), who approaches the past with a Marxist rather than a processual perspective, still makes similar assumptions about continuity in the state institutions of Andean culture:

> The class-stratified states that appeared in the fifth and sixth centuries A.D. derived their revenues from the labor of peasants [farmers], pastoralists, and fisherfolk and from goods they produced as part-time craft workers. Since the wealth of the ruling classes depended on the control of labor and, ultimately, on extending the agricultural base, the administrative and economic restructuring that occurred during the formation and subsequent development of these states was organized primarily to assess and collect tribute from subject communities. Some of the labor appropriated was employed to weave textiles that were placed in storehouses, to build pyramids, to dig irrigation canals, and to expand existing water management systems.

Clearly, the invasion-period descriptions of Inca political institutions constitute the basis for knowing about state organization in Andean culture. In the same fashion, later-sixteenth- as well as seventeenth- and early-eighteenth-century descriptions of Inca provincial administration of ethnic kingdoms that were incorporated into their empire determine ideas about the organization of pre-Inca polities in Andean culture.

This approach to knowing the Andean past was brilliantly pioneered by John Murra (1975a, 1975b, 1980) during the 1950s. Murra accepted John Rowe's (1946: 203) chronology for the Inca Empire, which permits no more than 100 years for the duration of Inca imperial development. He reviewed the earliest information about provincial Inca administration and later organized an interdisciplinary research project in Huánuco (see Ortiz de Zuñiga [1562] 1967 and 1972) that combined pre-*reducción* settlement documents with ethnographic community studies and archaeological investigations to help determine cultural continuities and changes. Murra concluded that provincial Inca governors employed previous ethnic divisions as administrative units, which in most cases remained under the leadership of their old chiefs and kings. Taxes demanded by the empire in labor, levied in agricultural tasks, military service, and other work, followed older, traditional patterns of obligation. Assessments were made by the Incas against former ethnic polities on the basis of the number of households they contained—determined by periodic censuses—and each group's leader or *kuraka* was obliged to oversee the delivery of required labor services, usually on a rotating basis established by Inca supervisors. *Kurakas* redivided tasks into *suyus* or parcels in accord with the number of divisions or *ayllus* in their kingdom or chiefdom, and the size of each *suyu* depended on the number of households in each *ayllu*. Finally, *ayllu* leaders were responsible for direct supervision of tributary work by the members.

In addition to the assessment of taxes in terms of *ayllu* and ethnic kingdom (perhaps in Andean thinking best referred to as minimal and maximal *ayllu*), land and resources were also conferred by the Incas in terms of these former kingdoms and their component *ayllus*. Early Spanish sources describe annual distribution of *ayllu* agricultural lands to household heads, according to the number of members. Subsequently, cultivation was conducted communally, beginning with tax obligations to imperial shrines and the state, then extending to lands allocated to the *kuraka* and ethnic shrines, and continuing till the fields of the householders were completed. John Murra argued that in less than 100 years the Incas could not have invented and imposed such a remarkably elaborate and efficient system of imperial administrative control. Rather, it must represent elaboration of basic and old Andean patterns that had existed for centuries. Labor given by *ayllu* members to their chiefs (*kurakas*) and shrines—cultivation of fields assigned these authorities and rotating services in their houses and temples—must have preceded and served as the model for Inca labor tax. In fact, Inca tributary institutions must have been superimposed on top of traditional service obligations, like the new layer of an onion, leaving the old institutions essentially unchanged.

Murra's research indicated that the Inca state was superimposed on the *kuraka* and ethnic kingdom and in much the same way the *kuraka* and ethnic kingdom were superimposed on the *ayllu* and its kin-based leader. Consequently, for reconstructing the prehistoric past, archaeologists could construct prestate Andean chiefdoms in the image of the ethnic administrative units of the Inca state or empire. As discussed above, they were described in Spanish administrative documents after about 1550.

If the institutions of *kuraka* leadership belong to a chiefly or protostate stage of Andean cultural evolution (the maximal *ayllu*), its antecedent must lie in the *ayllu* (or minimal *ayllu*). Modern and historic descriptions document small, essentially egalitarian *ayllus* that recognize one or more senior kinsmen as spokesmen and coordinators of resources. In the past it is clear that land and other resources were held in common by this group and usufruct rights were redistributed periodically in accord with perceived needs of individual households. Labor was also allocated communally, with many tasks conducted by large work parties. From the adaptive evolutionary point of view, *ayllu* as an institution must have originated earlier than chiefly, ethnic kingdoms.

The richest information about *ayllu* organization comes from modern ethnographies. Remote villages and hamlets remain imperfectly integrated into modern Andean nations, and subsistence economics mobilized by kinship and household characterize them. To appreciate how modern ethnographies and colonial ethnohistories have been woven together in the construction of adaptive evolutionism's interpretation of the Andean past we must briefly review the trends in Andean ethnography since the 1960s.

The directions that ethnographic studies of Andean culture took during the 1960s were significantly influenced by ethnohistorians John V. Murra and R. Tom Zuidema, who were both interested in identifying structural patterns underlying indigenous, pre-European Andean culture. But for much of the research, pre-European and non-European were little differentiated. Murra and his associates focused more on relationships of production, while Zuidema and his associates focused more on kinship, social organization, and worldview. The economic structure that emerged for Andean culture was initially described by Murra (1972, 1985a, 1985b) as the "vertical archipelago" or simply "verticality." Subsequently verticality was renamed "ecological complementarity." Murra's vertical ecological complementarity holds that the essential economic relationships upon which Andean culture developed were within-group reciprocity and sharing. These relations of production virtually precluded the development of interdependent cultural groups specialized in distinct environmental zones and products, integrated by exchange mechanisms. The Andean culture ideal was for each group to maintain direct access to all the diverse ecological tiers of vertical Andean topography necessary for its own subsistence. This could not be achieved by an independent household. The institution that appeared in response to this organizational challenge was a multihousehold social unit that held its resources in common and shared labor. This larger group could control a diversity of lands, water, and other resources; it could allocate the labor of its members; it would share the products communally. For Murra and his colleagues, this described the Andean *ayllu*. From this position it was easy for prehistorians to infer that *ayllu* organization was the initial adaptive response to the Andean environment, predating chiefly inequality and state bureaucracy.

Murra recognized vertical ecological complementarity in the Andes on the basis of colonial descriptions of Andean ethnic kingdoms, especially the Lupaca and Chupachu (Diez de San Miguel [1567] 1964; Ortiz de Zuñiga [1562] 1967 and 1972). While Murra focused on ethnohistoric studies, his students and colleagues undertook ethnographic research in remote modern Andean communities, discovering a vibrant subsistence economy based on the exploitation of diverse ecozones and on reciprocal labor exchanges. Since Karl Polanyi's (1944, 1957, 1959) work, capitalist, market-based institutions had been contrasted with precapitalist, kin-based institutions, and the latter were believed to depend on reciprocity. Noncapitalist, reciprocity-based subsistence economics in modern Andean villages were quickly assumed to represent precapitalist Andean culture surviving from Inca and earlier times.

In 1974 Giorgio Alberti and Enrique Mayer published an influential collection, *Reciprocidad e intercambio en los Andes peruanos*, that depicted numerous examples of Andean ecological complementarity operating in modern indigenous communities through mechanisms of reciprocity. Cesar Fonseca and Enrique Mayer (1978; Mayer 1977, 1985) initiated a systematic study of vertical ecology in Peru's Cañete Valley. Stephen Brush (1977) described modern highland strategies of ecological complementarity, developing a typology for different local environments, and Benjamin Orlove (1977a) described ecological zonation in relation to native systems of reciprocity.

During the same years Tom Zuidema was studying Inca ethnohistory to discover the structural principles underlying the organization of Cuzco (Zuidema 1964) as well as Andean systems of kinship (Zuidema 1977) and native calendrics (Zuidema 1981, 1982a, 1982b). He was also seeking the same principles in modern Indian communities, encouraging his students and colleagues to conduct formal studies in remote villages. It soon became apparent that modern Indians conceptualized their cosmos in terms of vertically differentiated space (Zuidema and Quispe 1968). Influenced by Zuidema, Billie Jean Isbell (1978) revealed structural principles governing vertically organized space and reciprocal complementarity in the modern village of Chuschi. Pierre Duviols (1973) showed similar principles underlying ethnohistoric chiefdoms. Only María Rostworowski (1970b, 1975, 1977, 1978, 1981b) challenged the universality of self-sufficient, reciprocal organization of vertical ecological complementarity in Andean culture. She discovered data for an alternative system based on specialization and trade on Peru's coast.

Andean ethnography revealed the economic importance of the nuclear family peasant household, more or less the same unit assumed to underlie production in precapitalist economies (Chayanov [1925] 1966; Valcárcel 1925, 1964). Furthermore, these ethnographic households were linked by two systems of reciprocity, *ayni* and *minka*, that were easily relegated to the Andean rather than the Hispanic sphere of culture. Since the popular theories of precapitalist economics emphasized social relations of production, and *ayni* and *minka* were key social relations of production in ethnographic Andean communities, they quickly assumed important roles in the processual evolutionary vision of primitive Andean culture. Ethnographically based definitions are as follow:

> An *ayni* exchange consists of one individual calling another to help him in a particular task. He must repay this individual with an equal amount of time spent in the same kind of work either by working himself or sending a member of his household in his stead. The assistant must be provided with food, coca leaf, and home-brewed barley or maize beer. The variation in the amount of work per day is quite small, and precise reckoning is kept of the time worked. (Orlove 1977a: 202)

> Like *ayni*, *mink'a* relationships are used to form work teams for different tasks. An individual organizes a *mink'a* work team by calling others to help him. He provides the assistants with food, coca leaf, and home-brewed barley or maize beer. However, *mink'a* exchanges involve goods and labor, rather than la-

bor alone as in the case of *ayni*. The repayment may be in two forms.

One form of *mink'a* is festive. There is better food in greater quantity than in *ayni* contexts, and *aguardiente* or alcohol is liberally supplied. Festive *mink'a* is used for nonseasonal labor, such as house construction, and for seasonal labor in which sizable groups must be assembled, such as shearing large herds of sheep. Workers are repaid with a feast rather than goods which they can consume later. Festive *mink'a* can be used for tasks which occur so infrequently as to make *ayni* impractical because of its precise reckoning and exact repayment.

The other form of *mink'a* is nonfestive; labor is repaid with goods or cash. An individual might arrange for other people to help shear his sheep by giving each one a fleece for every ten shorn. In other cases the payment would be by the day, rather than by a piece rate; workers at a potato harvest might be given a quarter sack of potatoes each day. (Orlove 1977a: 203)

While some researchers describe more variation in *minka* (Bradby 1982; Figueroa 1982; Fonseca 1974; Sánchez 1982), the fundamental characteristic is the receipt of goods in return for labor, with the *minka* sponsor, at least potentially, receiving a significant net gain.

Karl Polanyi (1944, 1957, 1959) and Marshall Sahlins (1972) argued that kinship was the universal context in which reciprocity was conducted. For Andean peasants this was clearly demonstrated by Billie Jean Isbell (1974), who showed how the concepts of *ayllu* and *karu ayllu* (close and distant *ayllu* members, respectively) mobilized reciprocal labor exchange. It quickly became apparent that *ayni* was symmetrical reciprocity, while *minka* represented asymmetrical reciprocity. In the evolutionary literature such noncapitalist forms of exchange were amply discussed as reciprocity and redistribution (Sahlins 1972). Reciprocity or balanced exchange between individuals or households was viewed as the universal means of exchanging goods and labor in egalitarian societies with little social and economic inequity. In contrast, redistribution was a form of reciprocity that funneled goods and labor through a central person or household, and it was considered the origin for institutionalized wealth differentials and rank society or chiefdoms. Redistribution was adaptively selected for when general access to products of several ecological resource zones conferred advantages to all—fish, taro, salt, and stone axes, for example—but could not be efficiently assured by direct individual relations of balanced reciprocity because of factors like different elasticity of demand—stone axes as opposed to taro or salt, for example. Equally important, redistribution also conferred the opportunity to accumulate wealth on the organizer of redistributional exchanges since exact balance in transactions was impossible.

For many processual evolutionists, *ayllu* was identified as the primordial social unit of Andean culture, with *ayni* and *minka* distinguished as archaic institutions of production that, preserved in modern culture, might represent successive evolutionary stages. I conclude that processual evolutionism postulates an early pre-Andean cultural stage of band organization that was succeeded by adaptation to vertical ecological complementarity through the development of *ayllu* organization in which households were formally associated with other households in communal landholding and symmetric reciprocity based on balanced relations of *ayni*. This was a stage of egalitarian society, although certainly not without any inequalities, as anticipated by theoretical expectations (Fried 1967) as well as modern community studies of *ayllu* organization (Bradby 1982; Figueroa 1982; Orlove 1977a; Sánchez 1982).

*Minka*, or redistribution, was the vehicle for constructing institutionalized privilege and chiefly organization in Andean culture, creating the next evolutionary stage. Probably by subverting *ayni* into *minka*, a transformation achieved by substituting unlike repayment, the richer household could accumulate more wealth and prestige, eventually transforming the influence of a "big man" into the institutionalized role of *kuraka* (chief, king). In the sixteenth century the *kuraka* received privileged use of land as well as agricultural labor and personal service from the members of his *ayllu*. In many cases this social unit was a maximal *ayllu* that was synonymous with an ethnic kingdom with thousands of members. Trappings of reciprocity were maintained in that the workers received food and drink while tributing labor, and they probably received other rights and goods when redistributions were made, especially at ritual occasions. Perhaps the asymmetry of *minka* was disguised in ritualized festivity, but *kurakas* were wealthy and powerful. This then represents a second stage in Andean cultural evolution. Chiefs and chiefly society arose through *minka*-based redistributional mechanisms within the *ayllu* that were adaptive for all while permitting concentration of wealth in the hands of a part-time managerial elite. Facilitated by *minka* and the adaptive advantage of redistribution, *kuraka*s created chiefly polities like those incorporated as administrative units within the Inca Empire.

The chiefly *kuraka* stage of Andean culture was the preadaptation for and the immediate antecedent of Andean states, which, as we have seen above, are conceptualized in terms of an Inca model. The specific evolution of Andean culture is thus reconstructed in terms of three broad stages based on information about Inca, colonial, and modern Indian culture. Cultural institutions have been unpacked and classified as Andean or Hispanic. Those assigned to Andean culture are transferred to a timeless construct, the parts of which can be projected backward through time in accordance with stages predicted by universal cultural evolution.

A scenario that more or less represents processual evolutionism may be stated as follows. Hunters and gatherers arriving in Andean South America more than 10,000 years ago were organized in terms of flexible bands consisting of family groups. We may suppose that they practiced symmetrical exchange, consistent with a deep structural canon of self-sufficiency. These immigrants adapted to the Andean environment, becoming progressively expert at exploiting its diverse resources based primarily on altitudinal variation. Different plants and animals were available at various elevations, some at the same and others at different times. Developing seasonally patterned transhumance from less organized nomadism, the use of complementary resources was becoming basic to subsistence by 8,000 years ago. Increasingly productive exploitation of the diverse resources promoted sedentism, or at least seasonal sedentism, and more formal relations of cooperation among several households. The subsistence strategy was within-group, kin-based reciprocity and sharing through vertical ecological complementarity, creating a new social unit, the *ayllu*. Archaeologists sometimes use timeless descriptions to communicate and emphasize these ideas. For example, using present tense, Michael Moseley (1992: 49) informs readers that agropastoral production in the Andes requires activities at the same time in different places and that labor demands often exceed the capacity of a nuclear family household. Consequently, while the household is the uncontested essential unit of Andean culture, it can only exist within a larger labor-sharing kin collective called the *ayllu*. This is especially true in the early stage of married life, when a couple have no grown children and may have to tend dependent infants, but must also build a house, cultivate new land, and undertake other expenditures that vastly exceed their resources. Thus, in the Andean environment, the survival of each and every household depends on participating in an *ayllu* that controls enough land and water, and manages enough labor, to insure the well-being of all its members. In fact, the larger—in terms of resources and working members—the *ayllu*, the more adaptive it becomes.

Moseley (1992: 94) affirms that by 6,000 years ago the archaeological record reveals kin groupings reminiscent of the *ayllu* and during the Initial Period—roughly the second millennium B.C.—construction of huge monuments on the coast of Peru reveals *ayllu*-like communities that were probably ancestral to those described by the Spanish in the sixteenth century (Moseley 1992: 127).

Alan Kolata (1993: 61–63) confidently states that in highland Bolivia first millennium B.C. Wankarani settlements contain house clusters that "reflect a minimal *ayllu* or lineage grouping." Like Moseley, Kolata also fails to specify what archaeological remains reveal the *ayllu*, but goes on to tell us that sculptures of llama heads from this culture were *ayllu* tutelary deities and that the *ayllu* units were bound together by kinship, economic relations, and shared religious cults into exchange networks that facilitated adaptation to the harsh environment. Joan Gero (1991), Patrick Carmichael (1995), and Helaine Silverman (1993) attribute *ayllu* organization to regional cultures of the Early Intermediate Period.

According to this popular scenario, *ayllu*-based chiefdoms, or maximal *ayllu*s, appeared as chiefs discovered how to manipulate redistributional exchange, employing conspicuous generosity and new luxury goods to avoid repayment in the form of equal work (Gero 1991: 135–138). These, too, were adaptive responses to the diverse Andean environment, where balanced reciprocity could not satisfy needs for access. Charles Stanish (1992) explicitly argues that the *ayllu* lost its egalitarian structure through the transformation of *ayni* into *minka*, promoting rank and offices such as the *kuraka*:

> ... price fixing market systems were absent in Andean indigenous economies. The dominant mechanism of exchange is either a symmetrical reciprocity based on kinship structures or an asymmetrical one based on redistribution. Redistribution

may be seen as a structural transformation of reciprocity in that political authorities manipulate traditional symmetrical relationships into unequal ones, setting up an economic system in which resources flow disproportionately to an elite group. (Stanish 1992: 24)

In the *minka* system, when one household suffers a temporary scarcity of resources, they are invited by another household (particularly by peasants in other ecological zones) as *minkakuna*. They are lodged and provided meals in return for agricultural labor. At the end of the harvest, part of the produce is redistributed to the *minkakuna*.... This process, incidentally, provides an insight into the dynamics of elite formation in traditional Andean society. By taking advantage of ecological fluctuation and by managing traditional value systems, a landowner possessing a stable productive base can become richer than other peasants....

According to Fonseca (1974), prehispanic Andean *kuraka*-peasant relationships were essentially structured by the *minka* system. (Stanish 1992: 25)

This explanation of Andean cultural evolution manipulates ethnographically described institutions—*ayllu, ayni,* and *minka*—to transform essentially egalitarian communities of the sort encountered in modern rural villages into chiefly societies of the kind implied by Spanish colonial accounts of the Inca provinces. *Kuraka* converted the exchange of labor among *ayllu* members into tribute by substituting *minka* payments for *ayni* obligations of equal work. Of course, the archaeological record plays a part, but its role is more to date critical transformations, to identify the actual locations, and to provide cultural correlates (for example, the demographic changes, the military developments, etc.) associated with universal stages of cultural evolution and the succession of institutions unpacked from Andean culture. Far too little effort has been made to identify rigorous archaeological criteria for verifying key institutions—such as *ayllu, minka,* or ethnic kingdom—by means of the archaeological record. Rather, it is common practice to interpret the past by simply inserting the institutions at the anticipated places and times. In the jargon of processual evolutionary archaeology, "middle range theories" are not being developed to show why remains excavated from the Andean past are best understood as the products of *ayllu*, *ayni*, and *minka* rather than some other institutions.

## CONTINGENT HISTORY AND THE RECENT *AYLLU* HYPOTHESIS

Construction of history by informed action assumes that culture is created and recreated in the actions of individuals. Institutions result from repeated and habitual activities and relations among actors who are subject to diverse pressures, including changing economic and political factors. Consequently, using modern cultural descriptions there is no basis for deciding which institutions are recent and which ones have been around for millennia. No one wants to deny long traditions of adaptation, cultural logic, worldview, or deep structure, but neither should we create continuity or deep structure with our methods and assumptions. Without convincing archaeological confirmation, projecting the modern *ayllu* back to the beginnings of Andean culture may be employing a bogus methodology that creates a counterproductive understanding of the past. Two principal criticisms must be taken very seriously.

First, processual evolutionary determination of the antiquity of institutions using the Andean culture construct employs oppositional thinking and circular argument. Oppositional thinking as described by Roseberry and O'Brien (1991) divides observed behavior into two classes, one usually considered modern, and its opposite, traditional behavior. Modern behavior is part of the global economic system and is being created in the present. Traditional behavior, by contrast, is not part of global economics so it must belong to the past. It is a living fossil. Cultural evolutionism provides a method for constructing pasts out of these survivalisms (cf. Herzfeld 1987). Of course, pasts constructed with this method confirm the antiquity of ethnic traditions, confirm institutional continuity, and confirm evolutionary theory—of course, because the argument is viciously circular.

> Comparative and historical understanding in general is often embedded in a variety of oppositional models taken to represent past and present. Whether expressed in terms of primitive versus civilized, traditional versus modern, folk versus urban,

natural economy versus market economy, community versus contract, underdeveloped versus developed, or other polar pairs, such models represent deductive constructs intended to present historical change as transition from one abstract pole to the other. The pole representing the past is often based upon naturalistic assumptions. Historical analysis then proceeds by sorting the mixed elements of any concrete reality into those left over from the past and those belonging to the emergent future. The analytic division of Third World societies into "traditional" and "modern" sectors is a familiar example of this procedure. The sectors are generally defined on the basis of assessments of the relative modernity of existing features of production, exchange, social organization, and so forth, without any rigorous attempt to account for the supposed sectors or their past and present interconnection. Rather than constructing social, political, and cultural changes in the past, this exercise reproduces a pseudohistorical process immanent in the categories themselves and derived from implicit evolutionary assumptions. (Roseberry and O'Brien 1991: 2)

I believe that Andeanists' division of ethnohistorical and ethnographic culture into an Andean sphere and a Hispanic, Western, or European sphere is often based on what Roseberry and O'Brien characterize as "oppositional models taken to represent past and present." Processual evolutionary constructions of the Andean past employ ideal Andean culture, conflating time and almost inverting changes documented historically. Prehistoric Andean state institutions are described in terms of Inca government as it existed during the Spanish invasion. Consequently, class-based organization of the sixteenth century is projected backward, sometimes a millennium or more. Supposedly earlier chiefly institutions are described from information about Inca provincial administration, which actually comes from colonial documents, so anthropologists are deciding what was authentically old and what was not. Furthermore, these data are conflated with modern ethnographic information about redistribution and *minka*, creating continuity between past and present, whether it existed or not. Finally, earlier stages of Andean culture rely on descriptions of the *ayllu*, *ayni*, dualism, and other modern information from community studies. Of course, historical descriptions are included, but evolutionary ideas as well as convictions about Andean culture usually contribute to the way historical documents are interpreted (cf. Netherly 1977, 1990). Consequently, what we see as culture change, and what we see as long-term continuity in Andean culture, from remotely pre-Inca to modern times, is created by anthropological methods and assumptions.

This is not to say that there is no continuity in Andean culture and that the very concept of Andean culture is nothing but a product of our methodological and theoretical inadequacies. What I am pointing out is that processual evolutionism and its vision of the Andean past must be critiqued and tested with independent information.

The second serious criticism of processual evolutionism and institutional continuity concerns the construction of Andean culture as an unchanging tradition. This promotes thinking about culture, not in terms of human relations but as a substantial, internally homogeneous thing that is a bounded entity capable of confronting similar entities on a field of cultural evolution and economic domination. As Eric Wolf (1982: 6) critically declares, "By endowing nations, societies, or cultures with the qualities of internally homogeneous and externally distinctive and bounded objects, we create a model of the world as a global pool hall in which entities spin off each other like so many hard and round billiard balls."

These kinds of ideas about culture have more basis in the politics of oppression, racism, and group subjugation than in social science (cf. Starn 1994). A contingent history approach to culture and the past rejects ethnic essentialism, arguing that neither cultural adaptation nor cultural meaning provides a universal key for inferring past from present. What is adaptive today, or what is deeply meaningful, is a result of recent history. Roseberry (1989: 198, emphasis added) argues that informed construction of the past benefits most from "a discussion of how we might think of *particular cases*."

Specific information about the prehistory and early colonial history of the *ayllu* is not abundant, but I do believe that we can show that this institution has not remained constant during the past 600 years or so. Important change-generating pressures can be identified. The first relates to the incorporation of local *ayllu*s into imperialistic states, first the Inca Empire, and subsequently the Spanish Viceroyalty. Both of these states employed the *ayllu* as a corporate, bureaucratic unit for censusing labor and allocating land, as well as for assigning work quotas and organizing rotation schedules. A later and quite different pressure relates to the articulation of the *ayllu* with a capitalistic economy in modern times. I suspect that the first set of influences promoted a more homogeneous *ayllu* throughout the Andes. Consistent with administrative impositions by both of these states it seems apparent that the *ayllu* must have become more focused around resources, including landholding, water rights, and the allocation of labor. The Spanish extirpation of idolatries campaign destroyed founder mummies and punished the worship of ancestors, eventually eliminating the religious element as well as the focus for the kin idiom that structured hierarchical organization within the *ayllu*. Bureaucratic government by the Incas and Spanish would have promoted a standard size for the *ayllu*, which was relatively small and internally undifferentiated except for the authority needed to assure effective management of resources necessary to meet external demands for labor.

More recently, modern pressures from capitalism would promote participation in wage labor that favors financially independent households. However, in view of low salaries and periodicity of work, a subsistence economy would be required with mechanisms for linking otherwise independent households in labor exchanges that did not require money.

Looking first for documentation of Inca and colonial transformations of the *ayllu*, historical information from Inca times is limited to general descriptive discussions and to dictionary definitions from decades following the Spanish invasion. However, John Murra's (1975b, 1980) studies of institutional continuity in *ayllu* and state organization are instructive for the contradictions they reveal. It is more than likely that Murra is correct in his conclusion that Inca administrators employed existing ethnic entities—*ayllu*s, both minimal and maximal—as units in terms of which land and other resources were assigned by the state and labor was deployed for state programs. But this is not to say that Inca use of the *ayllu* for the benefit of the state was without any consequences, for several significant changes are at least implied. First, the Inca policy of assigning land to each *ayllu* and mandating its periodic redistribution must have promoted an *ayllu* with little internal differentiation and strong corporate character. Second, labor obligations were levied on the entire *ayllu*, further fostering corporate responsibility. Third, early Spanish invaders recorded land inheritance laws among many ethnic groups that were inconsistent with corporate landholding and periodic redistribution of usufruct rights.

Murra accounts for this discrepancy by suggesting that households received the same land parcels year after year in accord with certain ideas about inheritance to promote land improvement and conservation. I suggest that the Spanish invaders recorded local laws that were being replaced by Inca policies of simplification and communalism being imposed on *ayllu* organization, organization that was probably quite heterogeneous from ethnicity to ethnicity at the onset of Inca conquests. Even among the Incas there is evidence for conflicts between civil or state policies and kin claims. Sherbondy (1982: 21) found that in addition to rules about corporate inheritance of an Inca king's lands by all *panaca* members, there was evidence that some parcels were designated to specific heirs. *Ayllu* and *panaca* may have been much less communal, and perhaps quite heterogeneous, before the Inca Empire.

Other evidence for Inca homogenization and simplification of the *ayllu* involves the division of conquered populations of households into units of standardized size based on decimal divisions. Murra suggests that this was primarily an administrative fiction, but Catherine J. Julien (1982: 129) found that early colonial Lupaca *ayllu*s did tend to contain about 100 households. Furthermore, the term *pachaca*—Inca for 100— was often used interchangeably for *ayllu* in administrative contexts during early colonial times. This practice is consistent with the inference that *ayllu* organization was being reshaped by the needs and policies of state administration.

Following the Spanish invasion, Europeans continued policies that influenced *ayllu* organization. At first Spanish provincial administrative units (*corregimientos*) correlated with the ethnic kingdoms recognized by Inca government ("recognized" by the Incas is not to say that they actually existed as pre-Inca political units—see Julien 1983: 35–62). During the early decades diverse Spanish interests competed for Indian labor, giving traditional *kurakas* room to maneuver and means to construct a power base (Larson 1988: 33–40; Stern 1982: 27–50). But beginning with the administration of Viceroy Toledo (1569–1581) the Spanish Crown adopted policies to secure government revenues that transformed the Andean order. First, the *reducciones* imposed a European model of the village with its local territory. As discussed above, Indians of a region were forcibly resettled into agglutinated towns, with minimal *ayllu*s allocated their own lands within one league of the settlement. Furthermore, *ayllu* members were obliged to reside in a defined section or *barrio* of the village (Spaulding 1984: 9). *Barrio* organization, long associated by anthropologists with the Andean rather than Hispanic cultural sphere, may be a colonial imposition. A long succession of laws regarding Indian lands mandated Indian ownership in terms of corporate *ayllu*s until republican government in the nineteenth century. Even then, excessive hacienda formation resulted in new legislation, such as the recreation of corporate Indian *comunidades* in Peru during the 1920s (Molinié-Fioravanti 1986).

Throughout the colonial era Spanish administration progressively cut traditional *kuraka*s out of the power loop by employing appointed officials. What is more, *reducción* policies and the progressive acquisition of lands by Europeans began a process that severely reduced complementary ecological archipelagos over which *kuraka*s had presided. Maximal *ayllu* kingdoms disappeared so completely before the end of the eighteenth century that John Murra and Nathan Wachtel (1986: 2) claim:

> . . . there is no way of projecting seriously from present-day practice to institutions four centuries earlier. Even when these [ethnographic] monographs provide interesting information, it is hard to use it to understand the Andean world: There is no way of knowing how these "communities [of modern Indians]" came to be the heirs of the large polities we know to have been prevalent in the Andes both before and after the Inka. In fact, the communities of today are recent colonial and even republican phenomena.

In addition to resettling the indigenous peoples, Viceroy Toledo instigated a labor tax payable to the central government. Called *mita* after the Inca labor draft, it sent about one-sixth of the Indian tributaries, on a rotating basis, to work in the mines of Potosí and Huancavelica, to work on haciendas producing food and other goods for Lima, or to work in the maintenance and provisioning of roads and waystations. The model for this tax was Inca, but not a tradition-based obligation. The inspiration seems to have been a late invention worked out in Cochabamba during the reign of the last precolombian Inca, Huayna Capac (Larson 1988: 60). Virtually the entire valley of Cochabamba had been depopulated, and outsider ethnic groups were imported on rotating bases to cultivate maize for the empire. Following this lead, in the colonial *mita*, minimal *ayllu*s from the new localized communities were the units in terms of which tributaries were counted and labor quotas were assessed. Workers were to be mobilized by appointed *ayllu* chiefs. At first only *ayllu* members were responsible for *mita*, because they alone received kin-based rights to land and other resources for their subsistence and reproduction in a *reducción* village (Spaulding 1984: 165). But as Europeans devised clever ways to separate lands from their Indian stewards, native households were also encouraged to abandon their *ayllu*, escape tribute obligations, and become sharecroppers for new foreign owners. A new class, termed *forasteros*—Indian residents in a town or place where their household lacked *ayllu* affiliation and land rights—became increasingly common. In fact, the number grew so large that the Crown eventually extended *mita* obligations to these Indians as well.

But in the meantime the exodus from *ayllu*s made the fulfillment of labor tax increasingly onerous for the members who remained. Official censuses were infrequent, and the *ayllu* bore the burden of providing all the labor that had been assessed in the last census, regardless of dwindling population. Clearly, this enforced corporate responsibility within the *ayllu*, as did the real conditions under which *mita* obligations were fulfilled. *Mita* workers sent to the mines in Potosí could not subsist on the wages they received during periods of service. Consequently, it was necessary to mobilize the resources of kin to fulfill subsistence and housing needs while away from home (Larson 1988: 62–63). Apparently it was common for *mita* payers to travel to the mines in entourages that included wives and kinsmen with food, tents, cooking utensils, clothing, and bedding packed on trains of llamas. While we may think of colonial *mita* tax payment as an individual or household obligation, in reality it involved and reinforced a new kind of *ayllu* organization.

These pressures clearly promoted a more corporate and communal *ayllu*, in terms of land ownership and labor allocation. They also promoted an *ayllu* that was small and lacking in significant internal hierarchy and separated from its former religious centerpiece, the founding ancestor. Maximal *ayllu*s and *kuraka* kings disappeared, to be replaced by egalitarian kin cooperatives capable of little more than subsistence and tribute obligations. Ancestor mummies also disappeared, to be replaced by Catholic saints and local mountain deities.

A new set of economic and political circumstances pressured *ayllu*s during the nineteenth and twentieth centuries. Communal *ayllu* lands were abolished in favor of individual Indian ownership, undermining the communal and corporate organization promoted by Inca and Spanish administrations. Wool production for the world market continued to support some degree of corporateness, but during the last fifty years communal, kin-based economic pursuits and corporate kin authority have declined more or less proportionately with direct Indian participation in wage labor. Cash wages encourage individualistic strategies. Furthermore, engaging in off-farm wage labor usually involves migration for several months at a time. The resulting withdrawal of a worker integral to communal farming and herding creates serious problems regarding rights to a share in *ayllu* products and hastens the emergence of the household as the independent social and economic unit (Collins 1988). But the realities of pricing oblige increasingly independent Indian households to participate in a second, simultaneous but radically different economy. Michael Painter (1991: 91–95) describes the way this has worked in the south highlands of Peru. Government policy—geared to promote industrial growth—and the market structure depressed the prices farm producers receive for basic products. But low food prices are not passed on to consumers. Indian cultivators respond by abandoning most efforts to farm for sale, placing more and more energy into off-farm wage labor. However, their modest wages do not buy much food, so it is necessary to continue to farm, but only for household subsistence. Employing the labor of children, the elderly, and adult men and women during times they are present on the farm, agriculture must apply labor-maximizing, extensive land use techniques. Production is low per unit of land, but sufficient to meet most of the needs of the household. What is essential for the success of this subsistence system is a mechanism to redistribute labor among increasingly independent farm households without expending hard-earned cash. *Ayni* and *minka* are the mechanisms. As observed by ethnographers, *ayni* and *minka* should be understood as institutions constructed historically under pressures from partial incorporation into the capitalist economy, which in turn demanded a new form of subsistence farming.

No one argues that *ayni* and *minka* are not old Andean terms and concepts. In his colonial Quechua dictionary Holguín ([1608] 1989:

40, 240) defines *ayni* more or less as equal repayment, whether referring to work, money, or revenge; and *minka* as renting or hiring help. Similarly, P. Ludovico Bertonio's seventeenth-century dictionary of Aymara ([1612] 1984, part 2: 28, 222) defines *ayni* as the obligation to return equal work and *minka* as hiring help, much as in the Quechua definition. But there is no proof that *ayni* and *minka* were the principal means of mobilizing labor in prehistoric *ayllu*s. Furthermore, there is no reason to assume that *ayni* and *minka* developed sequentially, in an egalitarian evolutionary stage followed by a chiefly evolutionary stage. This is really an example of constructing the past with "traditional" institutions assumed to be living fossils, ordered temporally to conform with the expectations of cultural evolutionism.

Contingent history assumes that the Andean *ayllu* cannot be an unchanged, primordial institution that has resisted external influences for centuries and perhaps millennia. Historical information supports this perspective. In Inca times it seems that heterogeneous *ayllu* groupings of diverse peoples were transformed into administrative units more standardized in size and function, in which land ownership and labor allocation were more emphasized by the state than the mythical histories of heroic ancestors that validated hierarchical rights, both within the *ayllu* and in relations among *ayllu*s. In colonial times *ayllu*s were reduced from corporate ethnic kingdoms consisting of hierarchically organized "kin" who shared the estate of a venerated ancestor founder to smaller landholding cooperatives with only modest internal differentiation. *Ayllu*s were localized into *reducción* community barrios, and mummy ancestors were abolished, to be replaced by Catholic saints. Under modern capitalistic economic pressures the *ayllu* has, in many cases, become little more than an association of households sharing a locational identity that facilitates community projects or subsistence agriculture through cooperative exchanges of labor.

Perhaps the strongest testimonies for contingent historical reconstruction of *ayllu* organization are the differences between modern Indian *ayllu*s in southern Peru and adjacent Bolivia, where adaptive pressures of environment can be considered more or less equivalent. In Peru, *ayllu*s exist as subdivisions of the village community. They include no more than a few hundred individuals. Pacariqtambo is a typical example, where Gary Urton (1992: 233) reports eleven *ayllu*s with fifteen to sixty families each. On the other hand, in Bolivia *ayllu*s integrate thousands of square kilometers, thousands of inhabitants, and many residential communities into a complex politico-religious hierarchy (Albó 1972; Harris 1978; Platt 1982a, 1982b; Rasnake 1988: 49–64). While these *ayllu*s shared the same organizational pressures of Inca and colonial administration, they differ in their experiences of the last 150 years in separate republican governments. Particularly, Peru's creation of local "indigenous communities" with political and juridical rights during the 1920s promoted village organization at the expense of the *ayllu*. In southern Peru the *ayllu* was transformed into an intervillage organization, terminating its broad regional functions. Across the international border, Bolivian *ayllu*s were affected by different laws and policies, so they, like Ecuadorian *ayllu*s, are strikingly different from their Peruvian counterparts, in spite of the shared indigenous name and Andean cultural origin.

It should be apparent that *ayllu*s of today do maintain an Andean cultural tradition, but many of their organizational features are responses to recent colonial and modern economic and political pressures, not adaptations to vertical Andean ecology by the first sedentary households more than ten thousand years ago. In fact, today's *ayllu*s may seem like archaic social units specifically because they have been simplified and homogenized by the administrative demands of Inca and colonial government and further deculturated by the incorporation of members into capitalistic wage labor in modern nation states.

## HYPOTHESES AND TESTS

Two competing approaches to knowing the past are responsible for two different visions of Andean prehistory. If the processual evolutionary perspective and scenario are reasonably accurate we should find evidence for *ayllu* organization long before the rise of the state—by 2000 B.C. or earlier. The *ayllu* should have originated among independent nuclear families in response to environmental challenges, particularly the need to exploit simultaneously the diversity of resources that characterizes the vertical Andean landscape. *Ayllu* organization should have employed *ayni* in its early stages, but later *minka* was developed and chiefly organization appeared. The state only made its appearance after the basics of corporately held land intended for periodic allocation to approved individuals, the fundamentals of labor tribute, and the nucleus of managerial administration by elites had been worked out within *ayllu* corporations.

A contingent history perspective refuses to construct scenarios of prehistoric change except for particular cases. It argues that prehistorians must seek specific information about each individual past, rather than employ general theory in conjunction with oppositional thinking about folk societies. These speculative prehistories tell us more about our categories and preconceptions than about the actual past. However, in its emphasis on continual reconstruction of institutions by knowledgeable actors, contingent history does suggest that we can anticipate that the *ayllu*, as it was described in early colonial times, must have had a fairly recent origin. The *ayllu* was a solution to communal control of labor and unequal access to resources, using the idiom of kinship rather than actual kinship or class as a basis for inequality. Its genesis was likely to have been in a politico-economic arena where definitions and distributions of unequal rights to resources were being contested. *Ayllu* origins could lie no earlier than rank society, but emphasis on unequal rights to resources suggests its origin in association with state-building processes. Rejection of class organization need not imply prestate origin but could signal that the *ayllu* had its beginnings in fairly recent times as a means for kin groups to resist state organization based on class and class prerogatives. Contingent history cannot propose a theory about the origin of *ayllu*, but it does suggest that archaeologists look in relatively recent times, and probably within the social turmoil that accompanied state-building processes in the central Andean past.

If the archaeological record for appropriate mortuary monuments reveals the early appearance of ancestor mummies and *ayllu* organization—a millennium or more before the beginning of our era—I would conclude that the data are consistent with a processual evolutionary construction of the *ayllu* in the Andean past. If, on the other hand, the archaeological record reveals a much later origin for the *ayllu*—significantly later than the emergence of agropastoral production representing successful adaptation to vertical zonation in the Andes, perhaps within our own era—then processual evolutionism could not be correct. A recent date for *ayllu* origins would support a contingent history approach and interpretation of the Andean past. If the appearance of the *ayllu* were as recent as the appearance of state administration, assumptions about agency and contingent history would be very strongly supported.

As a final note, remember that the *ayllu* I am discussing is the *ayllu* described in sixteenth- and early-seventeenth-century accounts from Cuzco and Huarochirí that I defined at the end of Chapter 3. This *ayllu* constitutes itself around its dead founder. It cannot exist without the focal ancestor, and it reconstructs itself in periodic rituals in the place where the ancestor mummy is housed. Mummy houses then provide the independent archaeological means for tracking the *ayllu* through prehistory. But mummy houses will not track *ayllu* organization if it is defined some other way. That is why Chapters 2 and 3 were devoted to determining the nature of the *ayllu* and our definition of it.

CHAPTER

V

The Open
Sepulcher

Andean prehistorians who employ the processual evolutionary approach, as discussed in Chapter 4, tend to view the *ayllu* as the primordial essence of Andean culture. Resisting change, it retained its basic form and function over millennia. Postprocessual contingent history postulates an *ayllu* that has been more dynamic and pliant, as a result of agents' construction and reconstruction of its organization under changing pressures from the political economy and other social powers. In accord with this view the *ayllu* could not have survived unchanged from the remote past. As described in the sixteenth century, it probably originated fairly late in Andean prehistory, perhaps in struggles over unequal access to resources associated with the origins of state government. We now turn our attention to identifying *ayllu* organization in prehistory. How can we trace the *ayllu* archaeologically? And does the archaeological record support one or the other origin scenario? In Chapters 2 and 3 we saw that the *ayllu* consisted of four components—a shared resource, a social group, organization based on the idiom of kinship, and a venerated ancestor mummy. Ideally archaeologists would like to identify all four features in the archaeological record before inferring the existence of *ayllu* organization for a particular prehistoric period, but such complete information is never available. Rather, prehistorians must argue on the basis of analogy—that the presence of one or more features of *ayllu* organization implies the existence of the others. Of course, this means that we must determine what features have the strongest connections with *ayllu* organization (Wylie 1985, 1988). Public works that reveal corporate labor by a social group are only weak indicators, for many groups that are not *ayllu* produce cooperative projects, from matrilineages to Boy Scout troops.

Consequently, Michael Moseley's (1992: 127) inference of *ayllu* organization in second millennium B.C. coastal communities—because of corporately constructed pyramids—is inadequate. Helaine Silverman (1993: 305–311) develops a similar argument for the temple compounds of Cahuachi constructed at the beginning of our era. She also discusses the association of small temple units with the large ceremonial complex as the spatial and architectural expression of a confederacy of kin groups, or *ayllu*s, into something that might be compared with the *llacta*, also discussed in Chapter 3. Using parallel lines of evidence like this creates a stronger analogy, but what I consider to be the most convincing material aspects of the *ayllu* are absent at Cahuachi.

Alan Kolata (1993: 61–63) attributes *ayllu* organization to first millennium B.C. Wankarani settlements because residences are spatially proximate. I feel that this demonstrates the existence of a residential community but not necessarily an *ayllu*. His inference that sculptures of llama heads represent *ayllu* tutelary deities for herd fertility is without ethnographic or historic analog. The religious object of the *ayllu* was its ancestor mummy, and it was the ancestor mummy that was beseeched for fertility and plenty, not llama images. Historically, idols were substituted for mummies if the ancestor's body was destroyed, or they served as secondary images that could travel about while the actual mummy remained carefully protected. But these idols seem to have incorporated some part of the deceased, even if only hair or fingernail trimmings. At a higher level, idols represented multi- or maximal *ayllu* polities, not local kin communities. But this discussion places us on the right track toward identifying convincing criteria for the *ayllu* in prehistory.

The *ayllu*, as it is described for Cuzco Incas (the *panaca*) in the early sixteenth century, and as it is described for Huarochirí in the early seventeenth century, used the idiom of kinship to determine the boundary of the group as well as its internal relations and resource allocations. The focal reference for real or fictional kinship was the ancestor founder. Behavior toward the founding mummy that was appropriate for a descendant, more than actual descent, determined *ayllu* membership (Salomon 1991, 1995). Furthermore, the ancestor mummy was the conceptual charter for *ayllu* wealth and its source of supernatural empowerment. The temple-tomb, where the mummy was carefully protected in an open sepulcher so that it was accessible to its descendant worshipers, was the place where *ayllu* members congregated for rituals as frequently as Christians attended church (Salomon 1987). The mummy and its temple-tomb placed the *ayllu* on the landscape, spatially structuring ritual, socializing time into calendrical rounds, and constructing power and social difference in competitive display of reverence and prestation. It was here that *ayllu* society and ideology were constructed and reconstructed in action that was both repetitive and innovative (cf. Agnew and Duncan 1989; Block 1989; King 1980, 1987; Markus 1993). I conclude that without the ancestor mummy in its open sepulcher there could be no *ayllu*.

The history of mummies is long in the Andes. At the beginning of sedentary life, perhaps as early as 5000 B.C., some bodies were receiving special treatment. At Paloma on the coast of Peru the dead were sometimes smoked, perhaps to better preserve the body, and then placed in graves under the floors of houses (Quilter 1989). Even more elaborate removal of organs and other mummification procedures were practiced by the preceramic Chinchorro peoples of coastal Chile, who buried their dead in sand dunes along the bays where they lived and fished (Rivera 1995). The attention lavished on some of these burials might imply that they were recognized as ancestors, functioning as focal founders for *ayllu*s similar to those of the sixteenth and seventeenth centuries.

I will return to this issue below, but I am not convinced that the mummies of Chinchorro or Paloma were objects of continuing cult, as required in *ayllu* organization. First, the human bodies were buried, even though efforts were made to promote their preservation. *Ayllu* organization constructed and reconstructed itself in ritual that required the body of the ancestor. I suspect that if *ayllu* organization had characterized these preceramic communities, Chinchorro and Paloma worshipers would have been digging up the bodies weekly, for offerings that promoted well-being and oracular prognostications seem to have involved direct address, and even physical embrace of the cadaver. Second, if *ayllu* ancestors had to be lavishly fed and dressed, how did Chinchorro and Paloma peoples deal with the foods and offerings if the body was reburied after each ceremony? Archaeologists should have found traces of many more gifts, renewed and renewed and renewed again. Finally, could rituals that brought together the members of the *ayllu* be conducted in Chinchorro or Paloma contexts? Cuzco was constructed around public plazas and household courts where mummy rituals were held, and even the modest open sepulchers of Huarochirí's peasants had their *cayan* courts. Such "places" are absent in the preceramic remains. Consequently, I consider Paloma and Chinchorro deserving of more study in regard to *ayllu* origins, but I cannot infer *ayllu* organization. I am convinced that the best way to track the *ayllu* in prehistory is the ancestor mummy and its open sepulcher.

The *ayllu* recreated itself around the ancestral founder, and nearly constant access to the mummy was required. Secure conservation of this body along with accessibility for veneration would require fairly significant facilities. The cadaver had to be available to groups that occasionally may have included most or all of the *ayllu* members. It had to be protected from decay and predation. And offerings and gifts to the mummy had to be stored somewhere, at least in the case of all but the poorest *ayllu*. For this reason I believe that the best tool for tracing the prehistory of the *ayllu* is the temple tomb or mortuary monument appropriate for preserving an ancestor mummy and its offerings. First we must define the phenomenon—what I call the "open sepulcher." In most cases, and particularly where natural conditions of preservation are poor, open sepulchers should leave recognizable material remains in the archaeological record. Since many were described by Peru's European invaders and colonial administrators, we can begin with their descriptions to help determine how to identify open sepulchers in the archaeological record.

## OPEN SEPULCHERS IN COLONIAL MORTUARY DESCRIPTIONS

In Chapter 2, I discussed Indian chronicler Guaman Poma de Ayala's ([1615] 1980) classification and description of Andean burial practices that he attributed to the time of the Inca Empire. From Poma's perspective all Andeans, except the natives of the eastern jungles, preserved the bodies of their dead in open sepulchers where periodic rituals were conducted that included the cadavers. Do other colonial descriptions support his claims?

Pedro Cieza de León's ([1553] 1959) marvelous descriptions were based on extended travels in Peru little more than a decade after the Spanish invasion. Much of what he described seems consistent with open sepulchers and ancestor veneration as chronicled by Guaman Poma:

[Speaking of the Colla area south of Cuzco] And it truly amazes me to think how little store the living set by having large, fine houses and the care with which they adorned the graves where they were to be buried, as though this constituted their entire happiness. Thus, all through the meadows and plains around the settlements were the tombs of these Indians, built like little four-sided towers, some of stone only, some of stone and earth, some wide, others narrow, according to the means or taste. Some of the roofs were covered with straw, others with large stone slabs, and it seems to me that the door of these tombs faced the rising sun. (Cieza de León [1553] 1959: 274)

... I have noted that Indians have different customs in this matter of graves, for in the province of the Colla they erect them in fields, in rows, as big as towers, some more, some less and some handsomely constructed, of matched stones with doors opening to the rising sun, and beside them (as I shall relate) they used to perform their sacrifices and burn certain things, and sprinkle the place with the blood of llamas and other animals. (Cieza de León [1553] 1959: 311*n*)

In the vicinity of Cuzco they bury their dead seated on magnificent stools, which they call *duhos*, dressed and adorned with their best finery.

In the province of Jauja, which is a very important place in these kingdoms of Peru, they put them in a fresh llama-hide, and sew them in it, shaping on the outside face, nose, mouth, and those who were chieftains and headmen are carried out at certain times of the year by their sons to their fields and villages in litters with great ceremonies, and sacrifices are made to them of llamas and even children and women.

In many valleys of the [coastal] plains, on emerging from the valley into the uplands of stones and sand, one finds great walls and divisions where each family has its allotted place to bury its dead, and for this purpose they have dug great hollows and cavities, each with its door, with all possible care. And it is a marvelous thing to behold the number of dead there are in those sand dunes and desert uplands; and separated one from the other, one sees a vast number of skeletons and their clothing, rotted and corroded by time. They call these places, which they hold sacred, *huacas*, which is a melancholy word, and many of them have been opened and, after the Spanish conquered this kingdom, despoiled of great sums of gold and silver. For in these valleys it was the custom to bury with the dead his wealth and the things he most prized, and many women and servants of those who were closest to the lord when he was alive. And it was the custom in olden times to open the tombs and renew the clothing and food that had been buried in them. (Cieza de León [1553] 1959: 311–312)

Cieza's reference to "burial" of bodies is problematic because it is explicitly nonburial that we are seeking. However, the English and Spanish languages make it virtually impossible to discuss treatment of the dead without using words like *entierro* and "burial." I have found it as difficult as Cieza apparently did, for in English even placement of a body in catacombs is referred to as "burial." Consequently, I conclude that Cieza de León's descriptions of Andean "burial" do tend to confirm Guaman Poma and provide us with additional information about open sepulchers. Furthermore, I too use the term "burial" here to describe placement of mummies in open sepulchers, for lack of an alternative word.

Writing three-quarters of a century later, Father Bernabé Cobo, our authority on Inca religion and shrines, furnishes us with what may be the most comprehensive analysis of Native American tombs:

A universal custom among all the Indian nations was to pay more attention to the dwellings that they were to have after death than to the one they had during their lifetime. . . . Though they made no effort to have big and attractive houses, they took great care in building and adorning the tombs where they were to be buried, as if all of their happiness resided there. These Peruvians observed the same custom, and with more care, style, and skill than any of the other peoples of the New World. Their pride and glory was to have the most lavish, impressive, and pompous burials and tombs possible, according to the importance of those to be buried. Most of the tombs were built in the countryside, some in the fields and others in the uninhabited pasturelands where livestock grazed, and in some provinces in their own houses. The form of the tombs was not the same throughout the whole kingdom. Since the provinces and nations were diverse, they also had different types of tombs. However, *we can assign them to two groups. The first, those that were dug out underground and the second, those that were built above ground.* Within the first group, some were very deep; many steps were provided for going down into them, and others were at ground level. The majority of these were square, and some were as large and deep as an ordinary room, with stone walls, and it was covered with a single stone slab, and some had a second slab under the first, and sometimes two more, very close together.

Tall tombs built above the ground were more common. But we also find a great variety of these because every Indian nation sought a new style of making them. . . . The tombs of the coastal Indians were unusually large; we see some of them that seem to be medium-sized hills. . . .

The Indians of the sierra do not make such big tombs as those of the coast. Nevertheless, the sierrans did not let the Indians of the coast outdo them in either the number of the tombs or the skill with which they made them. They made them in the pastures, grasslands, and uninhabited areas, some close to the towns, and others far from them. All the tombs were made in the form of small towers; the smallest ones were one estado [5½ feet] high, more or less, and the size of our fireplace chimneys, but a little larger, and the largest were four to six estados high. The doors on all of them face east, and these doors are as small and narrow as an oven door, for it is impossible to enter them without touching your chest to the ground. (Cobo [1653] 1990: 246–248, emphasis added)

Cobo's discussion is rich, and in most respects it supports the claims of both Guaman Poma and Cieza de León. Unfortunately, he seems to have based his classification of mortuary monuments on form rather than on the accessibility of bodies for rituals of veneration, but by the time of his observations ancestor mummies had become prohibited idols that were sought out and destroyed by Christian clerics. The tombs Cobo saw had probably ceased to function as open sepulchers, and any ceremonies still conducted there were probably kept secret by the Indian worshipers. Nonetheless, Father Cobo's division of tombs into those above ground and those excavated into the soil is a point of departure for differentiating open sepulchers from graves in which the dead are removed from the living. I suggest that above-ground tombs provide good preservation for cadavers and at least potentially leave them easily accessible. On the other hand, interment underground promotes deterioration of the flesh, and access is difficult if the body is covered by much dirt. This simple dichotomy may not work in all cases. Shaft tombs can provide excellent protection for a human mummy, especially in a dry climate or where the earth is well drained. The sand of the arid Andean coast preserves bodies very well without protective constructions at all. And, finally, underground tombs may be accessible if entered by tunnels that can be opened and closed quite easily. However, I believe that Cobo may have defined a general difference between easy-access sepulchers associated with *ayllu* organization and a different mortuary pattern or patterns.

As a caution, it is important to remember that *ayllu* organization hinged on the adoration of a founding ancestor mummy that was accessible in an open sepulcher, but that does not mean that everyone in the society had to be buried in open sepulcher conditions. Above-ground open sepulchers, and especially *machay* caves, seem to have been the favored burial sites for western Andean peoples around Huarochirí, whose testimonies were recorded in idolatries investigations. In fact, many of the trials revealed that kin who were buried in churchyard graves were secretly dug up and moved to the *ayllu machay*. However, Inca funerary practices certainly included burials in pit graves. Apparently those who were not venerated ancestors of the *ayllu* did not need to be preserved as mummies in open sepulchers. Consequently, we must be cautious not to conclude that the discovery of some burials in conditions inconsistent with the open sepulcher demonstrates the lack of *ayllu* organization. To imply that *ayllu* organization was absent we must seek to show that open sepulchers were not among the burial alternatives of a society or that important individuals who certainly would have founded *ayllu* descent groups, if *ayllu* organization existed, were not placed in open sepulchers.

The archaeological record reveals at least one popular Peruvian mortuary pattern that seems to have excluded burial in easy-access open sepulchers. In this pattern, that I at least provisionally call the "*huaca* cemetery," the body was sealed in an underground grave that was never intended to be opened. I conclude that *ayllu* organization, as described in the sixteenth and seventeenth centuries, did not exist among peoples who buried their principal members in a *huaca* cemetery.

## THE HUACA CEMETERY

Burial in underground tombs that were never intended to be reopened is best described for the Moche people by Christopher Donnan (Alva and Donnan 1993; Donnan 1976, 1995; Donnan and Castillo 1992; Donnan and Mackey 1978; Donnan and McClelland 1979). Burial was in a grave excavated into the ground, although the matrix might be the adobe of a mound or pyramid. Treatment of the body varied with rank. At the lowest level were individuals buried in extended positions wrapped in a simple mat. In fancier burials the mat might be rolled into a tube with a gourd plate at each end as a stopper. Sometimes a coffin was fashioned by wrapping a long cane mat around rectangular end pieces and carefully tying up the resulting box to give it rigidity. These coffin burials were accompanied by offerings that included clothing worn by the deceased as well as ceramic vessels and other objects, and it is clear that they were not intended to be reopened.

The most elaborate Moche burials were placed in wooden plank coffins fastened together with copper straps. Such coffins appear to have been decorated with symbols of the costumes worn by the deceased in life, and the body was dressed with fine cloth and marvelous jewelry, sometimes including many objects of gold. Archaeologists have excavated spectacular examples of such burials at Sipán, where a succession of male "warrior priests" was found, and at San José de Moro (Donnan and Castillo 1992) two graves of priestesses were unearthed (see Map 5.1). In life these individuals stood at the apex of their society and must have been the Moche equivalents of the Inca kings and queens. They were surely in the best position to conquer land, construct canals, and otherwise accrue estates they could pass to a corporate group of descendants. But their bodies were placed in remarkably deep graves and completely covered. At Sipán it is clear that "warrior priests" were placed in tombs excavated into the platforms of a temple. Not only were the graves refilled, but in subsequent architectural additions the entire platform might be covered (observe the location of graves in the illustration of Sipán's architectural sequence by Schuster 1992: 35). Consequently, these high-status bodies were never intended to be removed

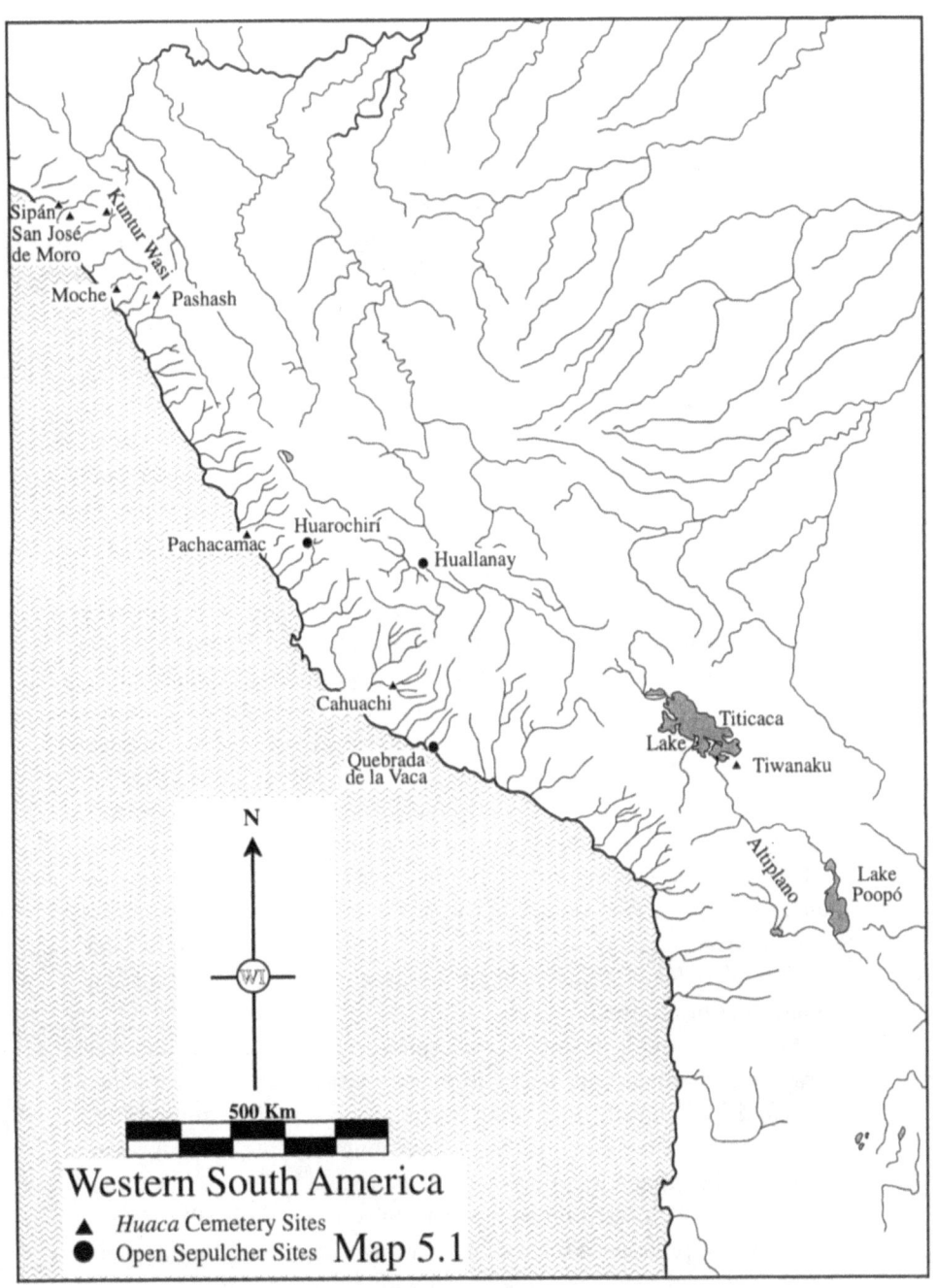

Map 5.1. Open Sepulchers and *Huaca* Cemeteries

from their tombs or to ever be viewed or touched again. According to my definitions, Moche's highest elite were not *ayllu* or *panaca* founders, and I conclude that *ayllu* (and *panaca*) organization could not have characterized Moche society.

The great temple and oracle of Pachacamac was a popular place for Andeans to be buried, for thousands of individual bodies were deposited within its precincts between the Middle Horizon and the Spanish Invasion (about A.D. 600 to 1535). Max Uhle ([1903] 1991: 18–21; Fleming 1986) excavated a large number of corpses, flexed and wrapped in many layers of cloth, that had been positioned around the base of this temple. Tom Patterson (1991: 33) interprets the discovery of a great many bodies in what appeared to be a single tomb on the side of another Pachacamac temple (Strong and Corbett 1943: 41) as retainers buried with a single elite. I cannot confirm this on the basis of the published data, so I must conclude that no burials from the Pachacamac region contain such elaborate offerings as those given Moche leaders at Sipán and San José de Moro. Nonetheless, the dead at Pachacamac were placed in cemeteries attached to great *huaca*s, and there are many reasons to think that these were the social elite who commanded the highest status. When Hernando Pizarro arrived to loot Pachacamac in January 1533, its pilgrims were required to fast twenty days in the outer precinct before entering the temple, and a special fast of a year was required before admission to the inner sanctuary. Cieza de León ([1553] n.d.: 372 [Ch. 72]) reported that around this temple only lords, priests, and pilgrims offering valuable gifts to the shrine could be buried. I conclude that the ideal burial for bodies of elites from the Pachacamac region was in a cemetery associated with the great *huaca*. There bodies were not preserved, and these lords could not have expected to become founders of *ayllu*s, with descendants curating their bodies and making regular offerings to them.

Another example of the *huaca* cemetery, although even less well known than Pachacamac, seems to be the Nasca culture (Carmichael 1995) and its Cahuachi site. Many burials, and especially those in the flatlands between the mounds, were made long after the site was abandoned. On the other hand, burials from the period of Cahuachi's ascendancy seem to be located on its mounds (Silverman 1993: 108). Again, I infer an elite preference for burial in graves excavated into important *huaca*s, not open sepulchers associated with *ayllu* organization.

All of these sites are on the coast. The Moche cemeteries belong to the Early Intermediate Period. Pachacamac and Cahuachi were founded during the Early Intermediate Period, but worship continued at Pachacamac until the arrival of the Europeans, and at Cahuachi, at least, burial continued long after the ceremonial center was abandoned.

Human burials are not as well preserved in the Andean highlands as on the coast, and far fewer are known. Nonetheless, the *huaca* cemetery may have been the preferred form of interment for elites, at least in early times. In the highlands adjacent to the Moche cultural region, recent excavations at the Early Horizon site of Kuntur Wasi (see Map 5.1) reveal a *huaca* cemetery (Kato 1993). One of the building complexes on the top of the Kuntur Wasi temple mound contains the remains of three elite males, an elite female, and a fourth male who may represent an individual of secondary status, perhaps a sacrificial victim. All were buried in underground tombs excavated into the platform fill. Two males have gold crowns, and the third has large gold ear plugs. The elite female has lesser gold ornaments. This material is discussed in more detail below, but it seems to follow a pattern similar to Moche burial preferences.

A variation on *huaca* cemetery interment of elites in religious monuments may have characterized highland valleys south of Kuntur Wasi, about A.D. 200. In a larger ceremonial precinct at the site of Pashash (see Map 5.1) a little temple seems to have been constructed over the body of an important person (Grieder 1978: 45–58). Perhaps a sacrificial body was included, as were rich offerings that were added at several points as the cloth-wrapped body was covered, and the walls, doors, and floor of the small ceremonial buildings were constructed above it. I wonder if this may actually represent some sort of transitional step in ancestor worship and origin of *ayllu* organization, for at more or less the same time—as we will see in Chapters 6 and 7—open sepulchers were first appearing in this region.

Tiwanaku is another highland ceremonial center with numerous burials in the ground (see Map 5.1). Unfortunately, archaeologists have not documented the kind of spectacular burials that would confirm in-ground interment of the elite, who should have been *ayllu* founders had that form of social organization existed. But the wealth of impressive Tiwanaku-style objects collected over the last century implies the discovery of high-status tombs by looters. While the case of Tiwanaku remains unclear, I suspect that below-ground burial was concentrated in the temple mounds and courts of Tiwanaku. Open sepulchers have not been documented for the site or its cultural sphere.

## THE OPEN SEPULCHER

For the central Andes, we have encountered a host of open sepulchers in the invaders' descriptions of Cuzco's royal mummies, in the testimonies of western Andean idolaters, and in the descriptions of chroniclers. The question is what were they like, and can we recognize open sepulchers in the archaeological record? Can they be identified with reasonable security, and can their absence be determined?

Evidence suggestive of the open sepulcher would be a well-made, above-ground building or cave that could be entered easily, with a flat *cayan*-like meeting space before it. The mortuary function would be proved if the building or cave contained mummies or human bones, like the *pucullo* illustrated by Felipe Guaman Poma de Ayala ([1615] 1980: 264–270; see Chapter 1). Many of the open sepulchers described below meet these formal criteria and also contain human remains, so they may be securely identified as open sepulchers. However, there are prehistoric buildings that do not have human remains, but whose forms imply open sepulchers. Should they be dismissed as something other than an open sepulcher, or can we identify open sepulchers on the basis of formal features alone, even when they have no human remains? My answer is that formal features alone must be sufficient. There are many reasons why human remains may have disappeared, and if we cannot identify open sepulchers on the basis of formal criteria, our record of this diagnostic kind of mortuary monument is bound to be inadequate for exploring *ayllu* origins.

Human remains have been systematically removed from open sepulchers for centuries. John Rowe (1995: 35) reports that on May 30, 1580, Viceroy Francisco Toledo ordered that the tombs of venerated ancestors should be demolished. Great pits should be excavated into which the bones of the mummies would be cast. Ossuaries from the campaign have been found by archaeologists. Fortunately some open sepulchers survived, for many descriptions were made by extirpators of idolatries in the seventeenth century. But their mission was also to destroy the ancestor mummies. The seventeenth-century transcriptions make it abundantly clear that priests burned vast numbers of cadavers. Father Arriaga's ([1621] 1968) instructions to the extirpators specified that they were to destroy every trace of the idols and *malqui*s to ensure that worshipers could not recover even tiny pieces or ashes that might continue to serve as cult objects.

I doubt that the removal of human remains from open sepulchers began in colonial times. It is clear that one's ancestor mummy was very valuable. The mummies were portable, especially among the Incas and in the Chinchaysuyu portion of the empire, where they were seated on litters and paraded about the country. Consequently, there is reason to doubt that if a defeated group were driven from its land, or a victorious group moved its capital to a more central location, the ancestor mummies would remain behind in the ruins of old monuments. Furthermore, we know that *huaca*s were objects of capture or destruction in warfare—idols and *malqui* mummies were included in the general class. For example, Atahualpa's soldiers are believed to have burned the mummy of Topa Inca because his descendants supported Huascar's claim to the throne. Western Andean idolatries testimonies are full of information about relations between conquerors and conquered, and it appears that peaceful relations included accommodation to one another's religious ideologies and shrines, including mummies. But had mummies been destroyed in earlier conflicts? Did new people replacing older occupants allow their shrines, and especially their ancestor mummies, to survive? We do not know with certainty the answer to this question, but it seems likely that in precolumbian conflicts many mummies and human remains were deliberately moved or destroyed.

Human remains are fragile. Unless they are cared for or are in environments favorable to preservation, the natural end is to deteriorate and disappear quite quickly.

Looters have contributed to the destruction of mummified human remains. *Malqui*s were dressed in fine clothing that included headbands, sometimes of gold. They were the recipients of rich offerings, and their veneration involved ritual paraphernalia from large offering vessels and drinking cups to horns and drums that may have been stored in the ceremonial centers with the bodies. Looters searching for wealth have been entering burial structures for centuries, scattering and damaging the human remains and often throwing the bones out where they are subject to rapid destruction.

In the late nineteenth and early twentieth centuries Andean mummies and human bones were collected for museums. During one of several trips to Peru to collect human skeletal remains for the Smithsonian

Institution, Ales Hrdlička visited the Huarochirí area (see Map 5.1). Describing mortuary monuments that probably belonged to Yauyos idolaters whose testimonies we have read, Hrdlička observed:

> And the explorations would have been prolonged had it not been found that the majority of the more approachable ruins had been visited by Tello and his native friends, who secured whatever seemed more valuable of the skeletal remains for the collection that was later sold to Harvard. The "Cinco Cerros" have fortunately escaped, though, like nearly all such locations in Peru the remains were despoiled by treasure hunters; and the writer found here some precious cases of trepanning as well as some interesting anthropological material. (Hrdlička 1914: 8)

Of course, Hrdlička removed the bones from "Cinco Cerros" as well, leaving little or nothing to reveal the function of the mortuary buildings of that site.

I believe that in the decades following these scientific collecting expeditions, when rural schools were first constructed by Peru's indigenous communities and government teachers assigned to them from more urban areas, looting of burial sites greatly increased. Schoolteachers traditionally make a yearly excursion with their students to an "old town" or other archaeological ruin within walking distance of the schoolhouse. Following a lecture about the children's Indian past, they spend the rest of the day digging among the buildings and tearing down walls in hopes of finding objects of value. Few rural schools are without a mummy or two, some textile fragments, and a few pots collected on these excursions. Over the years many of the objects have disappeared. Sometimes the mummies deteriorate in the dampness of the schoolhouses, so they must be discarded and replaced with others. I can document an example of this sort of destruction. In 1970 I surveyed the area around San Miguel in the Department of Ayacucho (W. H. Isbell 1977: Fig. 2). At Huallanay (see Map 5.1, Fig. 5.1) I observed foundations of small stone buildings, but neither standing walls nor human bones. Only thirty years earlier Victor Navarro del Aguila (1943) reported these same buildings, but they contained many human skeletons. He was provoked to write about them because looters had damaged the little buildings in their searches for valuables, and the bones they had protected for centuries had been scattered onto the surrounding ground. He was anxious to

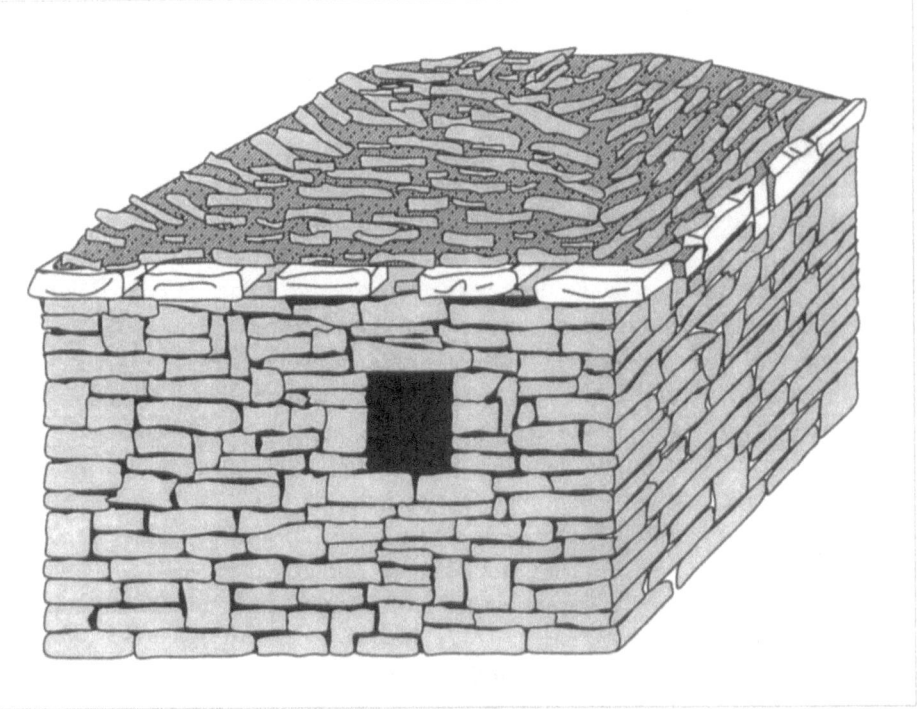

Figure 5.1. Huallanay Open Sepulcher (redrawn from Navarro del Aguila 1943: Plate I and Lumbreras 1974a: Figs. 37, 38)

praise a scientifically inclined individual who had collected the bones, including many skulls, protecting them from destruction. Of course, by 1970 these bones were no longer even remembered, and I had no idea that the Huallanay site had so recently included indisputable evidence for open sepulchers.

For these many reasons I conclude that we cannot depend on the presence of human remains to identify open sepulchers in the archaeological record. We must be able to identify a constellation of formal attributes if our sample is to reveal the history of ancestor mummies and *ayllu* organization.

Father Cobo's description of the open sepulcher is a good point of departure for abstracting formal attributes diagnostic of this kind of building.

All the tombs were made in the form of small towers; the smallest ones were one *estado* [5½ feet] high, more or less, and the size of our fireplace chimneys, but a little larger, and the largest were four to six *estados* high. The doors on all of them face east, and these doors are as small and narrow as an oven door, for it is impossible to enter them without touching your chest to the ground. (Cobo [1653] 1990: 248)

Are small east-facing doorways necessary and sufficient criteria for open sepulchers? It should be realized that this description of Cobo's refers to Colla sepulchers, south of Cuzco. John Hyslop (1976, 1977) surveyed Lupaca grave towers, and he does not confirm strict eastward orientation for all entrances. Eastern orientation is common, but not universal. I agree that the numerous stone and adobe towers in the *altiplano* were mortuary buildings, but their functional identification has not been systematically investigated. To avoid falling into a circular argument I prefer to test the generalizations about eastern orientation of entrances and small door size at a well-documented site known to have been occupied at the moment of the invasion. I also prefer a site with excellent preservation and abundant human remains, so that the mortuary function of open-sepulcher buildings cannot be doubted. An ideal site for which data are abundant is Quebrada de la Vaca, on Peru's south coast.

Quebrada de la Vaca (see Map 5.1) is a superbly preserved Inca period settlement (Howell n.d.; Riddell and Menzel 1954; Trimborn 1988). Glass beads in one of its mummy bundles show that it continued in use for at least several years after the Spanish invasion, confirming its contemporaneity with early written descriptions of ancestor mummies and open sepulchers. The settlement is a bay-side community on Peru's far south coast. It includes complex and well-preserved stone architecture distributed in several loci. On top of a high rocky point that projects into the sea is a shrine. From there a trail winds down between two enclosures and then north along the east side of the bay and ravine to an agglutinated community that covers slightly more than a hectare. There walls enclose courtyards and rooms on a terraced slope, suggesting residential and possibly also administrative or ceremonial functions. Small storage structures, both circular silos and subterranean cists, abound through the ruins, and the lower western edge of the community is defined by a massive wall, also full of subterranean bottle-shaped chambers. Continuing about 60 m north is a walled rectangular courtyard with a row of rooms across one side. It is flanked by another row of conjoined rooms, encouraging the inference that the entire complex functioned within the context of Inca state storage activities. There are additional supports for this thinking. Somewhat farther north and up the ravine is an area of irregular enclosures interpreted as corrals. Beyond this is a well-preserved section of the Inca highway. In the hills west of the main occupation area are a smaller number of ruins, including a rather ill-defined concentration of enclosures.

Associated with the various nuclei of ruins are three groups of mortuary buildings. The largest and most impressive group is located along terraced hillsides of the lower, west side of the canyon and bay, opposite the shrine, the residential community, and the rectangular courtyard. Highest on this western slope are the largest and most impressive tombs, at least three rectangular mortuary houses of stone, set on low platforms (Howell n.d., vol. 2: 1–12; Riddell and Menzel 1954: 15–32). The two best-preserved examples were 5 to 6 m long, about 3 m wide and some 2 m high (see Fig. 5.2). They have stone roofs, niches in the interior walls, and slightly projecting stone-slab eaves around the exteriors just below the roofs. Their platforms, about 8 to 10 m long by 6 to 8 m wide, are less than a meter high and ascended by steps. The long axis of both of the well-preserved mortuary houses is northeast-southwest, and a single small door in one long side faces southeast. Although all the mortuary buildings were looted many years ago, excavations of about two-thirds of burial house 2 by Riddell and Menzel (1954: 15–32) recovered remains of approximately 120 human bodies, including 56 adult skulls and the remains of some 50 infants. It was one of these infant bundles that contained a few glass beads. Santos's (Trimborn 1988: 145–152) excavations in burial house 1 revealed at least 30 individuals.

Somewhat lower on the west slope is a group of three smaller mortuary houses, also rectangular but only about half the size of those just described (Riddell and Menzel 1954: 14). While they also contained human remains, they lack the interior niches and the roof eaves of the larger buildings. Also, the doorway of one faces east, but the other two entrances face north. These buildings are on leveled ground, and one has a stone paved apron or small entrance platform before its doorway. Retaining walls and stone alignments across most of this slope form terraces and plazas among the mortuary buildings that are likely to have been the locations of rituals for the dead. Still lower on the slope are

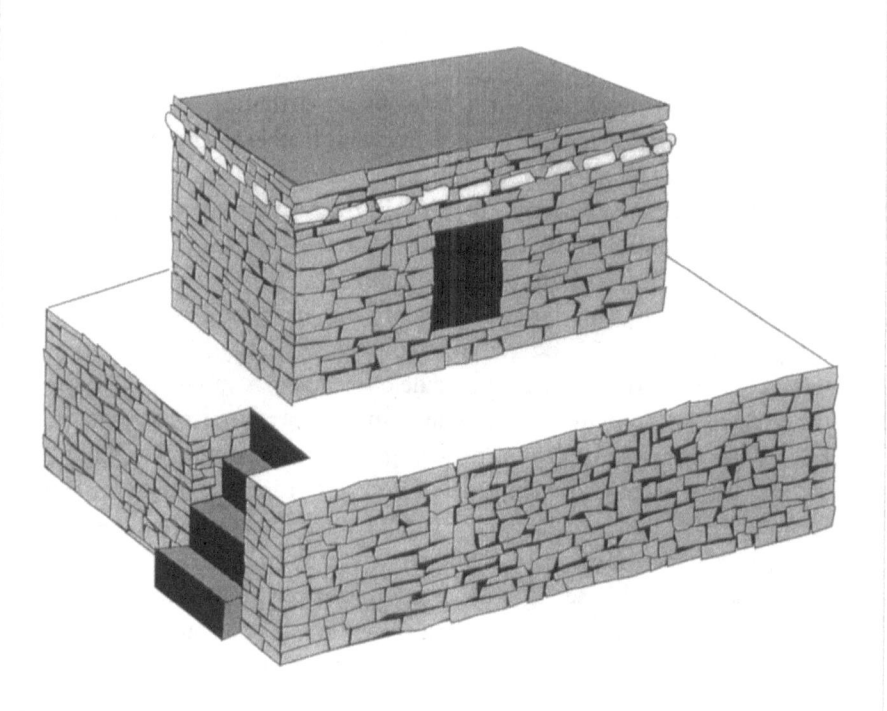

Figure 5.2. Quebrada de la Vaca Open Sepulcher Mortuary Monument (based on descriptions by Riddell and Menzel 1954)

many smaller buildings with diverse shapes and entrance orientations (Howell n.d., vol. 2: 1–12), but they lack human remains; Riddell and Menzel (1954: 36) suggest that they were used as storage units. Perhaps they served for storing ritual paraphernalia, offerings, and feast foods for the participants attending celebrations for *ayllu* ancestors.

Two smaller sets of mortuary buildings, with human bones scattered in and about them, are located between the agglutinated community and the rectangular courtyard complex and below the massive wall and across the bottom of the ravine from the agglutinated community. The first group consists of three beehive-shaped buildings now poorly preserved, but perhaps in the past opening to the northwest (Howell n.d., vol. 1: 36). The larger group across the ravine consists of at least six buildings, one rectangular, but most are beehive shaped. The largest and best preserved has its opening to the southwest.

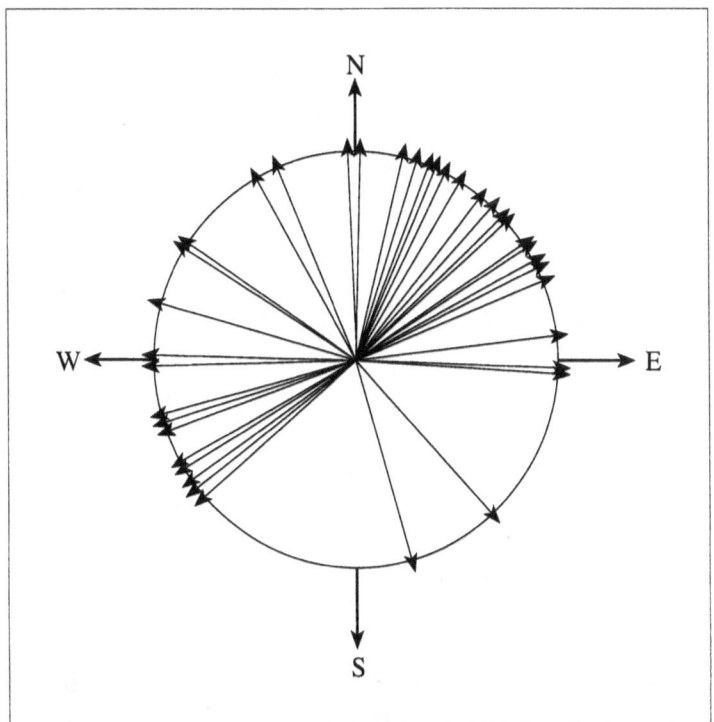

Figure 5.3. Orientations of Open Sepulcher Entrances, Toconce Site, Upper Río Loa, Chile (adapted from Aldunate and Castro 1981; orientation according to magnetic north)

This review of demonstrable mortuary buildings at Quebrada de la Vaca shows that the open sepulcher need not have an east-facing entrance. East was the most popular and, consequently, perhaps the ideal direction of orientation, but other directions occur quite frequently. A study of mortuary houses at Toconce in northern Chile suggests a preference for northerly orientation. Compass orientations were recorded for thirty-seven doorways (see Fig. 5.3), revealing that only 57 percent are oriented to the eastern half of the sky, while the northern half of the compass accounts for 65 percent.

Doorway size is not well preserved at Quebrada de la Vaca, for looting has caused damage to lintels and jambs. Still it appears that some of the buildings could have been entered without "touching your chest to the ground," as Cobo ([1653] 1990: 248) stated. What is perhaps most salient at Quebrada de la Vaca is the range of variation among the burial monuments. The finest examples were well built, close together, east facing, and surrounded by level terraces and plazas that probably constituted *cayan*s where *ayllu* members assembled. These buildings would have been recognized as open sepulchers even if they had not contained human remains. But the modest burial structures are less diagnostically located or shaped and resemble little more than beehive-shaped piles of stone accommodated in unoccupied space next to residential zones. Such simple and perhaps low-status sepulchers may be impossible to recognize unless actual human remains are preserved.

## CRITERIA FOR IDENTIFYING THE OPEN SEPULCHER

There can be little doubt that the most convincing evidence that a building was intended for mortuary purposes is the discovery of human remains within it. But human remains cannot be demanded as necessary before a building is classified as an open sepulcher burial house. We have seen that many events, none of them unlikely, might have removed or destroyed the human remains.

Some formal attributes of architecture help identify open sepulchers, but I do not believe that any one is definitive. Even a combination of several may be less than convincing. Among the affirmative features are an east-facing doorway, a small doorway, association of the building(s) with plazas or *cayan*s, and grouping of several similar buildings into a ceremonial complex. An ideal location is isolated from the community, but open sepulchers occur adjacent to, within, and overlooking residential areas. The buildings may be quite small, and ceilings are frequently low. Mortuary architecture is likely to be of considerably higher quality than domestic construction, and it is constructed with an eye for permanence and massiveness, both conceptual and real. It also seems that sepulchers often have niches and similar appointments where offerings and ritual paraphernalia were placed. The buildings might be constructed on platforms.

We can identify a number of criteria for the open sepulcher, but all these formal features seem a bit vague. I feel that in the long run convincing identification of open sepulchers will have to place them in stylistically defined regional and chronological traditions of mortuary architecture. Only by appreciating buildings in their fuller cultural contexts can we securely differentiate residential, storage, or administrative constructions from open sepulchers. Then, too, we can begin to appreciate the history of open sepulchers in fuller detail. What follows is a preliminary approximation of their history. It relies on human remains, formal architectural criteria, and local as well as regional traditions of mortuary monuments to the degree that these can be identified today. Rarely is it possible to show conclusively that a particular building was intended for mortuary purposes, but it should be clear that there is a general class of buildings with consistent distribution in space and time, in many cases already believed to have had mortuary functions, that are best understood as open sepulchers.

CHAPTER

# VI

# Distribution of Open Sepulcher Monuments

Does the distribution of open sepulchers support the processual evolutionary "ancient *ayllu* hypothesis" or the "recent *ayllu* argument" of contingent history? In this chapter we trace open sepulchers through the central Andean archaeological record, defining their spatial and temporal patterns. To the degree that data are adequate, this outlines the history of ancestor mummies and *ayllu* organization in the Andean past.

Since my goal is a global survey, it is impossible to examine every possible case of open sepulchers in depth, to evaluate each set of information, or to identify all types of mortuary behavior that may have been associated with *ayllu* mummies and their veneration. The result should be a meaningful, but admittedly preliminary, determination of the forms and distributions of open sepulcher monuments. Important objectives remain for the future, including more detailed studies and evaluations of poorly known cases, as well as the identification of other material cultural remains possibly associated with ancestor cults—for example, human sculptures such as those found in the Callejón de Huaylas (Schaedel 1948, 1952). We will also have to wait to adequately explore such important topics as why some open sepulchers seem to have contained a single body, while others contain several, and still others are "crammed full" of dozens or even hundreds of individuals. Closely related is the question why some *ayllu*s felt compelled to place all their dead in open sepulcher monuments while others seem to have been satisfied to curate only elite founders in special contexts. Before investigating these important issues we must make a general inventory of open sepulchers, establish the methodology, and confirm its usefulness by considering whether the spatial and temporal patterns revealed seem to make sense. Do patterns revealed for open sepulchers imply a more or less unified existence in space and time and consequently suggest a single meaning such as *ayllu* organization? Or does the distribution appear so random that a unified meaning seems impossible? Do the patterns suggest a broad distribution for *ayllu* organization or individual, localized traditions?

I intend to limit my discussion of open sepulchers to the Andean highlands, and I hope that this will not seriously affect the outcome. I have decided to do this because I believe that the architectural criteria in terms of which the open sepulcher is being identified may not be as meaningful for the coast because of the exceptional preservation provided by the dry coastal environment. Such excellent preservation encouraged me to select coastal Quebrada de la Vaca as my test for identifying formal features associated with mortuary architecture—high-quality construction, east-facing entrances, and the like—because the functions of these buildings were convincingly revealed by the human remains they contained. Even though all the sepulchers had been looted, skeletal remains, including still identifiable mummy bundles, were preserved. If Quebrada de la Vaca had been located in the highlands I believe that we would have had to infer the existence of human remains on the basis of architectural form and building location alone, especially for the more modest sepulchers. This, of course, would have contributed vicious circularity to the argument—identifying mortuary monuments by formal and locational attributes and then determining the formal and locational features of mortuary monuments based on the same buildings.

But the superb preservation of human remains on the coast means that venerated ancestors might be safely kept without constructing special sepulchers at all. At Quebrada de la Vaca it is pretty clear that the open sepulchers of masonry participated in a cultural tradition that included the highland Inca state. But it may be possible to preserve ancestor mummies in less formal contexts—perhaps nothing more than being wrapped in fabric and placed in a shallow pit in the dry sand. I think it unlikely that devout descendants would want to exhume their sacred founder from a hole in the ground each time they meant to honor him and then return his body to the pit, but there is evidence that coastal pit graves were carefully marked, and it is increasingly clear that some of the mummies were reburied.

I conclude that a careful study of coastal dead, evaluating the possibility that human bodies were treated in a manner consistent with *ayllu* ritual, requires thorough and lengthy treatment. Such a study should not focus so intensively on architectural monuments, as in the highlands, but look at graves and grave markers, the attachment of mummies to markers, depth of interments, the composition of mummy bundles, and the stratigraphy of cemetery sites that may reveal repeated access to the burials. I fear that the intensive looting of coastal cemeteries years ago may mean that much of this information is no longer available, but I hope that my highland study will encourage specialists experienced with coastal burials to conduct such studies. John Rowe (1995) has recently reviewed some of the data, especially those relevant to the important Paracas Necropolis mummies.

## CHULLPA: *A PRECOLUMBIAN TERM FOR THE OPEN SEPULCHER?*

Before beginning my review of open sepulchers in the highlands, area by area, it is important to discuss the term *chullpa*, with its meaning and history. Today throughout the central Andes the word *chullpa* refers to ruins, usually prehistoric, of above-ground tombs and burial houses. Here I use the term interchangeably with "open sepulcher." It seems only logical to ask whether this is a native term for the phenomenon I want to study, the open mortuary monument where venerated ancestor mummies were stored and revered.

In my experience the term *chullpa* is used in the central and north highlands to refer to the ruins of buildings, including multichambered buildings, believed to have served mortuary purposes. I am not familiar with its use for ruins assumed to have served other purposes, such as temples, forts, storage buildings, or houses. Stig Rydén (1947: 339–342), however, points out that at least in Aymara-speaking Bolivia the term may also be applied to grave chambers in the ground, and around Jesús de Machaca he found the term used for prehistoric graves as well as ruins and monuments of all sorts, including rustic structures erected today at traditional places of sacrifice. On the border with Argentina *chullpa* may refer to a walled-up cave with a small entrance doorway. Rydén believes that these caves were originally intended for the storage of products, but were sometimes reutilized for human remains.

There is no mention of the word *chullpa* in sixteenth-century chronicles and discussions of the Inca Empire, and Father Cobo's detailed seventeenth-century descriptions of the burial monuments around Lake Titicaca never employed the word. I believe that it came into popular use in southern Peru and the *altiplano* during the nineteenth century. According to Oscar Ayca (1995: 23), the French traveler Eugène de Sartiges identified the monuments of Sillustani as *chullpa*s following his visit on February 8, 1834. On the other hand, I did not find that Johann Jakob von Tschudi (1847) used the term in his accounts of grave monuments based on his Peru travels during the same decade. This is relevant, for Tschudi was very interested in open sepulchers and seems to have popularized a confusing functional controversy—whether burial houses served as domestic residences as well as mortuary monuments. He argued in the affirmative, referring to such buildings as house-grave or *casa-tumba*.

E. George Squier (1877) took the opposite position, asserting that burial houses were graves, but that they had been used as shelters by later travelers, accounting for the remains of hearths and other residential trash. I suspect that each was right, but for different areas. Tschudi's travels focused in northern and central Peru, and he was uninformed about *altiplano* sites. Indeed, in the central highlands there is much more evidence for the prehistoric storage of ancestor bodies in the houses of the living. On the other hand, Squier traveled extensively in the *altiplano*. In the account of his 1863–1864 trip through southern Peru and Bolivia Squier (1877) first encountered burial houses—little buildings of rough stone painted red, yellow, and white in coastal mountains above Tacna, east of the *altiplano*—and called them *chullpa*s. He subsequently traveled through the Lake Titicaca *altiplano* describing spectacular as well as modest *chullpa*s, including those at Sillustani (Squier 1877: 376–384). He is probably correct that these southern tower tombs were separated from the villages of the living; he observed that upon opening a *chullpa* that had no entrance he always found a single human skeleton, but those that had an entrance must have been family tombs, for they contained two to twelve individuals (Squier 1877: 386–389). Entrances tended to face east, but this was not universal—as I have proved at Quebrada de la Vaca.

Squier never entertained the possibility that there were significant differences between the *altiplano* burial houses and those of the central highlands. Had he read Guaman Poma's chronicle he would have seen that Poma recognized significant differences in the form and function of burial houses from one quarter of the Inca Empire to another. But this chronicle was not discovered for another seventy-five years. Rather, Squier (1877: 389) observed that north of the pass between the Titicaca Basin and the Vilcanota-Cuzco drainage, which he associated with the boundary between Aymara and Quechua speakers, he encountered only one group of *chullpa*s. He argued that the burial house was a building characteristic only of the Aymara peoples of Collasuyu and its presence elsewhere identified relocated Aymaras. We may speculate that, while burial houses were in fact more widely distributed, referring to them as *chullpa*s is a characteristic of the southern Aymara region, which originated in the nineteenth century.

In a footnote to Father Bernabé Cobo's seventeenth-century description of the burial towers of the *altiplano*, the famous editor D. Marcos Jiménez de la Espada (Cobo [1653] 1893: 236n1) stated that these buildings were now called *chullpa*s, but that this was improper usage, for they should be *amaya-uta*, meaning house (*uta*) of the dead (*amaya*). Unfortunately he does not discuss the source of the name *chullpa*, except that it originally referred to matting or basketry made of *ichu* grass or totora reeds that was used to bind human cadavers into tightly flexed mummies, as shown by Bertonio's ([1612] 1984) Aymara dictionary. Subsequently, Adolph Bandelier (1905: 51) cited Jiménez de la Espada's note in his discussion of *chullpa*s, as did Marion Tschopik (1946: 10) and Rydén (1947: 339–340). They all accepted the idea that the Aymara word *chullpa* for the binding of the mummy became generalized to the place where mummies were kept—above-ground mortuary houses.

I suspect that it was from Squier's book of 1877, or one of the other *altiplano* travel accounts, that Jiménez de la Espada learned that *chullpa* was the popular name for tower graves. By this time the name may already have been being disseminated beyond southern Peru by archaeological enthusiasts. For example, Antonio Raimondi (1874: 173–178), who described many ruins in northern Peru, employed the name *chullpa* during his visits to *altiplano* sites. He also met and discussed archaeology with Squier. At any rate, forty years later Pedro Villar Córdova ([1935] 1982: 300) described what he called house-grave or *kullpi* from the western Andes above Lima. He argued that *kullpi* must be a local variant of the word *chullpa* and that it was an inappropriate name, for it referred to mesh of agave fiber used to bind a mummy bundle. Does this name belong to an old linguistic substrate, or was it disseminated by reading Cobo and nineteenth-century archaeologists? If *chullpa* was a proto-Aymara term with variants in Lima (*kullpi*) and Tacna/Lake Titicaca (*chullpa*), how did a term for mummy wrappings become generalized to burial buildings in both areas? Rather, I believe that *chullpa* began to be used for the ruins of grave buildings in the far south around 1800. Because of spectacular grave buildings like those at Sillustani, travelers and archaeologists learned and popularized the name *chullpa* far beyond its region of origin. The history of the term *chullpa* needs more study, but I conclude that it was not the precolumbian Andean name for open sepulchers where *ayllu* ancestors were kept. In fact, its use in reference to above-ground tombs seems not to have been precolumbian at all.

## LAKE TITICACA, THE ALTIPLANO, AND THE SOUTHERN HIGHLANDS

Discussion of the term *chullpa* has taken us to the *altiplano* and southern Andes, as well as to Cobo, Squier, and other authors who emphasize the importance of mortuary monuments in the prehispanic architecture of that region. Consequently I begin our discussion of the distribution of open sepulchers with this southern area that centers on Lake Titicaca (see Map 6.1). From descriptions by Cieza de León ([1553] 1959), Guaman Poma ([1615] 1980), and Cobo ([1653] 1979) we know that accessible above-ground tombs were preferred by *altiplano* peoples during Inca and early colonial times. We also have Squier's (1877: 389) hypothesis that the *chullpa* belonged exclusively to Aymara culture of the *altiplano* and was never really a part of Quechua-speaking or Inca culture to the north. In recognition of this hypothesis Wendell Bennett (1949: 50) pointed out that many Andean prehistorians believed that the *chullpa* grave was an *altiplano* cultural trait. If the open sepulchers were limited to the Aymara and the *altiplano*, my survey would be very brief. However, if this were the case, the archaeological data would contradict Guaman Poma's ([1615] 1980) attribution of above-ground tombs to all the quarters of Tawantinsuyu except the residents of the eastern forests.

*Chullpa* burial houses of the *altiplano* region are described as circular, square, or rectangular buildings of stone or adobe with corbeled vault or slab roofs (see Fig. 6.1, Photos 6.1–6.7). Stone examples range

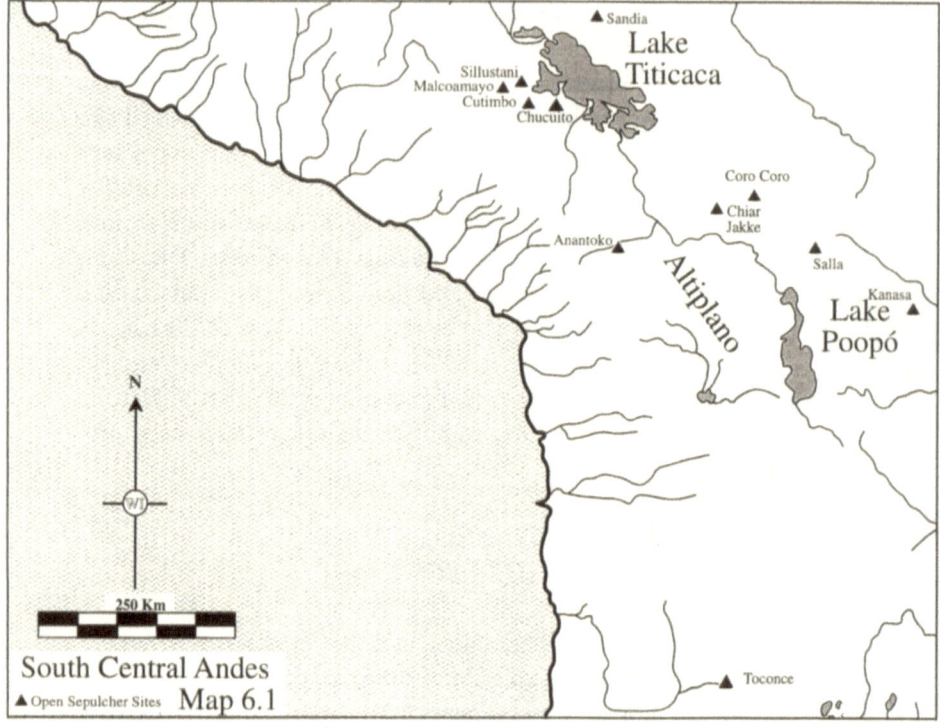

Map 6.1. Open Sepulcher Sites in the South-Central Andes

from very coarse construction in field stone to extremely fine ashlar masonry. Sometimes they are situated on a low rectangular platform. A small doorway, generally but not always facing east, is located close to the bottom of the building. Most common is a single door, but some *chullpa*s have a second doorway below ground that leads to a subterranean chamber. John Hyslop (1976, 1977) made an inventory of *chullpa*s in the northern *altiplano*, along the west side of Lake Titicaca. He found human skeletal remains in many that imply both single and multiple burials. Apparently there were no cases in which *chullpa*s contained dozens or hundreds of bodies, as described by idolatries judges for Huarochirí and observed at Quebrada de la Vaca. On the other hand, some *chullpa*s from Sandia (Photos 6.8–6.11), in the valleys east of the *altiplano*, were packed with skeletons (W. H. Isbell 1968). Many of these *chullpa*s also reveal traces of a mud plaster on the exterior walls that had been painted red.

Sometimes burials are found beneath the floors of *altiplano chullpa*s, or in stone-lidded chambers under the floor, similar to the *kullpi* to be described for the western Andes above Lima. Also, many *chullpa*s have sizable niches in the inner walls where mummies may have been seated. In fact, Hyslop (1977: 167) speculates that a mummy might have been placed under the floor after some time in one of these niches. These practices need more study. Perhaps *altiplano* mortuary ritual involved not only the curation of cadavers but their progression from one location to another within the tomb. Two features of *altiplano chullpa*s that occur only occasionally are a large stone protruding from the interior wall of the *chullpa* and relief carvings of animals on the exterior walls of the building.

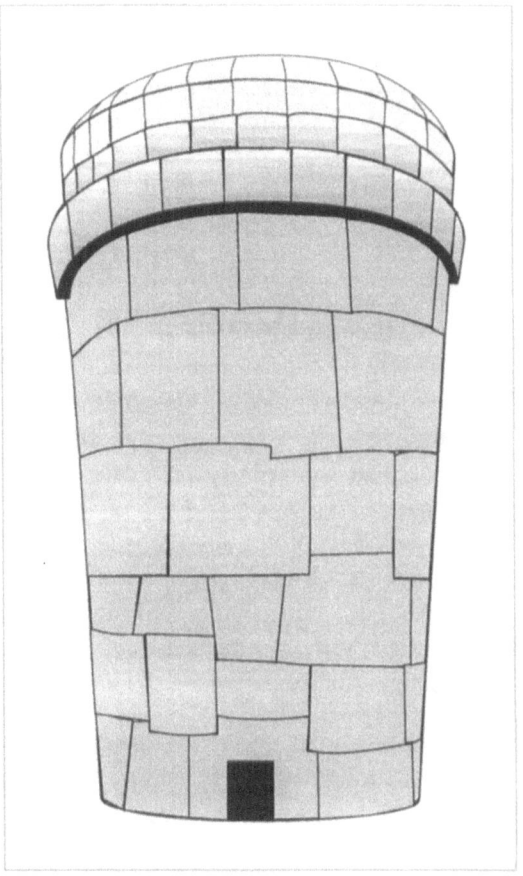

Figure 6.1. Open Sepulcher from Sillustani, Puno (redrawn from Gasparini and Margolies 1980: Fig. 140)

Syntheses of south highland *chullpa* information have been written by Erland Nordenskiöld (1906), Tschopik (1946: 10–20), Rydén (1947: 339–484, 1957) Hyslop (1976: 88–92, 1977), and Ayca (1995). In keeping with the identification of *chullpa*s with the *altiplano* it is common to attribute its origin to local evolution from earlier Tiwanaku burial patterns. The form of burial favored throughout the Tiwanaku sphere seems to have been a subterranean pit. In more elaborate graves the pit is lined with stones, usually flat slabs placed upright around the inside, and a stone cap formed by one or more additional slabs. Rydén

(1947, 1957, 1959) argued that urn burials by Tiwanakoid cultures in Cochabamba, southeast of the *altiplano*, were an alternative that responded to the lack of appropriate stone for slab-lined pits.

Late in Tiwanaku, perhaps after A.D. 1000, a few graves were placed on or above the surface of the ground. One way to achieve this was to create artificial mounds with fill to contain the tombs (Ayca 1995: 139–140). Some pit graves were also modified so that the tops of the slabs, or even several courses of rough stone wall, rose above the ground. These are described as collar tombs and proto-*chullpa*s (Ayca 1995: 141; Bermann 1994: 178–217, Fig. 12.20; Rydén 1947, 1957, 1959; Stanish, personal communication, 1992). The true *chullpa*, however—the kind of building that could have protected a venerated ancestor mummy—does not appear in the *altiplano* until Tiwanaku was replaced by Colla, Lupaca, Pacajes, and other cultures of the Late Intermediate Period.

Hyslop (1976: 88–92) is less satisfied with the gradual derivation of *chullpa*s from Tiwanaku graves. He points out that Nordenskiöld, Tschopik, and Rydén never found Tiwanaku ceramics in a *chullpa*, that on all Tiwanaku sites where *chullpa*s occur there are other signs of later occupation, and that the *chullpa*s on Tiwanaku sites are identical to *chullpa*s belonging to these later occupations. On the basis of his work west of Lake Titicaca he concludes that *chullpa* construction and burial was not part of the Tiwanaku culture, even of the late expansive phase, but originated with the disappearance of Tiwanaku, between A.D. 1000 and 1200.

I find Hyslop's arguments convincing, although his disagreement with Rydén, Ayca, Stanish, and others may be little more than an issue of defining the end of Tiwanaku and the beginning of the late *altiplano* cultures. At any rate, no one argues that open sepulchers of the *chullpa* type appeared before A.D. 1000, and Hyslop (1976, 1977) proposes that two phases of *chullpa* construction be recognized in the northwestern Lupaca region of the *altiplano*. The first he calls the Altiplano Phase, dating between about A.D. 1100 and 1450. The second phase, named Chuquito-Inca, is from A.D. 1450 to 1550. The proposed sequence has crude *chullpa*s of the Altiplano Phase (Photo 6.1) transform into impressive monuments of exquisite stonework under Inca influence during the Chuquito-Inca Phase (Photo 6.2). Beautiful cut stone *chullpa*s from this late phase occur at Sillustani (Fig. 6.1, Photos 6.2, 6.3), Cutimbo (Photo 6.4), and elsewhere in the *altiplano* (Photo 6.5). They

DISTRIBUTION OF OPEN SEPULCHER MONUMENTS • 167

Photo 6.1. Altiplano Phase *Chullpa* at Malcoamayo, Puno. Dated between A.D. 1100 and 1450, these open sepulchers were constructed of rough stones skillfully fitted into durable walls.

Photo 6.2. Chuquito-Inca Phase *Chullpa*. The Chuquito-Inca Phase dates between A.D. 1450 and 1550. In many cases, such as this partially destroyed example at Sillustani, it is clear that these burial towers resemble Altiplano Phase *chullpa*s except that they have an exterior covering of fine, Inca-style masonry.

Photo 6.3. Sillustani *Chullpa*s. *Chullpa*s at Sillustani are among the finest in the *altiplano*. They were contemporary with the Inca Empire, and many employ stonework similar to that of Cuzco.

include both circular and rectangular towers. For Hyslop, the rise of the *chullpa* mortuary pattern was intimately associated with the decline of Tiwanaku, announcing the appearance of a new form of religious expression.

The distribution of *chullpa*s continues far to the south of the Chuquito region investigated by Hyslop. On the Río Mauri, the western tributary of the Desaguadero that drains the Bolivian border with Chile and Peru, is the Anantoko site. Jorge Arellano López and Danilo

Kuljis Meruvia (1986) report forty-one *chullpa*s, surrounded by a stout stone wall with only a single entrance. Albeit smaller and less exquisitely finished, some of the *chullpa*s of Anantoko strongly resemble those of Sillustani. They have circular plans and are made of dressed stones, including some polygonal blocks. Horizontal cornices project out from the wall below corbeled vault roofs, and small doorways face east. However, the Anantoko mortuary group also includes rough stone *chullpa*s that taper toward the top in a distinctive conical shape, rectangular monuments of rough stone construction, and adobe *chullpa*s of rectangular form. All contain human osteological remains, reportedly limited to skulls and lower limb bones because of preservation, not original conditions of deposition. Each building contains between two and six individuals, including both male and female adults as well as children. Hyslop's chronology would predict that the rough conical buildings and the rectangular adobe towers belong to immediately pre-Inca Altiplano Phase kingdoms, while the Sillustani type might belong exclusively to the Inca period. Indeed, the Anantoko ceramics are described as belonging to the Mallku Kingdom and related to Sillustani Brown-on-Cream and Toconce of San Pedro de Atacama. However, exclusively Inca-period pottery is said to come from the rectangular adobe *chullpa*s, rather than the Sillustani types.

The distribution of *chullpa*s extends west into regions bordering the *altiplano*, where caravan trade and colonization apparently wove diverse local ethnic groups into a complementary economy. In the upper Río Loa Valley of Chile a study of *chullpa*s at Toconce was made by Carlos Aldunate del Solar and Victoria Castro Rojas (1981). These coarse little stone tombs seem to relate to the simple stone sepulchers at Anantoko. Thermoluminescence dates on associated ceramics imply that the Chilean sites came into use between the tenth and twelfth centuries, consistent with Hyslop's conclusions. In fact, there seems little doubt that throughout the southern central Andes the construction of *chullpa* burial houses represents a temporally unified tradition.

Rectangular *chullpa*s of adobe (Photo 6.6), although perhaps more correctly described as constructed of hand-modeled earthen slabs containing abundant straw, are the most common type of mortuary monument in the south *altiplano*, around Lake Poopó and beyond (Heredia Zavala 1991; Ponce Sanginés 1959a, 1959b; Portugal Ortiz 1988; Rivera Casanova 1989; Rydén 1947; Squier 1877). These *chullpa*s usually occur in groups, sometimes organized in lines, on hillsides and

Photo 6.4. Cutimbo *Chullpa*s

prominences. The buildings have square to rectangular plans, although they are generally elongated rectangles approximately 3.5 or 4 m long by 2 or 3 m wide. Some examples are smaller and some are much larger. A single doorway located in one of the elongated sides, often tall and narrow with pointed top, usually faces east. The inside burial chambers are also rectangular, with a false vault constructed of earthen bricks. Above the chamber the *chullpa* is solid for as much as a meter or more, to give the buildings total heights generally in excess of 3 m as well as considerable endurance in strong winds and seasonal rainfall. While few are completely enough preserved to supply all details about form, and there was significant variability through this large region, it does appear that these *chullpa*s had flat roofs. At least some roofs were of several layers, stepped back from the edge like a thin wedding cake. Carlos Ponce (1959a) describes three levels, in some cases each consisting of a layer of *ichu* straw held in place by hard clay and in others of clay alone. In some *chullpa*s one or more of the roof layers projected

Photo 6.5. Excellent Masonry of *Chullpa* at Cutimbo

beyond the line of the wall to produce a narrow cornice. It is also clear that some of the *chullpa*s were painted—red and red and yellow have been reported (Heredia Zavala 1991; Ponce Sanginés 1959b; Portugal Ortiz 1988; Rivera Casanova 1989; Rydén 1947; Squier 1877).

Chambers in many of the adobe *chullpa*s contain human bones. A comprehensive study is needed, but on a preliminary basis it seems that most contain the remains of several individuals but not multitudes of bodies. Ceramics in and around this type of *chullpa* are characteristically red slipped or painted black on red. The Black-on-Red style is post-Tiwanaku and often associated with the Pacajes Kingdom, especially during the time it was incorporated into the Inca Empire. As noted above, Arellano and Kuljis (1986) assert that the pottery from rectangular adobe *chullpa*s at Anantoko is limited to Pacajes Inca material.

In some cases the rectangular adobe *chullpa*s are built on low platforms. I observed one adobe *chullpa* at Chiar Jakke (Map 6.1, Photo 6.7), not far from Coro Coro, with the base of its walls of well-fitting

172 • MUMMIES AND MORTUARY MONUMENTS

Photo 6.6. *Chullpa* of Adobe near Coro Coro, Bolivia

Photo 6.7. *Chullpa* at Chiar Jakke, La Paz

dressed stones that include polygonal forms. In fact, the chamber of this *chullpa* has two floors, one below the ground level. The narrow, pointed entrance provides access to a typical chamber, except that the floor consists of large stone slabs. Below the slabs is a lower level, with a solid column of rocks in the center to support the middle of the floor. The lower-level chamber is constructed entirely of stone and has very large niches in its walls. Unfortunately, it was not readily apparent how the lower floor of this now partially damaged *chullpa* was entered in the past. Like the *kullpi* of highland Lima, the rectangular adobe *chullpa*s of the southern *altiplano* have been called house-graves where the living and the dead shared the same structure. However, Carlos Ponce Sanginés (1959a) argues that at the time of the Spanish invasion Pacajes peoples' residential houses were circular and dome shaped while the rectangular adobe towers were sepulchers.

Two samples of wood from rectangular adobe *chullpa*s were submitted for radiocarbon dating by Ponce Sanginés (1962). One sample from Salla (Province of Loayza, Department of La Paz) consisted of fragments of a wooden *kero* (tall drinking cup) that had been embedded in the wall of a *chullpa*. The resulting date, A.D. 1550 ± 150, implies that construction did not predate the Inca period or even early colonial times. A second radiocarbon sample from another wooden artifact associated with a similar *chullpa* in Kanasa (Province of Carangas, Department of Oruro) yielded the date of A.D. 1785 ± 150. While such a late date might seem surprising, in a circular house at the same site Inca and Black-on-Red pottery was excavated along with a rusted iron horseshoe.

On the Andean slopes to the east, *chullpa* burial towers occur with the late *altiplano* cultural influence. Most examples are little rectangular buildings of rough stone, with a small doorway, and a roof of flat stone slabs overhanging the walls to shelter them from rain (Photo 6.8). Some have traces of plaster and red paint (Photo 6.9), and they sometimes occur in large groups (Photo 6.10). Undisturbed examples may be packed full of human bones (Photo 6.11), but many *chullpa*s have been ransacked and damaged. However, it is likely that *chullpa* burial houses have suffered less deliberate destruction in the eastern forests than on the *altiplano*, and their frequency probably indicates that in the past modest open sepulchers were also very common in the *altiplano*.

In conclusion, there seems no doubt that the tower *chullpa* was the *altiplano* form of open sepulcher. It is not an archaic feature of *alti-*

Photo 6.8. Rough Stone *Chullpa* near Sandia. East of the *altiplano*, on the slopes into the Amazon, are numerous residential sites with *chullpa* sepulchers. While they are rather coarsely built, roofs with wide eaves protect the walls.

*plano* culture, but appeared with the decline of Tiwanaku styles, no earlier than A.D. 1000 and probably somewhat later. In the far southern *altiplano* the appearance of rectangular adobe *chullpa*s may be even later, dating to the time of the Incas or even the Spanish colonial era. I infer that the open sepulcher burial, and *ayllu* organization, appeared in the *altiplano* no more than five centuries before the Christian invasion. Hyslop (1976, 1977) seems to have been correct that the switch from Tiwanaku pit burial to open sepulcher, *chullpa* construction signaled a major religious and cultural transformation.

## CUZCO AND AREQUIPA

Contrary to Squier's belief, *chullpa* sepulchers have a continuous distribution from the *altiplano* to the north (Map 6.2), through the Peruvian departments of Arequipa and Cuzco (Bengtsson 1991). Rows of these

Photo 6.9. *Chullpa* at ColoColo, near Patanbuco, Sandia. At ColoColo, near Patanbuco on the eastern Andean slopes of the Andes, rough stone *chullpa* masonry was covered with clay plaster and painted red.

tombs are reported at Paucartambo (Fig. 6.2) as well as Nuñoa (Cornejo 1939: 42). Susan Niles (1987: 29) reports a likely example from the Valley of Cuzco, a circular foundation she considers to represent a *chullpa* predating Inca times. Lisbet Bengtsson (1991) describes *chullpa*s from near Ollantaytambo and Paucartambo. While some Cuzco *chullpa*s are well made and impressive, almost comparable to the spectacular Sillustani specimens, the *chullpa*s in Bengtsson's study are as modest as those of Toconce (see Fig. 6.3). All are located on hillsides

176 • MUMMIES AND MORTUARY MONUMENTS

Photo 6.10. "Village" of *Chullpa*s above the Site of ColoColo. Some Andean communities were accompanied by "villages" of the dead—a collection of *chullpa*s. At ColoColo the *chullpa*s are located on terraces above the residential area, perhaps to assure the mummies a good view of their descendants.

and made of rough stone work, with about a square meter of floor area and circular, square, or horseshoe-shaped plans. Some had traces of a mud coating covered with yellow plaster. Roofs are of flat stone slabs, and the buildings have cornices around them near the top. Each *chullpa* has a more or less rectangular entrance 55–85 cm high and 30–54 cm wide facing east, southeast, northeast, or west. They range in total height from about 1 to 1.8 m. Human skeletal remains were found in and around several of the *chullpa*s, as was pottery, mostly of Inca style, but a few sherds with earlier Lucre-style designs were also observed.

Radiocarbon samples were taken from four *chullpa*s, analyzed by the accelerator technique, and subsequently calibrated. Three are as follows:

A.D. 1420–1450 for *Chullpa* B
A.D. 1415–1454 for *Chullpa* 33
A.D. 1415–1454 for *Chullpa* 35

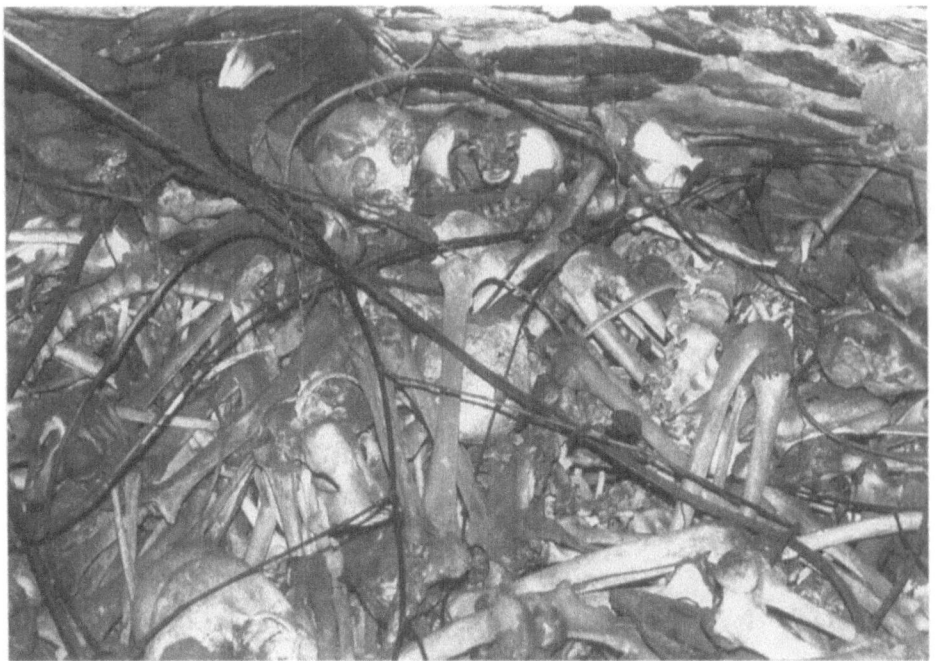

Photo 6.11. *Chullpa* with Human Remains. This *chullpa* is full of human remains, although the humid climate of the eastern slopes of the Andes has reduced mummies to bones. In many cases, however, all traces of the ancestor mummies have disappeared.

These dates are consistent with the Late Horizon or Inca period. Two additional dates were run on material from *Chullpa* 2, yielding earlier results:

A.D. 1277–1389 for *Chullpa* 2
A.D. 780–980 for *Chullpa* 2

The first of these dates belongs to the Late Intermediate Period, contemporary with Altiplano Phase *chullpas* to the south. The second belongs to the Middle Horizon, when Tiwanaku was the dominant culture of the *altiplano*. If correct, this date would reveal *chullpa* construction in Cuzco somewhat earlier than in the *altiplano*. However, a conclusion based on a single date must remain tentative. While *Chullpa* 2 does probably predate others at Ollantaytambo and Paucartambo, we must conclude that the radiocarbon dates only suggest the possibility of

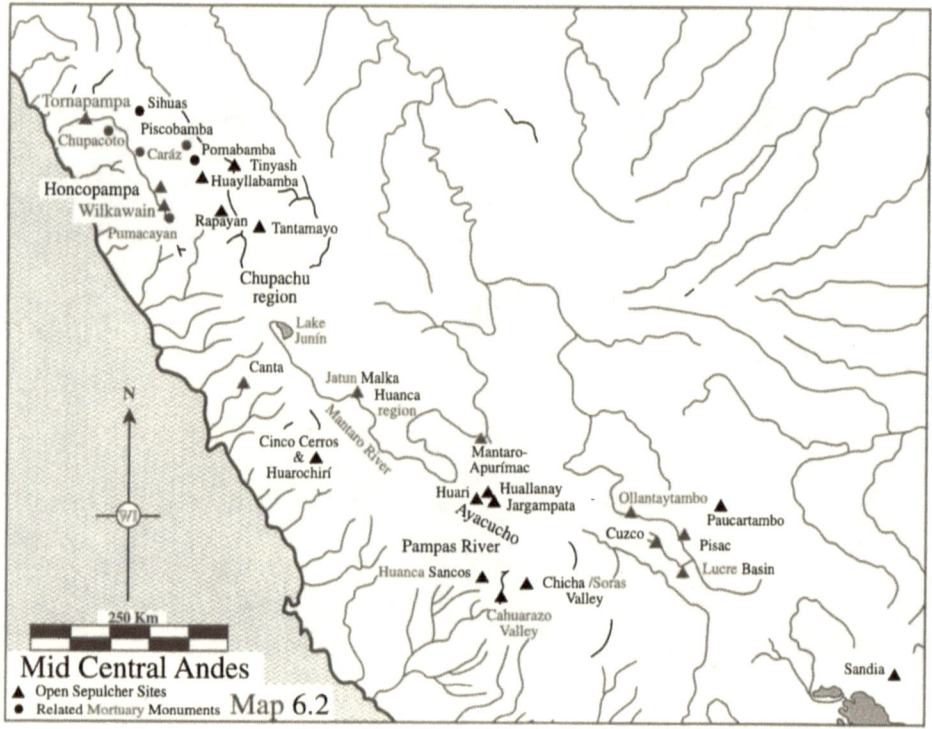

Map 6.2. Open Sepulcher Sites in the Mid-Central Andes

*chullpa* construction in Cuzco before the Late Intermediate Period and their appearance in the *altiplano*.

*Chullpa*s have been reported in the Lucre Basin, a few kilometers south of Cuzco (Niles 1987: 29). Unfortunately, they have not been described in detail or dated by association or radiocarbon, for the Lucre Basin contains the great Middle Horizon site of Pikillacta, as well as Choquepuquio, a big site probably constructed early in the Late Intermediate Period.

While *chullpa*s are conclusively documented in Cuzco, alternative forms of open sepulchers may have been popular as well. We must remember that the mummies of some Inca kings were kept in a special room of the Sun Temple. They were also kept in the palace the king had occupied during life, and others were kept in the buildings of their rural estates, in the care of their *panaca* members (Rowe 1995). At Ollantaytambo, in addition to the *chullpa*s studied by Bengtsson, Jean-Pierre

Figure 6.2. Open Sepulcher from Paucartambo, Cuzco (redrawn from Gasparini and Margolies 1980: Fig. 145)

Protzen (1993: 146–147) found a rock shelter with an entrance sealed by a stone wall to protect burials inside. These are reminiscent of the *machay* described in extirpation of idolatries testimonies from the western Andes, and Squier (1877: 491, 531–532) made it clear that when he visited Cuzco in the nineteenth century many such tombs could still be seen on the cliffs, walled, stuccoed over, and painted. He wrote of the sepulchers at Pisac:

> The cliff, which, for the length of a mile, and for the height of hundreds of feet, is literally speckled with the white faces of tombs, is called Tantana Marca ["the Steeps of Lamentation"]. Some of the tombs were elaborately built of cut stones, the rock being dug away behind them, so as to form large chambers; but these have all been broken into and rifled. Many of the others

Figure 6.3. Open Sepulcher from Kachiqhata, Ollantaytambo, Cuzco (redrawn from Bengtsson 1991: Fig. 2 and personal communication, 1993)

have also been desecrated, but most remain intact. They contain the desiccated, or dried, bodies of the dead, bent and in a sitting position, with their heads resting on their hands, and their hands on their knees, wrapped in coarse cotton cloth or mats of rushes, with a few rude household or other utensils and implements surrounding them. . . . (Squier 1877: 531–532)

The dates for these rock face burials have not been determined, although they are generally considered to have been Inca. Other information is also unclear. Could the bodies be reached easily? Were the cliffs furnished with plazas or other facilities for the ritual adoration of and offerings to important ancestors? What we do know is that Squier reached and inspected the tombs without difficulty; the tombs were designed to preserve the cadavers, and offerings accompanied the bodies. I suggest that Cuzco's cave, rock shelter, and cliff face tombs should be added to the list of open sepulchers.

Cuzco does not have a single and easily identified culture that preceded the Incas and Late Intermediate Period, such as Tiwanaku in the *altiplano*. Nor can we define a relatively unified burial technique predating the appearance of *chullpa* architecture or rock shelter graves. Consequently, I conclude that the limited evidence available supports the inference that open sepulchers for dead ancestors were popular in Cuzco in Inca times, and they can be traced back into the Late Intermediate Period and possibly the Middle Horizon, but no earlier. I suggest that the appearance of open sepulchers and *ayllu* organization in Cuzco is late and consistent with the record from the *altiplano*. There is no architectural evidence for *ayllu* ancestors earlier than five to seven centuries before the Spanish invasion.

## AYACUCHO AND THE SOUTH-CENTRAL HIGHLANDS

To the north and west of Cuzco, open sepulchers are abundant but little studied (Map 6.2). Speaking of the Ayacucho Valley and the adjacent Pampas River, Luis Lumbreras (1974a: 208, 213–218) associates *chullpa*s with sites dated to the Late Intermediate Period and Late Horizon. Katharina Schreiber (1993: 107) reports that open sepulchers of the *chullpa* variety are important features of post–Middle Horizon archaeology in the old Lucanas region that she calls the Carhuarazo Valley, a southern tributary of the Pampas River. Around the village of Queca above-ground tombs are rectangular, sometimes with rounded interior corners, and have stone-slab ceilings. They occur in isolation or in small attached groups on low hill tops. The *chullpa*s of Apcara and Andamarca are, by contrast, circular with corbeled vault ceilings. Near Apcara *chullpa*s occur only in habitation sites, sometimes attached to residential buildings, while around Andamarca they are found in both habitation sites as well as on hilltops.

Many of the open sepulchers of Ayacucho are found in poor condition, and many lack preserved skeletal remains. The Huallanay site, in a northern tributary of the Pampas River, discussed in Chapter 4, is an exception because it was documented in the 1940s before the last of its skeletal remains were destroyed or removed. Navarro del Aguila (1943) described trepanned and deformed skulls and reported eleven burial houses of rough stonework distributed in two groups. The largest sepulcher was oriented east-west, 3.6 m long and 3.05 m wide, with a small east-facing opening 1.2 m above the ground, about 50 by 65 cm in size, and somewhat north of the center of the wall (see Fig. 5.1). The second largest was 3 by 3.2 m in size with a small opening about 60 by 60 cm some 80 cm above the ground, also apparently in the east wall and offset to the north of its center. Roofs were said to have been of the false vault type, but the photographs and descriptions are not sufficiently complete to give me a secure impression of their technology. Consequently, for my reconstructive drawing I have also employed data given by Lumbreras (1974a), although all the *chullpas* in his sketches have small doors centered at the base of the walls. Unfortunately, none of the other nine *chullpas* at Huallanay were described, except that one had a niche in its inside south wall. My impression of the coarse ceramics of Huallanay in 1970 suggested a Late Intermediate Period date for the site (Isbell 1977), but the buildings had all but disappeared.

While it is apparent that many *chullpas* in Ayacucho have been damaged beyond recognition, Duccio Bonavia (1970) found well-preserved above-ground burial houses in the high forest or *montaña* in the northeastern corner of the department, where the Mantaro River joins the Apurímac River. Skeletal remains were preserved in some of the buildings. Unfortunately, the *chullpas* of the Mantaro-Apurímac junction are even less well dated than those of the Ayacucho and Pampas River valleys. In fact, they are simply considered to belong to the Late Intermediate Period through Late Horizon because that is the period to which *chullpas* are assigned.

Apparently, more common than interment in *chullpa* burial houses in the Ayacucho region was the placement of mummies in caves and rock shelters or *machays*. Sometimes the entrances were walled and even stuccoed and painted. When the walls are well preserved one can usually observe a small doorway providing access into the cave. Sites of this kind have never been inventoried, but they abound throughout Ayacucho and its neighboring department of Huancavelica (Ruiz Estrada 1983). Sometimes the abundance of human remains suggests hundreds of burials, but other caves seem to have contained only a few mummies. I have visited several such caves in the Pampas River Valley, where local peasants continue to bring bones and mummies out into the sunlight when rain is seriously needed. There has been little effort to date the remains in these caves, although most of the pottery that is found is coarse ware of the sort popularly ascribed to the Late Intermediate Period. However, there are some important data that bear on this. In the Chicha/Soras Valley, a tributary of the Pampas River, Frank Meddens (1991: 228–230 and Fig. 13) found a burial cave with fairly well-preserved mortuary architecture that contained pottery from Middle Horizon epoch 2 through Inca. I infer that this open sepulcher in a rock shelter (Fig. 6.4) was built sometime between A.D. 600 and 800, but utilized until Spanish colonial times. I am convinced of Meddens's evidence for Middle Horizon open sepulchers because he found a second walled shelter with a Middle Horizon offering that may once have included human remains (Meddens 1991: 224–227).

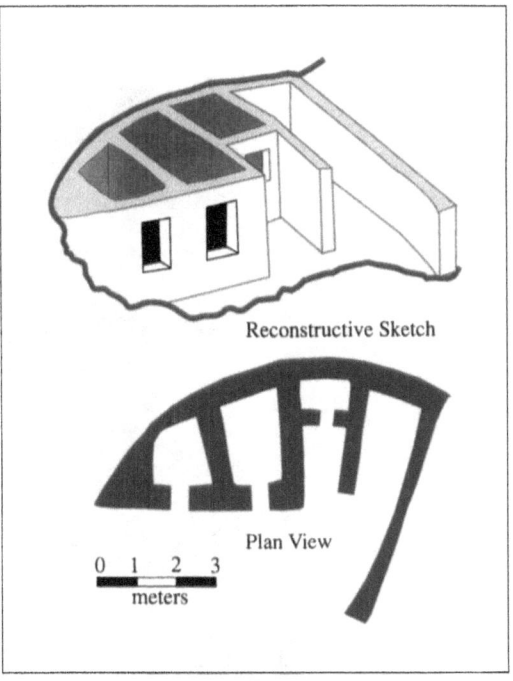

Figure 6.4. Rock Shelter with Open Sepulcher, Chicha-Soras Valley, Ayacucho (redrawn from Meddens 1985: 335 and reconstructive sketch by T. O'Brien)

Furthermore, in 1967 I visited several caves in the Pampas River Valley village of Huanca Sancos. The largest was sealed with a stone wall that was stuccoed and painted red, with a square doorway. Inside was a jumble of human bones that must have represented hundreds of individuals, for the bones covered the floor of the cave at least a meter deep. All had been turned over many times in search of valuables, and only in the low back of the cave could one see identifiable mummy bundles with evidence of having been bound in cloth and tied with rope. In the local school "museum" were textile fragments and copper *tupo* pins said to have come from the cave, and among them were many fragments of Huari tapestries. I photographed another piece of Huari tapestry in the school of the village of Sarhua, several days' walk from Huanca Sancos, although I did not visit the cave from which it was said to have come.

Photo 6.12. Mummy from a Cave near Saqsamarca, Ayacucho. This mummy and others occupy a dry cave above a remote archaeological site in southern Ayacucho. The bundle may have survived relatively undisturbed because it was wrapped in an animal skin instead of a fine textile.

Unfortunately this looting of fine Huari textiles has promoted the destruction of Middle Horizon mummy bundles, but I photographed a well-preserved mummy from a cave full of human remains where fine textiles were scarce. In fact, this ancestor's bundle may not have been violated because it was wrapped in an animal skin rather than a woven textile (Photo 6.12).

In concert, these data convince me that in the Ayacucho region during the Middle Horizon well-dressed bodies of dead ancestors were placed in modified caves and rock shelters. It would not have been difficult to visit these ancestors and make offerings.

At the archaeological site of Huari in the Ayacucho Valley, no *chullpa* burial towers are known, and no mummies have been found. However, there are a number of megalithic stone boxes that contain one or several chambers (see Photos 6.13, 6.14, 6.15). Some have two or three floor levels. All have been looted so intensively that it is almost impossible to determine even the original ground surface. Mario Benavides (1984, 1991), who has excavated extensively among these cham-

Photo 6.13. Megalithic Chamber in Cheqo Wasi Sector of Huari. When archaeologists first studied these stone chambers at Huari they were so completely looted that their function could not be determined. However, in view of the fact that human remains were found scattered about them it is likely that they contained burials and probably ancestor mummies.

bers, considers the probability that they originally served mortuary purposes. Many human bones were found in the looters' debris around the megalithic boxes. These constructions are massive stone boxes that were capped with heavy lids. They sometimes occur in groups that are surrounded by rough stone walls. It appears that the area within the enclosing wall was filled with earth during at least its later history, so that the structures may not have been freestanding but contained within a stone-faced mound. Some of the heavy lids have a circular hole about 10 cm in diameter cut through, and in some cases this hole corresponds with a half-circle groove down the interior east wall of the chamber.

In other parts of Huari simpler stone cists that contained human bones have been found under the floors of rooms. They, too, were capped with heavy stones with one or two holes cut through (Isbell, Brewster-Wray, and Spickard 1991: 33–36). At least some of these capped chambers contained human remains, although probably never entire cadavers. The lids of these chambers could have been removed by several people on special occasions when the bodies or bones were needed, and

Photo 6.14. Cheqo Wasi Megalithic Chamber

Photo 6.15. Overview of Megalithic Chambers at Cheqo Wasi, Huari

offerings could have been made to the dead inside the chambers through the holes in the lids at other times. It is probable that at least one such megalithic chamber exists at a peripheral Huari site in the Carhuarazo Valley (Schreiber 1992). I take this as additional evidence for open sepulchers in the Ayacucho region during Middle Horizon times.

In the Huari hinterland, Jargampata, a residential complex that I excavated in 1969–1970 (Isbell 1977: 22), contained human remains that probably included mummies placed in one of the rooms. Actually, two patterns of body disposal were discovered. Some bodies were interred in pits excavated in the kitchen and refuse areas at the edge of the house complex. Unfortunately, these burials were very poorly preserved, and I can say little more than that all were adults. The second pattern, inferred from the locations of human bones in strata looted from the central room of the complex, seems to have involved keeping the bodies in one room of the house, perhaps like the *kullpi* described below for the Lima highlands. At least three adult individuals seem to have received this treatment. This residential complex had horizontal rows of corbel stones that imply a second floor level, and perhaps the mummies were stored there. The upper building appears to have collapsed into the lower rooms, and later the main rooms were looted, so the original locations of the bodies cannot be securely determined. Jargampata's residential building belongs to Middle Horizon 2 on stylistic grounds.

I doubt that the open sepulcher has greater antiquity in Ayacucho than the Middle Horizon. First, it seems that in Huari times people were experimenting with mummies and easy access sepulchers. Second, there are no traces of the appropriate architecture in the earliest Huari remains or in Huarpa sites of the Early Intermediate Period (200 B.C.– A.D. 500). Rather, bodies seem to have been disposed of in subterranean burial. For example, a shaft tomb found at Conchopata (Lumbreras 1974a: 112–113) probably represents an important individual of the Huarpa culture, and slightly later early Middle Horizon burials at the same site were placed in stone-lined pits (Lumbreras 1974a: 172). If there was an important temple at Conchopata as I believe (Isbell and Cook 1987), these burials may be examples of the *huaca* cemetery pattern of interment.

I suggest that in Ayacucho during the Middle Horizon people began to experiment with several forms of open sepulchers and the curation of ancestor mummies, but most bodies probably continued to be buried underground in pits. Megalithic stone chambers at Huari may have been designed for elite individuals, while simpler cists under room floors served less influential persons. In a rural community, important ancestors' bodies were kept in a special room of the house, and elsewhere they were placed in walled-rock shelters. During the Late Intermediate Period and Late Horizon *chullpa* buildings and *machay* caves became standard receptacles for human bodies and virtually all the dead joined the venerated *ayllu* ancestors in these repositories.

I infer that *ayllu* organization appeared and began to gain popularity in Ayacucho during the Middle Horizon. But it was not the social organization that preceded Huari and to which Huari administration was added as another institutional level. Rather, open sepulchers seem to have appeared only at the end of epoch 1 or in epoch 2 of the Middle Horizon. Perhaps gains in the popularity of *ayllu* organization were related to the decline of Huari state power. In subsequent Late Intermediate Period and Late Horizon times *chullpa*s and *ayllu* organization seem to have been the regional norm, yielding a tradition of about 800 to 1,000 years in antiquity at the time of the Spanish invasion.

## NORTH-CENTRAL AND WEST-CENTRAL HIGHLANDS

The west-central highlands of Huancavelica, Jauja, and Junín as well as the adjacent western Andes above Lima appear to be the center for a distinctive kind of multistoried house-grave, round or rectangular, in which the bodies of deceased ancestors remained in houses with the living. In the second quarter of the nineteenth century, Tschudi (1847: 349) described the buildings as follows:

> In the departments of Junín and Ayacucho, I met with the ruins of great villages, consisting of dwellings of a peculiar construction, in the form of a tower. Each house is quadrangular, with a diameter of about six feet, and seventeen or eighteen feet high. The walls are from one to one and a half feet thick. The doors, which open to the east and south, are only a foot and a half high, and two feet wide. After creeping in (which is a work of some difficulty) the explorer finds himself in an apartment about five and a half feet in height, and of equal breadth, without any windows. In the walls there are closets or cupboards, which served to contain domestic utensils, food, etc. Earthen

pots with maize, coca, and other things, are still often found in the closets. The ceiling of the room is overlaid with flat plates of stone, and in the center an aperture, two feet wide, is left, forming a communication with the second floor, which is precisely like the first, but has two small windows. The roof of this apartment has also an aperture, affording access to the third floor, the ceiling of which forms the roof of the house, and consists of rather thick plates of stone. The upper room is usually less lofty than the two rooms below it, and seems to have been used as a provision store-room. I found in one of these upper rooms the mummy of a child very well embalmed. The family appear to have lived chiefly on the ground-floors. The place for cooking is often plainly perceptible. The second floor was probably the sleeping apartment. In the course of my travels, when overtaken by storms, I often retreated for shelter into one of these ruined dwellings.

If it was customary to use multistoried buildings both as dwellings and as tombs for the family dead, as seems also to be indicated for the Ayacucho site of Jargampata, identification of open sepulchers could depend on actual preservation of human remains. But this pattern does not seem to have been universal even in the west-central highlands. Big villages of round buildings, such as Jatun Malka and others around Jauja (Noriega 1935, 1937), seem to have consisted of single-floored dwellings, with separate above-ground tombs. Unfortunately, the archaeological sites of the Upper Mantaro River Valley and Lake Junín area remain little excavated. Even regional chronology is still a problem. Nonetheless, buildings that appear to have been open sepulchers are abundant and varied.

In the high elevations around Lake Junín, the earliest architecture discovered by Jeff Parsons, Charles Hastings, and Ramiro Matos (n.d.) appears to date to the end of the Early Intermediate Period and the Middle Horizon. From this first phase only one chamber attached to a wall might be interpreted as an open sepulcher. However, what they call "above-ground tombs" occur in sixty-one sites of the Late Intermediate Period and Late Horizon, and what they identify as storage buildings may also have served as mortuary monuments. The Mantaro Valley contains numerous hilltop settlements with well-preserved buildings that also date to the Late Intermediate Period. According to Terence

D'Altroy (1992: 55–57), *chullpa*-like tombs are present by Wanka II times (A.D. 1350–1460), but the scarcity of diagnostic architectural remains from earlier settlements makes it difficult to say whether this represents their first appearance. On the other hand, Tim Earle and his colleagues (Earle et al. 1987; Owen and Norconk 1987) found human burials in simple pits excavated into the ground in and around the architectural compounds of Huanca settlements of Late Intermediate and Late Horizon times, so there seem to have been several modes of burial.

In the north-central highlands of the Upper Marañón Valley where its headwaters interlace with the tributaries of the Upper Huallaga River, there are settlements that were occupied at the moment of the Spanish invasion. At least in the Inca period settlements of Chupachu ethnicity it was typical for several houses to be grouped around an irregular and walled patio that often included a storage chamber and an above-ground tomb (Grosboll 1993: 56–58). The tombs were small rectangular buildings with narrow doorways and domed ceilings constructed of overlapping slabs that produced a flat roof. In some sites one finds taller and more impressive towerlike structures with stone-slab roofs, tall windows, and small doorways, but also in association with the residential buildings. While lacking human remains, these fancy buildings are best interpreted as a variety of open sepulcher especially characteristic of the high Marañón Valley during the Inca period (Thompson 1968).

Somewhat farther down the Marañón are rather typical looking *chullpa*s as well as tall, multistoried, towerlike buildings in high-elevation sites of the Tantamayo region (Bonnier 1981; Flornoy 1949, 1957). This architecture includes courtyards and large niches where mummies might have been placed for rituals. Furthermore, the organization of the towers suggested kin groupings like the *ayllu* to Bertrand Flornoy and Elisabeth Bonnier. But definitive information about the content of these buildings is lacking, as are convincing dates. Primarily because of their excellent preservation these sites are assigned to the Late Intermediate Period and Late Horizon.

Also on the east side of the Upper Marañón River is Tinyash (Thompson and Ravines 1973), a high-altitude settlement with many exquisitely constructed buildings. Among them is a separate court with a complex of *chullpa*s. Three have preserved their stone-slab roofs, and two of these are very impressive.

> ... they contain three levels of rooms, the floors and ceilings of each constructed of heavy stone slabs, and access to each level is gained through its own low doorway. The interiors are divided into sections resembling rooms, although there are no true doorways between them. Moreover, each level has a different ground plan. The interior construction is crude but very solid. The exteriors, in contrast, are made of evenly laid masonry from which occasional stones and bits of crude tenoned sculpture—usually small heads—protrude. The roofs are steeply gabled and ingeniously designed with a series of overlapping slabs which allow the rain to drip from level to level. While those buildings probably served as burial houses, they have been so thoroughly looted that all apparent evidence of prior use has disappeared. (Thompson and Ravines 1973: 99)

No excavations have been made at Tinyash, and surface artifacts have few temporally diagnostic features. Like the Tantamayo sites, good preservation has contributed to convictions that Tinyash must be fairly recent, probably belonging to the Late Intermediate Period. Conversely, some consider it to be older—perhaps Middle Horizon. On the western bank of the Marañón there are village sites where burial was in small, rectangular buildings of stone, in beehive-shaped structures, or in caves (Thompson 1973b: 119–120), but here too there are no dates. From Rapayan to Huayllabamba are spectacular multistoried buildings that were probably for ancestor mummies (Amat 1978), but they are essentially unstudied.

In conclusion, it appears that the open sepulcher was a popular but highly varied architectural form in the west- and north-central highlands. Dating for these mortuary monuments is very unsatisfactory. They surely existed during the Late Intermediate Period and the Late Horizon. Perhaps they were already present by the Middle Horizon, but nothing earlier can be documented. It may be relevant to note that the only architectural monuments for the region that securely predate ruins with mortuary monuments are temples such as Kotosh and Shillacoto. They bear no resemblance to *chullpa*s or other open sepulchers. Much research remains to be done, but the north-central and west-central highlands patterns for open sepulchers are consistent with information from farther south. Open sepulchers and *ayllu* organization were late, perhaps appearing in the Middle Horizon, but becoming popular in the Late Intermediate Period and Late Horizon.

## WESTERN ANDES ABOVE LIMA

The western Andes above Lima includes the area from Cajatambo to Yauyos and from the high foothills of the Andes to the continental divide. While it lies across the continental divide from the Junín *puna* and Mantaro and Marañón rivers, ecologically and culturally the western Andes is highland. Huarochirí and the Yauyos ethnic group were at the approximate center of this region.

Much like adjacent Junín, above-ground tombs of the *chullpa* variety are very common in the western Andes, but they have not been investigated enough to date them definitively. Popular knowledge associates them with the people who occupied the area before the arrival of the Incas, implying a Late Intermediate Period date, with a continuation of the tradition into the Late Horizon and early colonial era.

The archaeological record for the western Andes is especially valuable because of the Huarochirí Manuscript (Salomon and Urioste 1991) and the transcripts of numerous idolatries trials. Descriptions of rituals for *ayllu* ancestors at local plazas or *cayan*s that constituted the *llacta* ceremonial centers might be investigated directly through systematic archaeological survey and excavation. Salomon (1991) reports that remains of old ceremonial centers with open sepulchers overlooking the ruins of residential communities were probably occupied when Viceroy Toledo ordered that Indians should be resettled into *reducciones*. The arguments have not been tested, but they are strongly supported by Ales Hrdlička's descriptions from the beginning of this century.

> Some of the largest burial houses seen at Five Peaks each contain the remains of over one hundred individuals, while the smallest ones might not shelter the bones of more than two or three bodies. . . . there existed in the midst of a group of such [burial] houses a moderate sized square, which may have served for ceremonies, and one isolated burial house at the same place was found surrounded by a circle of single large stones.
>
> . . . there were also found remains of what may have been clans in some of the settlements, with a more brachycephalic type of crania apparently approaching those of the coast. At the

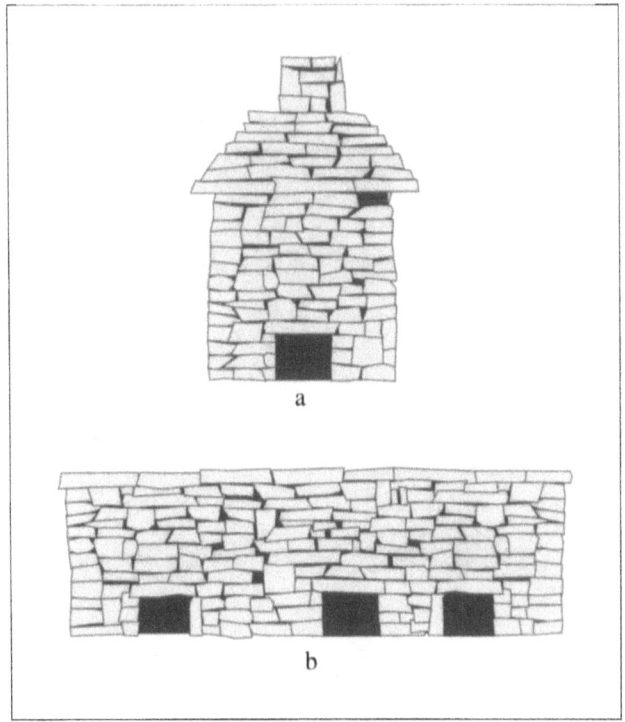

Figure 6.5. Open Sepulchers of the Huarochirí Area (redrawn from Hrdlička 1914: between 9 and 10)

"Cinco Cerros" ruin, the remains of the individuals of this type, who were in minority, occupied one separate burial house. (Hrdlička 1914: 9–10)

Hrdlička (1914: 7–13, Plate 3, Figs. 1 & 2, Plate 4, Plate 6, and Figs. 1 & 2) described four kinds of open sepulchers around Huarochirí. Apparently all were identified as tombs because they contained human remains. One common sepulcher form is the *machay*, created by placing the dead in caves or rock shelters that were generally but not always enclosed by a stone wall. Three styles of burial houses were observed. First are single-chambered, rectangular burial houses with a single little door at the level of the ground (see Fig. 6.5A). Second is an elongated burial house divided into two or three chambers inside, with multiple doors (Fig. 6.5B). Third is a burial house similar to the first but with a second story formed by slabs of stone.

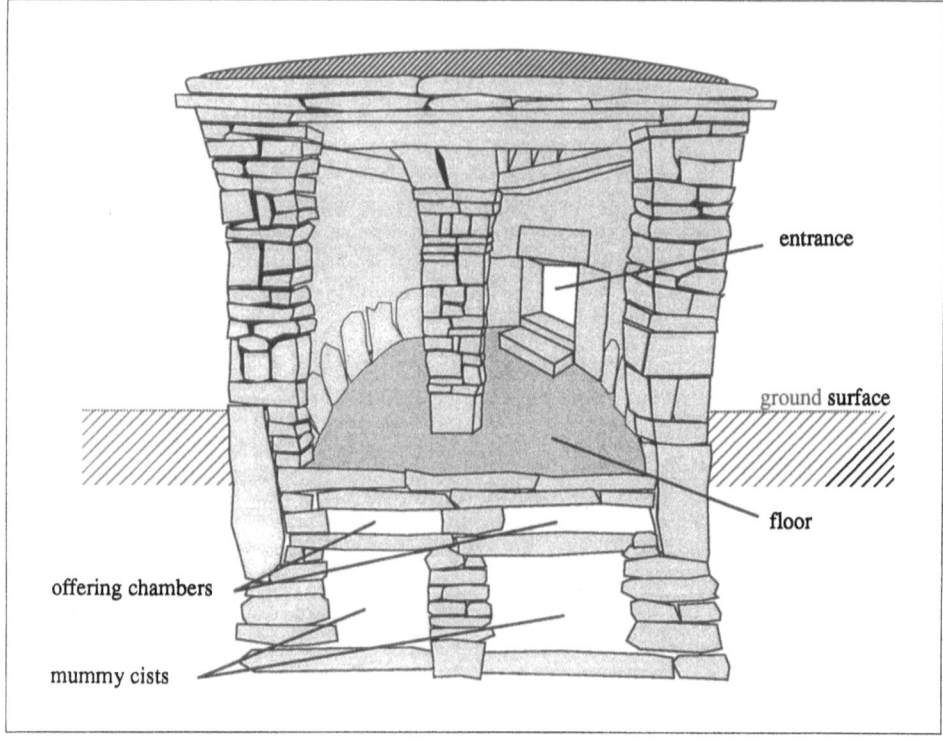

Figure 6.6. *Kullpi* House-Tomb from Canta, Lima: Cross-section Illustration (redrawn from Villar Córdova [1935] 1982: Fig. 43)

Pedro E. Villar Córdova (1923, [1935] 1982: 289–336) supplements information from Salomon and Hrdlička with extensive descriptions of archaeological remains slightly to the north of Huarochirí, in the headwaters of the Chillón and Chancay rivers around Canta. Besides burial caves and small burial buildings with two or more cadavers, Villar describes a larger kind of burial house that seems to combine residential and mortuary functions, including cult activities rendered to the dead. These cylindrical or rectangular "houses" are of well-fitted, rough-stone masonry and generally contain a large principal room as well as a number of small chambers (Fig. 6.6). They expand slightly toward the roof, where a cornice overhangs the walls and a roof of stone slabs covers the building. Sometimes, especially in the case of the cylindrical "houses," a central column of stones supports the roof, but the column may also be hollow and contain a passage to lower level chambers. The walls of the rooms and chambers often have large niches, and there are also cists under the floors where very well-preserved mummies have often been found, along with offerings of artifacts and llamas. Villar ([1935] 1982: 300) says that the natives call these house-tombs *kullpi*, a name he takes to be a local variant of the word *chullpa*. Cylindrical *kullpi*s are characteristic of the upper Chillon, but he insists that similar *kullpi*s were found in Huarochirí and Yauyos. If so, Hrdlička's description of burial contexts around Huarochirí may not have been exhaustive (Villar [1935] 1982: 302). In the Upper Chancay Valley, cubical versions of the *kullpi* are more common. These house-graves are taller than the round versions to the south and frequently have a small trapezoidal entrance framed by a tall trapezoidal niche that dominates the entire front of the building.

The popularity of open sepulchers and *ayllu* organization cannot be doubted for the western Andes above Lima in late prehistoric times. However, most of the information about the region is without temporal framework, so the antiquity of this architecture and its associated social organization cannot be determined. More research is needed.

## CALLEJÓN DE HUAYLAS AND ANCASH

The highlands of Ancash, and especially the Callejón de Huaylas and adjacent Cordillera Blanca, are full of monuments that appear to have been open sepulchers, although today human remains are no more frequent than in the monuments of Ayacucho and Junín. Antonio Raimondi (1873) visited many monuments over a century ago and even then mentioned few cases with human remains. Perhaps he simply omitted reference to bones unless they impressed him, as might be inferred by his argument that the Chavín "castillo" was not mortuary in nature because no human remains were found there.

In the vicinity of Sihuas human bones were found in sepulchers excavated into the bedrock. These tombs consist of a cylindrical shaft about half a meter in diameter and less than 1 m deep. Each shaft connects with four chambers located like a cross around the central one. In each cavity are human bones; all the skulls were reported to have been dolichocephalic. The circular entrances to the tombs had well-worked cut-stone lids that were covered with earth and stones (Raimondi 1873: 203–204). Near Piscobamba is a little granite hill with a cave that contained a great number of human bones (Raimondi 1873: 191–192). But the most interesting case came from the area of Pomabamba, where Raimondi (1873: 181–185) described a monumental cut-stone sarcophagus discovered in 1859. Inside there was not the single corpse of a great chief as Raimondi expected; in the four corners were circular holes, each covered by a stone, where bones were found along with objects of gold and silver. This is important because other examples of what are best identified as cut-stone coffins or sarcophagi were associated with severely damaged stone constructions, little more than mounds even in Raimondi's time, found throughout the Callejón de Huaylas. Near Caráz was a hill that looked natural, but was artificially constructed, with large walls in different levels. At the bottom of the hill a gallery was formed by two large stone walls with a ceiling of large horizontal stones. Inside was a stone "tank" with a channel on one side.

Raimondi pointed out that this might suggest that it was used to convey water, but since the hill was above the water level and there were no traces of an aqueduct, he concluded that the cut-stone box was used as a sarcophagus. Perhaps the channel was like the grooves of Huari's cut-stone chamber boxes, which may have functioned to make offerings into the box for mummies it could have contained. Raimondi found another "tank" but without such a channel in a comparable artificial hill named Pumacayan in the town of Huaráz. In Huaylas yet another such hill called Chupacoto was located. It was a favorite treasure hunting place, but Raimondi (1873: 106) says that nothing was found except human bones.

Raimondi's description of mounds with interior halls and megalithic sarcophagi is exciting, for it is without comparison in the Andes, except perhaps for the megalithic stone boxes at Huari. These impressive architectural remains seem to have been both temples and mortuary monuments, and I cannot help but suspect that they represent something intermediate between the *huaca* cemetery and the open sepulcher. Furthermore, I suspect that they were the original contexts for many of the human statues that now fill the museum in Huaráz. I feel that these ruined buildings represent a part of the archaeological record that has not received adequate attention from archaeologists of the twentieth century. Unfortunately, many of the monuments may be so thoroughly destroyed that their investigation today can produce only limited information. But the possibility that an entire class of mortuary monument might escape our attention should motivate an explicit campaign of research.

Figure 6.7. Callejón de Huaylas Open Sepulcher, Tornapampa Site (redrawn from Terada 1979: Plates 41–42 and Honcopampa data)

In addition to the big monuments described by Raimondi, the Callejón de Huaylas area has many open sepulchers that are quite consistent with *chullpa*s described for areas farther south. They range from little structures of rough stone work that sometimes employ large rocks for the corners, doorjambs, and lintel—similar to the Cuzco *chullpa*s of Ollantaytambo and Paucartambo—to large buildings of two and three floors, honeycombed with halls and rooms. The Japanese Scientific Expedition of 1975 (Terada 1979: 163–165, 178–179, and Plates 41–43) recorded nineteen of the smaller structures, which they called *chullpa*s, at Tornapampa (see Fig. 6.7).

> In general a *chullpa* is formed of bifacial walls on its four sides and the vault is corbeled by flat stones; it was, as we discovered, at least partially collapsed in many cases. Almost all of the plans were rectangular, but we found other shapes also. One had a round plan and another had four sides with rounded cor-

ners. A small entrance was made on one side of the wall, but is too small for an adult to enter. Its width is only 0.6–0.7 m and its height is almost the same. The entrance itself is carefully constructed of two vertical stones or posts and one horizontal flat stone which is set on the posts. Also, there is sometimes a threshold of large flat stones. The entrance commonly faces the southeast, but a few take the northeast or the east-north-eastern direction. Inside the *chullpas*, we found some fragments of bones, but nothing else. (Kato 1979: 163)

The more elaborate Tornapampa *chullpa*s stand on a large natural rock or a small platform and, in the case of an extremely fine example, on a two-stepped platform. Some have a cornice about the top of the wall. The cubical little buildings tend to be slightly longer in one axis than the other and not quite as tall as the shorter axis. They range from slightly less than 1.5 m long to over 3 m and in height from about 1.5 m to more than 2.5 m. Traces of mud plaster and red and white paint have been found on parts of the walls.

Ceramics from near the *chullpas*, assigned to the Tornapampa Period, relate to those of a circular building at La Pampa called the Rondán Circular Construction (Terada 1979). A radiocarbon date of A.D. 1310 for the Tornapampa Period is consistent with the Late Intermediate Period, but ceramics from around the *chullpas* include some with Huari-Tiwanakoid relations and others similar to the Cajamarca series, suggesting the possibility of construction and use as early as the Middle Horizon or even the Early Intermediate Period.

Located near Huaráz is Wilkawain, one of the most impressive *chullpas* in the Callejón de Huaylas (Photos 6.16–6.19). It was described by Wendell Bennett (1944: 14–53), and I cannot but wonder whether it is an example of what the rocky mounds of Pumacayan and Chupacoto, as well as the ones at Cara and other towns, might have been like before they were so completely destroyed. Bennett called Wilkawain's principal building a "temple." Its base is a platform 54 m by 35 m, but even this is surrounded by walls and a terrace. The building is 15.6 m by 10.7 m in plan and 9.25 m high. It consists of three floors and is surrounded by a terrace slightly more than 2 m wide. Each floor is entered from the exterior of the building, by a doorway on a different side of the building—first floor on the west, second toward the south, and third facing east. In the base terrace are large niches with openings to the north, although similar ones may have existed in the

DISTRIBUTION OF OPEN SEPULCHER MONUMENTS • 199

Photo 6.16. Wilkawain "Temple," the South Face. Wilkawain is a three-storied "temple" in the Callejón de Huaylas. Archaeologists found it deliberately filled with stones, but it may originally have contained ancestor mummies who were revered in the centuries immediately preceding 600 A.D. This doorway opens into the second floor.

Photo 6.17. Wilkawain "Temple," the North Face. The north face of Wilkawain has three large niches. The "temple" measures 15.6 m by 10.7 m in plan and 9.25 m high.

Photo 6.18. Wilkawain "Temple," the West End. The west end of the Wilkawain "temple" contains the entrance to the third floor. The structure was placed on a stone-faced platform measuring 54 by 35 m.

Photo 6.19. Interior of the Wilkawain "Temple." The interior of the Willkawain "temple" consists of three floors, each with seven rooms—three elongated halls and four rectangular chambers—linked by low doorways with massive lintels. The ceilings consist of huge flat slabs of stone that constitute the floors for the next level, except in the third floor, shown here, where ceiling slabs are steeply inclined to give slope to the roof.

south wall as well. Each floor of the building has seven rooms. A cornice and eaves project just below the barrel vault roof. Below the cornice the facade has a row of holes said to have contained tenoned heads representing felines. Construction is of rows of large stones with small chinking stones, alternating with rows of small, flat stones. Very large rocks surround doorways and form the roof.

In 1938, when Bennett excavated at Wilkawain, many of its rooms were full, or partially full, of stones. This deliberate filling may have protected Wilkawain from the degree of collapse reported by Raimondi for other buildings in the region, but it also entailed the removal of any contents that could shed light on the original function and date. Bennett also studied a similar but smaller three-storied temple half a kilometer to the southeast of Wilkawain and excavated what he called "houses," "deep stone-lined tombs," "direct burials," "stone box graves," and subterranean "Recuay galleries." In a few of the "stone box graves" and the "Recuay galleries" were traces of bones, but they were so poorly preserved that they were sometimes reduced to no more than powder. Except for the "Recuay galleries" and the graves, most of the structures seem to have been filled before abandonment. Ceramics from the "Recuay galleries" are White-on-Red and Recuay pieces of the Early Intermediate Period. Other structures contain a mixture of similar Early Intermediate Period pottery with polished black and polished red wares as well as polychrome pottery of the Middle Horizon. I suggest that subterranean tomb construction began early in the Early Intermediate Period and continued, but soon underground chamber burial was supplemented by above-ground, open sepulchers. Since their deliberate fills of stones contain Middle Horizon pottery it is likely that the buildings were abandoned about at that time or at least not a great deal later. With even the time of abandonment less than precise, the date of construction of the open sepulcher buildings remains to be determined. However, John Topic (personal communication, 1986) argues in favor of the Early Intermediate Period, roughly A.D. 200 to 600. He considers these buildings to have participated in a larger pattern of mausolea/temples that were built during the Early Intermediate Period, with their use continuing into the Middle Horizon, when they were deliberately abandoned.

Multistoried "temples" or *chullpa*s similar to but smaller than the one at Wilkawain are known at Honcopampa (Fig. 6.8, Photos 6.20, 6.21). Hernán Amat (personal communication, 1987), who excavated in the largest in 1961, found human skeletal remains as well as a Middle Horizon Huari sherd (he attributed it to the Viñaque style). My study of

Figure 6.8. Callejón de Huaylas Open Sepulcher from Honcopampa (based on Isbell 1987 field notes)

an isolated and smaller specimen more resembling the *chullpa*s of Tornapampa, located half a kilometer from the Honcopampa architectural concentration, also revealed human skeletal remains and Middle Horizon pottery (Isbell 1991a).

Augusto Soriano Infante (1939), priest and amateur archaeologist who assembled the collections of sculptures and ceramics in the modern museum of Huaráz, recognized single- and multiroomed burial buildings that were often several stories tall to be part of a prehistoric *chullpa* culture distributed through the entire Ancash region. He described many sites ranging from the western mountains above the Pacific to the eastern slopes of the Cordillera Blanca in the Marañón Valley (see Zaki 1978). As verified above, he noted that the buildings were associated with Huari-Tiwanaku pottery, but having been looted they lacked stone sculptures and contained only bones.

I suspect that the big *chullpa*s of the Callejón de Huaylas and greater Ancash region belong to a tradition of multistoried open sepulchers distributed through much of the Marañón River Valley. I have already mentioned examples along the west bank of the River from Rapayan to Huayllabamba (Amat 1978). On the east side are Tinyash (Thompson and Ravines 1973) as well as the Tantamayo ruins (Flornoy 1949, 1957; Bonnier 1981). Among these monuments are the tallest buildings

Photo 6.20. Group of Multistoried "Temples" at Honcopampa. A group of multistoried "temples" or *chullpa*s constitutes the southern portion of the Honcopampa site along the eastern side of the Callejón de Huaylas.

Photo 6.21. Largest *Chullpa* at Honcopampa. The largest of the *chullpa* buildings at Honcopampa was partially excavated in 1961 by Hernán Amat (personal communication, 1987), revealing human bones as well as some Viñaque-style pottery.

of precolumbian Peru, for some reached more than four floors high. There seems little doubt that at least some were *chullpa* buildings that protected mummies, but systematic research is much needed.

In the Callejón de Huaylas, open sepulchers and *ayllu* organization probably began during the Early Intermediate Period and continued through the Middle Horizon, Late Intermediate Period, and Late Horizon. But the archaeological record is incomplete and confusing, meaning that more research is required, beginning with the form and the dating of many of the mortuary monuments.

## THE NORTH HIGHLANDS

North of the Callejón de Huaylas the distribution of *chullpa*s continues into Pallasca, the Tablachaca Valley, and Huamachuco (see Map 6.3). On Cerro Amaru, in the Huamachuco Valley, Theresa and John Topic (1984: 5–41, Fig. 2) excavated poorly preserved remains of a small stone mausoleum of this type that was about 5 m by 6 m in plan (see Fig. 6.9). Its doorway was in the south wall. The interior was divided into an eastern and western half by a low stone wall. Three stone-lidded cists were found below the floor on the west side of this wall. Each cist contained human skeletal remains from several individuals in very poor condition, but only one cist was found undisturbed. This included the remains of at least one adult and one juvenile, although some additional teeth indicate that a second adult was present. The ceramics from the cist clearly belong to the Middle Horizon. Above the floor with the cists was a wooden loft, supported in part by the low wall. Scattered human remains, fine textile fragments, and many valuables show that the loft was a repository for mummies and their offerings. At some time the building was burned, accounting for the carbonization of the textiles. Four radiocarbon dates (T. Topic and J. Topic 1984: 73) come mostly from burned wood of the loft and/or roof of the *chullpa*.

   A.D. 330 ± 105
   A.D. 380 ± 65
   A.D. 405 ± 75
   A.D. 590 ± 65

These dates demonstrate what was inferred for the beginning of *chullpa*s in the Callejón de Huaylas—construction during the Early Intermediate Period, with occupation and use continuing into the Middle Horizon. This suite of dates confirms open sepulchers and *ayllu* reorganization in the north highlands during the Early Intermediate Period.

In the Huamachuco Valley archaeological remains that may represent open sepulchers are impressive and varied. At Marcahuamachuco, the most impressive site, stone buildings were truly spectacular, consisting of huge defensive walls around concentrations of oval enclosures, long halls, and high towers. John Topic (personal communication, 1990; J. Topic 1986, 1991; J. Topic and T. Topic 1983b, 1985; T. Topic and J. Topic 1984, 1987; also McCown 1945) considers many structures to have been mortuary buildings. Stanley Loten (1987) describes and illustrates four burial towers (see Fig. 6.10). The chambers located in several of the plazas (McCown 1945: Figs. 1 and 9) may also have been tombs, though they now lack human bones. The unexcavated towers certainly resemble *chullpas* from farther south, and human skeletal remains have been found, mostly scattered as if from looting, in many locations, including the great niched halls. These niched halls are large and have a flat terrace or walled court and huge elongated room with very large niches in one wall (Fig. 6.11). Some had more than one floor. I cannot resist thinking that the big niches were repositories for mummies and that niched halls were ceremonial open sepulchers where maximal *ayllu* groups conducted ritual gatherings in recognition of their common ancestors. The Marcahuamachuco buildings resemble the Cerro Amaru mausoleum and their Callejón de Huaylas relatives (J. Topic 1991: 154–155).

North of Huamachuco is the Cajamarca Valley, an enigma regarding open sepulchers. This is not because above-ground tombs are lacking; rather, there is such an abundance of what seem to be above-ground mortuary monuments, so varied in form and so little described that a meaningful overview is difficult to construct. Dan Julien (1988: 136–138) mentions several kinds of tombs, but most salient are large niches cut into the bedrock outcrops on hillsides where cadavers were deposited. They were sealed with mud and stones. Many such niches are found at Ventanillas de Otusco (Photo 6.22), near the city of Cajamarca, as well as other sites such as Combayo, Yanacancha, and Cerro Wallio de Cachicadan; they are distributed as far north as Bambamarca and as far south as Santiago de Chuco. Typically a niche measures 0.8 to 0.95 m high by 0.4 to 0.6 m wide. They usually occur in groups, arranged in horizontal rows. In addition, there are horizontal tunnels

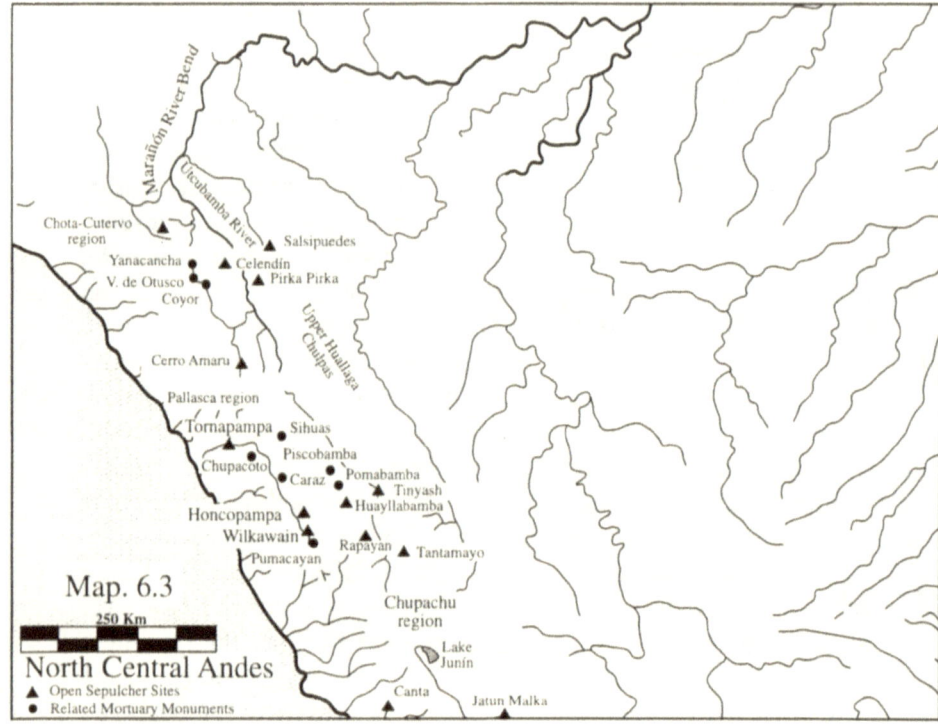

Map 6.3. Open Sepulcher Sites in the North-Central Andes

into hillsides, almost a meter in diameter and up to 4 m deep, that have several small chambers.

In Cajamarca another type of open sepulcher, also cut into a rock face, might be called the chambered shaft grave. It has a deep central tunnel penetrating horizontally into the stone, with a large chamber at the end. Symmetrically paired smaller chambers are cut into either side of the shaft, from one to three pairs. I observed several chambered shaft graves at Kolketín, near Ventanillas de Otusco (Photos 6.23, 6.24). Such cliff-face and bedrock tombs in Cajamarca recall Squier's descriptions of rock shelter tombs in Cuzco (Squier 1877: 491, 531–532). And like Cuzco, the Cajamarca niches and chambered shaft graves have been so extensively looted and completely cleared out that human remains are not found today.

In 1937 Julio Tello (1985: 177) explored megalithic mausolea in

DISTRIBUTION OF OPEN SEPULCHER MONUMENTS • 207

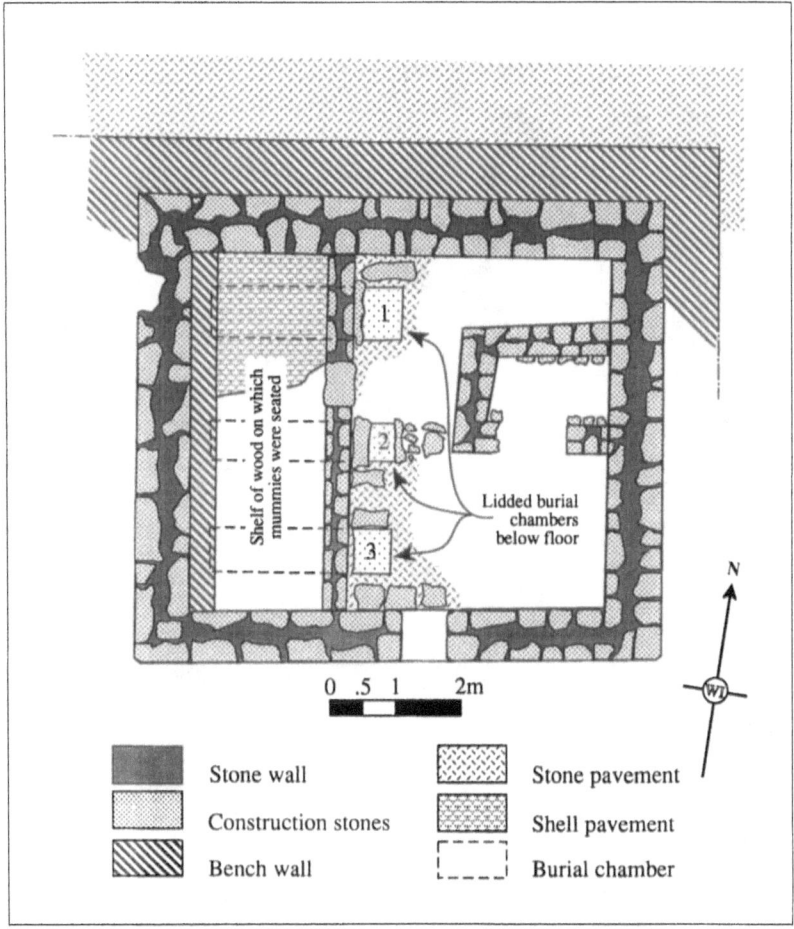

Figure 6.9. Cerro Amaru Mausoleum, Huamachuco (redrawn from T. Topic and J. Topic 1984: Fig. 2)

Yanacancha, north of the city of Cajamarca, that included both bedrock chambers and megalithic buildings (and a monolith). In view of this variety of tomb types, I am struck by the scarcity of *chullpa*-like structures similar to those so popular and widespread in regions immediately to the south. Perhaps deliberate destruction for reuse of materials in later buildings has been an important factor in eliminating some kinds of buildings. Charles Wiener's (1880: 130–133) archaeological descriptions

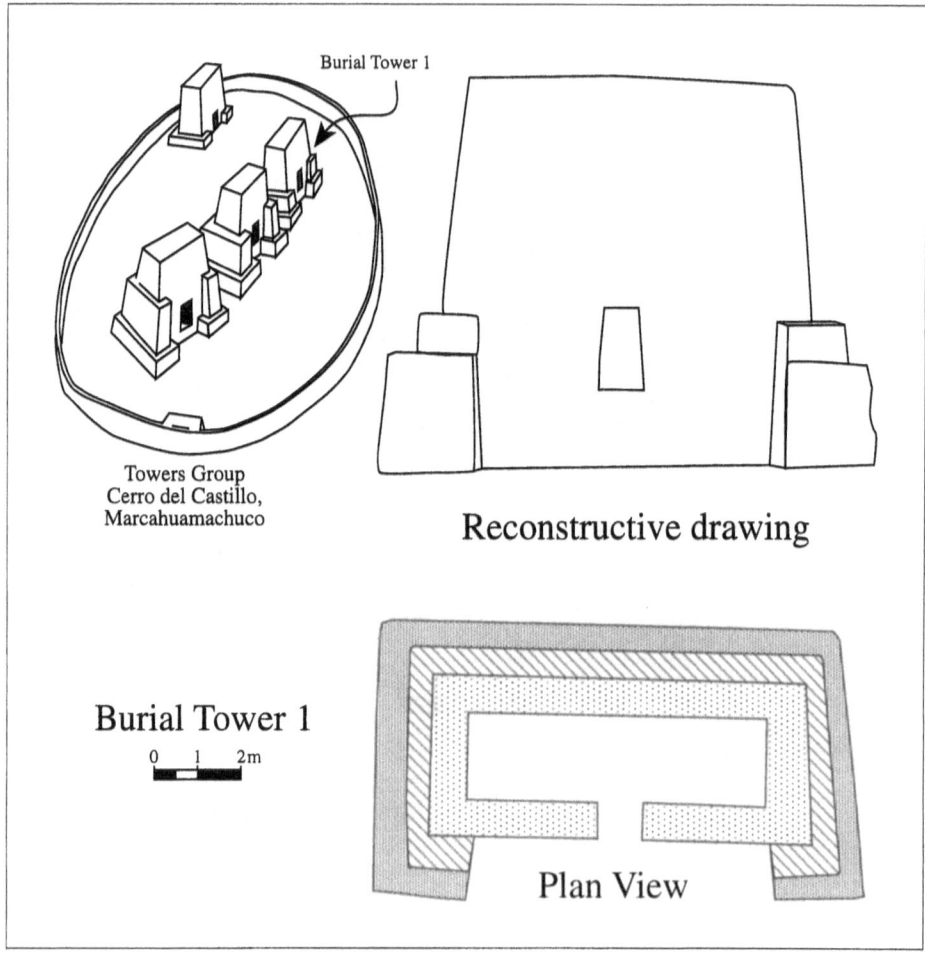

Figure 6.10. Burial Towers at Marcahuamachuco, Huamachuco (redrawn from Loten 1987: Figs. 3, 5, 7)

were often quite fanciful, but he described the Early Intermediate Period town of Coyor, southeast of the modern city of Cajamarca, as circles of masonry houses that ascended the hill. At the top were pyramidal mausolea for mummies. Few buildings remain at Coyor today, but the description of a pyramidal mausoleum recalls *chullpa*s from the Callejón de Huaylas, such as those at Honcopampa, and the general similar-

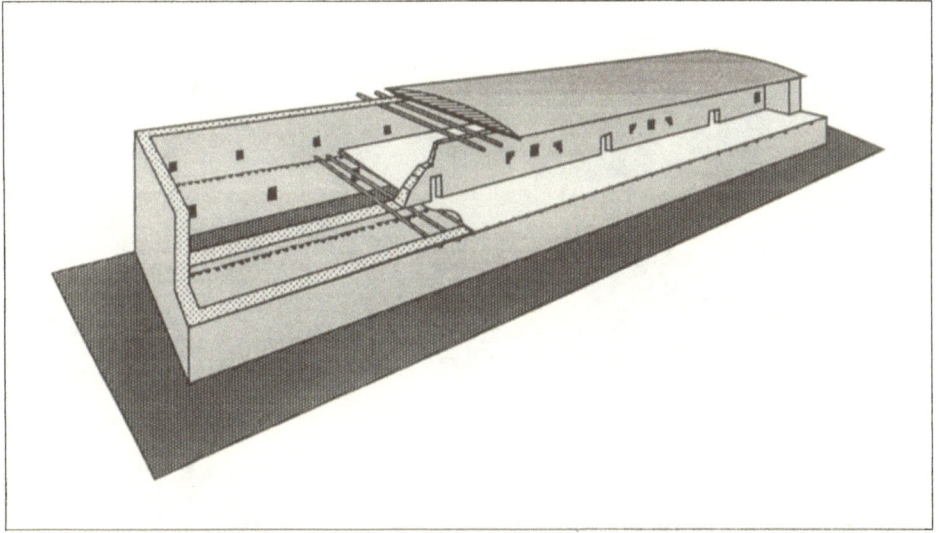

Figure 6.11. Niched Hall in Late Style, Early Intermediate Period, Marcahuamachuco (redrawn from J. Topic 1986: Fig. 6)

ity of this site to Pirka Pirka in the Uchumarca Valley across the Marañón (described below) lends credibility to the account.

East of Cajamarca, near Celendín, in the gorge of the Marañón River, Inge Schjellerup (personal communication, 1992) found small above-ground burial houses. They remain little investigated and undated.

On the east side of the Marañón River is the Uchumarca Valley. Donald Thompson (1973a, 1973b: 121–123, Photos 7 and 10) reports well-constructed prehistoric villages and a multistoried *chullpa* in a rock shelter. The site of Pirka Pirka contains many circular residential buildings around a hill, and at the top there is a monumental rectangular building with interior chambers that, although looted and lacking mortuary remains today, probably served that purpose originally. As elsewhere, in Uchumarca this inadequately dated site is tentatively assigned to the Late Intermediate Period or Late Horizon.

A major east bank tributary of the Marañón River is the Utcubamba Valley, famous for great ruins near the modern city of Chachapoyas. Here mortuary monuments are also common and varied. Some were obviously designed to be highly visible but virtually inaccessible. They

Photo 6.22. Niche Tombs, Ventanillas de Otusco, Cajamarca. At Ventanillas de Otusco, Cajamarca, niches a little less than a meter square are carved into vertical rock faces. These niches probably contained ancestor mummies, and in the past they may have been sealed with temporary walls or perishable screens.

are attached to steep cliff sides and include statuelike containers for individual mummies (Kauffman Doig et al. 1989; Savoy 1970: Plate 21) as well as masonry mortuary buildings (Kauffman Doig et al. 1989; Savoy 1970: Plates 27–29). Easy-access mortuary buildings are also common, and Gene Savoy (1970: Plates 35–36) shows tall, round *chullpa*s that include examples with four floors. Sometimes constructed against cliff walls, these *chullpa*s also share decorative masonry techniques with the Uchumarca example (Fig. 6.12). A similar *chullpa* exists at Salsipuedes (Jakobsen et al. 1986–1987: unnumbered [Torre funeraria, Salsipuedes]). A radiocarbon date for the Salsipuedes *chullpa* is A.D. 1485, suggesting Late Horizon occupation. Other *chullpa* sites in the same area were dated A.D. 910 and 1070. These dates, while very preliminary, reveal open sepulchers and *ayllu* organization in Late Intermediate Period and Late Horizon times, but possibly dating back to the Middle Horizon or earlier.

Photo 6.23. Entrance to a Chambered Shaft Grave at Kolketín. Chambered shaft graves are cut deep into rock outcrops at Kolketín in Cajamarca.

Photo 6.24. Interior of Chambered Shaft Grave at Kolketín. The interior of the chambered shaft grave at Kolketín, shown in Photo 6.23, has seven chambers. One large chamber is located at the end of the shaft, where archaeologist Daniel Morales is seated, and three smaller chambers are aligned along each side of the shaft.

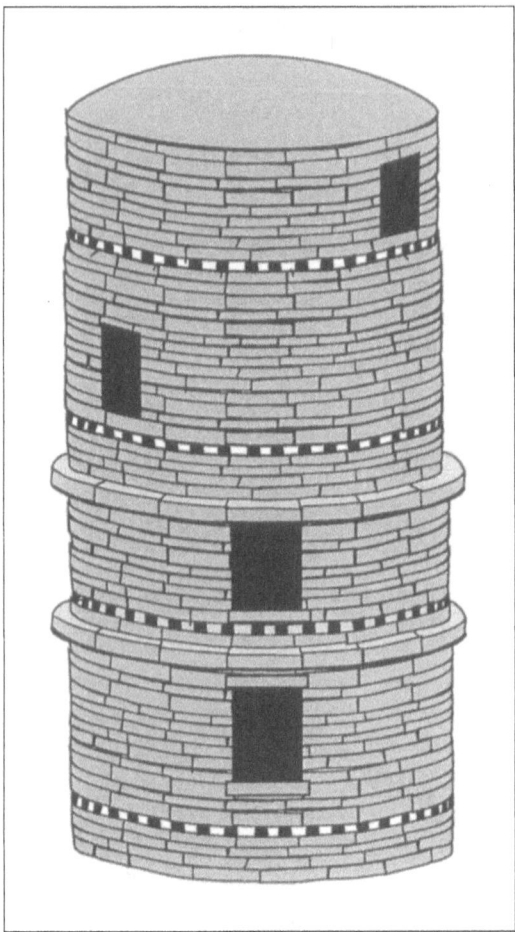

Figure 6.12. Utcubamba Open Sepulcher (drawn from Savoy 1970: Plate 36 and Jakobsen et al. 1986–1987, "Torre funeraria, Salsipuedes")

I suspect that the Uchumarca and Utcubamba open sepulchers, and especially the four-storied *chullpa*s, participated in the Marañón Valley tradition of multistoried mortuary monuments, and this tradition may have extended farther east. During an expedition to the site of Pajatén, across the divide between the Marañón River and the upper Huallaga River drainage, Federico Kauffman Doig (1984) found four *chullpa* mortuary monuments. They were only two stories high and built against a tall rock outcrop. What is exceptional about these open sepulchers is that one had broad eaves extending from the corbeled vault roof, and under these eaves hung several exquisitely preserved wooden sculptures of men in fancy headdresses. This is the only case in which such sculptures have been clearly associated with open sepulchers and mortuary ritual. For me they greatly enhance the probability that the stone statues of males in the Huaráz museum were also associated with ancestor worship and *ayllu* organization.

There can be no question that the open sepulchers distribution pattern supports the validity of the method for inferring the prehistory of *ayllu* organization. Open sepulchers reveal a continuous tradition of *ayllu* organization that is earliest in the north highlands, probably originating during the Early Intermediate Period. Consistent with theoretical expectations, the record for formal variation in open sepulchers is vastly more complex in the north, where the tradition seems to be oldest. Subsequently, *ayllu* organization and open sepulchers appear to have diffused south, reaching Ayacucho during the Middle Horizon and the *altiplano* in the Late Intermediate Period. But disappointingly, the archaeological record for the north highlands is confusing and not very well documented, especially if we hope to resolve such a weighty question as the origin of *ayllu* organization. For this reason I have saved information from a final area immediately north of the Cajamarca Valley, the headwaters of the Chotano River and its neighboring Upper Cuervo River, for a more detailed discussion. I want to focus on issues like the range of formal variation in mortuary monuments, dating the *chullpas*, and the possibility of identifying kinship models expressed in *chullpa* structures.

The north highlands from Huamachuco to the Chotano Valley lie adjacent to the core area for the definition of the "*huaca* cemetery" pattern of burial. *Huaca* cemetery interment seems to have characterized the northern highland valleys before and including the beginning of the Early Intermediate Period. *Huaca* cemetery burial was most magnificently expressed at Sipán and San José de Moro during the Early Intermediate Period by peoples of the Moche culture (see descriptions in Chapter 5). As a possible hypothesis we might suggest that the open sepulcher differentiated from the *huaca* cemetery in the north highlands and Marañón Valley during the Early Intermediate Period. With hopes of illuminating some of these problems, in the summer of 1990 I reexamined the *chullpa* sites reported for the Chotano and Cuervo valleys.

CHAPTER

# VII

## The Open Sepulchers of Chota-Cutervo

The spatial and temporal distribution of open sepulchers, in spite of how much information remains incomplete, certainly is not random. It defines an impressively clear pattern. In the *altiplano* of the southern Andes, above-ground tombs called *chullpas* first appeared with the decline of the Tiwanaku civilization, soon after A.D. 1000. As John Hyslop (1976, 1977) argued, complete alteration of mortuary custom must represent a major religious and cultural change in circum-Titicaca culture. I infer that *ayllu* social organization, as it was described in the sixteenth century, was spreading through the *altiplano* along with the advance of open sepulchers and venerated ancestor mummies. Consequently, the *ayllu* could not have been the social unit of Tiwanaku peoples or the antecedent from which a Tiwanaku state developed.

For more than a century many Andeanists associated the *chullpa* with the *altiplano* and its Aymara speakers, but a vast distribution of *chullpas* can be distinguished to the north of the *altiplano*. This includes Cuzco, through Ayacucho, to the headwaters of the Mantaro River, as well as the adjacent western Andes above Lima. Throughout this region it has become popular to associate the *chullpa* with the Late Intermediate Period and Later Horizon Inca Empire. Indeed, there are many sites with *chullpas* that do belong to these late prehistoric times. But there are hints of open sepulchers and venerated ancestor mummies in the central highlands during the Middle Horizon, sometime between A.D. 500 and

900, although probably not before A.D. 700. Described for Ayacucho, where the Middle Horizon is most studied, are burial caves, mummies in residential buildings, and looted megalithic stone boxes. I infer *ayllu* organization underlying the appearance, motivating the preservation, and demanding the accessibility of ancestor mummies.

A northern sphere of open sepulchers, focusing on the Marañón River Valley and its tributaries as well as some neighboring valleys such as the Callejón de Huaylas, can also be distinguished. Throughout this area open sepulchers seem to be highly varied, and for that reason they are often difficult to identify. They range from small chambers and niches cut into bedrock outcrops to huge buildings with several floors and many interior rooms. Unfortunately, too many of the Marañón open sepulchers contain few if any human bones, even though early reports occasionally confirm that bones were removed in the distant past. On the other hand, there is information placing some of these buildings and chambers in the Middle Horizon and even the Early Intermediate Period, during the first half millennium of our era. On the face of it, it appears that open sepulchers are 500 to 1,000 years older in the Marañón Valley of northern Peru than in the *altiplano* and that the central highland area has intermediate dates, implying a northern origin for the *ayllu* and its subsequent diffusion to the south. But the dating of northern mortuary monuments to the Early Intermediate Period is not robust, and certainly less than one would like for resolving such an important issue.

In this chapter we examine what I believe to be the most northerly example of open sepulchers (see Map 7.1). They come from neighboring valleys along the west side of the Marañón River, north of Cajamarca, that are the northernmost tributaries of the Marañón before it turns east into the Amazon jungle. The Chamaya Basin has a large southern headwater, the Chotano River, where *chullpas* are reported, but with little detailed information (Morales 1979; Shady and Rosas 1976). Curiously, I was actually motivated to study the region in August 1990 because I did not believe that the buildings could be mortuary monuments dating to the Early Intermediate Period. Following my excavations at Honcopampa in the Callejón de Huaylas (Isbell 1989, 1991a) I was preparing to argue that above-ground mortuary monuments at Honcopampa and elsewhere in the northern highlands dated no earlier than the Middle Horizon and was developing a theory that they originated at Huari. I supposed that having been developed in the megalithic boxes of Huari this pattern of mummy curation was spread to distant

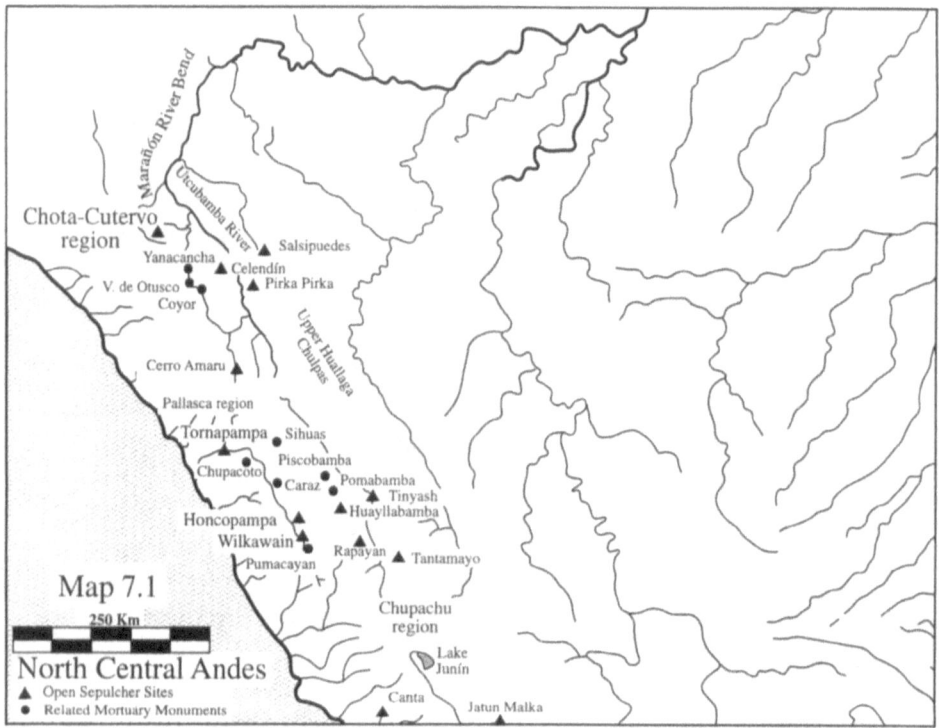

Map 7.1. Location of the Chota-Cutervo Region

provinces by Huari conquests. Several of the Callejón de Huaylas monuments do suggest Early Intermediate Period use, but there are underground buildings in these sites as well, and they might represent the only pre-Middle Horizon constructions. Of course, I had examined the Cerro Amaru mausoleum dates (T. Topic and J. Topic 1984) from the Early Intermediate Period and Middle Horizon. They might be discounted as reuse of old wood in roof construction if I could dispose of the argument that the Chota region also contained Early Intermediate Period mortuary monuments. I set out for Chota anticipating a case for the later date of these *chullpas*, if the buildings were mortuary monuments at all. But I returned convinced of their antiquity, for the reasons I will now describe.

Chamaya River Valley is a west bank tributary of the Marañón River. Like Cajamarca and Huamachuco to the south, it is a high, sec-

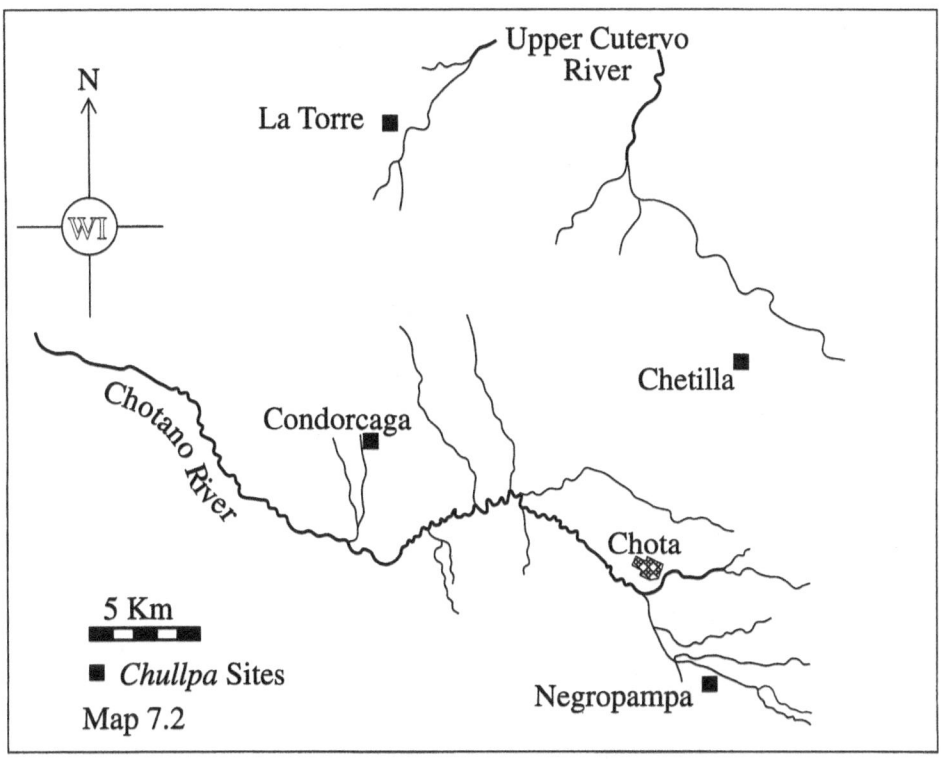

Map 7.2. Chota-Cutervo Area

ondary valley between the Marañón's long, narrow, tropical gorge and the headwaters of coastal rivers. Also like Cajamarca and Huamachuco, the Chamaya has a northern and a southern tributary making two headwater valleys. The northern affluent, the Huancabamba River, originates in Lake Shimbe, only 25 km from the border with Ecuador. To my knowledge this region has never been reconnoitered for archaeological remains, and it may hold significant surprises. This is the northern extreme of what is associated with the central Andean environment, and prehistoric cultures to the north have been classified into a different, even if related, culture area and social tradition.

The Chotano River is the southern of two affluents of the Chamaya (see Map 7.2). With its modern capital town of Chota in the southern headwaters, the Chamaya is best known for the early monumental ceremonial center of Pacopampa (Burger 1992: 104–109). It is also the center of a little-known but very impressive *chullpa* tradition. Ruth Shady and Hermilio Rosas (1976) reported three *chullpa* sites, and Daniel Morales Chocano (1979) described two. While they use different names, their discussions share one site in common, yielding an inventory of four known sites. I visited all four sites as well as local museums and collections, making notes and observations that constitute the basis for my descriptions and evaluations.

Actually the four *chullpa* sites are not in the headwaters of the Chotano River alone. Two are in the drainage of the adjacent, smaller Marañón tributary, the Cutervo River that joins the Bambamarca Valley that drains a small basin separating Chota from Cajamarca in the south. The two headwaters interlace, forming a more or less continuous zone, although the divide between them seems to function as a modest rain shadow. The Chotano Valley is more arid, while the Cutervo sites are in a wetter, lusher setting. For this reason I name the style the Chota-Cutervo Tradition.

The two sites in the Chotano drainage, Condorcaga and Negropampa, may have consisted of individual monuments. The Cutervo sites of Chetilla and La Torre have multiple *chullpa*s as well as indications of other prehistoric activities distributed over a considerable area. All four sites are located at similar altitudes, approximately 2,500 m above sea level, and well above the valley floor on slopes that are occupied and cultivated today. All but the Condorcaga site, which sits on elevated uplands well back from the lip of the valley, are on valley sides where they have commanding views and can also be seen from the surrounding lands. At the four sites, I was able to study the remains of six *chullpa* monuments, two at each of the Cutervo sites and one at each of the Chotano sites.

I want to begin this discussion with observations about the form and decoration of Chota *chullpa*s in order to make inferences about cultural patterns that governed their function and construction. Then I will describe the ruins of each site and make comparisons that bear on the antiquity and date of each monument. At the end of the chapter I will evaluate the Chota *chullpa*s in terms of four features that constitute *ayllu* organization—ancestor mummies in open sepulchers, social groups, communal resources, and organization based on the idiom of kinship—developed in Chapter 3. For the survey of open sepulchers in Chapter 6 we concentrated on the strongest material aspect of *ayllu* organization, the ancestor mummy in its open sepulcher. I argued that, by analogy, less materially manifest features of *ayllu* organization should also have been present. Now, in this more detailed examination of the Chota-Cutervo *chullpas*, we will try to do more. These *chullpas* seem to be among the earliest open sepulchers in the Andes and are probably the most elaborate. I believe that with them we are observing the material context in which *ayllu* organization was produced for the first time. Consequently, Chota-Cutervo *chullpas* must have had to communicate symbolic information very clearly and powerfully, since the goal of their rituals was not to reconstruct traditional patterns with only minor modifications, but to build a significantly new form of social organization. I infer that the powers of place (Agnew and Duncan 1989), the sensual experience of ritual (cf. Combs-Schilling 1989), and the organizational properties of building form (cf. Markus 1982, 1987, 1993) would all have been used to their maximum to achieve the transformation.

Since the clarity and redundancy of the message may have been quite exaggerated, we archaeologists should have a greater chance of meaningfully reading it after 1,500 or more years. I plan to see how much of the prehistoric text I can understand in terms of the characteristics of the *ayllu*—ancestor worship, a social group, communal resources, and ranked organization based on the idiom of kinship. We know that these were the features of *ayllu* organization among the sixteenth- and seventeenth-century Incas and Yauyos. If a convincing reading of the archaeological record from the earliest open sepulchers, about A.D. 200–300, suggests not only the existence but significant emphasis on them I will feel much more secure about associating these early *chullpas* with *ayllu* organization. Furthermore, I will conclude that it is not a great leap of faith to infer that the open sepulchers temporally and spatially between the Chota-Cutervo and the Inca/Yauyos examples, those discussed in Chapter 6, also communicated the four features of *ayllu* organization, recreating them in ritual action. These are the goals of this chapter.

The ideal original form that I imagine for Chota-Cutervo *chullpas* is based on observations I made on the six surviving examples (Fig. 7.1), including details of their construction, decoration, and preservation. Of course, my image is also informed by knowledge of other mortuary monuments and *ayllu* ancestors throughout the central Andes.

First, all Chota *chullpa* masonry is formally consistent (Photo 7.1). It employed large rectangular stones that were partially worked to achieve reasonably good fits with neighbors, and little or no clay mor-

Figure 7.1. Ideal Chota-Cutervo *Chullpa* (drawn by W. H. Isbell on the basis of field notes, 1991)

tar is visible in the outer surface of the walls. Each stone was unique in form and size, giving an appearance of less shaping than was often the case. Larger stones were used toward the bottoms of walls, including some over a meter in width and height that give a definite megalithic appearance to the masonry, but the average size of stones decreased with the height of the building. Building corners received especially large

Photo 7.1. Chetilla Tower 1, Masonry of the East Face. The masonry of the east face of the Chetilla Tower 1 is characteristic of Chota-Cutervo *chullpa* masonry. It employed partially worked, uniquely shaped stones that were usually rectangular to trapezoidal, but occasionally polygonal. Building stones were roughly fitted to neighbors to create an impressively megalithic yet natural and enduring effect.

blocks, much more completely and carefully worked than stones employed elsewhere in the walls. These corner stones are quite long but not very deep so that on one side of the corner they are long—perhaps 1 m or more—while on the other side they are short—perhaps no more than 30 cm. Alternating the long faces of the blocks between one side of the corner and the other produces a characteristic corner bond known as "long and short work." With slight variation this typifies all the *chullpa*s observed in Chota, and it also relates their architecture to Huamachuco and other north highland or Marañón regions. The *chullpa*s of Chota also achieve something of a megalithic polygonal appearance by avoiding blocks of uniform height that would produce even courses and by allowing some blocks, especially the larger ones, to have forms that are not rectangular. These irregular stones give the appearance of retaining much of their natural form and promote imprecise and accommodated fits. Finally, the masonry permits rather large gaps between stones, especially the vertical fittings. It may be that these were originally filled with clay and small stones that have now washed out.

Door lintels and doorjambs tend to be blocks that are fairly well shaped. They are often somewhat larger than the surrounding stones, and their fit with neighbors is often better than in the rest of the construction. Walls tend to be double faced, although many blocks are thick enough, especially those near the base of the monument, that they constitute the entire width of the wall. The outer face usually employs a small number of large stones, fairly well fitted. The interior face usually consists of smaller rocks with more clay mortar, but the fit is good, so mortar is not prominently visible. Sometimes the inner face is more of a patchwork around the irregularities of big stones whose fit is best achieved on the outer surface of the wall.

The effect of Chota *chullpa* masonry on the observer is powerful. Due to the joining of irregularly shaped stones and the use of rectangular blocks of varied size, wall faces have distinctively "natural" appearances that belie the degree of workmanship invested in shaping the stones. At the same time they achieve a harmony with the natural environment that promotes a sense of permanence, massiveness, and immobility that exceeds the size and weight of the stone employed. I conclude that the execution of *chullpa* masonry, with irregularities and imprecision of shape and fit, was deliberate and that it was a significant feature of the style. Furthermore, I feel that it contrasts with the earlier Pacopampa masonry that I observed at the type site. In my evaluation, Pacopampa stone masonry emphasized more rigid shaping and sizing of blocks as well as more precise fits among the stones. Pacopampa stonework expresses culture over nature, while the *chullpa*s emphasize culture in harmony with nature.

*Chullpa* facade stones were sometimes embellished with low to medium relief sculptural figures (Fig. 7.2, Photo 7.2; see also Photo 7.7),

Figure 7.2. Condorcaga Sculptural Detail (drawn by W. H. Isbell on the basis of field notes, 1991)

and some *chullpa*s have many sculptures on them. I believe that the sculptural decorations were added to the monuments after they were built, probably one or two at a time over a long period. This conclusion is based on the fact that some *chullpa*s have incompleted sculptures. While I admit that the eroded condition of many figures makes it difficult to determine what has been worn away and what was never cut into the rock, some sculptures are clearly unfinished. In the composition shown in Photo 7.2 the raised arm on the left side has less background removed than the area around the face and the other arm. The birds in the upper left are only outlined, with no background removed. These observations are not consistent with erosion.

If sculptural figures were added over a significant period, one or two at a time, their presence, their number, and probably their themes relate to the labor available and prestige commanded by those who

Photo 7.2. Unfinished Sculpture from Condorcaga *Chullpa*. This relief sculpture from the north side of the Condorcaga *chullpa* is clearly unfinished. The same theme occurs in the art of other north highland and north coast cultures during the Early Intermediate Period.

worshiped at the monument after it was constructed. I suggest that the sculptural figures provide at least some record of the history of each *ayllu* group associated with its *chullpa* monument. The figures of an individual monument probably relate to the achievements and negotiations effected by its community of worshipers—or from a participant's perspective the power of the ancestor mummy.

In the Chota region, in addition to sculptures on *chullpas* I observed stone blocks with figures like those on the *chullpas* but loose and in private collections or reused in the walls of modern buildings. I believe that these decorated stones have been removed from *chullpas*, perhaps some of the same ones I found partially destroyed but probably also undiscovered and perhaps even more severely destroyed monuments of the same cultural period. I conclude that sculpture robbery has contributed to the destruction of Chota's *chullpas* and may be the singularly most important factor. What this means is that destruction has

Photo 7.3. Chetilla Tower 1, Original Form of Chota-Cutervo *Chullpas*. Tower 1 at Chetilla reveals the ideal original form for Chota-Cutervo *chullpas*. They were four stories high, with an external doorway to each floor. This view of the north face shows the entrance to the third floor, although brush and debris around the base of the *chullpa* obscure at least a meter of the original height. This *chullpa* had no relief images carved on it and for that reason was not targeted for sculpture robbery, which appears to have contributed so severely to the destruction of other Chota-Cutervo *chullpas*.

been selective, eliminating the most elaborately decorated *chullpa*s most rapidly and most completely. If my inferences are correct, the best-preserved *chullpa*s should be the least decorated. Indeed, an example at the site of Chetilla has no sculptural decorations at all (Photo 7.3). It is the only specimen preserved from base to roof, although some parts of its walls have fallen and the roof is no longer totally complete. Even the partial destruction of the walls of the Chetilla *chullpa* may be attributable to human agency, as we will see when we discuss these remains. Nonetheless, I believe that this nearly complete *chullpa* furnishes the best information about the original form of Chota's *chullpas*, and my ideal reconstruction is based on it and the regularities it shares with less-preserved specimens.

We might ask why the Chetilla *chullpa* remained undecorated. Many possibilities come to mind. Its worshipers did not achieve success, gaining the necessary labor and making history that was worthy of recording on the stones of their ancestral sepulcher. The number of descendants declined. The site was abandoned not long after the monument was built, and worshipers ceased returning to the *chullpa* as a place of veneration. These explanations, while not intended to be exhaustive of all possibilities, impress me as probable.

Chota sculptural art and *chullpa* architecture are not newly discovered. Julio Tello (1940) mentioned these *chullpas*, although he did not make a systematic description. Richard Schaedel (1952) did not visit Chota, but he used photographs in an attempt to classify the relief figures in his impressive study of Andean stone sculpture. Shady and Rosas (1976) and Morales (1979) furnished the only descriptions based on site visits available at the time of my study in 1990. With so little known, the richness and complexity of Chota *chullpa* art is yet to be fully appreciated. I hope that by describing the four known sites and illustrating architecture and sculpture from each I can contribute to a fuller understanding of this important tradition, but I feel that a thorough survey is needed to determine the distribution of the distinctive architecture and collect a comprehensive corpus of the art. I suspect that more precise cultural and temporal assessments, including a stylistic seriation, should be possible with a larger sample of figures. Vigorous search will certainly reveal more sites and examples of the art, and excavations around the bases of the known monuments might reveal additional figures. The thematic variation, stylistic groupings, and technical aspects of Chota sculptural art are yet to be defined, and it may represent the least-known highland tradition of megalithic architecture associated with relief sculpture.

Relief sculptures I observed occur on the larger blocks, on the exterior faces of *chullpa* walls. The sculptural techniques range from outlining with incision, to low-relief champlevé, to fairly high-relief figures around which the background has been cut away several centimeters.

Some of the art appears unfinished, but much of it is poorly preserved and difficult to interpret. Erosion seems to have reduced the edges and angles of some pieces to soft curves that give the figures amoebalike qualities. A popular practice that has surely contributed to the destruction of the reliefs is outlining the figures with chalk or other soft, light-colored stone to enhance the visibility during modern visits. This causes alterations in surface color and even affects surface relief in a cumulative way, gradually destroying the original lines of the image and replacing them with modern visitors' conceptions of them.

## THE IDEAL CHOTA CHULLPA

The ideal Chota *chullpa* monument (see Fig. 7.1, Photo 7.3; see also Photos 7.13, 7.14) that I reconstruct had a small base of rectangular plan, ranging from 3.5 to 4.5 m long and 2 to 2.5 m wide. The walls varied from about 0.5 m to almost a full meter in thickness at the bottom and thinned toward the top. The building tapered as it ascended. The floor plan seems to prefer an orientation to cardinal directions, but there is considerable variation, perhaps for topography. The monument reached 7 to 8 m tall and consisted of four floors. Each floor had a single entrance to the outside, from 50 to possibly as much as 90 cm wide, but more commonly in the narrow range, and from 50 to 70 cm high. The door sill was level with or somewhat above the floor.

Two *chullpa* variants can be identified on the basis of doorway disposition (Fig. 7.3). The more common Type A *chullpa* had each of its four entrances in a different side of the building, with the first floor (east) opposite the second floor (west) and the third floor (north or south) opposite the fourth (south or north). Consequently the doorways rotate around the building, but not in a continuous spiral. Rather, the pattern alternates in zigzag (see Fig. 7.3, bottom). The small sample of Type A *chullpa*s has the longer axis of the building in a more or less north-south direction, with the first floor doorway facing east (ranging from southeast to northeast). The less common Type B *chullpa*, definitely represented by only the Condorcaga monument, had all the doors in the same wall, the south. (This is based on the first and second floors only as the third and fourth are now missing.) Significantly, the doorways are in the short axis of the building (Fig. 7.5).

The ground floor was simply of dirt, but upper floors consisted of one to four large stone slabs, 20 cm or more thick, inserted into the ma-

228 • MUMMIES AND MORTUARY MONUMENTS

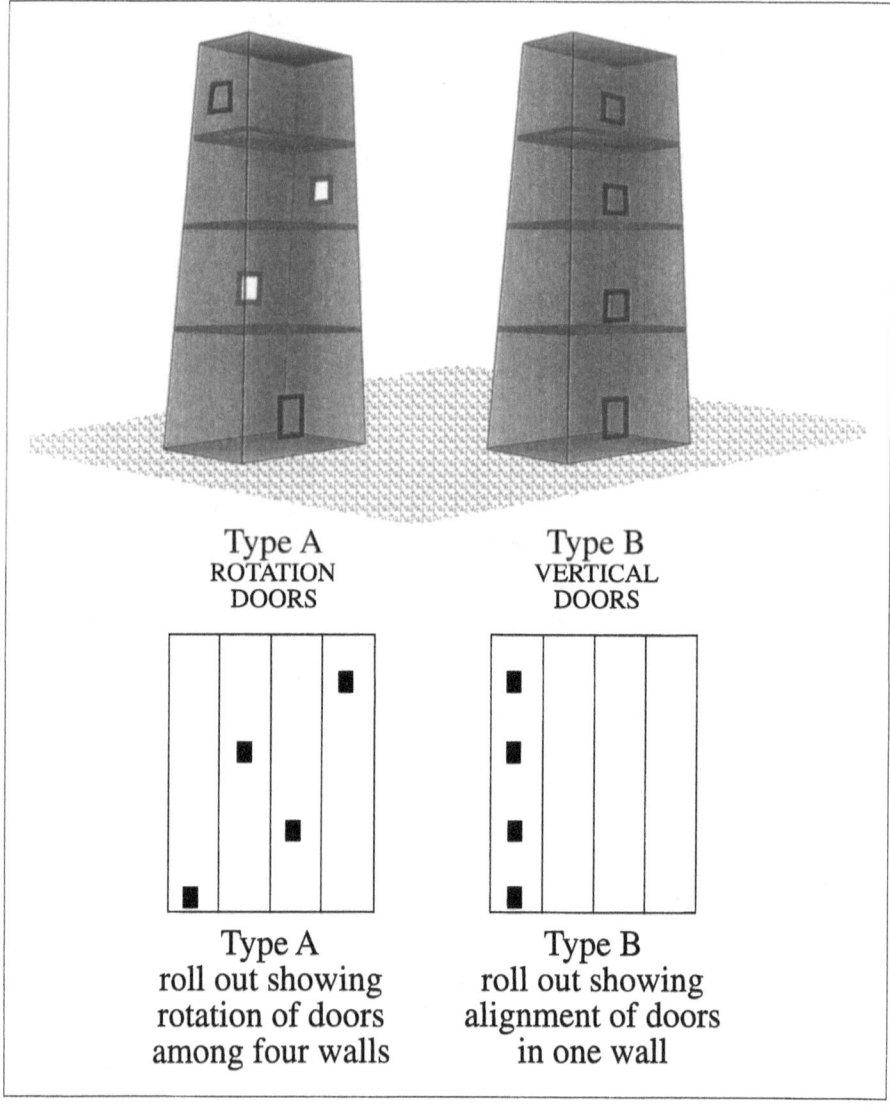

Figure 7.3. Wire Frame Perspective of *Chullpa* Types (drawn by W. H. Isbell on the basis of field notes, 1991)

sonry of the walls. Corbels were not employed, and the technological limitations of these floors probably constrained the dimensions of the rectangular floor plans, especially the maximum dimension of the short axis. No roof is preserved enough to fully determine the original form, but on the best-preserved *chullpa* at Chetilla large slabs cap the fourth floor and a few stone blocks preserved on their top suggest a paving that may have been more or less flat. That is how I have reconstructed the ideal *chullpa* in my drawing, though it would not surprise me if the stone blocks on the top counter balanced a projecting stone cornice or eaves of thin, flat rocks that would have helped protect the sides and foundation of the building from frequent rains. Excavations around the bases of a few of the *chullpa*s should show whether slabs of the appropriate shape and size have fallen, to collect there.

Sometimes one or more of the entrances to an upper floor, the third floor in the reconstructive illustration (Fig. 7.1, Photo 7.14), may have a stone sill projecting beyond the wall, forming a small porch or balcony.

The heights of the floor levels within *chullpa*s vary, even within the same monument, and I cannot discern a pattern based on the few well-preserved monuments in my sample. The first floor room of the well-preserved *chullpa* at Chetilla is 2.05 m high inside, while the second, third, and fourth floors are 1.66, 1.2, and 1.48 m, respectively. The first floor of the well-preserved La Torre *chullpa* is 0.96 m, while the second and third floors are 1.65 and 1.84 m, respectively, with the fourth floor impossible to determine.

There are stains of red on two of the buildings, most apparent on inner walls of rooms, and a yellowish color on one of the sculptures. This may imply that the *chullpa*s were painted or perhaps even plastered and painted. If so, red was apparently the preferred color. However, it is wise to remember that the *chullpa*s of Chota have been inspected by hundreds and perhaps thousands of visitors over the centuries since they were constructed. Just as their current poor condition probably relates to deliberate robbing of sculptures and building stones, color stains may represent activities of recent visitors rather than original conditions.

## CONDORCAGA

The Condorcaga *chullpa* is on the upper northern side of the Chotano Valley (see Map 7.2, Figs. 7.2 and 7.4–7.6, Photos 7.2 and 7.4–7.7), far enough back from the lip of the valley to obstruct the panoramic view of the basin where the modern city of Chota is located. Shady and Rosas (1976) reserved the name Condorcaga for a nearby area of valley slope where they found surface artifacts and called the location of the *chullpa* Churucancha. The *chullpa*, which seems to have stood on a low platform with a companion building about 2.5 m to its east

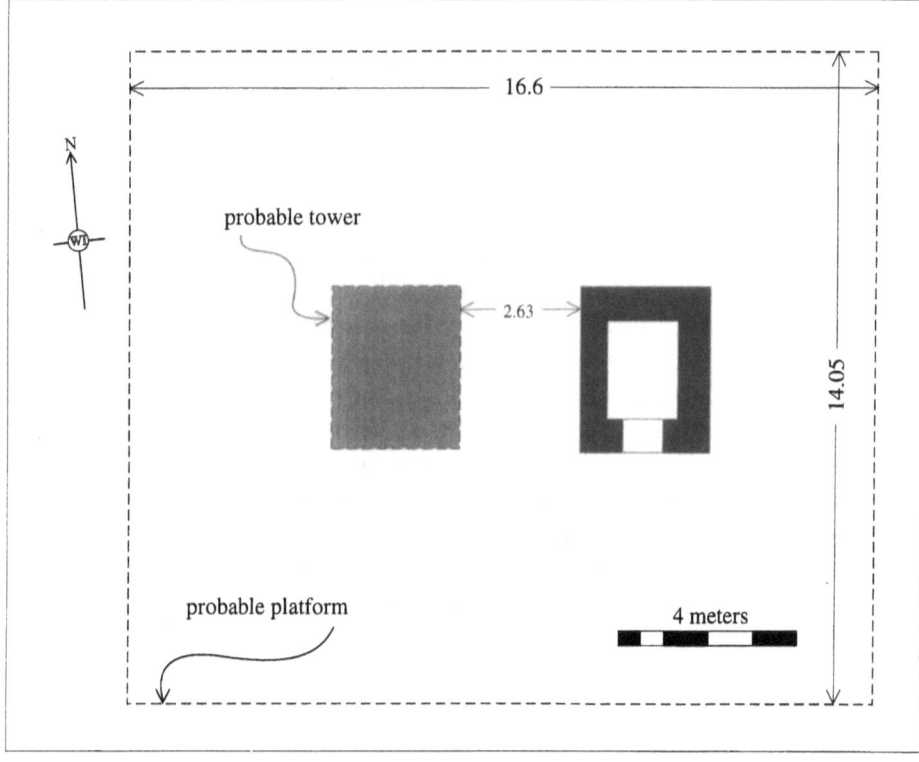

Figure 7.4. Platform and *Chullpa* at Condorcaga (drawn by W. H. Isbell on the basis of field notes, 1991)

(Fig. 7.4)—perhaps another *chullpa*—is isolated and neither other architecture nor diagnostic ceramics were found in the vicinity. It was constructed in an area of natural rock outcrops that may have provided the building stone. This monument is less prominent in the rolling uplands than are the other *chullpas* I visited, although the south-facing entrances are toward the valley (Photo 7.4). Today a foot trail between the towns of Chota and Cutervo passes close by, a peasants' homestead is located only 50 m north of the *chullpa*, and there are cultivated fields nearby. In the immediate area of the site the soil seems to be too thin for cultivation, and there are many rock outcrops. However, a thick scrub vegetation obscures any other traces of prehistoric occupation, so while I doubt that there was a community immediately surrounding this *chullpa* I cannot reject the possibility. I would be more inclined to

Photo 7.4. Condorcaga *Chullpa* Showing Aligned Doorways. The Condorcaga *chullpa* seen from the south reveals doorways to the first and second floors directly above one another. Sculpture A is on the lintel above the lower doorway.

guess that in the precolumbian past the settlement pattern was similar to that of today, with homesteads and fields widely dispersed across the landscape.

Only the first and second floors of the Condorcaga *chullpa* are preserved today, and the entrances were both in the south face, one above the other (Fig. 7.5, Photo 7.4). There is a very small lip projecting from the sill of the second floor entrance, probably representing a tiny porch. The inside of the *chullpa* is now so full of fallen stone that its technology and interior dimensions could not be determined with accuracy. In spite of its poor condition, Condorcaga possesses diagnostic long and short work corners and block masonry with greater vertical than horizontal spaces. It also has important relief figures on the larger stones, including both of the entrance lintels, a feature unique to this *chullpa*. Only Condorcaga's lower lintel figures are well enough preserved to be drawn (Fig. 7.6A).

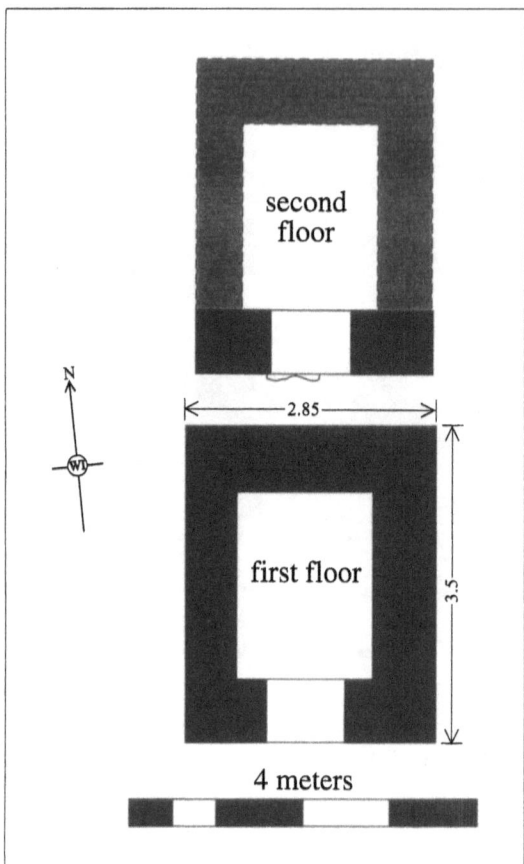

Figure 7.5. Condorcaga Tower 1 (drawn by W. H. Isbell on the basis of field notes, 1991)

On the north side of the Condorcaga *chullpa* is a carving of birds attacking a human, especially the head, that I discussed above as unfinished (Fig. 7.2, Photos 7.2, 7.7). The body of the bird in the upper left as well as parts of the human figure are defined by fine lines, but the bird's head and the human head in the center of the illustration are in relief formed by removing the background stone. The wing of the bird in the upper right is incompletely defined, as are the bird in the lower right and other parts of the sculptural representation. I conclude that this figure was begun late in the use history of the *chullpa* and that the monument was abandoned before the representation was completed. Consequently, I infer that this and many of the other relief figures were made after the *chullpa* was constructed, probably at different times during its history.

The theme of a human surrounded by and being pecked by birds is diagnostic of the Early Intermediate Period, appearing in the art of both Moche (Lavallée 1970: Plate 32d) and Recuay (Grieder 1978: Figs. 147, 151; Lumbreras 1974b, Fig. 125 lower left). Further stylistic similarities link the Chota example with Moche and Recuay, strongly implying an Early Intermediate Period date for this sculpture on the Condorcaga *chullpa*.

THE OPEN SEPULCHERS OF CHOTA-CUTERVO • 233

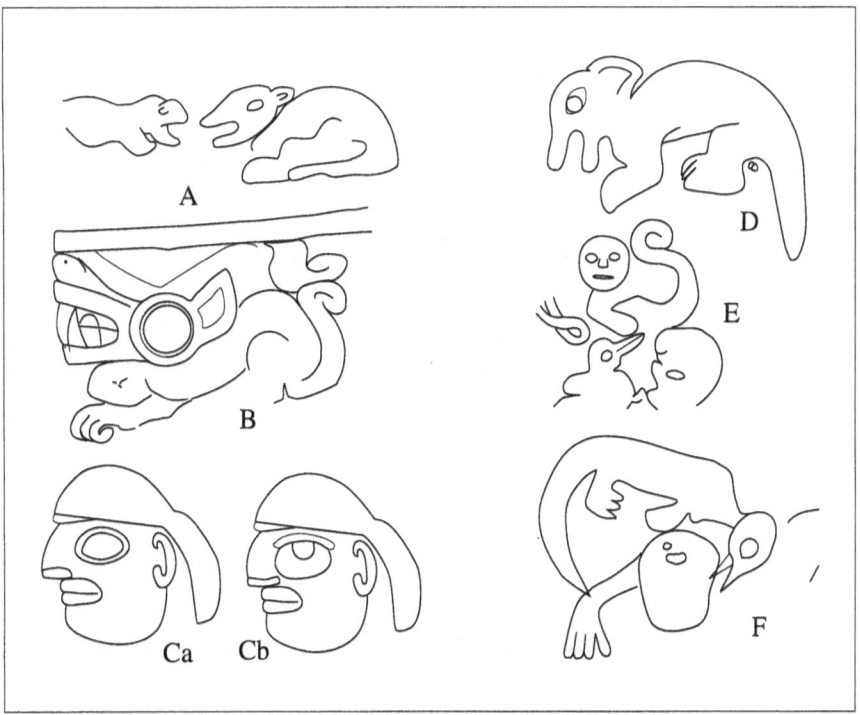

Figure 7.6. Condorcaga Relief Sculptures (drawn by W. H. Isbell on the basis of field notes, 1991)

On the east face of the *chullpa* is a figure I consider to be a feline with salient teeth (Fig. 7.6B). It may have a head ornament or crest and is obviously related to a very similar Recuay cat (Grieder 1978: Figs. 156, 157, 163, 164, 165). Moche has a comparable feline (Lapiner 1976: Figs. 282–286), and so does Vicús (Banco Popular del Perú 1979: 46, 93, 101). Interestingly, in Recuay the feline is usually shown with an elaborate head ornament or crest. This crest often appears on the feline in Moche (Lavallée 1970: Plate 81; Lapiner 1976: Fig. 252; and Banco Popular del Perú 1979: 150, 151, 170), sometimes with a crescent moon (Lavallée 1970: Plate 82). In this form—crested feline or Moon Animal—Karen O. Bruhns (1982) argues that the same feline appears at San Augustín, Colombia, implying an Early Intermediate Period date for at least some of the Colombian sculptures. If she is correct, the crested feline had a very wide distribution in the central and north Andes during the Early Intermediate Period, appearing in this and several other variants on the Chota-Cutervo *chullpa*s.

On the same block as the crested feline is a human head in profile (Fig. 7.6C). I offer two alternative constructions of the eye, one based on my photographs and the other based on a photo published by Shady and Rosas (1976: Photo 14). I cannot account for such difference unless it is due to the annoying practice of outlining or "redrawing" sculptural figures with chalk, a technique apparent in most of the Shady and Rosas photographs. The pointed-end oval eye comes from the Shady and Rosas publication and is consistent with much Early Intermediate Period art, such as profile Moche Moon Animals (Fig. 7.6C-*a*), while my reconstruction with the upward-looking pupil looks more Chavinoid (Fig. 7.6C-*b*). Shady and Rosas suggest that the head is wearing a fox skin cap, a feature often associated with coastal culture and mentioned by extirpation of idolatries documents in relation to mortuary celebrations.

Also on the east face of the Condorcaga *chullpa*, on a corner stone above the former figures, is an animal with a droop ear, possibly another feline or perhaps a dog or fox (Fig. 7.6D, Photo 7.5) that is similar to certain Recuay figures (Donna McClelland, personal communication, 1991; Grieder 1978: Figs. 131, 132). Its distinctive ear reminds one of the Middle Horizon droop ear. Perhaps this ear distinguishes an animal that is different from the feline with upward-pointing ear. The position of the tail is also unlike that of felines with upright ears, for it points down and has no curve. The edges of the sculpture are ill defined, soft, and rounded, leaving me uncertain whether the figure is badly eroded or unfinished—or perhaps both. An amorphous figure (Fig. 7.6E, Photo 7.6) from the west side of the *chullpa* is difficult to interpret but may also relate to Moche iconography (Christopher Donnan, personal communication, 1991), which includes some complex and multifigured scenes reminiscent of this. Another from the west face (Fig. 7.6F, Photo 7.6) also defies my ability to make sense of the preserved images. Perhaps it is both unfinished and eroded.

## NEGROPAMPA

The Negropampa *chullpa* is located in the south end of the basin of Chota, on the divide between the Chotano and the Bambamarca valleys

Photo 7.5. Condorcaga *Chullpa*, East Side, Sculptures B, C, and D

(see Map 7.2). Shady and Rosas (1976) recognized two names, Negropampa and Andamayo. The site is a moderate promontory partway up the valley side, where it has a commanding view of the immediately surrounding lands as well as the open valley. Only one *chullpa* is in evidence, although there are level areas and patterning in the positions of large stones that suggest a small ceremonial area. I suspect that the stones for the *chullpa* were quarried from the promontory and shaped here, which probably accounts for some of the modifications to the natural form of the Negropampa hillock, and further study would almost certainly confirm terraced courts and assembly areas.

Ceramics are present around Negropampa, but scarce, and I collected only a handful of undecorated body sherds useless for stylistic

Photo 7.6. Condorcaga *Chullpa*, West Side, Sculptures E and F

comparisons. Furthermore, there are numerous peasant houses within a few hundred meters of the site and many cultivated fields, so human activities have probably been considerable and continuous since the *chullpa* was built.

Only the ground floor of the Negropampa *chullpa* and part of the second floor are preserved (Fig. 7.7, Photos 7.8 and 7.9). While many of the stones seem nicely shaped, vertical spaces between them are considerable. This prompted me to consider whether they had separated by a process like settling in the foundation. To determine this I drew each block into the computer independently as it appeared in a photograph of the east side of the building, which has the ground floor doorway. Then I pushed the blocks together on the computer screen, leveling some stones and especially the large broken block in the upper right (Photo 7.8). What I found was that in order to tighten the fit of the blocks in the east face of the monument enough to significantly reduce the size of the vertical fissures two blocks had to be compressed to a centimeter or

Photo 7.7. Condorcaga *Chullpa*, North Side, Unfinished Sculpture. The north side of the Condorcaga *chullpa*, showing the sculpture in Fig. 7.2 and Photo 7.2.

two less than their actual size. While this can be done with computer drawings, it cannot be done with stone constructions. Consequently, I conclude that rather wide vertical spaces between blocks were an original feature of this *chullpa* and its masonry style.

This conclusion introduced another possibility: were the stones robbed from an earlier monument and reused? Some distinctively polygonal stones in the east face seemed very well shaped but did not fit their neighbors accurately. Could they have been taken from an earlier monument, perhaps characterized by a slightly different masonry style, and reused in the *chullpa*? Of course, if this were the case it would also be necessary to question whether the stones brought from earlier monuments were already decorated with relief sculptures. I sought to test this by identifying all the blocks that on the basis of their form and finish seemed to distinguish themselves as candidates for a slightly different style. Then I removed these blocks from their architectural matrix and tried to fit them together—on the computer screen, of course—rather

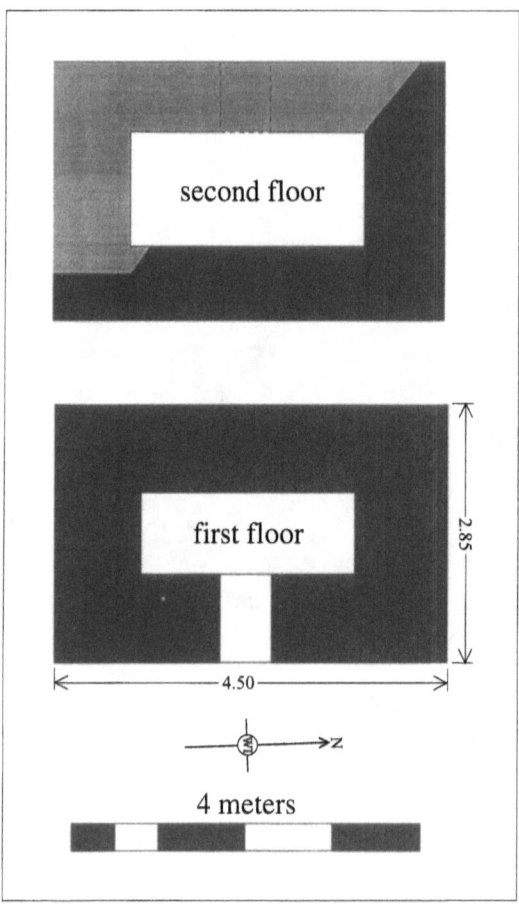

Figure 7.7. Negropampa *Chullpa* (drawn by W. H. Isbell on the basis of field notes, 1991)

like pieces of a jigsaw puzzle. I failed to find any better fits. While this does not absolutely eliminate the possibility that some blocks might be stones from earlier monuments, perhaps characterized by polygonal block construction, I concluded that Chota *chullpa* masonry, and sculpture, belongs to its own tradition. First, there is no hint of an earlier polygonal masonry tradition at Pacopampa or elsewhere in the Chota region. Second, I was unable to achieve better fits among the more polygonal stones of Negropampa. Third, the four *chullpa* sites that have been studied are so similar in their masonry, including features like the rather broad vertical fissures between stones, the occasional irregularity of predominantly rectangular masonry blocks, and the long and short work corners, that the independence of this tradition must be recognized. I infer that the blocks were prepared for the Negropampa *chullpa*.

Four sculptural figures and a possible fifth were observed on the ruined base of the Negropampa *chullpa* (Photos 7.8 and 7.9, Fig. 7.8). These sculptures distinguish themselves from Condorcaga by employing more of an incised line technique and less excision of the background. Two well-preserved reliefs and the possible additional figure are located on the east wall where the doorway of the ground floor is

Photo 7.8. Negropampa *Chullpa*, East Side, Sculptures A and B

(Photo 7.8). Two more figures are on the north wall (Photo 7.9). The other walls have so few blocks standing above the modern ground surface that no sculpture can even be expected. I suspect that stone robbery rather than natural destruction accounts for nearly complete collapse of this spectacular *chullpa*.

On the east side of the building is a front-view face or disembodied head (Fig. 7.8A). It has concentric oval eyes, a mouth with N-shaped canines, and a domed head with a downward projecting peak in the center. The dome-shaped top of the head is separated from the eyes by a fillet or band. The nose is distinctive, appearing to be formed by a continuous sweep from the fillet, but separated from it by a deep depression at the bridge. The ears have two big lobes, one above and a second below. This icon is best interpreted as the Chota variant of a figure well known in Moche art (Donnan, personal communication, 1991; see Alva and Donnan 1993: Fig. 163, upper string; Lapiner 1976: Fig. 247) and in Vicús (Shady and Rosas 1976: Photo 7; see also Banco

Photo 7.9. Negropampa *Chullpa*, North Side, Sculptures C and D

Popular del Perú 1979: 148, 149, 160, 169). Several conventions such as the shape of the ears and the low-bridged nose clearly link Moche, Vicús, and Chota.

Also on the east side of the Negropampa *chullpa* is a profile body, apparently with down-curving tail, with a front-view face that has prominent N-shaped canine teeth, concentric-circle eyes, bilobed ears, and other features shared with the head described above (Fig. 7.8B). The figure wears a distinctive collar with pendant volutes and a headdress or coiffure with a deep groove in the middle. While the foot of the figure is human, but four-toed, the hand has three pointed fingers or claws that do not look human at all. The groove in the top of the head appears on disembodied heads in the Moche style from Sipán (Alva and Donnan 1993: Fig. 163, lower string of heads). The theme shares with poorly dated Callejón de Huaylas sculpture the profile presentation of a body with full front view of the head. It shares other stylistic details with Moche and Vicús, in the form of the ears, for example.

THE OPEN SEPULCHERS OF CHOTA-CUTERVO • 241

Figure 7.8. Negropampa Relief Sculptures (drawn by W. H. Isbell on the basis of field notes, 1991)

On the north side of the *chullpa* is a front-view, spread figure (Fig. 7.8C). I interpret the pose to represent a squatting or seated position, with elbows resting on the knees. The difference between the hands and feet parallel those of the profile-bodied front-face figure with the down-turned tail from the east wall. Like it, this figure wears a collar with pendent volutes and has a groove in the top of the head. It has prominent canine teeth, but the condition of the stone precluded me from determining whether it may have both lower and upper canines. The eyes appear to be blank circles, while the nose forms a continuous sweep with the eyebrows. The ears are bilobed but not quite like those of the former two figures. This may be significant, for Alana Cordy-Collins (personal communication, 1991) has observed that two ear forms characterize the head-shaped beads of two necklaces from Tomb 2 of Sipán (Alva and Donnan 1993: Fig 163; compare the upper and lower string of heads). Significantly, these ear forms correlate, one with a domed-head shape like the disembodied head at Negropampa and the other ear form with a head that has a groove in the top, like the profile and the squatting figures at Negropampa. I suspect that the two Negropampa figures can be identified with the same mythical personages that appear in Moche art.

The squatting figure has a crescentlike object with three ovals between its legs, perhaps male sex organs, but the form may represent a *tumi* knife suspended from the waist or even a breechcloth. This squatting position is also prominent in both Moche (Lapiner 1976: Fig. 247) and Vicús (Banco Popular del Perú: 148, 149) pottery, where a mythical personage with canine teeth is shown squatting with arms resting on knees.

The final recognizable figure at Negropampa (Fig. 7.8D), also on the north wall, depicts a feline, but it is in poor condition. Shady and Rosas (1976: Fig. 2) depicted it in a drawing, but I believe they made several errors. Like them I was unable to detect some features of this feline, and I have left sections of the drawing blank. I suspect that it had a tongue projecting from the mouth, but since I could not distinguish the lines accurately I have omitted it. This feline shares a recurved tail with the Condorcaga crested feline (Fig. 7.6B). While the end of the tail is eroded away, it almost surely depicted a second head. That is a very specific icon shared with Moche (see Photo 7.17; Patricia Lyon, personal communication, 1991; Lavallée 1970: Plates 5, 64). Still, there is a strong Vicús flavor to this cat, especially apparent in the profile of the head with its projecting nose (Lapiner 1976; Fig. 390).

## CHETILLA

Chetilla is located in the wet Cutervo drainage (see Map 7.2), partway up a lush hillside where it is highly visible and has a commanding view of the surrounding country. A magnificently preserved *chullpa* with no relief sculptures perches on a slight prominence that might have accommodated a group of worshipers (Photos 7.3 and 7.10), but vegetative cover is thick and no other remains were observed. Several hundred meters higher on the valley side, and perhaps a kilometer northeast, is another *chullpa*, which was described by Shady and Rosas (1976: 17–18: Photos 22–25, Fig. 3). We were warned that there was a nest of coral snakes in its ruins so I made no new investigations. This *chullpa*, which I have designated Tower 2, is now heavily overgrown and is poorly preserved in comparison with Tower 1. Two walls are standing slightly more than about 3 m high amidst a pile of rubble from the collapse of the other walls and upper floors. The ground floor is the only one with doorway and roof still intact. Tower 2 has a single small sculptural figure that has been identified (Shady and Rosas 1976: Photo 25, Fig. 3) that looks like a lizard with two feet, N-shaped canine teeth, a back-curved nose fillet, long tongue, and curving tail. Surrounding Tower 2 is an area replete with traces of walls and terraces, for more than half a kilometer of the valley side. Much of this has been cleared for cultivation, and several homesteads are located close by. In spite of numerous walls and other indications of environmental modifications I found only nondiagnostic sherds while walking several plowed fields.

The newly discovered *chullpa* at Chetilla, Tower 1 (Photos 7.1, 7.3, 7.10, 7.11 and Fig. 7.9), is complete from foundation to roof. It is the best representative of the form I imagine for all Chota *chullpa*s, consisting of four floors within the narrow, towerlike construction. Only the upper part of the south wall has fallen, revealing the interior chambers of the third and fourth floors, as well as their great slab floors and roofs (Photo 7.11). Curiously, one of the floor slabs of the third floor level has disappeared. Initially, I thought that the third and fourth floors communicated though this opening, but examination of the walls revealed the slot to hold the original slab. I conclude that this slab was deliberately removed and that its removal required the destruction of the south wall of the third floor and, by implication, the fourth-floor wall as well. Such large and flat slabs are frequently used in modern buildings for door lintels, and if they are wider they are popular for bridge spans. If my inferences regarding damage to this *chullpa* are correct, the only destruction not attributable to human agency is the loss of some roof stones and the collapse of a small part of the north face of the fourth floor.

The east side of the building has an entrance to the ground floor (Photo 7.1) with well-shaped lintel and jambs. Elsewhere the masonry stones are less rectangular, and the long and short work corner stones frequently retain irregular shapes. Inside the ground floor room (Photo 7.12), which is barely more than a meter wide, are traces of red paint on the big construction stones as well as the smaller infill rocks.

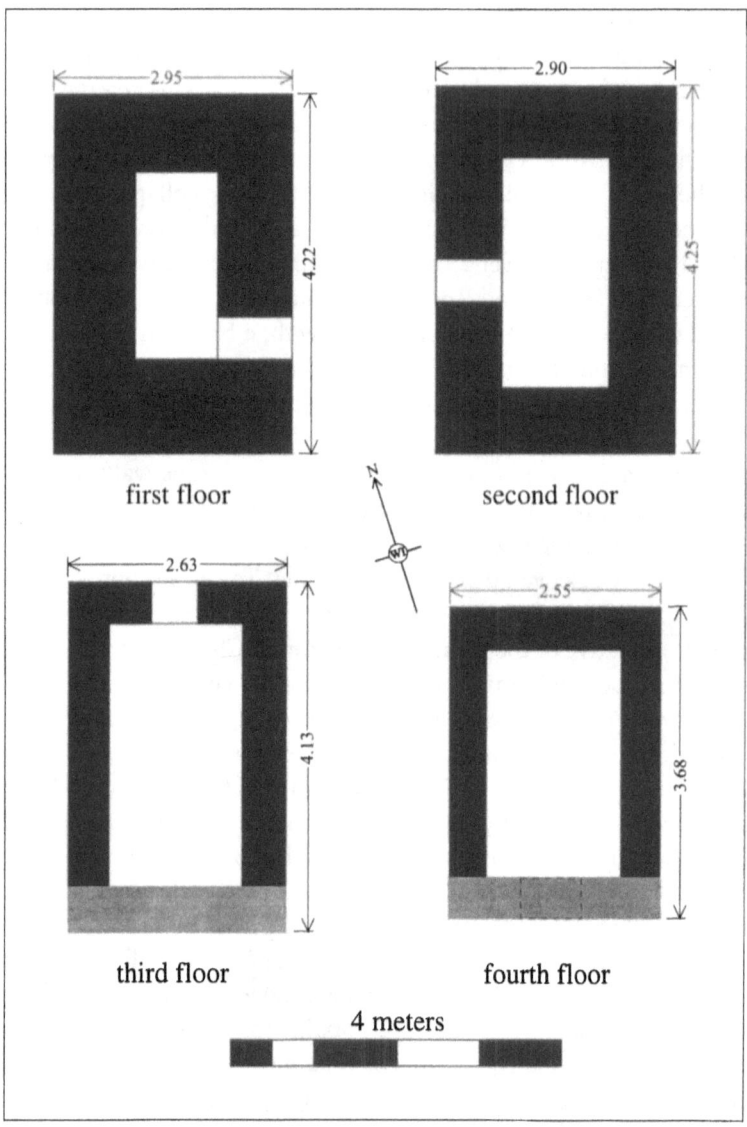

Figure 7.9. Chetilla Tower 1 (drawn by W. H. Isbell on the basis of field notes, 1991)

Plans of the four floors show the size of the building, locations of the entrances, the thinning of the walls, and the tapering of the entire building (Fig. 7.9). The second floor, with its entrance to the west (Photo 7.10), is the only interior chamber of all the Chota *chullpas* where fragments of human bones were observed. The third floor had its entrance to the

Photo 7.10. Chetilla Tower 1, West Side, Second Floor Doorway

north (Photo 7.3), and the fourth must have been open to the south (Photo 7.11).

About the Chetilla hillside are a number of other concentrations of rubble, terraces, and small platformlike features. Some may have been additional *chullpa*s, for Shady and Rosas (1976: 17) reported a total of four *chullpa* buildings at the site. I, however, was unable to confirm more than two *chullpa*s.

## LA TORRE CHIGURIP

La Torre Chigurip is also located in the Cutervo drainage (Map 7.2). The village of Chigurip is a sizable settlement in a natural little bowl.

Photo 7.11. Chetilla Tower 1, South Side. The south side of Chetilla Tower 1 shows the third and fourth floors through the collapsed wall. The entrance to the third floor is in the north face of the tower, while the entrance to the fourth floor must have been in the now missing south wall. Deep debris against the base of the *chullpa* accounts for some of this wall collapse, but a big floor slab from the third floor has been removed, and other stones may also have been taken away.

About a kilometer upslope is a hamlet called La Torre that overlooks Chigurip. Climbing to La Torre one has a nice view of the village and the surrounding valley and one passes a cave full of rock crystals. The name "La Torre" must come from the *chullpa* against which the chapel of the hamlet was built, so it might serve as the bell tower (Photo 7.13). I call this Tower 1. Three floors of this building are fully preserved, and

Photo 7.12. Chetilla Tower 1, Interior of First Floor, South End. The south end of the first floor room in Chetilla Tower 1 is just over a meter wide. It is roofed with massive stone slabs. Evidence of frequent visitors includes graffiti on many of the larger stones, so it is not surprising that no human remains have been preserved.

it appears that the old fourth floor blends into recent masonry modifying the top of the tower to contain the bell. If the ideal *chullpa* form (Type A, Fig 7.3) is correct, with a door in each of the four sides of the building, the fourth-floor entrance of the La Torre *chullpa* is against the roof of the church, facing northeast. Perhaps it serves as a passage into the bell tower from the attic or roof of the church, but I was unable to confirm this since the church was locked and the key unavailable. Plans of the floor levels show the size and orientation of the building and the

Photo 7.13. La Torre Tower 1, Southeast Face. The southeast face of Tower 1 at La Torre shows the ground floor doorway. This *chullpa* was used as a bell tower for a Christian chapel by constructing the recent building against the northwest wall of the mortuary monument.

hypothetical fourth-floor entrance oriented to the northeast (Fig. 7.10).

A small stone balcony projects below the third-floor doorway in the southwest face of the tower (Photo 7.14). This doorway has two vertical jambs with rather high-relief sculptural images that cannot now be recognized. Perhaps their details have been eroded, but they may have been unfinished. In addition, the northwest wall, with the second floor entrance, has three sculptural figures. On the lintel above the second floor entrance is a simple face (Photo 7.15, Fig. 7.11B). Traces of

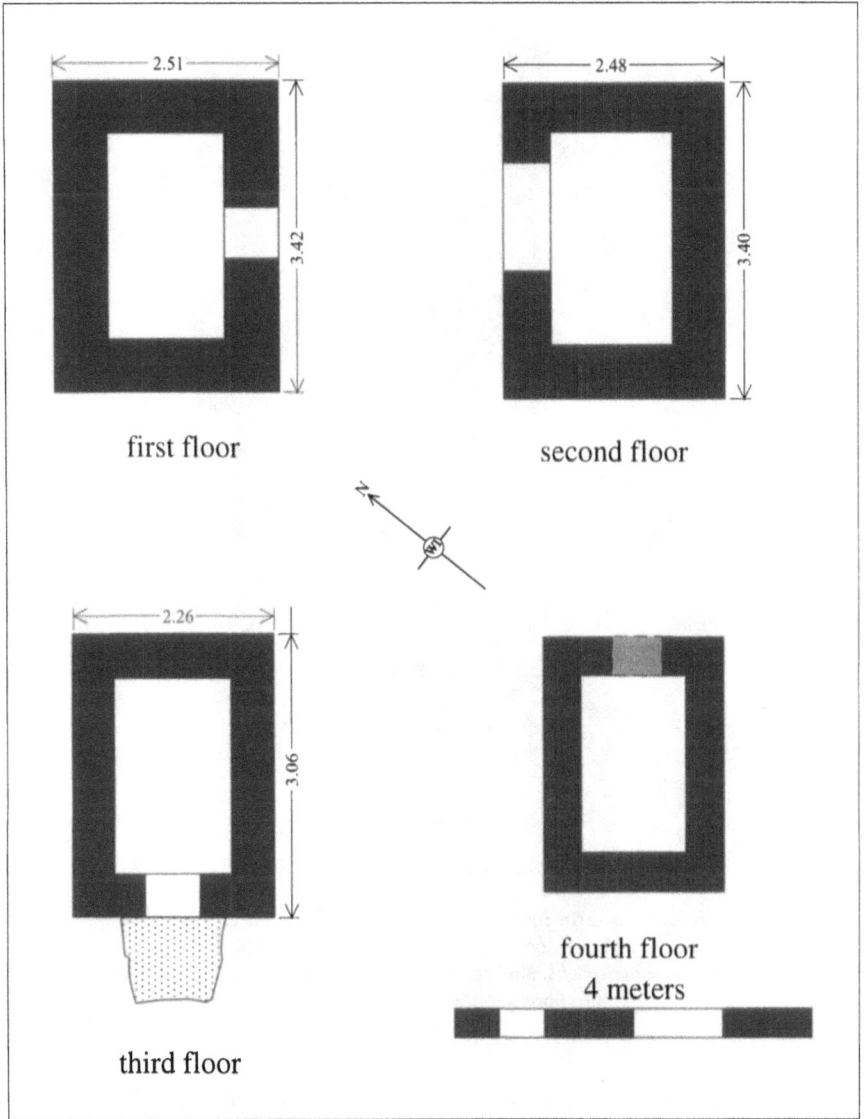

Figure 7.10. La Torre Tower 1 (drawn by W. H. Isbell on the basis of field notes, 1991)

stain on the lintel, both red and yellow, may be precolumbian. On the same wall between the second and third floor is a feline (Photo 7.16, Fig. 7.11A). Its body is represented in profile, while the head is turned to provide a full-face view. The tail curves up over the back and there is a ball at the tip of the cat's tail that surely represented a second head—be-

Photo 7.14. La Torre Tower 1, West Side. Tower 1 at La Torre from the west shows doorways to the second and third floors. Also visible are relief sculptures A, B, and C, as well as the balcony of the third floor and the sculptures on its doorjambs.

fore the sculpture was exposed to erosion—like the cat from Negropampa and the Moche felines (Photo 7.17). In its depiction of the body in profile but the head turned front face, the La Torre feline resembles many Huaráz figures (Schaedel 1948: 73, Figs. 67, 68), although it is more realistic than most Huaráz sculpture.

The final relief is a squatting profile human (Photo 7.18, Fig. 7.11C) rather crudely illustrated on the end of one of the big corner stones. I suspect that it may have been unfinished, for some of its lines are very

Photo 7.15. La Torre Tower 1, Sculpture B

angular and preliminary in appearance. The posture resembles the Negropampa front-face squatter, with knees drawn up and arms resting on the knees. This individual wears a tall pillbox hat or fez. His ear contains insufficient detail for comparisons, and the eye is a simple almond-shaped oval.

A second *chullpa* at La Torre, Tower 2, is located about a quarter kilometer from the first. Although it has been reduced to only one level (Fig. 7.12), it has what may be the region's most impressive art, especially on its west-face blocks (Photo 7.19). One interesting figure is a profile feline (Photo 7.20, Fig. 7.13A) that obviously relates to the crested felines or Moon Animal discussed above and so well known in Recuay art (Grieder 1978: Figs. 156, 157, 163, 164, 165). This feline has no crest, but it shares a different feature, a projecting tongue that may have a head at the tip, with some Moche felines (with and without tongue: see Lapiner 1976: Figs. 282–286) and also Vicús (Banco Popular del Perú 1979: 46, 93, 101).

Next to the feline is a long corner block with several representa-

Figure 7.11. La Torre Tower 1 Relief Sculptures (drawn by W. H. Isbell on the basis of field notes, 1991)

tions that may be a narrative scene (Photo 7.21, Fig. 7.13C). At the left side is a feline with profile body but front-face head. Its C-like body and both the position and form of the front and rear paws are consistent with other Chota-Cutervo felines, implying that it is another variant of a related group of icons. However, it has long eyebrows, a feature occasionally observed on profile-body front-face feline sculptures in the Callejón de Huaylas. And it appears that the top of the head was intended to be deeply grooved, like several anthropomorphic figures at Negropampa. Only lower canine teeth could be identified in the poorly preserved face, and many other features were difficult to determine. At the right end of the block is a standing human figure grasping a staff or weapon in the raised left hand. The right hand is also raised and prob-

Photo 7.16. La Torre Tower 1, Sculpture A. A profile feline, sculpture A, adorns one of the corner stones in the northwest wall of Tower 1. Although eroded, or perhaps unfinished, it may have held a trophy head in one paw and had another head at the tip of its tail.

ably grasps something flexible that may be attached to the figure in the center of the illustration, which cannot be adequately interpreted. It may be a captive, a trophy head, or perhaps a tethered llama. The front-face human figure wears a distinctive pillbox hat and there are suggestions of a shirt. The hands as well as the feet are obviously human, and the ears have no hint of the bilobed form characteristic of the toothy figures from Negropampa.

Some of the figures on Tower 2 at La Torre were either never completed or have been so badly eroded that they are now unrecognizable (Photos 7.19, 7.21, 7.22). Blocks above the narrative scene have traces of feet and hands pointed downward, as though they belonged to a human walking on all fours. A figure to the left seems to be a standing humanoid (Photo 7.22, upper center, Fig. 7.13C). A more complete standing human with prominent canine teeth was observed in the Chota Colegio Museum collection, although its provenience is not known.

Photo 7.17. Moche Ceramic Feline Sculpture (from Lothrop 1964: 165). This Moche culture modeled vessel shows a feline with a trophy head in its paws and an additional head at the tip of its tail. This theme seems to have been widely distributed in northern cultures of the Early Intermediate Period.

On the north side of Tower 2, on the same block as the narrative scene, is a pair of humans, embracing or wrestling (Photo 7.22, Fig. 7.13D). They wear pillbox hats, but with more rounded contours than the front-face human with staff. The relief is rather high, and the artist seems to have been seeking to depict depth in a way that I have not seen in other Andean stone sculpture. Embracing wrestlers is a theme shared

Photo 7.18. La Torre Tower 1, Sculpture C

with Vicús (Banco Popular del Perú 1979: 10, 40, 41) and perhaps Recuay (Lapiner 1976: Fig. 411 and Figs. 51, 52, respectively). However, there may be two separate themes here, with the Chota and Vicús examples most likely representing male wrestlers in combat, while Recuay and Tembladera representations seem to depict male and female in amorous embrace.

The east side of Tower 2, with the entrance to the ground floor, also had at least one sculptural relief, but it cannot be reconstructed for lack of detail. The south face of this *chullpa* is almost completely destroyed.

256 • MUMMIES AND MORTUARY MONUMENTS

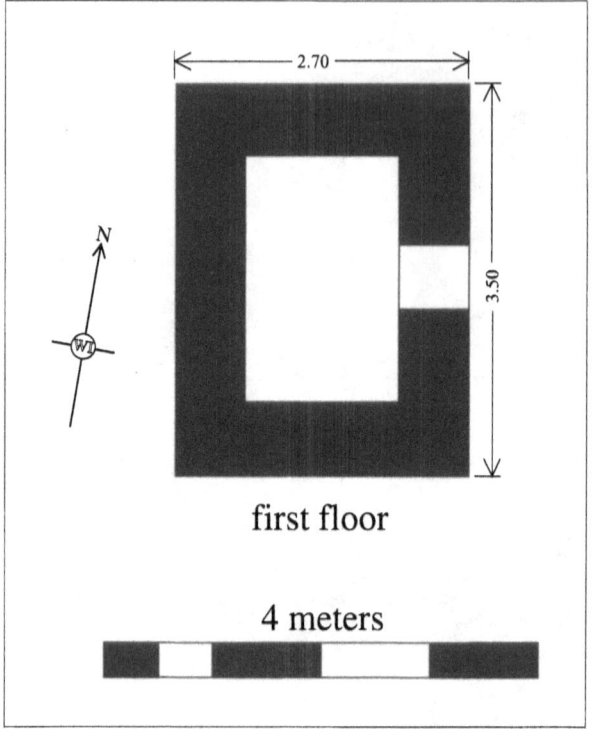

Figure 7.12. La Torre Tower 2 (drawn by W. H. Isbell on the basis of field notes, 1991)

I suspect that in its original condition this *chullpa* had many more figures and was probably pulled apart for that reason. Perhaps confirming the suspicion that Tower 2 and maybe even others were dismantled for their lovely sculpted stones is the abundance of relief-sculpted blocks in the buildings of the La Torre Chigurip hamlet. The largest collection is now in the facade of the chapel (Photos 7.23, 7.24; Fig. 7.14), but most are sufficiently eroded to make it very difficult to recognize the original representations. In fact, I was not even secure about the original orientation. Other stones are in the walls of private houses, and one is in the wall of a water well. All these are consistent with construction stones from *chullpa*s, but there is also an elongated stone with sculptured relief images set up like a stele near the hamlet plaza (Photo 7.25, Fig. 7.14). It seems too thin to have been an effective construction stone,

Photo 7.19. La Torre Tower 2, West Wall, Sculptures A, B, and C. Tower 2 at La Torre is one of the most elaborately sculpted burial monuments in the Chota-Cutervo region. Such fine art probably attracted sculpture robbers, accounting for the demolition of this building almost to its foundation. This view of the west wall shows sculptures A, B, and C as well as an undefined figure.

so perhaps its original use was not in a *chullpa* wall. Was it a monolith, and if so, how was it used? Does it belong to the Chota-Cutervo tradition, or is it perhaps something of a transition between the Pacopampa sculptures and those of the *chullpas*? Unfortunately the surviving relief is sufficiently eroded that the original depictions are difficult to define. The animal with tail curved over the back looks at home with other Chota-Cutervo sculpture, but the abstract figure is less so. However, the Chota-Cutervo sculptural tradition as defined here is still based on a small corpus of art. I should not dismiss the possibility that it included nonrepresentational themes, and perhaps even some of the La Torre chapel reliefs, which are so confusing, actually depict abstract themes.

Pottery sherds can be found in the plowed fields among the houses of the La Torre hamlet. My collection reveals a light-colored ware with

Photo 7.20. La Torre Tower 2, West Wall, Profile Feline. The profile feline is a frequent theme in Chota-Cuervo mortuary sculpture as well as Early Intermediate Period Recuay, Moche, and Vicús art.

shallow bowls decorated on the inside with two or three colors, a dark gray to black, red-brown, and a darker red-brown (Figs. 7.15, 7.16). Decoration emphasizes diagonal bands with geometric elements that bear at least general resemblance to Cajamarca IV or Cajamarca Medio ceramics (Reichlen and Reichlen [1947] 1985; Terada and Matsumoto 1985). Fragments of low ring bases probably come from the same open-bowl shapes, but jar necks and basin rims were also found. These sherds tend to support the Early Intermediate Period dating for La Torre, but without further study there is no assurance that this pottery belongs to the same period as the *chullpas*.

## MORTUARY FUNCTION AND THE CHOTA-CUTERVO CHULLPAS

Julio Tello (1940) wrote of the Chota-Cutervo *chullpa*s: "These kullpi [of Chota] . . . are not habitations or shelters; they are buildings con-

Figure 7.13. La Torre Tower 2 Relief Sculptures (drawn by W. H. Isbell on the basis of field notes, 1991)

structed expressly for funerary rites; they are mausoleums where one always finds the complex remains associated with the cult to the dead" (Tello 1940: 65, quoted in Shady and Rosas 1976: 18).

Is it possible that more than fifty years ago, when Tello discussed the Chota-Cutervo towers, they contained human remains? Indubitably, the presence of human bones is the most conclusive way to identify a

Photo 7.21. La Torre Tower 2, West Wall Sculptural Group. Such concentration of sculpture on a single block is unusual in Chota-Cutervo mortuary art. Perhaps this represents a narrative scene. The profile feline with front face resembles many other sculptures, but the human with staff as well as the figure in the middle are unusual in the currently known sample of Chota-Cutervo art.

mortuary monument, but in Chapter 4 I concluded that the modern absence of human remains cannot be taken as proof that a monument never held ancestors' bodies. Among the *chullpa*s of Chota-Cutervo we discovered human remains in the second floor of the Chetilla Tower 1. Significantly, this is the best-preserved tower, and the second floor neither has suffered deliberate destruction, as the third and fourth floors have, nor is it as accessible as the first floor, which bears many recent graffiti.

How should we interpret the scarcity of human remains in the Chota-Cutervo *chullpa*s? Several have collapsed so completely that they no longer have rooms or chambers at all. Chetilla Tower 2 and the Condorcaga *chullpa* are examples. None of these buildings has been excavated. At Negropampa and La Torre Tower 2, only the ground floors of the buildings remain. Finally, it would be surprising if precolum-

Photo 7.22. La Torre Tower 2, Northwest Corner, Sculptures C and D. This view of the northwest corner of Tower 2 at La Torre shows sculptures C and D, as well as other figures too eroded—or perhaps never completed—to be identified.

bian bodies or skeletal remains were permitted to remain in La Torre Tower 1, the bell tower of the Christian chapel. In retrospect, the presence of human remains in one floor of one of the remaining *chullpa*s may actually be a fairly positive indicator of the mortuary function inferred for the Chota-Cutervo *chullpa*s.

Sixteenth-century chronicles identified east-facing doorways, as well as small entrances, as defining features of mortuary monuments. In my attempt to define open sepulchers in the central Andes in Chapter 5 I recognized that these generalizations seemed to be based on *altiplano* burial towers. Furthermore, monuments at Quebrada de la Vaca and elsewhere that are indisputably mortuary buildings tend to open to the east, but this is not an absolute rule. The ideal Chota-Cutervo *chullpa* tower probably had four doorways, and in many cases each doorway faced a different direction. Consequently, it was impossible for "the doorway" to face east, but it seems more than coincidence that among

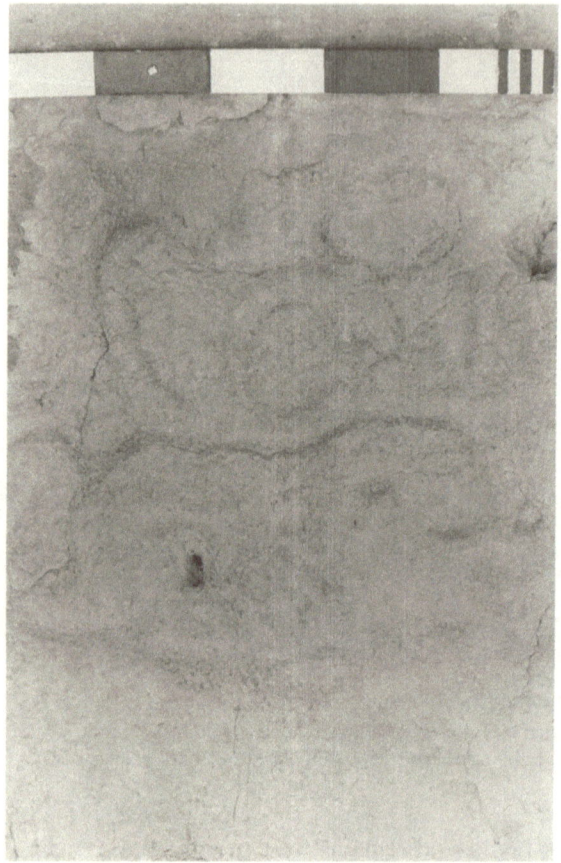

Photo 7.23. La Torre Sculptures in Modern Buildings. Sculptures almost certainly robbed from mortuary monuments like Tower 2 are common in La Torre buildings, especially the facade of the chapel. This figure, which remains unidentified, is illustrated in Fig. 7.14C.

the Type A *chullpa*s four have their ground-floor doorway oriented toward the east. Only the single example of a Type B *chullpa*, Condorcaga, has all of its doorways facing south.

Small doorways are common in mortuary monuments, but the study of Quebrada de la Vaca showed that this is not an absolute criterion either. Entrances to the Chota-Cutervo *chullpa*s are usually small and

Photo 7.24. La Torre Sculpture in Modern Chapel Facade. This sculpture, located in the facade of the chapel of La Torre, is illustrated in Fig. 7.14B.

quite difficult to enter. They range from 50 to 70 cm high and from 50 to as much as 90 cm wide, but it is clear that jamb stones have been removed from several of the wider entrance casings, for these broad doors are off center in the building faces, and the surviving jamb stones are not well shaped or finished. Comparing the third floor entrance visible in Fig. 7.3 with the upper entrance of Fig. 7.4 shows that a jamb stone has been removed from the right side of the doorway of the latter building, and perhaps from both sides of the entrance in Fig. 7.15. Consequently, the doorways of the Chota *chullpa*s were quite small, supporting the probability that the buildings were intended for mortuary functions.

According to the sixteenth-century chroniclers, mortuary monuments tended to be better built and to have more effort lavished on them than residential architecture. They were sometimes raised on platforms and often associated with terraces or plazas where worshipers could

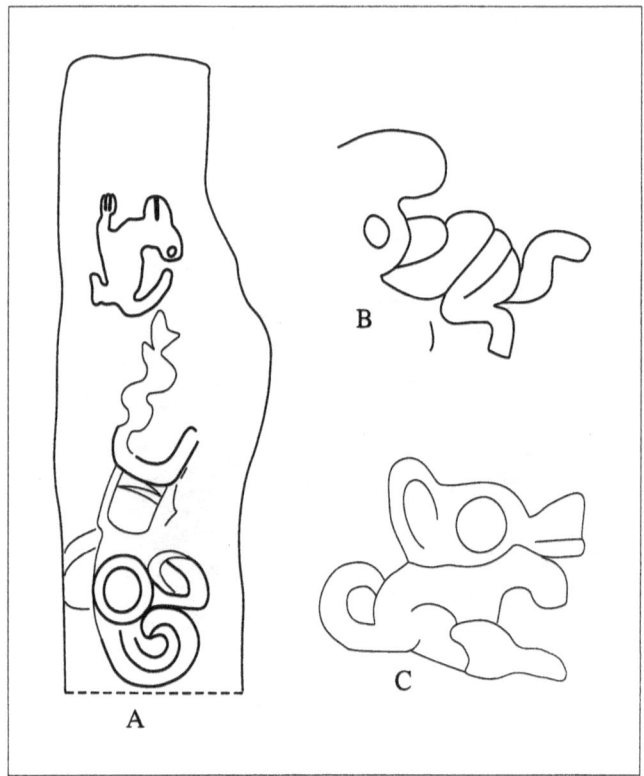

Figure 7.14. La Torre Sculptures (drawn by W. H. Isbell on the basis of field notes, 1991)

congregate. Locations for burial monuments varied from culture to culture. Sometimes they were within, or attached to, houses. Some burial monuments were in the communities of the living, but in separate buildings. Sometimes the dead had their own little communities, overlooking the hamlets and villages of the living. Sometimes the tombs were in the distant fields and pastures, individually or in groups. In at least some cases the tombs were part of a ceremonial center that was the heart of the polity, as in the case of Cuzco.

The Condorcaga tower was probably built on a platform. Negropampa is sited on a promontory where traces of terraces and courts suggest a small ceremonial complex. Chetilla has walls and terraces in much

Photo 7.25. La Torre Stelelike Sculpture. This stelelike slab, illustrated in Fig. 7.14A, has been placed upright near the plaza of La Torre. Its shape is unusual for masonry blocks used in Chota-Cutervo mortuary monuments. Perhaps it is transitional, relating to an earlier sculptural style such as that of Pacopampa.

of the area that has been sufficiently cleared to reveal ruins less massive than the big towers. Only the La Torre towers were not associated with additional architecture that might be of ceremonial nature. But the La Torre monuments are found attached to the modern chapel and among modern houses, so it is likely that prehistoric terraces and landscaping walls would have been obliterated by recent construction activities.

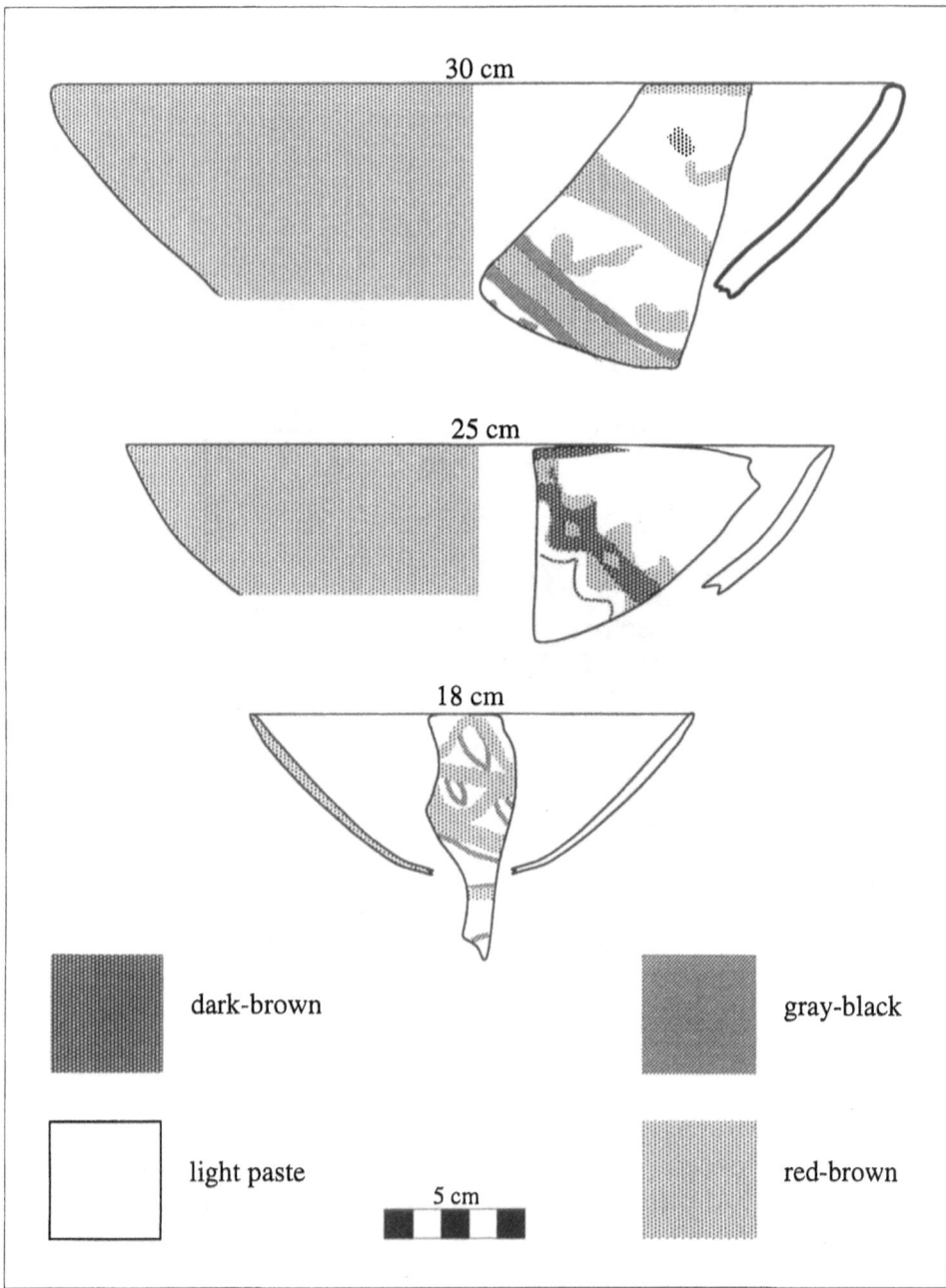

Figure 7.15. La Torre Decorated Ceramics (drawn by W. H. Isbell on the basis of field notes, 1991)

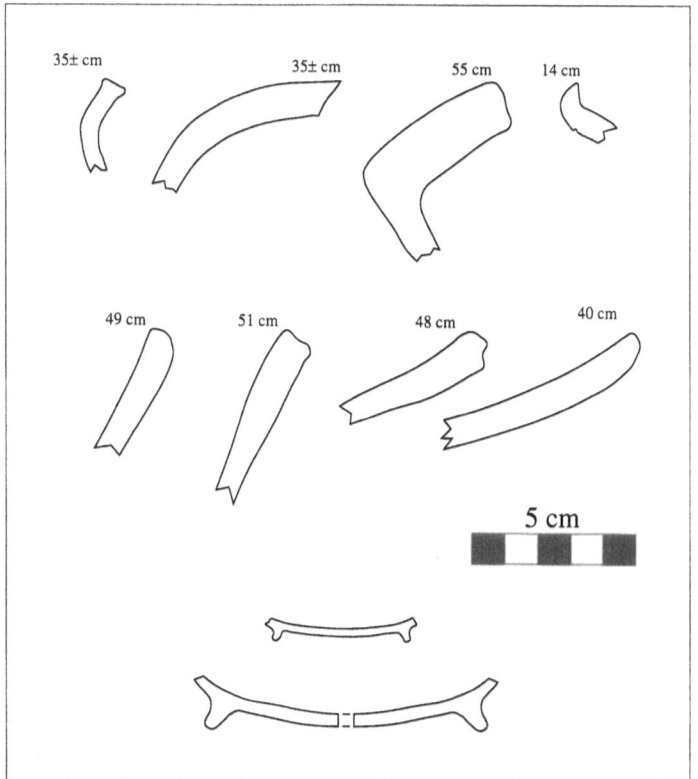

Figure 7.16. La Torre Plainware Ceramics (drawn by W. H. Isbell on the basis of field notes, 1991)

At La Torre there were several *chullpa* monuments, perhaps within a residential community or perhaps on the edge of it. Chetilla probably also included several towers, but there is less evidence of occupation. Perhaps it represents a ceremonial center only periodically visited. Negropampa was almost surely an isolated ceremonial complex, and so was Condorcaga, although they may have had residential homesteads and hamlets scattered nearby.

The impressive masonry of the Chota-Cutervo *chullpa*s distinguishes itself, expressing a special, nondomestic nature. Far more effort was lavished on shaping blocks, selecting and transporting large stones, and creating distinctive long and short work corners than would have been necessary for a functional building. Finally, decorating the larger stones with sculptural figures, many of apparent mythical origin, reinforces the separation of these buildings from the activities of domestic life.

The small floor area, more or less low ceilings (that range from 0.96 m in the lowest example to 2.05 m in the highest, but average 1.54 m), and small doorways also support the inferred mortuary function. Any activities that required several persons would have been virtually precluded. On the other hand, the height of the Chota-Cutervo *chullpas*, which must have been intended to draw attention to them, would have made any kind of storage that required periodic access to and movement of heavy goods extremely inconvenient. Access to upper floors requires tall ladders. Negotiating entry and exit through the tiny doorways from the top of a ladder demands considerable athletic skill.

The final aspect of mortuary monuments that I want to consider is the regional cultural context for the Chota-Cutervo *chullpas*. In Chapter 5, probable mortuary monuments to the south of the Chota-Cutervo region were discussed. While it is unfortunate not to be able to evaluate all the sites through personal visits, to develop a critical new synthesis of mortuary monuments in the north highlands, there can be little doubt that the Marañón Valley, including east and west tributaries, and parallel valleys such as the Callejón de Huaylas are characterized by megalithic mortuary monuments that often tend to be tall and multistoried buildings. The Chota-Cutervo *chullpas* seem to be one variant among many, which include two- to four-storied mortuary towers from Uchumarca and Utcubamba, three-storied examples at Tinyash, and possibly four- or more storied buildings among the Tantamayo and Rapayan remains. In the Callejón de Huaylas there are multistoried chamber buildings as well as smaller, single chamber structures. I have excavated human remains from one of the smaller types (Isbell 1991a), and human remains are said to have been found in some others. Huamachuco also has tall towers believed to have been mortuary *chullpas*. One mausoleum, again a rather small example, was excavated (T. Topic and J. Topic 1984) and found to contain human remains, as well as burned textiles, apparently from mummy bundles. More significantly, radiocarbon dates from this Cerro Amaru *chullpa* show that this mortuary monument was built and used through the late half of the Early Intermediate Period and into the Middle Horizon.

In the Junín-Tarma region and in the western Andes above Lima the identification of often multistoried monuments as mortuary relies more on old reports by Villar Córdova and Hrdlička than on systematically published archaeological research. Even at Huari, frequently multifloored megalithic stone boxes can be associated with human bodies only by indirect evidence—fragmentary human bones and the luxury goods scattered about the exteriors of these buildings when they were looted in the past.

Systematic and detailed evaluations of probable mortuary monuments in the Marañón Valley as well as other areas of the central Andes are desperately needed. But in the meantime it seems that the weight of the evidence is too great to ignore. There appears to be a long, important, and variable tradition of mortuary monuments from the Junín Pampa and surrounding valleys in the south to the bend of the Marañón in the north. The Chota-Cutervo *chullpa* towers fit very comfortably within this tradition. Throughout the region there are monumental mortuary buildings that tend to be very tall, with two, three, four, and perhaps more floors. While these big buildings capture most of the attention, such impressive above-ground tombs probably coexisted with modest sepulchers, like those of Tornapampa or the little grave buildings at Tinyash.

## DATING THE CHOTA-CUTERVO CHULLPAS AND SCULPTURE

When I went to Chota I expected to find evidence discounting the Early Intermediate Period date inferred for the Chota-Cutervo *chullpa*s. Instead, I found sculptures that irrefutably confirmed that temporal assignment. Unfortunately, we still have no dates from radiocarbon and few from ceramic styles, but the sculptural remains are numerous and explicit. Sculptural depictions on the buildings consistently reveal relations to neighboring Early Intermediate Period cultures, including Moche, Vicús, and Recuay. Perhaps the most salient shared icon is the feline or the group of feline variants. Similar felines occur in Recuay stone sculpture and in the ceramics of Moche and Vicús. In some cases comparisons are quite specific, such as the second head at the end of the tail or the crested feline. Equally salient are comparisons with Moche based on anthropomorphic figures, one with domed head and canine teeth, the other with grooved head and canine teeth. The shared theme of birds attacking a human and the wrestlers in firm embrace also link the Chota-Cutervo style with Recuay, Vicús, and Moche.

Moche, Vicús, and Recuay all belong to the Early Intermediate Period, which lasted from about 200 B.C. till about A.D. 500. At least

Moche and Recuay have earlier Early Intermediate Period styles, Salinar and White-on-Red, respectively, so these cultural styles belong more to the second half of that time span. The chronological position of Vicús remains little investigated. On the basis of the Moche and Recuay relations I place the Chota-Cutervo *chullpa*s and sculptural style in the second half of the Early Intermediate Period, most likely between A.D. 200 and 500. This clearly confirms the dates obtained by Theresa and John Topic (1984) from the open sepulcher mortuary monument in Huamachuco, with radiocarbon dates from A.D. 330 to 590. The latest date from this suite probably relates to the Middle Horizon pottery found in part of the mausoleum, associated with the final use of the mortuary building.

## CHOTA-CUTERVO CHULLPA *TRADITION* AND AYLLU *ORGANIZATION*

I have reached the conclusion that the Chota-Cutervo *chullpa*s were open sepulchers where ancestor mummies were stored. This is the kind of mortuary practice on which *ayllu* organization was based in the sixteenth century. In addition to embodying itself around rituals venerating a visible and handled ancestor mummy who was at once the "owner," multiplier, and justification for community resources, I have argued that the *ayllu* consisted of a social group, with communal resources, and a hierarchical organization in terms of a kinship idiom.

Successful construction of one of the Chota-Cutervo monuments documents the existence of a social group with some degree of internal organization and identity. First, the construction of such an impressive monument required the cooperation of a significant social group, although it may not have been a particularly large group. I suspect that the construction required no more labor than could be contributed by a pool with as few as one hundred adults, even if no more than 10 percent to 20 percent ever worked at the same time. Furthermore, the distribution of the monuments implies deliberate dispersal across the landscape. Locations on promontories with local visibility might suggest an association with land and symbolic statements about the control of fields and territory.

Second, the Chota-Cutervo *chullpa*s also have sculptural art that probably commemorated mythical and historical events significant to the group associated with each monument. We can infer a geographical landscape with numerous mortuary monuments of the same type. Some of the monuments became richly decorated, while others remained plain. The corresponding social landscape was almost certainly one with competition among basically similar groups that resulted in marked difference in relative success, including its symbolic expression. Some groups had a great deal to commemorate on the walls of their shrine, while others had little or no success to declare.

In the Huarochirí myths, among the Incas, and in the seventeenth-century extirpation of idolatries testimonies, events that were allegorized in myth and history by groups of descendants concerned claims to privileges based on descent from powerful origin figures; claims to territory based on conquests and discoveries conducted by the group's ancestor; rights to resources based on construction of canals or reclamation of lands by an ancestor; and spiritual authority based on visions and sacrifices by an ancestor who subsequently established a local shrine. I suggest that similar events were allegorized in the sculptures cut on the blocks of Chota-Cutervo *chullpa*s. The members of each group were striving to create and commemorate the pedigree and history they wished to have accepted among themselves and, perhaps even more importantly, by allied and competitive groups.

I infer that *chullpa* relief figures shared with other cultures—for example, the two anthropomorphic figures with prominent canine teeth, one with domed head and one with grooved head, shared at least with Moche and Vicús and best represented at Negropampa—refer to regionally recognized *huaca*s or deities. Comparisons from the Huarochirí myths might be Paria Caca, Huallallo Caruincho, Chaupi Ñamca, and Pachacamac. The Huarochirí myths show that such *huaca*s were recognized and revered by several ethnic groups but considered founder and patron by only one or two of the groups. The mythic exploits of the *huaca*s allegorically described relations among the diverse peoples. Mythical figures shared in the Early Intermediate Period iconography of Chota-Cutervo, Recuay, Moche, and Vicús may imply a similar situation. I would suggest that the depiction of such regional *huaca*s on one's *chullpa* probably related to claims about ultimate priorities among mythical founders of competitive ethnic groups, implying competition between ethnicities at more than a local scale. Perhaps such icons participated in the creation of rights to represent one's fellows in inter-group politics.

On the other hand, the narrative scene at La Torre Tower 2 looks like a simple victory statement. A menacing feline, possibly with a groove in the middle of its head, is at one end of this block. In Moche iconography one sees that the feline was virtually an alternative for a human warrior, often in the act of sacrificing another warrior (Alva and Donnan 1993; Donnan 1975, 1978). A human with no mythical attributes is at the other end of the same stone. Probably a male, as indicated by his shirt, this figure holds a staff or weapon in his left hand and something else, perhaps a trophy head, a captive, or a tethered llama, in the right. Another feline is located on the block adjacent to the victory scene. At this time I am hesitant to speculate whether Chota-Cutervo sculptural images on adjacent stones should be read as separate statements or perhaps linked into a single narrative. Be that as it may, the narrow end of the victory stone shows two men locked in embrace, probably wrestling. Such conflict may commemorate titanic combat that created the topography recognized as one's homeland, such as Paria Caca's struggle with Huallallo Caruincho (Salomon and Urioste 1991: 68). However, these figures lack mythical attributes such as canine teeth and lobed ears.

It is well to remember that combat between pairs, expressing individual prowess and valor, was at the heart of Moche military scenery (Alva and Donnan 1993: 129). More than a thousand years later, while in captivity, Atahualpa challenged Francisco Pizarro to a wrestling match between champions (Hemming 1970: 55). The Indian wrestler Tucuycuyuche gained the initial advantage in the single pair combat, but Spanish champion Alonso Díaz rallied and strangled his competitor, greatly enhancing the military esteem accorded the Spanish. I suspect that this *chullpa* sculpture could commemorate such combat between champions, one that the worshipers of La Torre Tower 2 claimed as a significant victory for their faction.

The scene of birds pecking a human (Photo 7.2, Fig. 7.2) found at Condorcaga seems to be a sacrificial theme. In the Moche version of this theme the human is often shown bound to a post (Lavallée 1970: Plate 32d). I infer that what is depicted is a human sacrifice, perhaps one that validated an ancestor's claim to supernatural authority by establishing a shrine and cult in his name. In the extirpation of idolatries trials we learned that Caque Poma (Zuidema 1973) was elevated to the status of *kuraka* by the Inca after giving his daughter for human sacrifice. But first he distinguished himself by organizing the construction of a multicommunity irrigation canal.

Human representations, such as the crouched figure on the La Torre Tower 1 monument (Photo 7.18, Fig. 7.11C), may represent an actual ancestor, in the flexed position so characteristic of mummies. Perhaps the human head with a hat (Fig. 7.6C) that Shady and Rosas (1976) identified as a fox skin relates to privileges reserved for members of this *chullpa* group, expressed in terms of ritual paraphernalia associated with the office. The Huarochirí myths are full of specific explanations for privileges given particular ancestors. In one sequence the *huaca* Collquiri created a great spring and dammed a lake. He taught a man of the Concha *ayllu* named Llacsa Misa to measure the elevation of the water behind the dam with stones so he would know when to open the canal and irrigate the corn (Salomon and Urioste 1991: 141). We also learn of mythical ancestors who arrived early and made important conquests, but whose brothers arrived late and their descendants therefore remained landless.

While we cannot know what the Chota-Cutervo sculptures meant to their makers I feel that this reading, in terms of the Huarochirí myths, is attractive. It presents the *chullpa*s as embodiments of long-lived social groups composed of informed actors involved in garnering privileges and advantages for themselves and their fellows.

Archaeological remains rarely reveal prehistoric kinship or its use as an idiom for organizing and ranking, but the Chota-Cutervo *chullpa*s may prove an exception. First we must seek instructions that will help us read these texts. The study of Inca and Andean kinship (Lounsbury 1964; Zuidema 1977, 1990b, 1990c) has focused much attention on a genealogical model drawn by Juan Pérez Bocanegra (1631). It depicts a male ancestor with a four generation-line of descendant sons, an identical line of descendant daughters, and information about the degree of relationship in both Spanish and Inca (Fig. 7.17).

In their pioneering studies, Zuidema and Lounsbury assumed that Pérez Bocanegra illustrated Inca or Andean kinship as he had learned about it from informants. Consequently the model should be a European effort to represent an Andean conceptualization. Recently Frank Salomon and John Rowe (personal communications, 1990) have both questioned this. They assert that Pérez Bocanegra's drawing came from a European model known in 1574 from a non-Andean context—although, of course, without the Andean faces and names that Pérez Bocanegra added to his 1631 rendition. Zuidema (1990c: 24) has responded that Pérez Bocanegra must have selected this European depiction very carefully, for it captures Andean ideology precisely. I hope to see this paradox debated to resolution, but in the meantime I will accept

Figure 7.17. Pérez Bocanegra Diagram of Inca Kinship (from Pérez Bocanegra 1631)

Zuidema's position for I find the similarities between the Pérez Bocanegra drawing and the Chota-Cutervo *chullpa*s too specific to ignore.

It is wise to remember that Zuidema, as we have seen from our discussion of his structural interpretation of the Inca dynasty and mummies in Chapter 1, argues that kinship terminology was not so much about descent as it was about confirming social status and establishing groups and classes with different rights and privileges. He shows that Inca hierarchy focused on the living king, who was addressed by noble Incas with kin terms for ancestor that recognized varying degrees of removal (Zuidema 1990b, 1990c). Persons addressing the king as great-great-grandfather (four generations' distance) belonged to a group lacking high rank. Persons allowed to use closer terms of address belonged to groups accorded greater privileges.

One of the important privileges of rank was license to marry more endogamously, and by marrying a close relative a man fathered descendants that retained the rank of the two parents rather than descending to a lower and more distant position relative to the living king because an additional generation intervened. (Remember that the Inca king's own sons by secondary, non-Inca wives did not address their father with an agnatic term but were required to use a term for a cross uncle—mother's brother—with generational distinctions added [mother's mother's brother, etc.] in accord with the boy's mother's status relative to her Sapa Inca husband.) An Inca king's sons were eligible for his title only if their mother was his full sister. Similarly, high noblemen married a half sister or a parallel cousin. Somewhat lesser nobility were permitted to marry a cross cousin, yet lesser nobility a second cross cousin, and so on. As Zuidema reconstructs the system, when a man married his father's father's father's sister's daughter's daughter's daughter (third cousin, or great-great-grandfather's great-great-granddaughter) no relationship was recognized, no prohibitions were imposed, and no status was conserved. For Zuidema, this is one of the key Andean concepts represented in the Pérez Bocanegra diagram: that up to the third cousin—or grade 4 relationship—intermarriage was subject to rules governing the formation of status groups.

Now let us explore the implications of the Pérez Bocanegra genealogical diagram for commoner *ayllu* organization and then return to the *chullpa*s of Chota-Cutervo. First, we know that marriage was supposed to be within the *ayllu*. That is, a man married a woman who belonged to the same *ayllu* to which he belonged. Second, the ideal was for a family to reciprocate the receipt of a bride with a kinswoman—ideally the groom's sister—in marriage to a man of the other group, ideally the bride's brother. This is called sister exchange by anthropologists, although another relative of the right sex and age will do just as well as a sister (or brother). Third, if marriage closer than third cousin was controlled it is apparent that an original couple would require marriage partners for their son (and daughter), son's son (and daughter's daughter), and son's son's son (and daughter's daughter's daughter) before their son's son's son's son could marry their daughter's daughter's daughter's daughter (see Fig. 7.18, a reconceptualization of Pérez Bocanegra's genealogy into a contemporary anthropological kinship diagram showing the spouses required from other families or groups within the *ayllu*). What all this means is that a minimum of three other "families" or kin groups would be required to make the endogamous *ayllu* work, if marriage was prohibited among relatives closer than third cousin. Consequently, if the *ayllu* required four intermarrying family lines or kin groups to function as an endogamous social group, the ideal *ayllu* can be modeled in terms of the potentials and the constraints that such a structure—in the context of preferential sister exchange—implies.

Andean peoples' kinship was probably based on parallel descent. Zuidema and others have concluded that the Incas and probably other Andeans recognized a form of parallel descent in which women counted their descent through women, from mother to daughter, and men counted descent through men, from father to son. This is another key Andean principle illustrated by Pérez Bocanegra in his genealogical diagram. This means the Andean kin group was unlike that with which we are familiar, because a man's sister was not part of his immediate group, for he belonged to his father's group, but she belonged to her mother's group.

Let us consider this in terms of the other constraints listed above (see Fig. 7.19). If a man and woman of the same kin group (Group A) marry (*caru* generation), their male and female children belong to the same group, the males by descent from the father and the females by descent from the mother (*collana* generation). The children of the *collana* generation cannot marry closer than third cousin, so must seek marriage partners outside their immediate kin group, although within the *ayllu*. Let us also assume and represent the ideal, brother-sister ex-

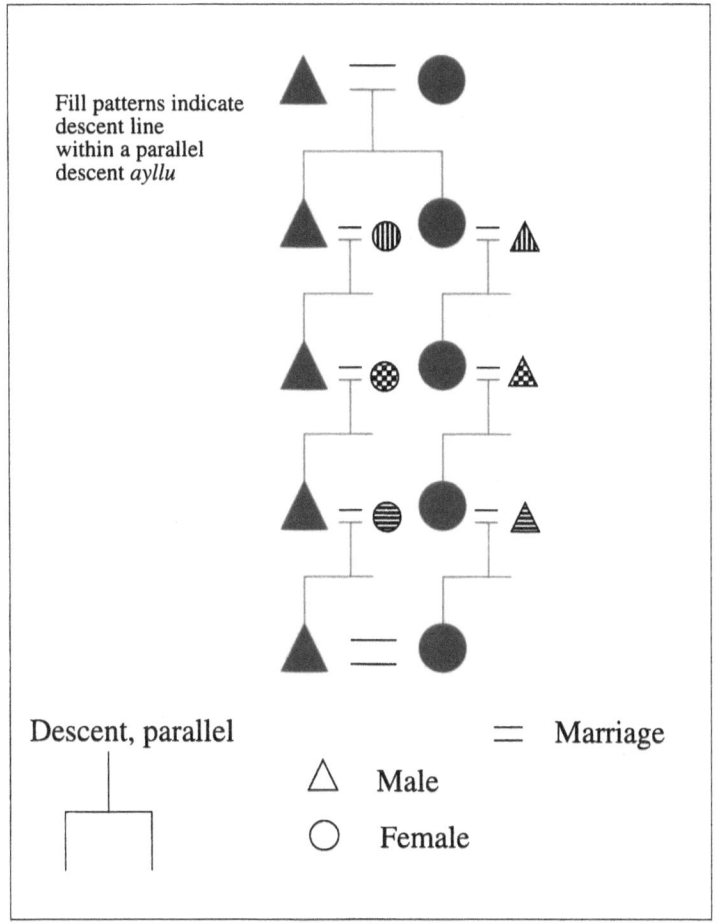

Figure 7.18. Four-Generation *Ayllu* Marriage Cycle (drawn by W. H. Isbell)

change in marriage. Once achieved, the (*payan* generation) male children of the sons belong to the same kin group (Group A), but not their sisters, who belong to their mother's kin group (Group D). On the other hand, the daughters of Group D men belong to Group A because these men all married the sisters of the males to whom they gave wives. In the next generation marriage among these first cousins is prohibited, so this set of siblings and cousins must also seek more distant spouses within the *ayllu*. In the *cayao* generation the male and female children that

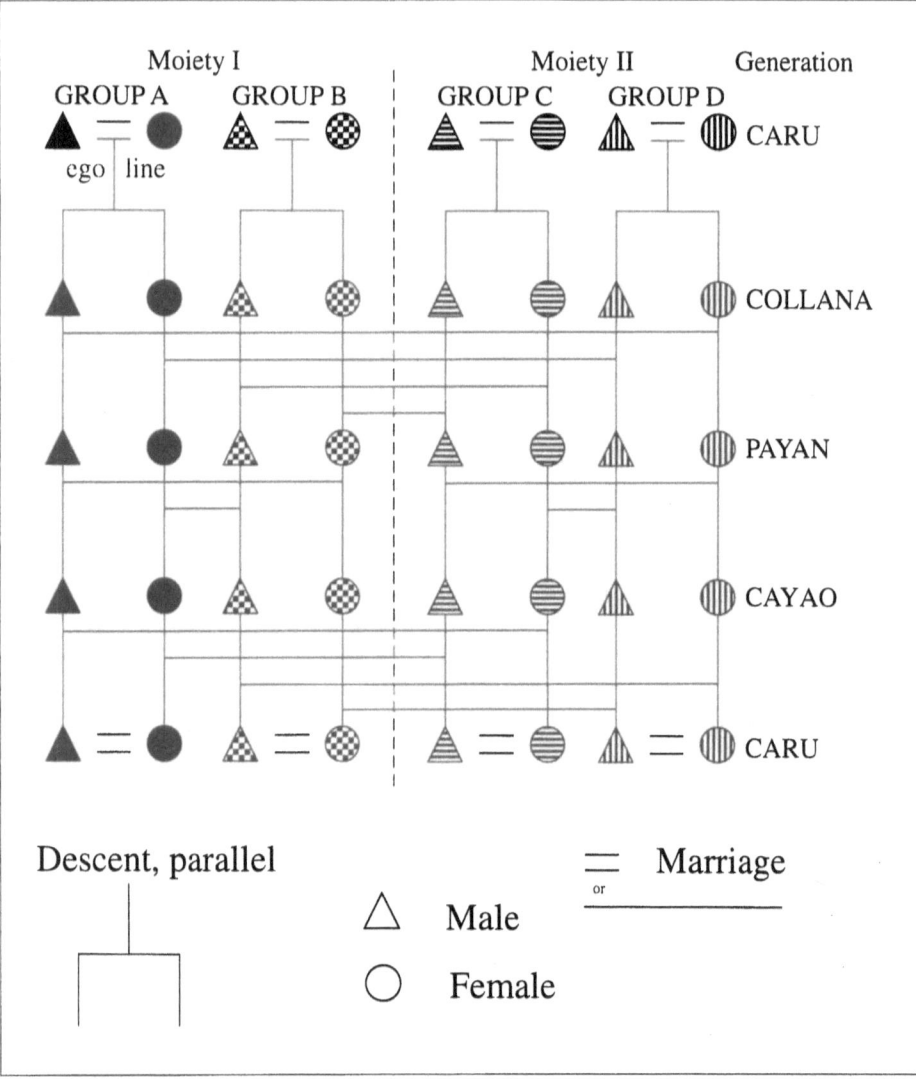

Figure 7.19. Four-Generational *Ayllu* Kinship Structure. This chart represents ideal *ayllu* organization as it was supposed to be structured by marriage alliances. The *ayllu* was to be composed of four descent lines that exchanged spouses, and marriage was to repeat the same pattern in cycles of four generations. (drawn by W. H. Isbell)

belong to Group A are second cousins. Their siblings and first cousins belong to other groups within the *ayllu*. They are all too closely related to intermarry and so must seek more distant partners, in Group C. In the next generation the males and females born into Group A are third cousins. Their siblings, first cousins, and second cousins are distributed through the other three groups of the *ayllu*. They can and, indeed, must marry one another (*caru* generation). Consequently, they repeat the "within group marriage" made by their great-great-grandfather and great-great-grandmother, and they renew a system based on cycles of four generations among four kin groups that allows the *ayllu* (at least in theory) to go on forever as an endogamous social unit.

Neither Tom Zuidema nor I mean to imply that real *ayllu* members conformed to these ideals, always marrying only in terms of the options explained above. Rather, this was the idea that furnished concepts in terms of which a less orderly reality was made universally intelligible. It was the ideal behind kin idioms that did organize the *ayllu*.

For example, examining Figure 7.19 we can see why quadripartite and dual or moiety organization was characteristic of Andean societies founded on *ayllu* organization. We see why a founder—the *caru* generation—was an essential point of reference for Andean organization modeled on the *ayllu*, but we should also see that the Andean founder was not like a European founder of a dynasty in linear, historiographic time. The Andean founder represented a relative position in terms of which others computed their places in a sequence of cycles that repeated itself after four generations. The fifth generation was equivalent to the first. In Inca society each Sapa Inca reconstructed the social universe about himself, becoming the *caru* ancestor, with three ascending agnates representing the other groups, marriage classes, or status categories, and a fourth ascending founder—equivalent to the living king—who represented the unity of the entire group. This is why Zuidema argued that each of the two living kings of Cuzco's two moieties would always have four agnatic ascending ancestors for a total of ten kings in Cuzco.

I want to show that the structure of the Chota-Cutervo *chullpa*s expresses the ideal *ayllu* model as depicted by Pérez Bocanegra and reconceptualized in Figure 7.19. The ideal *chullpa*s have four floors and four sides—corresponding with four generations and four kin groups. Furthermore, they express the two basic perspectives that everyone in an

280 • MUMMIES AND MORTUARY MONUMENTS

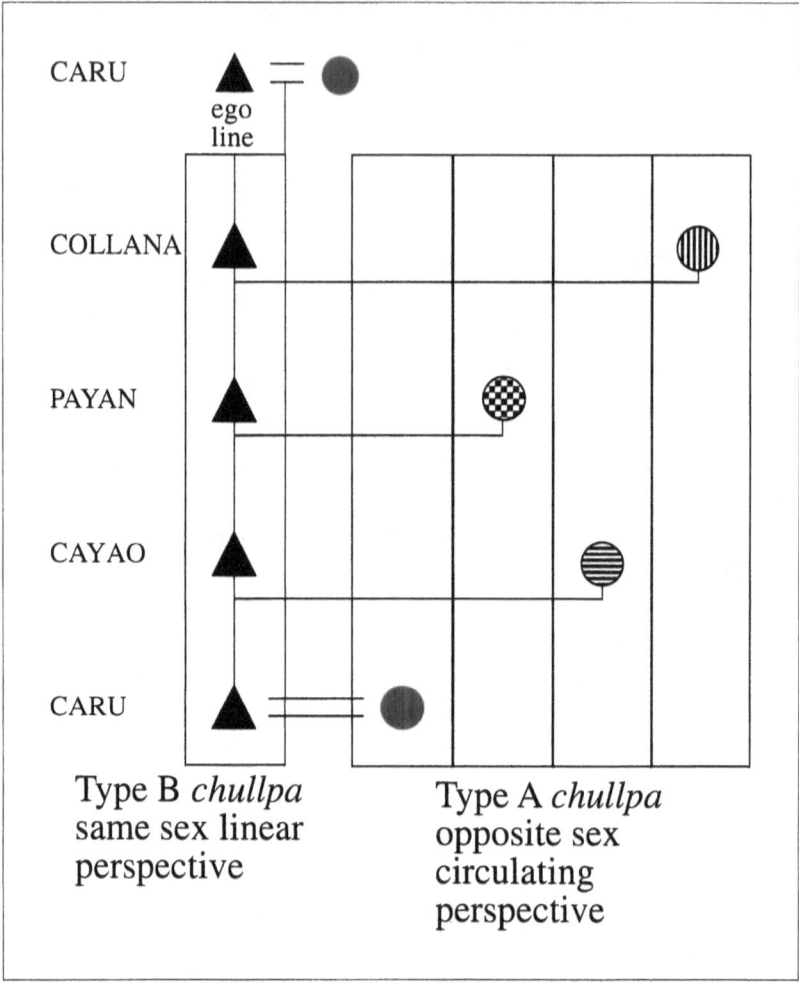

Figure 7.20. *Ayllu* Kinship and Chota-Cutervo *Chullpa* Types. Structural relationships created by *ayllu* marriage patterns were designed into Chota-Cutervo *chullpa*s, suggesting that these *chullpa* towers were models of, and perhaps mnemonic devices for organizing, *ayllu*-based society. (drawn by W. Isbell)

Andean *ayllu* had to consider. These may be termed same sex unilineal descent and opposite sex circulation. From the same sex perspective—suppose a male perspective (see Fig. 7.20, where a male perspective has been adopted)—the four groups and four generations came into focus as one agnatic line. From the other perspective this line or group was wife taker and wife giver to all three other groups. From the point of view of the wife's social location—illustrated here, although a man's sister would follow exactly the same pattern—the kinswomen cycle through all the four groups, a different one in each generation, until in the fourth generation women return to male ego's own lineal group, but based on the descent through the female line. Representation of these two perspectives in a simplified anthropological kinship chart recapitulates Chota-Cutervo Type A and Type B *chullpa*s (compare Fig. 7.20 with Fig. 7.3). Type B *chullpa*s have four floors with four walls—generations and kin groups—and all the entrance ways are in line with one another in the same wall, expressing a same sex unilineal lineal view, either agnatic or uterine. Type A *chullpa*s have four floors and four walls with each doorway in a different wall, circulating through the four walls—kin groups and generations—as a succession of sons' marriage partners and sisters would, in the ideal *ayllu*, and in terms of not a spiral but a zigzag progression.

I infer that the Chota-Cutervo *chullpa*s were architectural representations of the ideal *ayllu* model. The representation probably was not intended to regulate marriages as much as to present the structure underlying the kinship idiom that organized society. Each *ayllu* modeled itself as a sustainable social unit capable of its own production and reproduction, with internal order and hierarchy using moieties, quadripartition, and the *collana, payan, cayao,* and *caru* categories. With these categories they could incorporate members and define rights among participants whose actual relationships with one another were not known or were perhaps flexible and subject to negotiation.

## CONCLUSION

I conclude that the multistoried towers of the Chota-Cutervo region were mortuary monuments. In fact, they participated in a widespread tradition of open sepulchers that characterized the Marañón River Basin and neighboring valleys. These megalithic buildings probably coexisted with more modest mortuary constructions, but these lesser examples have not been reported or investigated. Perhaps they have not survived. I infer that the big monuments of Chota-Cutervo were constructed and used during the latter half of the Early Intermediate Period, from about A.D. 200 to 500. Their construction reveals the existence of a social group with corporate projects requiring the allocation of labor.

The locations of and the sculptural art on the Chota-Cutervo *chullpas* are consistent with moderate-sized social groups that were using ritual to mediate competition for resources and status. Sculptural decorations on the buildings seem to have included regional deities at the level of major natural phenomena, which probably represented widespread ethnic associations, and the negotiations of relations among them. But representational themes also included human sacrifice, individual combat, and military victory that asserted the individual kin group's rights to lands, to water, and to superordinate/subordinate relations in the social geography within which these resources also participated. In my view, iconography supports the corporate interests of the social groups responsible for each *chullpa*.

We have also seen that the Chota-Cutervo *chullpas* can be understood as models of *ayllu* kinship structure. Their two variants express gendered views of ideal *ayllu* organization: the same sex perspective and the opposite sex view. While much is yet to be determined about Andean kinship and its representations, the correspondence with Chota-Cutervo *chullpa* forms is too great to dismiss. I conclude that the monuments served as models, and perhaps even mnemonic devices, that promoted creative use of a kinship idiom for organizing the members associated with each *chullpa*—the *ayllu* of "descendants" from the venerated ancestor mummy.

The meanings that material cultural items had for prehistoric makers and users can never be known with assurance. However, in this chapter I have presented plausible arguments associating Chota-Cutervo *chullpas* with each element of *ayllu* organization, as defined in Chapter 3. I have shown the association of the Chota-Cutervo *chullpa* with a social group and that this social group almost certainly had corporate resources and interests. We have seen that the social group preserved some of its dead in an open sepulcher monument. Finally, I have reviewed reasons to believe that the *chullpa* group constituted itself around that ancestor and monument, using an idiom of kinship of the kind associated with *ayllu* organization in later Andean culture.

I feel justified in asserting that the Chota-Cutervo *chullpas* represent people who were organized in terms of the *ayllu*, more or less as it was described in the sixteenth and seventeenth centuries. Furthermore, no earlier evidence has been discovered for *ayllu* organization anywhere in the central Andes. We cannot designate an exact place for the invention of *ayllu* organization since in Chota-Cutervo, Huamachuco, and the Callejón de Huaylas people began to build the appropriate kinds of mortuary monuments at about the same time, during the latter part of the Early Intermediate Period. Perhaps this entire area participated in the social upheavals that prompted people into social actions that created the *ayllu*. At any rate, there seems little doubt that the people of Chota-Cutervo and their southern neighbors along the western Marañón created this important Andean institution no more than ten to thirteen centuries before the arrival of the Spaniards.

CHAPTER

# VIII

## Origin of the *Ayllu* and the Andean Past

Open sepulcher mortuary monuments have a clear and meaningful distribution in highland Andean space and time. The definition of this pattern is sufficiently continuous to validate the study of mortuary monuments as a window into prehistoric Andean social organization, in spite of the numerous inadequacies of research, especially accurate dating. If the choice of open sepulcher burial had not been based on strong ideological expectations, we would expect to find such tombs here and there, scattered more or less randomly in time and space. If the choice of the open sepulcher depended on highly differentiated local custom, we would expect to find spatial and temporal pockets of *chullpa*s, surrounded by cultures practicing significantly different forms of dealing with the corpses of the dead. But that is not what is revealed by our survey of the space-time distribution of *chullpa*s in Chapter 7. The archaeological information reveals a place and time of origin for open sepulchers—the north highlands of Peru during the latter half of the Early Intermediate Period. Within the north highlands, formal variation in *chullpa*s is extremely great. While this makes for confusion it is also consistent with the "age area hypothesis" that proposes that cultural traits become most varied where they are oldest. Clearly, there are likely antecedents and close relations of the open sepulcher in the north highlands, which include well-built chamber tombs—sometimes with massive stone sarcophagi—as well as bedrock chambers and windowlike niches in stone cliffs. Much remains to be studied, but there seems little doubt when and where prehistoric Andeans first began constructing above-ground *chullpa*s to protect their deceased ancestors' mummies in such a way that they were accessible for rites of veneration that constructed and reconstructed social groups of descendants.

The archaeological record reveals a southward diffusion of open sepulchers from the north highland origin area, reaching the central highlands after several hundred years and the south highlands following two to four more centuries. The open sepulcher certainly is mortuary behavior with spatial and temporal integrity.

In Chapter 2 of this study we saw that an ancestor mummy was the essential focus of the royal *ayllu*, named *panaca*, of Inca nobles. This mummy was protected in an open sepulcher that could be a burial house called *pucullo*, a special room of the Sun Temple, or the palace and other buildings of the mummy's estate. On ritual occasions the royal mummies were brought out into the plazas of Cuzco for public rites, at which time each body was specially attended by its *panaca* descendants.

Chapter 3 showed that an ancestor mummy was the focus of each *ayllu* among the Yauyos people of the western Andes, around Huarochirí. The mummy was placed in an open sepulcher, a *machay* cave, or a *chullpa* monument that usually had its *cayan* plaza for ritual assembly of the mummy's descendants, who constituted his (or her?) *ayllu*. In many cases several mummies and *ayllu*s participated in one ritual calendar and their open sepulchers constituted a ceremonial center of mummy idols, known as a *llacta*. While Cuzco appears to have been a special example of an imperial *llacta*, the *llacta*s of Huarochirí were the "old towns" referred to in extirpation of idolatries testimonies by Indians obliged to explain their continued veneration of ancestor mummies with references to the myths of origin that chartered their *ayllu* lands and water.

At the end of Chapter 3 I defined the *ayllu* on the basis of shared features that were documented in Cuzco during the sixteenth century and in Huarochirí at the beginning of the seventeenth century. Four attributes were identified. In the sixteenth and seventeenth centuries, the *ayllu* consisted of people who recognized themselves as a definite social group. These *ayllu* members shared certain resources, and its senior associates acted as stewards of the resources, administering them for the mutual, albeit not necessarily equal, benefit of all the members. *Ayllu* members were organized in terms of the idiom of kinship. While most *ayllu* members were probably kin descending from the founder, it was behavior appropriate for kin and participation in *ayllu* activities that were essential for *ayllu* membership, not actual genealogy. Fourth and finally, the linchpin of the *ayllu* was the ancestor mummy, for the mummy was the putative biological founder, the source of resource entitlements, and focus of the kin idiom organization of unequal rights and privileges within the *ayllu*. In rituals of veneration to the ancestor mummy, each *ayllu* embodied itself, confirming the unity of its members, while stating its corporate status and goals.

In Chapter 5 we considered how to identify the open sepulchers of *ayllu* founding mummies in the archaeological record, employing written descriptions and architectural remains from Inca and early colonial times. In Chapter 7 we saw that prehistoric *chullpa* sepulchers of Chota-Cutervo can be associated with all of the features of the *ayllu*. Each of these monuments implies a social group of builders, and each group had at least some corporate interests. We have seen that the monuments were almost certainly open sepulchers for ancestor mummies and that the distribution of doorways in the four-floor and four-sided buildings reproduces an ideal kinship model for *ayllu* organization. While we can never be completely sure that these prehistoric architectural texts were intended to be read in this way, the coincidences are too many to be dismissed. Consequently, interpreting Chota-Cutervo *chullpa*s as *ayllu* mortuary monuments is the most plausible explanation.

The sculpted figures found on the Chota-Cutervo *chullpa*s are Early Intermediate Period in date, confirming radiocarbon dates from an open sepulcher at Cerro Amaru (T. and J. Topic 1984) in the Huamachuco Valley. So the Chota-Cutervo *chullpa*s are among the oldest in the Andes, but the open sepulcher does not date back to a primordial inception of Andean culture, millennia before the beginning of our era. The open sepulcher first appeared in the second half of the Early Intermediate Period, or about A.D. 200.

In Chapter 6 it was not possible to explore each example of an open sepulcher with the intensity and detail lavished on the Chota-Cutervo *chullpa*s in Chapter 7. Furthermore, many open sepulcher sites are too little known for such detailed examination. However, I believe that the spatial and temporal unity of *chullpa* monuments implies a cultural and ideological unity in which the four features of *ayllu* organization—a social group, corporate resources and management, kin idiom organization, and mummy ancestor—can be inferred for the spatially and temporally neighboring cultures on the basis of their selection of the open sepulcher for ancestor bodies. I have identified the four features of sixteenth- and seventeenth-century *ayllu* organization at both ends of the *chullpa* continuum, at its Early Intermediate Period beginning and at its colonial era end. I take the open sepulchers in between as valid indicators and necessary material cultural associates of *ayllu* organization.

The spatial and temporal distribution of open sepulchers, reviewed in Chapter 6, indicates that the prehistoric distribution of *ayllu* organization can be summarized more or less as follows. The *ayllu* and open sepulcher originated in the north highlands of Peru, among the secondary tributaries and close neighbors of the great Marañón Valley, during the second half of the Early Intermediate Period. The valleys for which we have convincing archaeological records as early as A.D. 200–500 are Chota-Cutervo and Huamachuco, followed by less demonstrable but suggestive data from the Callejón de Huaylas. Cajamarca, between Huamachuco and Chota-Cutervo, must have participated in the process, but its archaeological record and especially the architectural remains are poorly known. Other neighboring valleys, including Utcubamba, Uchumarca, Tantamayo, and other Upper Marañón regions around Tinyash and Rapayan, all have rich histories of open sepulchers and possibly related means of storing mummies, but their archaeological records remain poorly described. Furthermore, there is much confusion about dating because of inadequate regional chronologies. The valleys across the watershed into the Huallaga River drainage also seem to have participated in the open sepulcher phenomena, but their archaeological records and cultural chronologies are even less known.

By Middle Horizon 2, the open sepulcher reached Huari in Ayacucho. It may have leapfrogged to this capital city with soldiers and other travelers moving about within more or less open imperial territory, but architectural records for intervening areas are so scant that we cannot dismiss the possibility of a more continuous spread through space and time. The open sepulcher also became popular in rural Ayacucho, and it may have reached Cuzco before the end of the Middle Horizon.

During the Late Intermediate Period the open sepulcher *chullpa* seems to have become the most prominent form of mortuary monument in the Andean highlands. During this time open sepulchers are documented in the north highlands as well as the central highlands, from the bend in the Marañón to Cuzco. In fact, the popularity of the open sepulcher has promoted potentially dangerous circular reasoning—that any site with *chullpa* burial monuments must belong to the Late Intermediate Period. If we permit ourselves to indulge in this sort of typological dating we risk obscuring the temporal development of open sepulchers and *ayllu* organization.

Significantly, the Late Intermediate Period was the time when *chullpa*s appeared in the *altiplano* and far south highlands. They are conclusively documented no earlier than A.D. 1000 to 1200, and many are later, implying continued spread through the Late Horizon and perhaps even into early colonial times. Consequently, I have disproved Squier's (1877: 389) hypothesis that *chullpa* burial monuments belonged to the culture of Aymara speakers from Collasuyu. Certainly the spectacular *chullpa*s of Collasuyu represent an impressive subtradition of open sepulchers, but the *chullpa* was characteristic of many other Andean culture areas, and its origin was not in the *altiplano*. The open sepulcher became a part of southern, Aymara culture quite late in Andean prehistory.

In Chapter 4 we examined two alternative theories about the origin of the *ayllu*. Processual evolutionism emphasizes the validity of knowledge about modern and recent cultures for constructing visions of the past. There is a strong tendency to assume that cultures consist of institutions that have a great deal of internal integrity and durability. Cultural evolution takes place by the addition of new institutions, in response to new environmental challenges. Consequently, complex cultures consist of more institutions than simple cultures, and their large inventories of institutions represent additions that have taken place over many millennia. Because institutions are durable and resistant, the ones a culture already has will not change much with the later addition of new institutions; in fact, that is why we can construct the past on the basis of the present. These ideas are consistent with a doctrine of survivalism, and cultures can be conceptualized as layers of institutions, some very old and at the core of behavior, others more recent and lying on the top like a veneer. I suggested the onion as a model for culture conceptualized as layers of institutions added at different times during a culture's developmental history. In the onionlike institutional layers conceptualization, fundamental institutions like the family and household must be very old, representing the core to which later institutions were added.

This logic of processual evolutionism and institutional layers encourages some Andean prehistorians to argue that the *ayllu* is a fundamental institution that must have originated thousands of years ago. In Chapter 4 I discussed this vision as the ancient *ayllu* hypothesis. In this hypothesis the *ayllu* developed in response to the Andean environment thousands of years ago. Indeed, Moseley (1992: 94) suggests *ayllu*-like groupings by 6,000 years ago and *ayllu*-like organization during the second millennium B.C. (Moseley 1992: 127). Kolata (1993: 61–63) infers the minimal *ayllu* in the *altiplano* by 1000 B.C.

We have seen that the *ayllu* is not documented by open sepulchers and ancestor mummies before the second half of the Early Intermediate Period, even in its place of greatest antiquity. This means that *ayllu* organization appeared more than 1,000 years to as much as 4,000 years later than predicted by the ancient *ayllu* hypothesis of processual evolutionism.

I conclude that on the basis of the archaeological record the *ayllu* was not a primordial Andean social institution. I also argue that the relatively late origin for the *ayllu* discredits the entire processual evolutionary scenario for Andean culture. In Chapter 4 we examined the construction of the ancient *ayllu* argument, not from the archaeological record, but in a carefully conflated tapestry of analogies with the present. According to this developmental scheme the earliest and most fundamental feature of Andean culture was symmetrical exchange of labor in accord with the principles of *ayni*, an Andean institution whose description is based on modern ethnographic accounts from numerous peasant communities. Andeanists implicitly consider *ayllu* and *ayni* to represent the egalitarian condition out of which rank and state organization developed. By subverting symmetrical *ayni* into asymmetrical *minka*, aspiring elites created redistribution, wealth differentials, and rank. Subsequently, administrative responsibilities and their privileges were institutionalized by these elites, creating a class that managed community resources, especially labor, and directed some surplus to their own use. Since the history of open sepulchers shows that *ayllu* organization did not significantly precede the development of state authority, there is no basis for inferring *ayni* as another primordial institution for allocated labor within the *ayllu*. In the absence of *ayni* as a primordial institution, there is no basis for inferring that its transformation, *minka*, was the evolutionary vehicle for generating rank and wealth. In fact, in the demonstrated absence of *ayllu* organization, Andean prehistorians must admit that discussions of the institutions that preceded Andean states are mostly speculations based on theoretical expectations.

Contingent history and the recent *ayllu* hypothesis, offered in Chapter 4 as an alternative to processual evolutionism and the ancient *ayllu*, also have not been proven by this study of open sepulchers. Of course, a contingent history approach did not offer a narrative account of the past, but a critique of inadequacies in the ancient *ayllu* argument. Contingent history does theorize that the *ayllu* will not turn out to be a resistant survival from primordial times, for culture is produced and reproduced in the actions of people. It is not determined by deep structure. But more importantly, Roseberry (1989: 198) admonished us to focus our attention on the individual case. We cannot construct the past on the basis of anticipated sequences of culture change, using assumptions of survivalism to identify primordial institutions. Following this advice, and using the archaeological record to create a particular "history" of open sepulchers, I have produced an alternative past for the *ayllu*.

Perhaps the most significant discovery of this research is that the open sepulcher and associated *ayllu* organization were not antecedents of the state in Andean cultural evolution. Rather, they appear to have developed at a time when intense state formation processes were already influencing the lives of many people in Peru's north highlands. If *ayllu* organization developed along with state building processes we should examine this idea theoretically and in terms of archaeological information that may illuminate it.

By the second half of the Early Intermediate Period, when open sepulchers and *ayllu* organization made their appearance in the central Andean north highlands, inequality and rank had existed for centuries, if not millennia. Northern Peru seems to have been an early center for these developments. Preceding the Early Intermediate Period, during the Early Horizon, Chavín-related cults promoted social privilege and wealth differences, as vividly revealed by the elite burials at Kuntur Wasi, in the mountains a few kilometers west of the Cajamarca Valley. Several centuries before the beginning of our era, below-ground graves were dug into a central room on top of Kuntur Wasi's pyramid temple. Later, these graves were covered by a new architectural addition. Four tombs were found, belonging to two elderly men, a middle-aged male, and an elderly woman (Kato 1993: 216–224). The old men probably both had deformed skulls, and their tightly flexed, squatting bodies had been sprinkled with cinnabar. Each was accompanied by a spectacular gold crown and other impressive ornaments. The middle-aged man also had a deformed skull and cinnabar but no crown. Instead he had large gold ear plugs and other ornaments. The elderly woman lacked skull deformation but had cinnabar and two small gold pendants as well as numerous beads, a stone cup, and several ceramic vessels. A fifth burial in an adjacent room on the temple seems to have been a secondary location of lower social status, or perhaps even a human sacrifice. This robust male of forty to fifty years had an undeformed skull with a hole in the left side that seems to have caused his death, and no cinnabar. His ornaments were restricted to two small copper disks and beads of bone and stone.

These finds reveal two important facts. First, the mortuary behavior fits the "*huaca* cemetery" pattern. Given the long popularity of this form of disposal of the dead on the adjacent north coast I propose that this was the preferred mortuary behavior for people occupying some, if not all, of the north highlands before *ayllu* organization was invented. Society's most important men and women were placed in appropriately important locations within the *huaca* temple, and their bodies must have disappeared forever because access to their graves was frequently made impossible by subsequent architectural expansions. These elite could not have been venerated founders of *ayllu*s who could be seen and embraced during rites of propitiation. Second, the Kuntur Wasi finds prove that highly differentiated elites existed within north highland societies during the first millennium B.C. While we may not want to concern ourselves with identifying the moment that state government originated, as processual evolutionism does, it is likely that by A.D. 200 class formation processes had been putting intense pressure on kin organizations for several centuries.

Tom Patterson (1991: 9–41) and Christine Gailey (Gailey and Patterson 1987; Gailey 1987) discard sequences of cultural evolutionism in an effort to discover a generalization about culture in process rather than content. Culture change, they argue, is promoted by violence and conflict, and both are especially intense when kin communities and class-based economic extraction exist simultaneously.

> The state, then, represents a rough, crisis-ridden series of institutional mediations between producers, on the one hand, and those who benefit from the forcible extraction of goods and labor on the other. The mediating institutions aim at containing discontent while ensuring the continuation of a class structure, although not necessarily the existing class structure. The state cannot provide a long-lasting resolution to the disruptions created from the extraction process, because it would challenge the

very basis on which the state institutions depend. Most theories of the state ignore this dynamic; they adopt the rationale of rulership, namely, that the state is crucial for orderly social progress. (Gailey 1987: 28)

I believe that in the *ayllu* we should recognize a powerful institution for defending kin interests while challenging class-based difference and privilege. Descent and, much more emphatically, primary allegiance to the kin group and behavior appropriate for kin—and that behavior clearly focused on participation in and contribution to mutually beneficial undertakings—were the prerequisites for *ayllu* membership. In turn, *ayllu* membership was required for access to virtually all resources. The resources were "owned" not by any living persons, but by dead ancestors. This placed a barrier on the formation of class prerogatives. The living, at the most, were only stewards of lands and waters acquired by mummy forefathers. Leaders were charged with administering the resources for the benefit of all the mummy's "descendants," who were the leaders' younger brothers and sisters, not their peasant workers. Despite inequality within the *ayllu*, all the descendants petitioned the same ancestor for abundance and shared in the results. None were dependent on a class that owned productive resources or monopolized knowledge required for religious access. We may assume that if elite *ayllu* leaders acted too much in their own interest their very membership in the commune could be placed at risk. In terms of the information discussed in Chapters 2 and 3, only the Inca emperor constituted his *ayllu* or *panaca* around his person—instead of his ancestor—so that his actions were not subject to critical review.

If, as Gailey and Patterson argue, state construction is a wrenching and long-term process in which an upper class seeks to impose civil demands on kin groups, reducing them to a uniform class of exploited peasants, kin groups can be expected to resist the impositions by strengthening the reproduction of kin organization. Similarly, civil order resists kin-group attempts to reproduce society at the kin level. This often results in conflicts about tribute, military or corvée service, and other issues of class and state privileges. Numerous and rapid changes take place. Ethnic groups that may have existed for centuries can disappear, and new ethnic identities are likely to develop very rapidly in the wake of new experiences and new interests. I suggest that the appearance of the *ayllu* represents the formation of a new kind of kin group—

an ethnogenesis based in resistance to the demands of civil society. Of course, successful resistance of class institutions varies in time and space. From time to time state institutions are more successfully imposed and from time to time more successfully resisted, so that the dynamic is one of changing forms and degrees of imposition, resistance, collaboration, and co-option accompanied by temporary resolutions often based on force.

Tom Patterson (1991: 26–41) believes that in the central Andes the Early Intermediate Period was the crucial time for the dynamics of state building. Following a temporarily successful state during the second millennium B.C. in the lower Casma Valley, the final centuries before our era and the first half millennium of this era witnessed the initial impositions of several state governments in Peru. Gailey (1987: 25–26) is explicit that state building is not indicated by simple difference in wealth and privilege. What is essential is to distinguish wealth and privilege that were coming from a new source: class relations of civil society. Unfortunately, Patterson does not discuss the archaeological criteria he considers indicative of class relations and state government or specify how the Andean archaeological record may be interpreted to distinguish class-based differences in wealth and privilege from those based on other forms of accumulation. His review is brief, and it remains to be evaluated in terms of specific and systematic criteria. However, the north coastal Moche culture of the Early Intermediate Period, to which he devotes several pages, is a compelling case, and perhaps an exceptionally explosive and vibrant example, of state building.

Class-based civil society among the Moche is implied by spectacular tombs with vast material wealth as well as human sacrifices. Their contrast with modest graves seems to lie beyond any simple form of wealth difference. Furthermore, these elite graves fit into a complex symbolic dialogue of difference and privilege expressed in ritual sacrifice (see Alva and Donnan 1993; Donnan and Castillo 1992; Donnan and Mackey 1978; Donnan and McClelland 1979). The vehicle of symbolic expression was Moche iconography, which also depicts specialization and differentiation that seem to exceed anything characteristic of kin-organized society. Donnan (1978) shows that Moche artists depicted only ceremonial themes, implying a ritual elite in control of esoteric knowledge. Within the precinct of ritual iconography are depictions of women weavers making headdresses, male metallurgists making head ornaments, shamans with special paraphernalia, *chicha* beer makers, sea lion hunters, deer hunters, runners who probably represent some sort of messengers, warriors in special regalia, elites on thrones, and even impressive processions with musicians. Moche pottery was made by specialist artists, for different vessels come from the hands of the same master painters. Finally, it is likely that labor for *huaca* pyramid construction drew on many communities (Hastings and Moseley 1975), and some of the pyramids held palace buildings, not just temples.

In spite of strong emphasis on unifying ritual and ideology in Moche art, Patterson (1991: 33–35) argues that cultural heterogeneity was endemic and opposed interest groups were confronting one another constantly. Old kin-based communities, new elite classes, and probably emerging regional groupings were competing for power and control. Influential ritual art was pressed into the service of elite classes who employed stylistic archaism to claim antiquity and legitimacy. The imitation of earlier representations of supernatural beings is documented archaeologically in the fancy ceramics of the Moche, at least during Early Intermediate Period 6–7 (about A.D. 400) and again at the beginning of the Middle Horizon (about A.D. 600). Regional styles appeared, and perhaps even the pantheon of supernaturals found in Moche art of the final centuries of the Early Intermediate Period reveals competing cults. Each cult may have given voice to a regional, kin, or class interest in an ongoing struggle for power.

During this same time—the first half millennium of our era—open sepulchers, ancestor mummies, and *ayllu* organization were established in Chota-Cutervo, Huamachuco, and probably the Callejón de Huaylas. The archaeological record for Moche state formation processes is unusually rich and well studied. With much less research in the adjacent highlands, can we justify the inference that peoples in the north highlands valleys were experiencing at least some of the same pressures and processes of state formation? I believe so. First, we should remember that the Kuntur Wasi graves revealed significant rank difference in Cajamarca several hundreds of years earlier than Moche culture and long before the appearance of *chullpa* monuments. Second, there is abundant evidence of interaction between Moche and the Early Intermediate Period highland cultures of Huamachuco, Cajamarca, Chota-Cutervo, and the Callejón de Huaylas. As we will see below, the forms of contact included military conflicts, so state institutions existing on the coast were making themselves felt in the highlands.

Moche scene painting on ceramics, especially of the second half of the Early Intermediate Period, frequently depicts combat between elite warriors outfitted with fine garments and accouterments for individual contest. This type of scene probably relates to others that show victorious warriors leading nude captives with a rope around the neck. The victor carries the clothes, weapons, and other objects of the costume of the vanquished. A third scene from this ritual scenario is the taking of the captive's blood for offering, apparently by cutting his throat (Alva and Donnan 1993). Some of the combat scenes show warriors whose costumes distinguish them from ethnic Moche. The headdresses, clubs, and other items of one set of warriors on a fine bottle (Donnan 1978: Fig. 68) have generally been identified as those of a group of highland neighbors of the Moche. This implies that Moche military elites engaged in combat with highland warriors, certainly promoting a highland warrior class, whether by expansionism or by imitation.

Theresa Topic (1991; see also Wilson 1988) presents direct archaeological evidence for warfare and conflict between the Moche and their highland neighbors during the late Early Intermediate Period. Many forts and defensive walls were built in intermediate territory, and concentrations of fist-sized stones within a sling-throw of the walls indicate assaults on these fortifications. There is also abundant evidence for trade and even for colonial enclaves in different ethnic territories of the north coast and highlands (J. and T. Topic 1983a). It is not my intention for this review to show that one ethnic group conquered or occupied the other, but to reveal an intensively interacting regional context within which state building processes that are archaeologically documented in any one area must be assumed, to at least some degree, throughout the region. While unequal development certainly existed, the power of state governments to mobilize trade expeditions, to launch military campaigns, and to appropriate and defend resources would promote similar institutions in neighboring territories. Other mechanisms of cultural influence probably included exchange of marriage partners and sharing religious rituals and ideology in peace-making ceremonies.

I infer that during the late Early Intermediate Period state building processes were affecting highland peoples adjacent to the Moche. However, the monuments, population centers, and iconography of the Callejón de Huaylas, Huamachuco, Cajamarca, and Chota-Cutervo do not indicate that state governments and class structures were enduringly instigated. Many processual evolutionists conclude that developmental processes failed to achieve state organization, perhaps because of environmental limitations in small highland valleys, so during the Early Intermediate Period societies remained at the level of chiefdoms. However, from a contingent history perspective we should consider the possibility that the lack of state governments might indicate that highland people discovered more effective behavior for resisting the impositions of class-based elites who sought to institutionalize new privileges. Christine Gailey (1987) is clear about this:

> In their attempts to continue production to serve kin-defined ends, community members come into opposition to the civil authority, whether or not this opposition is recognized. In other words, the very efforts to reproduce kin-based relations become resistance to state penetration. (Gailey 1987: xii)

> Unlike other life crises, marriages may represent the indivisibility of production and reproduction in kinship societies. In marrying, a person acknowledges his or her responsibility to the group as a whole to help continue the group, in terms of both provisions and demographic replacement; the responsibilities show a fusion characteristic of kinship societies between public and domestic activities. In the establishment of at least potentially a new household, the new couple *owe their adulthood to their kin*. They can only reciprocate over time—to the nexus of people who validated and made possible their growing personhood. (Gailey 1987: 11)

An institutionalized group of descendants organized around their ancestor mummy, all dependent on the mummy as well as the kin-organized commune for marriage, resources, labor, and spiritual well-being, certainly promotes reproduction of the kin community. Its rituals emphasize the individual's dependence on and duties to the ancestor mummy, who in turn embodies the social descent group. For the *ayllu*, the ancestor's life and death legitimized the rights of the corporate group of descendants. These rights emphasized every member's responsibility for and participation in the management of resources. As the focus of a kin-based idiom of organization, the founding ancestor defined differences in status and privilege that were conceptualized in terms of seniority, cognatic and affinal links, and other principles of kinship. While differential privileges legitimized in this way were apparently established by appropriate behavior, within the *ayllu* they were not based on class. In fact, the kin idiom excluded class differences, for ultimately all *ayllu* members were brothers and sisters responsible to one another in their service to the mummy founder.

I suggest that the *ayllu* developed in the context of state formation, to defend kin group interests. Mummified ancestors, the most powerful symbol of kinship and tradition, were transformed into the embodiment of the *ayllu* and the symbolic focus of the kin group's strategies for reproducing itself. At least in part, the success of *ayllu* organization probably lay in its ability to accommodate to state demands. For the Inca and early Spanish administrations it was easier to employ the *ayllu* within a system of indirect rule than to reorganize the entire population. So state revenue depended on continuity of the *ayllu*. But *ayllu*s were always ready to take advantage of weakness in the state, from hesitating to pay tribute to establishing complete political independence.

*Ayllu*s had enough internal specialization to operate independently, for significant power was lodged in leaders' rights to manage resources. As described in the sixteenth and seventeenth centuries, independent *ayllu*s could become allied and even united as descendants of a more senior ancestor and founder. Of course, state governments did have effects on *ayllu* organization, for both the Spanish and Incas reduced their size and internal differentiation of big *ayllu* polities. For example, the Spanish Viceroyalty awarded Indians their access to land on the basis of *ayllu* affiliation, but it replaced kin-based leadership with centrally appointed officials.

I believe that the archaeological record for open sepulchers supports the inference that *ayllu* organization appeared in the north Peruvian highlands during the final centuries of the Early Intermediate Period and that this was a time of widespread state formation. *Ayllu*, mummy, and open sepulcher represent creative responses by supporters of kin community interests, in a struggle to protect local control and resist the demands of an increasingly influential and privileged class of elites. The objectification of the kin group, the intensification of a kin-based idiom for social organization, and the allocation of resources through an ancestor mummy promoted the maintenance of kin communities and their leaders. These leaders—perhaps new rather than customary leaders—appropriated ancestral bodies to represent the kin corporation and legitimate claims to authority in antiquity and tradition. In at least some ethnohistoric cases it is clear that mummy priests spoke with the divine voice of the ancestor himself.

I suspect that in the Early Intermediate Period north highlands, ancestors' bodies were available for these roles because *huaca* cemeteries had employed tombs cut into bedrock, stone crypts deeply buried in platform mounds, or deep shaft tombs that effectively excluded many conditions detrimental to the preservation of a body. In effect, the north highland crypt preceded and made possible the open sepulcher, and the mummy ancestor became the visible object of recurrent ritual, required for consultation, divination, and adoration, and vitally prerequisite for fertility and abundance. Production and reproduction became securely linked to the benevolence of the common ancestor. Even kings and nobles could not legitimately alienate what a divine ancestor had bequeathed his children, except through force. And such alienation risked the wrath of the mummy founder, who would visit famine and disease on those who opposed his rights and will. In fact, a good deal of ethnohistoric information about Andean religion seems to have been concerned with appropriating the ancestors of conquered peoples so that their spiritual powers could be harnessed for the good of the conquerors, rather than their destruction.

Similarly, this aspect of *ayllu* structure probably led Andean peoples to fashion early resistance to Spanish colonialism in the Taki Onqoy, the dancing sickness of the 1560s. The *huaca*s were going to defeat the Christian God, destroy the invaders along with all their collaborators, and bring paradise to loyal Indian believers. What was new about the Taki Onqoy was its pan-Indianism and the consequent focus on high and distant members of the Andean pantheon rather than on individual *ayllu* mummies.

The discovery that *ayllu* organization originated in the late Early Intermediate Period not only shows that this form of organization must have been born in contexts of state building, but also yields major new insights into Andean geopolitics. First, the *ayllu* did not spread north from the Marañón, at least not significantly. I conclude that this was because defense of the kin group may not have been necessary in the northern societies, perhaps because the pressures of state formation were absent. On the other hand, *ayllu* organization spread south, where it probably contributed to the failure of two great states, first Huari and a couple of centuries later Tiwanaku. The collapse of these big expansionist states has not been convincingly explained. Military defeat does not seem to be indicated, climate change hypotheses are weak, and there is little evidence for intrusive new peoples in either area. Much more interesting is the notion of internal disruption. Processual evolutionism prompts us to assume that collapse represents the failure of adaptive governmental administration, but a contingent history approach suggests that we should look at each case individually, including mechanisms of resistance developed by kin communities. When we do this we find *ayllu* organization in the right places at the right times to provide local kin communities with strategies for subverting state control by returning wealth to mummy founders and their legitimate descendants.

In the sixth or seventh century there can be no question that Huari penetrated the north highland Marañón Basin. Huari was instrumental in the selection of new architectural forms at the big site of Honcopampa in the Callejón de Huaylas (W. H. Isbell 1989, 1991a), and Huari military architects laid out a huge administrative center at Viracochapampa in Huamachuco (W. H. Isbell 1991b). But Huari's effective control of the north has been questioned (cf. J. Topic 1991), and this is an important issue. One set of information relevant to the discussion is the apparent abandonment of big open sepulchers built several centuries earlier in Huamachuco and probably also in the Callejón de Huaylas. It certainly does seem that at least initially these northern architectural forms associated with resistance to state institutions suffered during Middle Horizon Huari intrusion. But they were eventually replaced, as shown by the little *chullpa*s of Tornapampa (Terada 1979) and by many other Late Intermediate Period mortuary houses throughout the north, so the open sepulcher and *ayllu* organization survived Huari.

Very surprising is what I take to be the appearance of open sepulchers and founder mummies in Huari's heartland. They appear both in the city and in provincial contexts. By late Epoch 1 or early Epoch 2 of the Middle Horizon it seems that chamber mausoleums were being built at the Cheqo Wasi sector of Huari and in a rural Huari community or two. At least part of this must represent mortuary activities by powerful elites, for the central location of the chambers, their massive construction, and the apparently rich offerings imply considerable control of labor and wealth. Could it be that the descendants of successful Huari conquerors were so anxious to aggrandize themselves and to secure kin-based claims to spoils accumulated by their ancestor that they unwittingly reproduced in Ayacucho a northern institution capable of combating class structure that had mobilized Huari expansionism in the first place? I propose this as a hypothesis for further research.

In support of the inference that mummy veneration and *ayllu* organization reached Huari by Middle Horizon Epoch 2 is a house group at the rural settlement of Jargampata. One room had been set aside for the remains of deceased (W. H. Isbell 1977). I infer that the bodies were curated in the form of mummy bundles and that they represented the group founder and primary descendants. At more or less the same time, *machay* caves were becoming popular means of dealing with the dead (Meddens 1991). By Middle Horizon 3, Huari was abandoned, and small hilltop villages and hamlets suggestive of more kin-oriented communities seem to have replaced the state, with its central controls and class difference.

The spread of open sepulchers into Cuzco and the *altiplano* needs much more documentation. Tiwanaku was flourishing when Huari experienced its dramatic decline around A.D. 900. Within a few centuries, probably between A.D. 1000 and 1200, Tiwanaku's fancy pottery styles disappeared, monumental construction at the Tiwanaku capital declined, and the capital city was more or less abandoned (Albarracin-Jordan and Mathews 1990; Kolata 1993). Most traces of a Tiwanaku state and elite culture disappeared. What may have been a politically unified *altiplano* broke up into smaller chiefdoms, and open sepulchers became the most prominent monuments and the preferred means of dealing with the dead. As in the central highlands of Ayacucho, there is little evidence for an invasion or population replacement so it seems that the same Aymara speakers created Tiwanaku only to reject it in favor of kin-based organization. I suggest that the adoption of *ayllu* organization, ancestor founders, and the open sepulcher played a key role in this return to a classless social formation.

## PROCESSUAL EVOLUTIONISM OR CONTINGENT HISTORY?

We have completed this archaeological examination of the development of *ayllu* organization, so it is time to return to evaluating competing theoretical approaches to the Andean past. Processual evolutionism produced the ancient *ayllu* hypothesis, ascribing *ayllu* or *ayllu*-like organization to the beginning of Andean culture. As cited above, Moseley (1992: 94) suggests a date of about 6,000 years ago. While most processual evolutionists are less specific, none have questioned the existence of *ayllu* organization among Peru's first monument builders by 2000 B.C.

A contingent history approach to the Andean past critically questions whether any institution remains unchanged for centuries. The production and reproduction of culture by human agents accommodating to changing conditions of daily life means that institutions also change. They respond to different goals and aspirations, to new demands and requirements, and to improved technologies or the availability of new goods and the opportunity for accumulation. Of course, the contingency or specificity of history makes it impossible to determine when the *ayllu* appeared on the basis of theoretical convictions, but this approach does argue that culture change is greatest during times of social conflict. State building processes are notorious for violence and discord, so a contingent history approach to the Andean past might look for the *ayllu* as recently as the era of state building. This focuses attention on the Early Intermediate Period and the Middle Horizon—about 200 B.C. to A.D. 900.

The archaeological record for open sepulchers shows that processual evolutionism's ancient *ayllu* hypothesis failed disastrously, missing the mark for *ayllu* origins by thousands of years. On the other hand, contingent history's recent *ayllu* hypothesis anticipated the results of archaeological research quite accurately. The *ayllu* does not seem to be an archaic adaptation to the Andean environment. Rather, it seems to have developed as a social innovation that enabled kin groups to perpetuate themselves, while resisting class formation and combating state authority. The *ayllu* did not make Andean agropastoralism possible, but it may explain the long endurance of kin-based agropastoral communities. *Ayllu* organization may also explain the relative lack of success experienced by Andean states, especially in the highlands. In the vision of the Andean past that I am proposing, following its invention the *ayllu* spread far to the south, destabilizing elite classes at Huari and Tiwanaku. Spread of the *ayllu* ushered in an era of local, kin-group autonomy that lasted for centuries. In the north highlands, the home of the *ayllu*, state government may never have gained more than brief control before the Inca incursion. Vibrant local cultures seem to have enjoyed demographic growth, spectacular art, wealth, and regional exchange—as well as gender inequality, warfare, and human sacrifice—without large, bureaucratically organized state governments. In the central highlands, Huari government may have destructed as *ayllu* membership replaced state obligations with powerful duties to ancestor and kin. In the old Huari core territory, the Late Intermediate Period appears to have been a time of population growth and cultural success, but without significant class differentiation.

Tiwanaku may have faded more gradually in the competition between state administrators and *ayllu* mummies. I suspect that Tiwanaku was less bureaucratic and less class-based than Huari, so it may have offered a social context in which *ayllu* organization combined more with older cultural institutions and where clash was less violent. At any rate, several scholars think that there was a late transitional phase in which Tiwanaku pit tombs slowly transformed into open sepulcher *chullpas*. It is also interesting to note that in the south highlands post-Tiwanaku *ayllu*s or ethnic kingdoms were probably the largest and most complex in the Andes. Furthermore, it was nearby in Cuzco that the ongoing struggle between kin and class resulted in a new and solid victory for state organization. The Incas put together a remarkably successful administration by ethnic Inca nobility, who constituted the core of their expansionist military force. *Ayllu* organization participated in the Inca state, but the Inca king usurped the position of the ancestor mummy.

According to Tom Zuidema's model, the ascension of a new emperor required the Incas of Cuzco to restructure their *panaca* and *ayllu* to focus on the new king. Using the idiom of kinship the elite class was reorganized, constructing the new emperor as the founding ancestor. The most remote creator and ancestor of the Inca nobility, Viracocha, was credited with creating the most remote ancestor of all *ayllu*s throughout the Andes. While colonial testimonies show that Indians' allegiance diminished with the distance of ancestors, idols, and shrines, this ideology did constitute the Inca Empire as one super *ayllu*, in which the Inca emperor was the living founder. Furthermore, the Incas forcibly took part of the land and water of each incorporated *ayllu*. It was removed from the political and supernatural domain of the *ayllu* ancestor and transferred to the supernatural and political domain of the Inca king or one of his shrines, with many rituals to validate the "recreation" of these resources.

## METHOD AND THEORY IN ANDEAN ARCHAEOLOGY

The study of open sepulchers as a window into the prehistory of the *ayllu* has produced an account that differs remarkably from the Andean past envisioned by processual evolutionism. Considering that this vision is the most popular Andean past, at least among English speakers, and is being disseminated in many current books and films, there is reason for concern. An error of such magnitude regarding a key institution implies that problems may be even more extensive, and we should reconsider the methods and theories on which this approach to the Andean past bases itself. Furthermore, we should look into the possibility that errors similar to that regarding the *ayllu* have occurred with other prehistoric institutions and events.

I believe that the error regarding the significance, nature, and antiquity of the *ayllu* springs from three methodological and theoretical inadequacies that have far-reaching implications for representations of Andean prehistory. I will describe each so that other research conclusions based on similar procedures and assumptions may be identified, questioned, and reexamined in hopes of moving toward a more rigorous and more accurate past for Andean peoples and cultures. The first problem requires us to reconsider the use of ethnographic analogy for constructing visions of the Andean past and the role played by the construct "Andean culture." The second inadequacy springs from the way that the theory of cultural evolution is used to create an Andean past. The third inadequacy relates to archaeological tests of the analogies, scenarios, and visions of the past that we prehistorians construct.

The first problem is perhaps the most serious: it concerns the way ethnographic and ethnohistorical descriptions have been used by Andeanists to infer prehistoric culture. Inference about prehistoric culture on the basis of more recent cultural descriptions is what archaeologists call "analogy" or "ethnographic analogy." When applied within the same culture it is often referred to as the "direct historical approach." It is interesting that this method was convincingly employed by Andeanist scholar John Murra (1975a, 1980) to infer that Inca state organization was primarily an elaboration of earlier institutions that characterized most pre-Inca Andean societies. On the other hand, Murra and his colleague Nathan Wachtel disavowed the same approach in another situation, arguing that ethnographic descriptions of modern Andean communities cannot furnish meaningful information about preconquest Andean polities (Murra and Wachtel 1986: 2). This implies that there are conditions in which analogies from recent or historic cultures can be convincingly applied to earlier cultures and other circumstances in which they cannot. What conditions constrain the use of ethnographic analogies?

Unfortunately, Murra and Wachtel do not explain why they deny the validity of inferences about prehistoric Andean political formations based on modern ethnographic communities, except to say that these latter are not of the "Andean world," but represent colonial and even republican era phenomena. While Murra and Wachtel are not more specific about the matter of applying cultural analogies to prehistory, there is an extensive archaeological literature about this important technique for knowing the past.

Analogical constructions of the past are based on the assumption that cultures are integrated and functioning systems and that if some aspects of an archaeologically known culture are similar to those of an ethnographically or historically described culture then other aspects may also be similar, including behaviors that are difficult to detect in the archaeological record. Analogies allow the archaeologist to infer past cultural institutions on the basis of known human behavior, rather than just making it up from the artifacts. When appropriate methods are employed, analogy is one of the most important tools that archaeologists have for constructing visions of the past, but, as I shall argue, analogy has been inappropriately used in constructing processual evolutionism's vision of the Andean past.

A rigorous archaeological approach to analogical reasoning requires a source culture—the modern or recent culture for which descriptions exist—and a subject culture—the prehistoric culture for which only archaeological remains exist and about which inferences will be made. Comparisons between the source and the subject cultures should be detailed and specific. The moment in time on which the source descriptions are based should be specified, taking care not to mix descriptions of institutions separated by decades or centuries so that the essential integration or systemic nature of the culture is not violated. A moment in time must also be determined for the subject culture, for the same reason (Stahl 1993: 249; 1994). Institutions and behavior that the archaeologist considers inferring from the source to the subject culture must be examined very carefully, identifying their material cultural contexts and correlates. It is important to consider how the relevant institutions and behavior that do and do not leave material records were related and interdependent in the source culture and then in the subject culture. Analogical comparisons between the two should include these relations as well as comparison of actual material remains (Wylie 1985: 94–95).

It is also essential that the archaeologist carefully document differences as well as similarities between source and subject cultures (Stahl 1993). In this way the prehistorian decides what behavior should be inferred from the source culture and what behavior should not. In fact it may be desirable to examine a number of analogies to construct pasts that are not simply duplicates of ethnographic and ethnohistorical cultures. Stahl (1993: 244) refers to analogies based on these rigorous methods as "specific analogy."

During the 1960s and 1970s there was extensive dialogue among archaeologists regarding the application of analogical logic (Ascher 1961, 1962; Binford 1967, 1968; Gould 1978, 1980; Gould and Watson 1982; Hodder 1982; Kleindienst and Watson 1956; Rowe 1953; Schrire 1980, 1984; Steward 1942; Strong 1936; Trigger 1982; Tringham 1978; Watson 1978a, 1978b, 1982; Watson et al. 1971). Initially it was argued that analogies must be set up as hypotheses for explicit testing with the methods of logical positivism. But with fuller appreciation of the impossibility of ever confirming a hypothesis, a less scientist and more practical approach to testing the application of analogies from source culture to subject culture emerged (Stahl 1993, 1994; Wylie 1985, 1988, 1989). Of course, an analogical inference can never be proved, but properly applied analogy can be tested for plausibly developing the most satisfying description of prehistoric culture available. However, not all schools of analogical thinking employ the rigorous application techniques developed over the past few decades.

One popular approach to analogy in prehistory concerns itself with validating source descriptions as representative of the subject culture, but then ignores criteria for application to the archaeological culture, as well as specific material cultural tests. This less rigorous approach explored two bases for similarities, those founded on historical continuities between source and subject and those based on similar environmental adaptation and/or relations of production (Ascher 1961). It is the former, based on historical continuity, that we must consider to understand processual evolutionism's visions of the Andean past.

Archaeologists recognize that removal of behavioral descriptions from their historical and cultural contexts, to be attributed to a prehistoric people, can result in erroneous descriptions of the past. A popular solution to this problem has been to make analogies within the same cultural tradition—using contemporary or recent cultures that are related to the past culture by a continuous tradition (Ascher 1961; Clark 1951: 55). As Alison Wylie (1985: 70) points out, "the assumption seems to be that if historical continuity is established, then 'historical context' can be assumed to be more or less constant." Essentially, the archaeologist assumes cultural stability.

Once archaeologists assume stability within cultural traditions they also tend to assume that as long as they stay within one tradition all analogies across time are equally valid. First, they need not employ the rigorous methods of analogical reasoning described above—that analogies be drawn between a specific source culture and a specific subject culture; that specific moments in time be identified for both source and subject cultures; that relations be established between material and nonmaterial behavior that the archaeologist is interested in inferring into the past; that the material record of the past subject culture be examined and meticulously compared with source culture data, along with evaluations of the probability of similar relations between material and nonmaterial domains; and that differences as well as similarities be considered when behavior is inferred from source to subject. Second, when specific historical context is considered irrelevant it becomes possible to describe the past in terms of cultural behavior conflated from many different source cultures and many different moments in time, just so long as all are identified with the same tradition (Hall 1984; Huffman 1982, 1986, 1989; Vansina 1989). As pointed out above, this violates the very basis for analogical thinking, based as it is on the integration of culture and the probability that the identification of some similarities between two cultures is likely to mean additional similarities. Ann Stahl (1993: 246–249) refers to this tendency to conflate across temporal and social boundaries as "homogenized analogy." Finally, concomitant with the assumption of cultural stability it becomes increasingly difficult for archaeologists to visualize the past in terms of anything but the ethnographic present, in spite of the limitations ethnography and ethnohistory always afford (Clifford and Marcus 1986; Upham 1987).

The majority of analogical thinking employed to construct the Andean past has been of the "homogenized analogy" variety. Homogenized analogy rarely identifies a specific source culture, and in many cases even a specific prehistoric object culture is not defined, leaving both social and temporal boundaries open and inclusive. Little effort is made to build detailed and convincing material contexts or interactional relations for homogenized analogies. Of course, when an institution inferred into the past is actually an abstraction inferred by an anthropologist from bits and pieces in various accounts, such as Patricia Netherly's model of dual organization for north coast polities (Netherly 1990) or Zuidema's construction of Inca dynastic organization (Zuidema 1990b), there can be no specific behavioral contexts and correlates, for the behavior was never actually observed. Finally, even if material contexts are discussed when homogenized analogies are applied, similarities are emphasized while differences are almost ignored.

Andeanists employ a legitimizing process or decontextualizing operation to obscure the assumptions that underlie homogenized analogy—that culture is timeless, changeless, and normative. This decontextualizer is "Andean culture." While the concept of Andean culture as a tradition may have many positive uses, archaeologists are employing it to decontextualize specific cultural behavior, to generalize and idealize that behavior, to mix descriptions of cultural institutions from different times and places, and then to insert institutions from composite Andean culture into convenient prehistoric slots with no more tests than conformity with the expectations of cultural evolutionism. The logic seems to go more or less as follows. Andean culture is an essence shared by all indigenous peoples of the central Andes. The adaptive basics, as well as the structure and logic of Andean culture, have remained little changed for hundreds and even thousands of years. Adaptive necessities and deep structure work in favor of institutional continuity, so institutions established hundreds and even thousands of years ago have remained little changed.

Membership in Andean culture is established by pedigree, and the institutions of any culture with an Andean pedigree can and should be added to the ideal construct. Differences found among examples of a single widely spread institution, such as the modern *ayllu*, reveal its antiquity and challenge investigators to discover the original and true essence. These exercises have become major research goals, and Andean culture is regularly characterized in terms of such essences.

For the archaeologist, potential sources of analogies as well as prehistoric subjects of analogies are equally mixed into Andean culture. A researcher need only show that a prehistoric or early colonial group lived within the culture area to qualify for addition to the construct. A culture may be denied validity as an analogy for prehistory only by refusing Andean culture pedigree. This is what I believe that Murra and Wachtel (1986: 2) intend when they assert that modern ethnographic descriptions do not belong to the "Andean world," but to colonial and republican cultural contexts. But many archaeologists and ethnographers ignore even this caution and employ what Stahl (1993: 240, 250) calls "ubiquity" or simply the wide diffusion of a cultural trait to accept it as a survival from the archaic past. Furthermore, thinking in terms of dichotomous oppositional models like traditional/modern (Roseberry and O'Brien 1991) or Andean/Hispanic and in terms of evolutionary concepts or typological time (Stahl 1993) validates the inclusion of contemporary Andean institutions like the *ayllu*, the nuclear family, *ayni*, and *minka* in Andean culture. The more remote a modern community is, the more popular an indigenous language remains among its inhabitants, and the more its economic institutions contrast with those of capitalism, the more authentic its Andean culture pedigree is taken to be. When an institution enters Andean culture it becomes part of a timeless and idealized domain. From there it is a simple step, violating no rules of logic, to insert institutions into actual archaeological cultures without concern for validation.

The theory of cultural evolutionism has had the second most important influence on the way processual evolutionists construct the Andean past. In many respects this discussion of cultural evolutionism simply expands the critique of analogical thinking, for nineteenth-century theories of cultural evolution were the first systematic use of ethnographic analogy for reconstructing the past (Ascher 1961). Contemporary evolutionism continues to be based in ethnography and the projection of ethnographic information into the past by means of analogy. As it has been practiced it is social philosophy of progress, not scientific study of past cultures (Dunnell 1980; O'Brien and Holland 1992). But before I continue the discussion I want to affirm that cultural evolution happens, and I have no desire to deny it. It is not the concept of cultural evolution but its current practice in constructing Andean prehistory that I am critiquing.

Theories of cultural evolutionism depend on a universal sequence of culture change, from one idealized culture type to another. This sequence is created by organizing descriptions of contemporary ethnographic cultures into a logical or typological succession, not by actual chronologies of change from the prehistoric past. The goal is to explain the ideal sequence considered more or less universal and, in so doing, to identify the general rules of cultural evolution that influence or direct all cases of culture change. I believe that it is erroneous thinking if anyone believes that the ideal sequence of culture types describes the changes actually experienced or the stages actually passed through by any real culture. The ideal sequence is a model deliberately designed to exclude the historical particulars that affect individual real cultures. Only by excluding individual and unique occurrences and events—the process emphasized by the contingent history approach—can evolutionism have universal application. Perhaps general cultural evolution is like a model of motion in physics that ignores the realities of friction. It effectively reveals universal relationships, but it does not describe any example of motion in the real world.

In anthropology this is demonstrated by Morton Fried's (1975) argument that tribal organization, once considered a universal evolutionary stage, was actually a response by real egalitarian societies to real contacts with states. Consequently, tribes could not be explained by universal evolutionary change so they should be (and were) removed from the concern of cultural evolutionism. The underlying idea is that particular historical contacts and events create particular sequences of culture change. Only by excluding such contacts may theorists discover the ideal course of evolutionary change, and it is this ideal course that is explained by evolutionary theory. Historical particulars experienced by individual real cultures defy explanation, requiring understanding in terms of individual and particular cases.

Ideal cultural stages may be fine for evolutionistic insights into technological progress, demographic growth, social organization, and other interests. But the Andean past is the past of real cultures and real peoples. I assert that the ideal succession of stages is of limited use for constructing this real past. In fact, it seems naive for anyone to think that real Andean societies would have followed ideal evolutionary trajectories. But, unfortunately, that is how the Andean past is being created. As in the case of homogenized analogy, ideal Andean culture plays a key role. Remember that in popular thinking Andean culture consists of many institutions that are resistant to change. Each of these institutions entered Andean culture at a different time in its evolutionary history. Consequently it may be assumed that when Andean culture is unpacked its component institutions may be reorganized to recreate Andean cultural evolution in terms of the sequence we have learned to expect from cultural evolution. This intellectual error is compounded by considering each real prehistoric culture as a perfect example of Andean culture and the change it experienced. Andeanists unpack Andean culture and infer seemingly egalitarian institutions like *ayni* and *ayllu* into the earliest components of their local sequences. *Minka* or redistribution is placed in the local sequence in somewhat more recent time, as rank and inequality increased. Inca-like labor tax collection is inserted into succeeding phases if they reveal statelike complexity. Adaptation to vertical ecological complementarity is considered the constant selective force behind change, and particulars of individual histories are not relevant.

As I have shown above, this procedure is problematic in itself because institutions like *ayllu*, *ayni*, and *minka* are unlikely to have remained static since the remote prehistoric past. As described in modern contexts they are institutions constructed and reconstructed under the influences of national laws, migration for wage labor, market exchange, and other influences. Even *mita* labor tax experienced change in the hands of colonial officials from Spain, and the Incas seem to have been active inventors as well, devising new taxation policies to deal with the lush Cochabamba Valley. But Andean prehistorians compound the error when they deconstruct the timeless, normative, and idealized model and use it to construct a sequence of development for a real local culture (cf. Gero 1991; Kolata 1993; Moseley 1992). Very few archaeological studies infer historical processes atypical of ideal evolutionary progress, such as ethnogenesis and ethnocide, tribal alliances, resistance to state institutions, or the rejection of complexity in favor of simpler organization. Rather, change is virtually always progress, with all innovative behavior contributing to increases in social differentiation, hierarchy, and centralization as well as adaptive management of the environment. In fact, Andean prehistorians seem to be very uncomfortable with culture change that is contrary to the evolutionary ideals of progress. Cultures such as Moche and Tiwanaku, in which complexity seems to have decreased when unifying styles disappeared, are not interpreted in terms of cultural processes that include conflict, resistance to authority, and ethnocide. They are considered cultures making good adaptive progress until overwhelmed by an exceptional natural disaster (Kolata 1993; Moseley 1978; Ortloff and Kolata 1993).

Cultural evolutionism and homogenized analogy combine in the methods of processual evolutionism to create a problem more serious than might be produced by either alone. This problem was recognized by Murra and Wachtel (1986) when they rejected analogous inferences about precolumbian polities based on information about colonial and modern behavior among Andean peoples. Clearly Murra and Wachtel posited a cultural hiatus brought on by the Spanish conquest and across which human behavior altered so severely that general cultural similarities should not be assumed. At this point we should remember that institutions like *ayni* and *minka*, as well as household organization and agropastoral production, that are imputed to the earliest Andean communities of thousands of years ago are best known from modern ethnographic descriptions. I conclude that Murra and Wachtel would disallow these cultural analogies across the hiatus of the Spanish conquest, an attitude that parallels convictions of scholars advocating contingent history, as described in Chapter 4. Apparently Murra and Wachtel would agree that the construction of archaic Andean society on the basis of family, community, and labor-sharing organization described for modern cultures that are marginal to but dependent on capitalism is spurious, even though these institutions most resemble those considered early and egalitarian by processual evolutionism. But this caution to the contrary, processual evolutionism's images of sedentary life in the Andes thousands of years ago are heavily determined by analogies with twentieth-century communities.

Contingent history theorists argue that change characterizes all cultures in all times. The Andean past, even before the great hiatus created by the European invasion, was not static. Analogies between Inca institutions and earlier Andean cultures should not be assumed on the basis of homogenized analogy, but they should only be inferred when the methods of specific analogy are employed. I believe that this study of the *ayllu* proves this point. *Ayllu* organization should not be imputed to the beginning of Andean culture simply because the *ayllu* was a ubiquitous feature of the Andes in the sixteenth century, it appears in modern indigenous communities, it has been pedigreed into Andean culture, and it looks like the lineages and clans that cultural evolutionism ascribes to an archaic stage of human society.

The fact that the history of *ayllu* organization can now be shown to have been quite different from what was predicted by evolutionary theory, homogenized analogies, and ideal Andean culture implies that the pasts of other institutions that have been constructed with the same methods must be reexamined. I believe that vertical ecological complementarity and the collection of tribute in the form of a labor tax are important examples. In fact vertical ecological complementarity takes on new relevance in the context of recent origins for the *ayllu*. The *ayllu*'s ideal emphasis on economic independence makes far more sense as part of a strategy of resistance to state organization than it does as a primal Andean cultural essence. Furthermore, the collection of tax in labor fits in this context as well. One must recognize that the Inca state developed in a real historical context in which the *ayllu* was a strongly established institution capable of resisting certain kinds of external power. In fact, it seems likely that the strength of the *ayllu* lay in its periodic recreation of the links among land, other crucial resources, their products, and the ancestor mummy, whose benevolence and supernatural authority chartered exclusive possession by the corporate body of descendants. In developing a strategy for state taxation the Incas might well have recognized the desirability of avoiding overt challenge to such a powerful institution. Perhaps they found a solution by focusing on the creation of new land and resources, to become associated with the state ancestor—the Inca king and his divine descent line in Cuzco. New lands would be farmed by the members of *ayllu*s throughout the kingdom, taking labor but avoiding the alienation of products created on the mummy estate through the ancestor's benevolence. Constructions that impute *ayllu* organization, vertical ecological complementarity, and tribute collection in the form of labor tax to the early Andean past do so simply because they are part of ideal Andean culture. They should not be taken for granted, but require testing.

Andean prehistory's third and final inadequacy is the scarcity of archaeological tests of the inferences, scenarios, and narratives constructed by Andeanist prehistorians. In part this concern has already been expressed, for homogenized analogy ignores rigorous methods dictated by specific analogy. However, the topic deserves separate treatment because it holds the solution to the problematic situation in which Andean prehistory finds itself.

Andean archaeologists have demonstrated little concern for testing the inferences they have made about the Andean past. Rather, they seem to feel remarkably satisfied visualizing the past in terms of models and then interpreting the archaeological record as perfect expressions of these models. In some cases the model comes from homogenized analogy based on Andean culture, such as Moseley's (1992: 182) inference that the Incas, Chimú, and Moche all used the same form of indirect rule on the north coast of Peru. In some cases the model comes from the reordering of Andean culture in terms of evolutionary theory, such as Gero's (1991: 135–138) discussion of balanced reciprocal labor exchange within the egalitarian *ayllu* slowly transforming into redistribution as *ayllu* elites became wealthy enough to substitute conspicuous feasting and display of scarce goods for their obligation to participate in communal work, including cultivation of fields under their control. In some cases models come from sources unrelated to the Andes, such as

Kolata's (1993: 88) model of Tiwanaku as cosmological map, adopted from Paul Wheatley's (1971) study of ancient Chinese and southeast Asian capitals.

As shown above, Andean culture is an ideal construct, and its manipulation is not a reliable way of knowing the pasts of real Andean cultures. Models constructed on the basis of other cultures do not promise greater accuracy in representing the pasts of actual Andean cultures. The confidence that Andean prehistorians feel in analogies and models has been misplaced, but there is no need to discard all these ideas and models out of hand. If analogies and models are carefully tested in accord with the methods of specific analogy, they can provide important insights into Andean prehistory. If proposals about individual cultural pasts, at defined times, are based on analogies or other models whose material correlates and relational contexts are carefully worked out and these relations and correlates are then examined in the archaeological record—giving as much attention to differences as to similarities—there is reason for feeling confidence in the resulting inferences. It is only when analogies and models are assumed to be true because of some inherent reliability, such as belonging to Andean culture and conforming to evolutionary expectations, that archaeologists slip into speculative idealizations.

We have seen the degree of error in processual evolutionism's assertions about *ayllu* origins, but let us briefly examine another case to see if it suggests comparable error. Current descriptions of Andean culture indicate that Andean peoples resisted paying taxes in goods, but readily paid state levies on labor. This timeless generalization indicates that all Andean states collected and managed labor as the basis for class differentiation. I know of no archaeological tests of this, in spite of the fact that it seems to have become accepted doctrine. Using characteristic timeless prose, Michael Moseley (1992: 65) informs readers that money was rarely if ever the form in which Andean polities collected revenue. Andean cultures extracted tribute in labor.

> The agricultural labor tax was not an invention of the Inca, but an ancient feature of the Andean social landscape. Throughout the Andes, local political leaders and ethnic lords had extracted surplus labor in community owned fields from their subjects for generations before the coming of the Inca. (Kolata 1993: 209)

The class-stratified states that appeared in the fifth and sixth centuries A.D. derived their revenues from the labor of peasants [farmers], pastoralists, and fisherfolk and from goods they produced as part-time craft workers. (Patterson 1991: 33–34)

If we were to test this idea in terms of the methods of specific analogy we should look at Inca tax collection at the moment of the Spanish invasion for the source of the analogy. In fact, Inca labor tax collection was associated with provincial politico-ceremonial centers that had large storage facilities. Relations between the architectural facilities of these administrative centers and the institution of labor tax were based on the fact that workers for the state were not required to provide any goods to the state, even their own food. Consequently, the feeding and final feasting of state workers required storehouses for foods, barrackslike housing for the women who prepared the food and *chicha* corn beer, as well as other facilities well preserved and thoroughly identified in the archaeological record (Morris 1974, 1982, 1992; Morris and Thompson 1985). Once these relations and material correlates are worked out for the Incas, a subject culture and time must be identified—let us say Tiwanaku at A.D. 500. The archaeological record of Tiwanaku for that period must then be compared with the Inca information. Equal attention must be paid to differences as well as similarities if we want to avoid limiting our knowledge of the past to the knowledge of more recent cultures (Stahl 1993; Upham 1987; Wylie 1985).

Significantly, I believe we can already affirm that Tiwanaku at A.D. 500 was not constructing anything like the Inca facilities for food storage, housing for women workers, and other intimately related material associates of the Inca state labor tax. Neither did any other Andean culture of the Early Intermediate Period that we currently know, and even data for the Middle Horizon and Late Intermediate Period are inconclusive. I believe that the almost universally accepted association between Andean states and the collection of taxes in the form of labor is a construct of homogenized analogy that fails rigorous tests of specific analogy.

I suggest that we need to reevaluate another doctrinaire feature of Andean prehistory, vertical ecological complementarity. It, too, comes to us from homogenized analogy and idealized Andean culture. It need not be rejected as a part of the Andean past, but it must be tested in terms of methods identified with specific analogy. At present, creative archaeological studies of verticality are being conducted (cf. Aldenderfer 1993; Aldenderfer and Stanish 1993; Dillehay 1976, 1977, 1979; Muñoz 1993; Stanish 1989a, 1989b, 1992; Stanish et al. 1993), but they could benefit from more conscious identification of source and subject cultures, direct historical techniques (Stahl 1994), and careful consideration of differences as well as similarities in the archaeological record.

In conclusion, I find that the *ayllu* is unlikely to be the only institution that has been inferred for the early Andean past from Andean culture on the basis of untested homogeneous analogy. Other institutions have become important parts of the Andean past through the same methods and theoretical assumptions that allowed the *ayllu* to be attributed to the earliest stages of Andean development and to become conceptualized as an ancient cultural essence. I recommend that tests like this study of *ayllu* organization and antiquity be conducted for institutions such as vertical ecological complementarity and state taxation in labor before they are included in our visions of the Andean past. I also conclude that untested inferences about the Andean past that are based on homogenized analogies tend to confirm processual evolutionism's vision of prehistory, seeming to validate this approach, its assumptions, and its theory. However, the appearance of confirmation springs from circular logic and faulty methods that construct the past in terms of the practitioner's expectations.

For the future of Andean archaeology I advocate an approach that recognizes contingent history grounded in informed action. I recommend specific analogy and rigorous study of relations between material contexts and social action before inferring behavior into the past. Differences must be as important in these studies as similarities. I also advocate a focus on people as informed agents to counterbalance the traditional concern with institutions, systems, and adaptation. While cultural evolutionism should not be ignored, it should not simply provide the framework of expectations in terms of which archaeologists organize chronologies for real cultures in the past. In these ways we may better know the Andean past, constructing, testing, and revising accounts, making them more plausible and consistent with the archaeological remains. Rigorous methods and theories allow archaeologists to gain meaningful knowledge—even though that knowledge always retains its subjective quality, remaining less than proven.

BIBLIOGRAPHY

Agnew, John A., and James S. Duncan, eds.
1989 "Introduction." In *The Power of Place*, edited by John A. Agnew and James S. Duncan, pp. 1-8. London: Unwin Hyman.

Albarracin-Jordan, Juan V., and James E. Mathews
1990 *Asentamientos prehispánicos del Valle de Tiwanaku*. La Paz: Producciones CIMA.

Alberti, Giorgio, and Enrique Mayer
1974a "Reciprocidad andina, ayer y hoy." In *Reciprocidad e intercambio en los Andes peruanos*, edited by Giorgio Alberti and Enrique Mayer, pp. 13-33. Perú Problema no. 12. Lima: Instituto de Estudios Peruanos.
1974b *Reciprocidad e intercambio en los Andes peruanos*. Perú Problema no. 12. Lima: Instituto de Estudios Peruanos.

Albó, Javier
1972 "Dinámica en la estructura inter-comunitaria de Jesús de Machaca." *América Indígena* 32(3): 773-816.

Aldenderfer, Mark S., ed.
1993 *Domestic Architecture, Ethnicity, and Complementarity in the South-Central Andes*. Iowa City: University of Iowa Press.

Aldenderfer, Mark S., and Charles Stanish
1993 "Domestic Architecture, Household Archaeology, and the Past in the South-Central Andes." In *Domestic Architecture, Ethnicity, and Complementarity in the South-Central Andes*, edited by Mark S. Aldenderfer, pp. 1-12. Iowa City: University of Iowa Press.

Aldunate del Solar, Carlos, and Victoria Castro Rojas
1981 "Las Chullpa de Toconce y su relación con el poblamiento altiplánico en el Loa Superior período tardío." Licenciado en Filosofía. Universidad de Chile, Santiago.

Allen, Catherine J.
1982 "Body and Soul in Quechua Thought." *Journal of Latin American Lore* 8(2): 179-196.
1988 *The Hold Life Has: Coca and Cultural Identity in an Andean Community*. Washington, D.C.: Smithsonian Institution Press.

Alva, Walter, and Christopher B. Donnan
1993 *Royal Tombs of Sipán*. Los Angeles: Fowler Museum of Culture History.

Amat Olazábal, Hernán
1978 "Los Yaros: Destructores del imperio Wari." In *El hombre*

y la cultura andina: III Congreso Peruano, vol. 2, edited by Ramiro Matos, pp. 614–640. Lima: JERM.

Appaduri, Arjun
1988 "Introduction: Place and Voice in Anthropology." *Cultural Anthropology* 3(1): 16–20.

Arellano López, Jorge, and Danilo Kuljis Meruvia
1986 "Antecedentes preliminares de las investigaciones arqueológicas en la zona circumtitikaka de Bolivia (sector occidental sur)." *Prehistóricas*: 19–28. La Paz: Universidad Mayor de San Andrés, Facultad de Ciencias Sociales, Carrera de Antropología y Arqueología.

Arnold, Dean E.
1993 *Ecology and Ceramic Production in an Andean Community*. Cambridge: Cambridge University Press.

Arriaga, Father Pablo José de
[1621] 1968 *The Extirpation of Idolatry in Peru*. Translated by L. Clark Keating. Lexington: University of Kentucky Press.

Ascher, Robert
1961 "Analogy in Archaeological Interpretation." *Southwestern Journal of Anthropology* 17(4): 317–325.
1962 "Ethnography for Archaeology: A Case Study from the Seri Indians." *Ethnology* 1: 360–369.

Avila, Francisco de
[1608] 1966 *Dioses y hombres de Huarochirí: Narración quechua recogida por Francisco de Avila (¿1598?)*. Translation by José María Arguedas. Lima: Instituto Francés de Estudios Andinos/Instituto de Estudios Peruanos.
[1611] 1966 "Relación que yo el Dr. Francisco de Avila, cura y beneficiado de la ciudad de Guánuco, hize por mandato del Sr. Arcobispado . . ." In *Dioses y hombres de Huarochirí: Narración quechua recogida por Francisco de Avila (1598?)*, edited by José María Arguedas, pp. 255–259. Lima: Instituto Francés de Estudios Andinos/Instituto de Estudios Peruanos.

Ayca Gallegos, Oscar
1995 *Sillustani*. Tacna, Peru: Instituto de Arqueología del Sur.

Banco Popular del Perú
1979 *El arte y la vida Vicús*. (Text by Luis G. Lumbreras.) Lima: Colección del Banco Popular del Perú.

Bandelier, Adolph F.
1905 "The Aboriginal Ruins at Sillustani, Peru." *American Anthropologist* 7(1): 49–68.
1910 *The Islands of Titicaca and Koati*. New York: Hispanic Society of America.

Barrett, John C.
1988 "The Field of Discourse: Reconstituting a Social Archaeology." *Critique of Archaeology* 7(3): 5–16.

Bastien, Joseph
1978 *Mountain of the Condor: Metaphor and Ritual in an Andean Ayllu*. New York: West Publishing Co.
1995 "The Mountain/Body Metaphor Expressed in a Kaatan Funeral." In *Tombs for the Living: Andean Mortuary Practices*, edited by Tom D. Dillehay, pp. 355–378. Washington, D.C.: Dumbarton Oaks.

Bauer, Brian S.
1992 *The Development of the Inca State*. Austin: University of Texas Press.

Benavides C., Mario
1984 *Carácter del estado Wari*. Ayacucho: Universidad Nacional Mayor San Cristóbal de Huamanga.
1991 "Cheqo Wasi, Huari." In *Huari Administrative Structure: Prehistoric Monumental Architecture and State Government*, edited by William H. Isbell and Gordon E. McEwan, pp. 55–69. Washington, D.C.: Dumbarton Oaks.

Bengtsson, Lisbet
1991 "Grave Chambers at Kachiqhata and Markaqocha in the District of Ollantaytambo, Cusco Department, Peru." Paper presented at the 47th International Congress of Americanists, New Orleans.

Bennett, Wendell C.
1944 *The North Highlands of Peru: Excavations in the Callejón de Huaylas and at Chavín de Huantar*. Anthropological Papers, vol. 39, pt. 1. New York: American Museum of Natural History.
1946 "Archaeology of the Central Andes." In *Handbook of South American Indians*, vol. 2, *The Andean Civilizations*, edited by Julian Steward, pp. 61–147. Bureau of American Ethnology Bulletin 143. Washington, D.C.: Smithsonian Institution.
1949 "Religious Structures." In *Handbook of South American Indians*, vol. 5, edited by Julian Steward, pp. 29–51. Bureau of American Ethnology Bulletin 143. Washington, D.C.: Smithsonian Institution.

Berezkin, Yury
1978a "Chronologie des étapes moyenne et tardive de la culture Mochica (Pérou) [in Russian]." *Sovetskaya archeologiya* (Moscow) 2: 78–96.
1978b "The Social Structure of the Mochica through the Prism of

Mythology (Ancient Peru) [in Russian]." *Vestnik drevnei istorii* (Moscow) 3(145): 39–59.

Bermann, Mark
1994 *Lukurmata: Household Archaeology in Prehispanic Peru*. Princeton: Princeton University Press.

Bertonio, P. Ludovico
[1612] 1984 *Vocabulario de la lengua aymara*. Cochabamba: Centro de Estudios de la Realidad Económica y Social.

Betanzos, Juan de
[1551] 1987 *Suma y narración de los Incas*. Edited by María del Carmen Martín Rubio. Madrid: Ediciones Atlas.

Binford, Lewis R.
1962 "Archaeology as Anthropology." *American Antiquity* 28(2): 217–225.
1964 "A Consideration of Archaeological Research Design." *American Antiquity* 29: 425–441.
1967 "Smudge Pits and Hide Smoking: The Use of Analogy in Archaeological Reasoning." *American Antiquity* 32(1): 1–32.
1968 "Methodological Considerations of the Archaeological Use of Ethnographic Data." In *Man the Hunter*, edited by Richard B. Lee and Irving DeVore, pp. 268–273. Chicago: Aldine.

Bloch, Maurice
1989 "From Cognition to Ideology." In *The Past and the Present: The Collected Papers of Maurice Bloch*, edited by Maurice Bloch, pp. 106–136. London and Atlantic Highlands, N.J.: Athlone Press.

Bonavia, Duccio
1970 "Investigaciones arqueológicas en el Mantaro Medio (1967–1968)." *Revista del Museo Nacional* 35: 211–294.

Bonnier, Elisabeth
1981 "Las ruinas de Tantamayo: Vestigios de una ocupación tardía." *Boletín de Lima* 14(3): 38–53.

Bradby, Barbara
1982 "Resistance to Capitalism in the Peruvian Andes." In *Ecology and Exchange in the Andes*, edited by David Lehmann, pp. 97–122. Cambridge: Cambridge University Press.

Brewster-Wray, Michael
1988 "Kinship and Labor in the Structure of the Inka Empire." Ph.D. dissertation. Department of Anthropology, State University of New York, Binghamton.

Browman, David
1974 "Pastoral Nomadism in the Andes." *Current Anthropology* 15(2): 188–196.

Bruhns, Karen O.
1982 "Dating the Sculpture of San Augustín: A Correlation with Northern Peru." In *Pre-Columbian Art History*, edited by Alana Cordy-Collins, pp. 193–204. Palo Alto: Peek Publications.

Brumfiel, Elizabeth M.
1992 "Distinguished Lecture in Archaeology: Breaking and Entering the Ecosystem—Gender, Class, and Faction Steal the Show." *American Anthropologist* 94(3): 551–567.

Brush, Stephen B.
1977 *Mountain, Field and Family: The Economy and Human Ecology of an Andean Valley*. Philadelphia: University of Pennsylvania Press.
1980 "The Environment and Native Andean Agriculture." *América Indígena* 40(1): 161–172.

Burger, Richard
1992 *Chavín and the Origins of Andean Civilization*. London: Thames and Hudson.

Cabello de Balboa, Miguel
[1586] 1951 *Miscelánea antártica*. Lima: Instituto de Etnología. Universidad Nacional Mayor de San Marcos.

Camino D. C., Alejandro
1982 "Tiempo y espacio en la estrategia de subsistencia andina: Un caso en las vertientes orientales sud-peruanos." In *El hombre y su ambiente en los Andes centrales*, edited by Luis Millones and Hiroyasu Tomoeda, pp. 11–38. Senri Ethnological Studies no. 10. Osaka: National Museum of Ethnology.

Carmichael, Patrick H.
1995 "Nasca Burial Patterns: Social Structure and Mortuary Ideology." In *Tombs for the Living: Andean Mortuary Practices*, edited by Tom D. Dillehay, pp. 161–187. Washington, D.C.: Dumbarton Oaks.

Carneiro, Robert
1962 "Scale Analysis as an Instrument for the Study of Cultural Evolution." *Southwestern Journal of Anthropology* 18: 149–169.
1981 "The Chiefdom: Precursor of the State." In *The Transition to Statehood in the New World*, edited by Grant D. Jones and Robert R. Kautz, pp. 37–79. Cambridge: Cambridge University Press.

Casenelli, Amalia, Marcia Koth de Paredes, and Mariana Mould de Pease, eds.
1981 *Etnohistoria y antropología andina*. Lima: Museo Nacional de Historia.

Castro-Klarén, Sara
    1990        "Discurso y transformación de los dioses en los Andes: del Taki Onqoy a 'Rasu Ñiti.'" In *El retorno de las huacas: Estudios y documentos sobre el Taki Onqoy, siglo XVI*, edited by Luis Millones, pp. 407–423. Lima: Instituto de Estudios Peruanos.
Castro Pozo, Hildebrando
    1946        "Social and Economico-Political Evolution of the Communities of Central Peru." In *Handbook of South American Indians*, vol. 2, *The Andean Civilizations*, edited by Julian Steward, pp. 483–499. Washington, D.C.: Smithsonian Institution.
Chayanov, Aleksandr V.
    [1925] 1966    *The Theory of Peasant Economy*. Holywood, Ill.: Richard Erwin.
Cieza de León, Pedro
    [1553] 1959    *The Incas of Pedro Cieza de León*. Edited by Victor von Hagen. Norman: University of Oklahoma Press.
    [1553] n.d.    "La crónica del Perú." In *Crónicas de la conquista del Perú*, edited by Julio Riverend, pp. 125–497. Mexico City: Editorial Nueva España.
Clark, John Grahame D.
    1951        "Folk Culture and the Study of European Prehistory." In *Aspects of Archaeology in Great Britain and Beyond: Essays Presented to O. G. S. Crawford*, edited by William Francis Grimes, pp. 49–65. London: H. W. Edwards.
Clifford, James
    1988        *The Predicament of Culture: Twentieth Century Ethnography, Literature and Art*. Cambridge, Mass.: Harvard University Press.
Clifford, James, and George Marcus, eds.
    1986        *Writing Culture: The Poetics and Politics of Ethnography*. Berkeley: University of California Press.
Cobo, Bernabé
    [1653] 1892    *Historia del nuevo mundo*, vol. 3. Seville: E. Rasco.
    [1653] 1893    *Historia del nuevo mundo*, vol. 4. Seville: E. Rasco.
    [1653] 1964    *Obras del P. Bernabé Cobo I & II*. Madrid: Real Academia Española.
    [1653] 1979    *History of the Inca Empire*. Translated and edited by Roland Hamilton. Austin: University of Texas Press.
    [1653] 1990    *Inca Religion and Custom*. Translated and edited by Roland Hamilton. Austin: University of Texas Press.
Collins, Jane L.
    1986        "The Household and Relations of Production in Southern

Peru." *Comparative Studies in Society and History* 28(4): 651–671.
1988 *Unseasonal Migration: The Effects of Rural Labor Scarcity in Peru.* Princeton: Princeton University Press.
Colvin, Howard
1991 *Architecture and the After-Life.* New Haven: Yale University Press.
Combs-Schilling, M. Elaine
1989 *Sacred Performances: Islam, Sexuality and Sacrifice.* New York: Columbia University Press.
Conkey, Margaret W.
1990 "Experimenting with Style in Archaeology: Some Historical and Theoretical Issues." In *The Uses of Style in Archaeology*, edited by Margaret W. Conkey and Christine Hastorf, pp. 5–17. Cambridge: Cambridge University Press.
Conkey, Margaret, and Joan M. Gero
1991 "Tensions, Pluralities, and Engendering Archaeology: An Introduction to Women and Prehistory." In *Engendering Archaeology: Women in Prehistory*, edited by Joan M. Gero and Margaret W. Conkey, pp. 3–30. Cambridge, Mass.: Basil Blackwell.
Conkey, Margaret, and Janet Spector
1984 "Archaeology and the Study of Gender." *Advances in Archaeological Method and Theory* 7: 1–38.
Cornejo Bouroncle, Jorge
1939 "Las momias incas: Trepanaciones craneanas en el antiguo Perú." In *Actas y trabajos científicos del 27 Congreso Internacional de Americanistas*, vol. 1, pp. 35–49. Lima.
Crapanzano, Vincent
1992 *Hermes' Dilemma and Hamlet's Desire: On the Epistemology of Interpretation.* Cambridge, Mass.: Harvard University Press.
D'Altroy, Terence N.
1992 *Provincial Power in the Inka Empire.* Washington, D.C.: Smithsonian Institution.
D'Andrade, Roy, and Nancy Scheper-Hughes
1995 "Objectivity and Militancy: A Debate (with Commentary)." *Current Anthropology* 36(3): 399–440.
Diamond, Stanley
1951 "Dahomey: A Proto-State in West Africa." Ph.D. dissertation. Columbia University.

Diez de San Miguel, Garci
[1567] 1964 *Visita hecha a la provincia de Chuquito por Garci Diez de San Miguel en el año 1567*. Documentos Regionales para la Etnología y Etnohistoria Andina, vol. 1. Lima: Casa de la Cultura del Perú.

di Leonardo, Michaela
1991 "Gender, Culture and Political Economy: Feminist Anthropology in Historical Perspective." In *Gender at the Crossroads of Knowledge: Feminist Anthropology in the Postmodern Era*, edited by Michaela di Leonardo, pp. 1–48. Berkeley: University of California Press.

Dillehay, Tom D.
1976 "Competition and Cooperation in a Prehistoric Multiethnic System in the Central Andes." Ph.D. dissertation. University of Texas, Austin.
1977 "Tawantinsuyu Integration of the Chillón Valley, Peru: A Case of Inca Geo-Political Mastery." *Journal of Field Archaeology* 4: 397–405.
1979 "Pre-Hispanic Resource Sharing in the Central Andes." *Science* 204(6): 24–31.
1995a "Introduction." In *Tombs for the Living: Andean Mortuary Practices*, edited by Tom D. Dillehay, pp. 1–26. Washington, D.C.: Dumbarton Oaks.
1995b *Tombs for the Living: Andean Mortuary Practices*. Washington, D.C.: Dumbarton Oaks.

Disselhoff, Hans Dietrich
1967 *Daily Life in Ancient Peru*. New York: McGraw-Hill.

Donnan, Christopher B.
1975 "The Thematic Approach to Moche Iconography." *Journal of Latin American Lore* 1(2): 147–162.
1976 *Moche Art of Peru*. Los Angeles: Museum of Culture History, University of California, Los Angeles.
1978 *Moche Art of Peru: Pre-Columbian Symbolic Communication*. Los Angeles: Museum of Culture History, University of California, Los Angeles.
1995 "Moche Funerary Practices." In *Tombs for the Living: Andean Mortuary Practices*, edited by Tom D. Dillehay, pp. 111–159. Washington, D.C.: Dumbarton Oaks.

Donnan, Christopher B., and Luis Jaime Castillo
1992 "Finding the Tomb of a Moche Priestess." *Archaeology* 45(6): 38–42.

Donnan, Christopher B., and Carol J. Mackey
1978 *Ancient Burial Patterns of the Moche Valley, Peru*. Austin: University of Texas Press.

Donnan, Christopher B., and Donna McClelland
    1979          *The Burial Theme in Moche Iconography*. Washington, D.C.: Dumbarton Oaks.

Doyle, Mary E.
    1988          "The Ancestor Cult and Burial Ritual in Seventeenth and Eighteenth-Century Central Peru." Ph.D. dissertation. University of California, Los Angeles. Ann Arbor: University Microfilms.

Duncan, James S.
    1990          *The City as Text: The Politics of Landscape Interpretation in the Kandyan Kingdom*. New York: Cambridge University Press.

Dunnell, R.
    1980          "Evolutionary Theory in Archaeology." *Advances in Archaeological Method and Theory* 3: 35–99.

Duviols, Pierre
    1966          "Un procès d'idolatrie, 1671." *Fénix, Revista de la Biblioteca Nacional* (Lima) 16: 198–211.
    1973          "Huari y Llacuaz: Agricultores y pastores, un dualismo prehispánico de oposición y complementaridad." *Revista del Museo Nacional* 39: 153–191.
    1976          "'Punchao,' ídolo mayor del Coricancha: Historia y tipología." *Antropología Andina* (Centro de Estudios Andinos, Cuzco) 1–2: 156–183.
    1986          *Cultura andina y represión: Procesos y visitas de idolatrías y hechicerías, Cajatambo, siglo XVII*. Cuzco: Centro de Estudios Rurales Andinos "Bartolomé de Las Casas."

Earle, Timothy, Terence D'Altroy, Christine Hastorf, Catherine Scott, Cathy Costin, Glenn Russell, and Elsie Sandefur
    1987          *Archaeological Field Research in the Upper Mantaro, Peru, 1982–1983: Investigations of Inka Expansion and Exchange*. Monograph 28. Los Angeles: Institute of Archaeology, University of California, Los Angeles.

Engels, Frederick
    1972          *The Origin of the Family, Private Property and the State (with Introduction and Notes by Eleanor Burke Leacock)*. New York: International Publishers.

Espinoza Soriano, Waldemar
    1981          "El fundamento territorial del ayllu: Siglos XV y XVI." In *Etnohistoria y antropología andina*, edited by Amalia Casenelli, Marcia Koth de Paredes, and Mariana Mould de Pease, pp. 93–130. Lima: Museo Nacional de Historia.
    1987          *Los Incas: Economía, sociedad y estado en la era del Tahuantinsuyo*. Lima: Amaru.

Fabian, Johannes
　　1983　　　　　*Time and the Other: How Anthropology Makes Its Objects*. New York: Columbia University Press.
Farabee, William Curtis
　　1922　　　　　*Indian Tribes of Eastern Peru*. Papers of the Peabody Museum of American Archaeology and Ethnology, vol. 10. Cambridge: Harvard University.
Feld, Stephen
　　1982　　　　　*Sound and Sentiment: Birds, Weeping, Poetics and Song in Kaluli Expression*. Philadelphia: University of Pennsylvania Press.
Figueroa, Adolfo
　　1982　　　　　"Production and Market Exchange in Peasant Economies: The Case of the Southern Highlands of Peru." In *Ecology and Exchange in the Andes*, edited by David Lehmann, pp. 123–156. Cambridge: Cambridge University Press.
Fleming, Stuart
　　1986　　　　　"The Mummies of Pachacamac: An Exceptional Legacy from Uhle's 1896 Excavations in Peru." *Expedition* 28(3): 39–45.
Flornoy, Bertrand
　　1949　　　　　*Exploration archéologique del'Alto Marañon (des sources du Marañon au Rio Sarma)*. Institut Français d'Etudes Andines 5: 51–81.
　　1957　　　　　"Monuments de la région de Tantamayo (Pérou)." *Journal de la Société des Américanistes* 46: 207–225.
Fonseca Martel, César
　　1974　　　　　"Modalidades de la Minka." In *Reciprocidad e intercambio en los Andes*, edited by Giorgio Alberti and Enrique Mayer, pp. 86–109. Perú Problema no. 12. Lima: Instituto de Estudios Peruanos.
Fonseca Martel, César, and Enrique Mayer
　　1978　　　　　"La economía 'vertical' y la economía de mercado en las comunidades alteñas del Perú." *Debates en Antropología* 2: 25–51.
Fried, Morton H.
　　1967　　　　　*The Evolution of Political Society*. New York: Random House.
　　1975　　　　　*The Notion of Tribe*. Menlo Park, Calif.: Cummings.
Friedrich, Paul
　　1989　　　　　"Language, Ideology, and Political Economy." *American Anthropologist* 91(2): 295–312.
Fritz, John, and Fred Plog
　　1970　　　　　"The Nature of Archaeological Explanation." *American Antiquity* 35(4): 405–412.

Fuenzalida, Fernando
    1979        "Los gentiles y el origen de la muerte." *Revista de la Universidad Católica* 5: 213–222.

Gad, G., and D. Holdsworth
    1987        "Corporate Capitalism and the Emergence of the High-Rise Office Building." *Urban Geography* 8: 212–231.

Gailey, Christine Ward
    1987        *Kinship to Kingship: Gender Hierarchy and State Formation in the Tongan Islands*. Austin: University of Texas Press.

Gailey, Christine Ward, and Thomas C. Patterson
    1987        "Power Relations and State Formation." In *Power Relations and State Formation*, edited by Thomas C. Patterson and Christine Ward Gailey, pp. 1–26. Washington, D.C.: Archaeology Section, American Anthropological Association.

Gasparini, Graziano, and Luise Margolies
    1980        *Inca Architecture*. Bloomington and London: Indiana University Press.

Geertz, Clifford
    1973        *The Interpretation of Cultures*. New York: Basic Books.
    1983        *Local Knowledge: Further Essays in Interpretive Anthropology*. New York: Basic Books.
    1984        "Distinguished Lecture: Anti Anti-Relativism." *American Anthropologist* 86: 263–278.

Gell, Alfred
    1992        *The Anthropology of Time: Cultural Constructions of Temporal Maps and Images*. Oxford: Berg.

Gero, Joan M.
    1991        "Who Experienced What in Prehistory? A Narrative Explanation from Queyash, Peru." In *Processual and Postprocessual Archaeologies: Multiple Ways of Knowing the Past*, edited by Robert W. Prucel, pp. 126–139. Center for Archaeological Investigations Occasional Paper no. 10. Carbondale: Southern Illinois University.

Giddens, Anthony
    1979        *Central Problems in Social Theory: Action, Structure and Contradictions in Social Analysis*. Berkeley: University of California Press.
    1981        *A Contemporary Critique of Historical Materialism*. Berkeley: University of California Press.
    1984        *The Constitution of Society*. Berkeley: University of California Press.

Gillet, David W.
    1992        *Covering Ground: Communal Water Management and*

the State in the Peruvian Highlands. Ann Arbor: University of Michigan Press.

Godelier, M.
1977a "The Concept of 'Social and Economic Formation': The Inca Example." In *Perspectives in Marxist Anthropology*, edited by Maurice Godelier, pp. 63–69. Cambridge: Cambridge University Press.

1977b "The Non-Correspondence between Form and Content in Social Relations." In *Perspectives in Marxist Anthropology*, edited by Maurice Godelier, pp. 186–195. Cambridge: Cambridge University Press.

Golte, Jürgen
1980 *La racionalidad de la organización andina*. Lima: Instituto de Estudios Peruanos.

Gould, Richard A.
1978 "The Anthropology of Human Residues." *American Anthropologist* 80: 815–835.

1980 *Living Archaeology*. Cambridge: Cambridge University Press.

Gould, Richard A., and Patty Jo Watson
1982 "A Dialogue on the Meaning and Use of Analogy in Ethnoarchaeological Reasoning." *Journal of Anthropological Archaeology* 1: 355–381.

Grieder, Terence
1978 *The Art and Archaeology of Pashash*. Austin: University of Texas Press.

Grosboll, Sue
1993 "And He Said in the Time of the Ynga, They Paid Tribute and Served the Ynga." In *Provincial Inca: Archaeological and Ethnohistorical Assessment of the Impact of the Inca State*, edited by Michael A. Malpass, pp. 44–76. Iowa City: University of Iowa Press.

Guaman Poma de Ayala, Felipe
[1615] 1936 *Nueva corónica y buen gobierno*. Paris: Institut d'Ethnologie.

[1615] 1980 *Nueva corónica y buen gobierno*. Edited by John V. Murra and Rolena Adorno with translation by Jorge L. Urioste. 3 vols. Mexico City: Siglo XXI.

Guillén Guillén, Eduardo
1983 "El enigma de las momias incas." *Boletín de Lima* 28(5): 29–42.

Gupta, Akhil, and James Ferguson
1992 "Beyond 'Culture': Space, Identity, and the Politics of Difference." *Cultural Anthropology* 7(1): 6–23.

Hall, Martin
1984 "The Myth of the Zulu Homestead: Archaeology and Ethnography." *Africa* 54(1): 65–79.
Halperin, Rhoda, and James Dow, eds.
1977 *Peasant Livelihood.* New York: St. Martin's Press.
Hanson, Allan
1989 "The Making of the Maori: Culture, Invention and Its Logic." *American Anthropologist* 91(4): 890–902.
Harris, Olivia
1978 "El parentesco y la economía vertical en el ayllu Laymi (norte de Potosí)." *Avances* 1: 51–64.
1982 "Labour and Produce in an Ethnic Economy, Northern Potosí, Bolivia." In *Ecology and Exchange in the Andes*, edited by David Lehmann, pp. 70–96. Cambridge: Cambridge University Press.
Hastings, Charles M., and Michael E. Moseley
1975 "The Adobes of Huaca del Sol and Huaca de la Luna." *American Antiquity* 40(2): 196–203.
Hastorf, Christine A.
1990a "The Ecosystem Model and Long-term Prehistoric Change: An Example from the Andes." In *The Ecosystem Approach in Anthropology: From Concept to Practice*, edited by Emilio Moran, pp. 131–157. Ann Arbor: University of Michigan Press.
1990b "The Effect of the Inka State on Sausa Agricultural Production and Crop Consumption." *American Antiquity* 55(2): 262–290.
1992 *Agriculture and the Onset of Political Inequality before the Inka.* Cambridge: Cambridge University Press.
Hemming, John
1970 *The Conquest of Peru.* New York: Harcourt, Brace, Jovanovich.
Heredia Zavala, María de los Angeles
1991 "Arqueología para Culli-Culli: Primeros resultados." *Textos antropológicos: Revista de la Carrera de Antropología-Arqueología* (Universidad Mayor San Andrés) 2: 97–114.
Hernández Príncipe, R.
1923 "Mitología andina: Idolatrías de Recuay, 1622." *Inca* 1: 25–68.
Herzfeld, Michael
1987 *Anthropology through the Looking Glass: Critical Ethnography in the Margins of Europe.* Cambridge: Cambridge University Press.

Hobsbawm, Eric, and Terence O. Ranger, eds.
   1983        *The Invention of Tradition*. Cambridge: Cambridge University Press.

Hodder, Ian
   1982a      *Symbolic and Structural Archaeology*. Cambridge: Cambridge University Press.
   1982b      *Symbols in Action*. Cambridge: Cambridge University Press.
   1983        "Archaeology, Ideology and Contemporary Society." *Royal Anthropological Institute News* 56: 5–7.
   1984a      "Archaeology in 1984." *Antiquity* 58: 25–32.
   1984b      "Burials, Houses, Women, and Men in the European Neolithic." In *Ideology, Power and Prehistory*, edited by Daniel Miller and Christopher Tilley, pp. 51–68. Cambridge: Cambridge University Press.
   1985        "Post-Processual Archaeology." In *Advances in Archaeological Method and Theory*, vol. 8, edited by Michael B. Schiffer, pp. 1–26. New York: Academic Press.
   1986        *Reading the Past*. Cambridge: Cambridge University Press.
   1989        *The Meaning of Things: Material Culture and Symbolic Expression*. London: Unwin Hyman.
   1991        *Reading the Past*. 2d ed. Cambridge: Cambridge University Press.

Holguín, Diego G.
   [1608] 1989  *Vocabulario de la lengua general de todo el Perú: Llamada lengua Quichua, del Inca*. Lima: Universidad Nacional Mayor de San Marcos.

Horkheimer, Hans
   1944        *Vistas arqueológicas del noroeste del Perú*. Trujillo, Peru: Librería e Imprenta Moreno.

Howell, Carol J.
   n.d.         Photographic Record of Quebrada de la Vaca. (Unpublished report.) Sacramento: California Institute for Peruvian Studies.

Hrdlička, Ales
   1914        *Anthropological Work in Peru in 1913, with Notes on the Pathology of the Ancient Peruvians*. Smithsonian Miscellaneous Collections, vol. 61, no. 18. Washington, D.C.: Smithsonian Institution.

Huaman Poma, Felipe
   [1615] 1978  *Letter to a King: A Peruvian Chief's Account of Life under the Incas and Spanish Rule*. Translated, arranged, and edited by Christopher Dilke. New York: E. P. Dutton.

Huertas V., Lorenzo
1981a    *La religión en una sociedad rural andina (siglo XVII)*. Ayacucho: Universidad Nacional Mayor San Cristóbal de Huamanga.
1981b    "Poblaciones indígenes en Huamanga colonial." In *Etnohistoria y antropología andina*, edited by Amalia Casenelli, Marcia Koth de Paredes, and Mariana Mould de Pease, pp. 131–144. Lima: Museo Nacional de Historia.

Huffman, Thomas N.
1982    "Archaeology and Ethnohistory in the African Iron Age." *Annual Review of Anthropology* 11: 133–150.
1986    "Iron-Age Settlement Patterns and the Origin of Class Distinction in Southern Africa." In *Advances in World Archaeology*, vol. 5, edited by Fred Wendorf and Angela E. Close, pp. 291–338. New York: Academic Press.
1989    "Ceramics, Settlements and Late Iron Age Migrations." *African Archaeological Review* 7: 155–182.

Hyslop, John
1976    "An Archaeological Survey of the Lupaca Kingdom and Its Origins." Ph.D. dissertation. Department of Anthropology, Columbia University.
1977    "Chulpas of the Lupaca Zone of the Peruvian High Plateau." *Journal of Field Archaeology* 4(2): 149–170.

Inojosa, José María Franco
1937    "Informe sobre los sestos arqueológicos de las cabeceras del Paucartambo." *Revista del Museo Nacional* 6(2): 255–277.

Inojosa, José María Franco, and Alejandro González
1936    "Exploraciones arqueológicos en el Perú, departamento de Puno." *Revista del Museo Nacional* 5(2): 157–183.
1939    "Arqueología del Cusco: Ruinas de Chamankalla, Quillarumi, Yunkaracay y Salakaka." *Revista del Museo Nacional* 8(2): 250–264.

Isbell, Billie Jean
1974    "Parentesco andino y reciprocidad: Kuyaq, los que nos aman." In *Reciprocidad e intercambio en los Andes*, edited by Giorgio Alberti and Enrique Mayer, pp. 110–145. Perú Problema no. 12. Lima: Instituto de Estudios Peruanos.
1978    *To Defend Ourselves: Ecology and Ritual in an Andean Village*. Austin: University of Texas Press.

Isbell, William H.
1968    "New Discoveries in the Montaña of Southeastern Peru." *Archaeology* 21(2): 108–114.

1977  The Rural Foundation for Urbanism. Illinois Studies in Anthropology no. 10. Urbana: University of Illinois Press.
1978a  "Cosmological Order Expressed in Prehistoric Ceremonial Centers." Actes du LXII Congrès International des Américanistes (Paris) 4: 269–297.
1978b  "El imperio Huari: Estado o ciudad?" Revista del Museo Nacional 43: 227–241.
1989  "Honcopampa: Was It a Huari Administrative Center?" In The Nature of Wari: A Reappraisal of the Middle Horizon in Peru, edited by R. Michael Czwarno, Frank M. Meddens, and Alexandra Morgan, pp. 98–115. International Series, 525. Oxford: British Archaeological Reports.
1991a  "Honcopampa: Monumental Ruins in Peru's North Highlands." Expedition Magazine 33(3): 27–36.
1991b  "Huari Administration and the Orthogonal Cellular Architecture Horizon." In Huari Administrative Structure: Prehistoric Monumental Architecture and State Government, edited by William H. Isbell and Gordon E. McEwan, pp. 293–315. Washington, D.C.: Dumbarton Oaks.
1995  "Constructing the Andean Past or 'As You Like It.'" In Current Research in Andean Antiquity, edited by Ari Zighelboim and Carol Barnes. Journal of the Steward Anthropological Society 25(1–2): 1–12.

Isbell, William H., Christine Brewster-Wray, and Lynda Spickard
1991  "Architecture and Spatial Organization at Huari." In Huari Administrative Structure: Prehistoric Monumental Architecture and State Government, edited by William H. Isbell and Gordon E. McEwan, pp. 19–53. Washington, D.C.: Dumbarton Oaks.

Isbell, William H., and Anita G. Cook
1987  "Ideological Origins of an Andean Conquest State." Archaeology 40(4): 27–33.

Jakobsen, Jan, J. Balslev Jakobsen, L. Kempfner Jorgensen, and Inge Schjellerup
1986–1987  "'Cazadores de Cabezas' en sitios pre-Inca de Chachapoyas, Amazonas." Revista del Museo Nacional 48: 139–185.

Julien, Catherine J.
1982  "Inca Decimal Administration in the Lake Titicaca Region." In The Inca and Aztec States, 1400–1800: Anthropology and History, edited by George A. Collier, Renato I. Rosaldo, and John D. Wirth, pp. 119–151. New York and London: Academic Press.
1983  Hatunqolla: A View of Inca Rule from the Lake Titicaca Region. University of California Publications, Anthropology, vol. 15. Berkeley: University of California.

| | |
|---|---|
| 1991 | *Condesuyo: The Political Division of Territory under Inca and Spanish Rule.* BAS 19. Bonn: Bonner Amerikanistische Studien, Estudios Americanistas de Bonn. |

Julien, Daniel
1988     "Ancient Cuismancu: Settlement and Cultural Dynamics in the Cajamarca Region of the North Highlands of Peru, 200 B.C.–A.D. 1532." Ph.D. dissertation. Department of Anthropology, University of Texas at Austin.

Karp, Ivan, and Steven D. Lavine
1991     "Introduction: Museums and Multiculturalism." In *Exhibiting Cultures: The Poetics and Politics of Museum Display*, edited by Ivan Karp and Steven D. Lavine, pp. 1–9. Washington, D.C.: Smithsonian Institution Press.

Kato, Yasutake
1979     "Chapter 8: Chullpas at Tornapampa." In *Excavations at La Pampa in the North Highlands of Peru*, edited by Kazuo Terada, pp. 163–166. Tokyo: University of Tokyo Press.
1993     "Resultados de las excavaciones en Kuntur Wasi, Cajamarca." In *El mundo ceremonial andino*, edited by Luis Millones and Yoshio Onuki, pp. 203–228. Senri Ethnological Studies, no. 37. Osaka: National Museum of Ethnology.

Kauffman Doig, Federico
1984     "Pucullo y figuras antropomorfas de madera en el Antisuyo." *Cielo abierto* 10(29): 45–52.

Kauffman Doig, Federico, Miriam Salazar, Daniel Morales, Iain Mackay, and Oscar Sacay
1989     *Andes amazónicos: Sitios intervenidos por la expedición Antisuyo 1986.* Arqueológicas 20. Lima: Museo Nacional de Antropología y Arqueología.

King, Anthony
1980     "Introduction." In *Buildings and Society*, edited by Anthony King, pp. 1–33. London: Routledge and Kegan Paul.
1987     "Cultural Production and Reproduction." In *Environmental Perspectives: Ethnoscapes: Current Challenges in the Environmental Social Sciences*, edited by David Canter, Martin Krampen, and David Stea, pp. 72–98. London: Grower.

Klein, Herbert S.
1993     *Haciendas and "Ayllus": Rural Society in the Bolivian Andes in the Eighteenth and Ninteenth Centuries.* Stanford: Stanford University Press.

Kleindienst, Maxine R., and Patty Jo Watson
1956     "'Action Archaeology': The Archaeological Inventory of a Living Community." *Anthropology Tomorrow* 5: 75–78.

Kolata, Alan L.
1993  *The Tiwanaku: Portrait of an Andean Civilization.* Cambridge, Mass., and Oxford, U.K.: Blackwell.

Kosso, Peter
1991  "Method in Archaeology: Middle Range Theory as Hermeneutics." *American Antiquity* 56(4): 621–627.

Kuper, Adam
1994  "Culture, Identity, and the Project of Contemporary Anthropology." *Man* 29: 537–554.

Lagos, María L.
1994  *Autonomy and Power: The Dynamics of Class and Culture in Rural Bolivia.* Philadelphia: University of Pennsylvania Press.

Langlois, Louis
1940a  "Utcubamba: Investigaciones arqueológicas in este valle del departamento de Amazonas (Perú)." *Revista del Museo Nacional* 9(1): 33–72.
1940b  "Utcubamba: Investigaciones arqueológicas in este valle del departamento de Amazonas (Perú)." *Revista del Museo Nacional* 9(2): 224–249.

Lapiner, Alan
1976  *Pre-Columbian Art of South America.* New York: Harry N. Abrams.

Larson, Brooke
1988  *Colonialism and Agrarian Transformations in Bolivia: Cochabamba, 1550–1900.* Princeton: Princeton University Press.

Lavallée, Danièle
1970  *Les représentations animales dans la céramique mochica.* Mémoires 4. Paris: l'Institut d'Ethnologie.

Lehmann, David
1982  "Introduction: Andean Societies and the Theory of Peasant Economies." In *Ecology and Exchange in the Andes*, edited by David Lehmann, pp. 1–26. Cambridge: Cambridge University Press.

Leone, Mark P.
1995  "A Historical Archaeology of Capitalism." *American Anthropologist* 97(2): 251–268.

Lévi-Strauss, Claude
1969  *The Elementary Structures of Kinship.* Boston: Beacon Press.

Long, Norman
1992  "From Paradigm Lost to Paradigm Regained? The Case for an Actor-Oriented Sociology of Development." In

Battlefields of Knowledge, edited by Norman Long and Ann Long, pp. 16–43. London and New York: Routledge.

Loten, Stanley H.
1987　　　　Burial Tower 2 and Fort A, Marcahuamachuco. Occasional Papers in Anthropology no. 3. Peterborough, Ontario: Trent University.

Lothrop, Samuel K.
1964　　　　Treasures of Ancient America: Pre-Columbian Art from Mexico to Peru. Geneva: Editions d'Art Albert Skira.

Lounsbury, Floyd G.
1964　　　　"Some Aspects of the Inca Kinship System." Unpublished paper.

Lumbreras, Luis G.
1974a　　　 Las fundaciones de Huamanga. Lima: Editorial Nueva Educación.
1974b　　　 The Peoples and Cultures of Ancient Peru. Washington, D.C.: Smithsonian Institution.

MacCormack, Sabine
1991　　　　Religion in the Andes: Vision and Imagination in Early Colonial Peru. Princeton: Princeton University Press.

MacGaffey, Wyatt
1986　　　　"Epistemological Ethnocentrism in African Studies." In African Historiographies: What History for Which Africa? edited by B. Jewsiewicki and D. Newbury, pp. 42–48. Sage Series on African Modernization and Development, no. 12. Beverly Hills, Calif.: Sage.

Marcus, George, and Michael Fischer
1986　　　　Anthropology as Cultural Critique: An Experimental Moment in the Human Sciences. Chicago: University of Chicago Press.

Marcus, Joyce, and Jorge Silva
1988　　　　"The Chillón Valley 'Coca Lands': Archaeological Background and Ecological Context." In Conflicts over Coca Fields in XVIth-Century Peru, edited by María Rostworowski de Diez Canseco, pp. 1–32. Memoirs of the Museum of Anthropology, no. 21. Ann Arbor: University of Michigan.

Markus, Thomas A.
1982　　　　Order in Space and Society. Edinburgh: Mainstream.
1987　　　　"Buildings as Classifying Devices." Environment and Planning B: Planning and Design 14: 467–484.
1993　　　　Buildings and Power: Freedom and Control in the Origin of Modern Building Types. London and New York: Routledge.

Masuda, Shozo, Izumi Shimada, and Craig Morris, eds.
1985   *Andean Ecology and Civilization: An Interdisciplinary Perspective on Andean Ecological Complementarity.* (Papers from Wenner-Gren Foundation for Anthropological Research Symposium, no. 91.) Tokyo: University of Tokyo Press.

Mayer, Enrique
1974   "Las reglas del juego en la reciprocidad andina." In *Reciprocidad e intercambio en los Andes,* edited by Giorgio Alberti and Enrique Mayer, pp. 37–65. Perú Problema no. 12. Lima: Instituto de Estudios Peruanos.
1977   "Tenencia y control comunal de la tierra: Caso de Laraos (Yayos)." *Cuadernos* 24–25: 59–72.
1985   "Production Zones." In *Andean Ecology and Civilization,* edited by Shozo Masuda, Izumi Shimada, and Craig Morris, pp. 45–84. Tokyo: University of Tokyo Press.

McCown, Theodore D.
1945   *Pre-Incaic Huamachuco.* University of California Publications in American Archaeology and Ethnology, vol. 39, no. 4. Berkeley: University of California Press.

Meddens, Frank M.
1985   "The Chicha/Soras Valley during the Middle Horizon: Provincial Aspects of Huari." Ph.D. dissertation. University of London.
1991   "A Provincial Perspective on Huari Organization Viewed from the Chicha/Soras Valley." In *Huari Administrative Structure: Prehistoric Monumental Architecture and State Government,* edited by William H. Isbell and Gordon E. McEwan, pp. 215–231. Washington, D.C.: Dumbarton Oaks.

Mena, Cristóbal de
[1534] 1967   "La conquista del Perú, 1534." In *Las relaciones primitivas de la conquista del Perú,* edited by R. Porras Barrenechea, pp. 79–101. Lima: Instituto Raúl Porras Barrenechea, Universidad Nacional Mayor de San Marcos.

Menzel, Dorothy
1959   "The Inca Occupation of the South Coast of Peru." *Southwestern Journal of Anthropology* 15(2): 125–142.

Millones, Luis
1971   "Las informaciones de Cristóbal de Albornoz: Documentos para el estudio del Taki Onqoy." Sondeos no. 79. Cuernavaca, Mexico: Centro Intercultural de Documentación.
1990   *El retorno de las huacas: Estudios y documentos sobre el Taki Onqoy, siglo XVI.* Lima: Instituto de Estudios Peruanos.

Molinié-Fioravanti, Antoinette
1986 "The Andean Community Today." In *Anthropological History of Andean Polities*, edited by John V. Murra, Nathan Wachtel, and Jacques Revel, pp. 342–358. London: Cambridge University Press.

Moore, Henrietta
1988 *Space, Text, and Gender*. London: Cambridge University Press.

Morales Chocano, Daniel
1979 "Prospección arqueológica en Tacabamba." In *Arqueología Peruana*, edited by Ramiro Matos Mendieta, pp. 49–63. Lima: Universidad Nacional Mayor de San Marcos con la Comisión para Intercambio Educativo entre Los Estados Unidos y el Perú.

Morris, Craig
1974 "Reconstructing Patterns of Non-agricultural Production in the Inca Economy: Archaeology and Documents in Institutional Analysis." In *The Reconstruction of Complex Societies: An Archaeological Symposium*, edited by Charlotte Moore, pp. 49–60. Chicago: American School of Oriental Research.
1982 "The Infrastructure of Inka Control in the Peruvian Central Highlands." In *The Inca and Aztec States*, edited by George A. Collier, Renato I. Rosaldo, and John D. Wirth, pp. 153–171. New York: Academic Press.
1992 "The Technology of Highland Inka Food Storage." In *Inka Storage Systems*, edited by Terry Y. LeVine, pp. 237–258. Norman: University of Oklahoma Press.

Morris, Craig, and Donald E. Thompson
1985 *Huánuco Pampa: An Inca City and Its Hinterland*. London: Thames and Hudson.

Morris, Craig, and Adriana von Hagen
1993 *The Inka Empire and Its Origins*. New York: Abbeville Press.

Moseley, Michael E.
1975 *The Maritime Foundations of Andean Civilization*. Menlo Park, Calif.: Cummings.
1978 "An Empirical Approach to Prehistoric Agrarian Collapse: The Case of the Moche Valley, Peru." In *Social and Technological Management in Dry Lands, Past and Present, Indigenous and Imposed*, edited by Nancy Gonzales, pp. 9–43. Selected Symposia, 10. New York: American Association for the Advancement of Science.
1992 *The Incas and Their Ancestors: The Archaeology of Peru*. London: Thames and Hudson.

Muñoz Ovalle, Ivan
   1993            "Spatial Dimensions of Complementary Resource Utilization at Acha-2 and San Lorenzo." In *Domestic Architecture, Ethnicity, and Complementarity in the South-Central Andes*, edited by Mark S. Aldenderfer, pp. 94–102. Iowa City: University of Iowa Press.

Murra, John V.
   1960            "Rite and Crop in the Inca State." In *Culture in History*, edited by Stanley Diamond, pp. 393–407. New York: Columbia University Press.

   1964            "Una apreciación etnológica de la visita." In *Visita hecha a la provincia de Chucuito por Garci Diez de San Miguel en 1567*, edited by John V. Murra, pp. 421–444. Documentos regionales para la Etnología y Etnohistoria andinas, vol. 1. Lima: Ediciones de la Casa de la Cultura del Perú.

   1967            "La visita de los Chupachu como fuente etnológica." In *Iñigo Ortiz de Zuñiga, visita de la provincia de León de Huánuco en 1562*, edited by John V. Murra, pp. 381–406. Huánuco: Universidad Hermilio Valdizán.

   1968            "An Aymara Kingdom in 1567." *Ethnohistory* 15: 115–151.

   1972            "El 'control vertical' de un máximo de pisos ecológicos en la economía de las sociedades andinas." In *Iñigo Ortiz de Zuñiga, visita de la provincia de León de Huánuco en 1562*, edited by John V. Murra, pp. 429–476. Huánuco: Universidad Hermilio Valdizán.

   1975a          "El torno a la estructura política de los Inka." In *Formaciones económicas y políticas del mundo andino*, edited by John V. Murra, pp. 23–44. Lima: Instituto de Estudios Peruanos.

   1975b          *Formaciones económicas y políticas del mundo andino.* Lima: Instituto de Estudios Peruanos.

   1980            *The Economic Organization of the Inka State.* Greenwich, Conn.: JAI Press.

   1982            "The Mit'a Obligations of the Ethnic Groups in the Inka State." In *The Inca and Aztec States, 1400–1800*, edited by George A. Collier, Renato I. Rosaldo, and John D. Wirth, pp. 237–262. New York: Academic Press.

   1985a          " 'El archipiélago vertical' Revisited." In *Andean Ecology and Civilization*, edited by Shozo Masuda, Izumi Shimada, and Craig Morris, pp. 3–14. Tokyo: University of Tokyo Press.

   1985b          "The Limits and Limitations of the 'Vertical Archipelago' in the Andes." In *Andean Ecology and Civilization*, edited by Shozo Masuda, Izumi Shimada, and Craig Morris, pp. 15–20. Tokyo: University of Tokyo Press.

Murra, John V., and Nathan Wachtel
1986     "Introduction." In *Anthropological History of Andean Polities*, edited by John V. Murra, Nathan Wachtel, and Jacques Revel, pp. 1–8. Cambridge: Cambridge University Press.

Murra, John V., Nathan Wachtel, and Jacques Revel, eds.
1986     *Anthropological History of Andean Polities*. Cambridge: Cambridge University Press.

Nagel, Thomas
1986     *The View from Nowhere*. Oxford: Oxford University Press.

Navarro del Aguila, Victor
1943     "Los Pukullos de Huayanay." *Revista del Museo Nacional* 12(1): 97–107.

Netherly, Patricia
1977     "Local Level Lords on the North Coast of Peru." Ph.D. dissertation. Cornell University.
1990     "Out of Many, One: The Organization of the North Coast Polities." In *The Northern Dynasties: Kingship and Statecraft in Chimor*, edited by Michael E. Moseley and Alana Cordy-Collins, pp. 461–487. Washington, D.C.: Dumbarton Oaks Research Library and Collection.

Niles, Susan
1987     *Callachaca: Style and Status in an Inca Community*. Iowa City: University of Iowa Press.
1993     "The Provinces in the Heartland: Stylistic Variation and Architectural Innovation near Inca Cuzco." In *Provincial Inca: Archaeological and Ethnohistorical Assessment of the Impact of the Inca State*, edited by Michael A. Malpass, pp. 145–176. Iowa City: University of Iowa Press.

Nordenskiöld, Erland
1906     *Arkeologiska Undersökningar I: Perus Och Bolivias Gränstraker 1904–1905. Svenska Vetenskapsakademiens Handlingar* 42(2).

Noriega, Carlos G.
1935     "Jatun Mallka." *Revista del Museo Nacional* 4(1): 105–110.
1937     "Ciudadelas chullparias de los Wankas." *Revista del Museo Nacional* 6(1): 43–51.

O'Brien, Jay, and William Roseberry, eds.
1991     *Golden Ages, Dark Ages: Imagining the Past in Anthropology and History*. Berkeley: University of California Press.

O'Brien, Michael J., and Thomas D. Holland
    1992           "The Role of Adaptation in Archaeological Explanation." *American Antiquity* 57(1): 36–59.

Orlove, Benjamin
    1977a         "Inequality among Peasants: The Forms and Uses of Reciprocal Exchange in Andean Peru." In *Peasant Livelihood: Studies in Economic Anthropology and Cultural Ecology*, edited by Rhoda Halperin and James Dow, pp. 201–226. New York: St. Martin's Press.
    1977b         "Integration through Production: The Use of Zonation in Espinar." *American Ethnologist* 4: 84–101.

Ortiz de Zuñiga, Iñigo
    [1562] 1967    *Visita de la provincia León de Huánuco en 1562*. 2
    & 1972           vols. Huánuco: Universidad Nacional Hermilio Valdizán.

Ortloff, Charles, and Alan Kolata
    1993           "Climate and Collapse: Agro-Ecological Perspectives on the Decline of the Tiwanaku State." *Journal of Archaeological Science* 20(2): 195–222.

Owen, Bruce D., and Marilyn A. Norconk
    1987           "Appendix 1." In *Archaeological Field Research in the Upper Mantaro, Peru, 1982–1983*, edited by Timothy Earle, Terence D'Altroy, Christine Hastorf, Catherine Scott, Cathy Costin, Glenn Russell, and Elsie Sandefur, pp. 107–123. Monograph 28, Institute of Archaeology. Los Angeles: University of California, Los Angeles.

Painter, Michael
    1991           "Re-Creating Peasant Economy in Southern Peru." In *Golden Ages, Dark Ages: Imagining the Past in Anthropology and History*, edited by Jay O'Brien and William Roseberry, pp. 89–106. Berkeley: University of California Press.

Parsons, Jeffrey R., and Charles M. Hastings
    1988           "The Late Intermediate Period." In *Peruvian Prehistory*, edited by Richard W. Keatinge, pp. 190–229. Cambridge: Cambridge University Press.

Parsons, Jeffrey R., Charles M. Hastings, and Ramiro M. Matos
    n.d.            "Prehispanic Settlement Patterns in the Upper Mantaro and Tarma Drainages, Depto. de Junín, Peru, vol. 1: The Tarma and Chinchaycocha Regions." Manuscript in preparation, University of Michigan.

Patterson, Thomas C.
    1987           "Tribes, Chiefdoms and Kingdoms in the Inca Empire." In *Power Relations and State Formation*, edited by Thomas C. Patterson and Christine Ward Gailey, pp. 117–127. Washington, D.C.: American Anthropological Association.

| | |
|---|---|
| 1991 | *The Inca Empire: The Formation and Disintegration of a Pre-Capitalist State.* New York: Berg Publishers. |

Pease, Franklin
    1965    "Causas religiosas de la guerra entre el Cusco y Quito." *Historia y Cultura* 1(1): 127–136.

Pérez Bocanegra, Juan
    1631    *Ritual formulario e institución de curas, para administrar a los naturales de este Reyno los sanctos sacramentos* . . . Lima: n.p.

Pizarro, Pedro
    [1571] 1917    *Descubrimiento y conquista del Perú.* Colección de libros y documentos referentes a la historia del Perú, vol. 6. Lima: Sanmartí.
    [1571] 1921    *Relations of the Discovery and Conquest of the Kingdoms of Peru.* Translated into English and annotated by Philip Ainsworth Means. New York: Cortes Society.
    [1571] 1978    *Relación del descubrimiento y conquista del Perú.* Lima: Pontificia Universidad Católica del Perú.

Platt, Tristan
    1982a    *Estado boliviano y ayllu andino.* Lima: Instituto de Estudios Peruanos.
    1982b    "The Role of the Ayllu in the Reproduction of the Petty Commodity Regime in Northern Potosí." In *Ecology and Exchange in the Andes,* edited by David Lehmann, pp. 27–69. Cambridge: Cambridge University Press.

Polanyi, Karl
    1944    *The Great Transformation.* New York: Reinhart.
    1957    "The Economy as Instituted Process." In *Trade and Markets in Early Empires,* edited by Karl Polanyi, Conrad M. Arensberg, and Harry W. Pearson, pp. 243–270. New York: Free Press.
    1959    "Anthropology and Economic Theory." In *Readings in Anthropology,* vol. 2, edited by M. Fried. New York: Crowell.

Polanyi, Karl, Conrad M. Arensberg, and Harry W. Pearson, eds.
    1957    *Trade and Markets in Early Empires.* New York: Free Press.

Poma, Huaman
    [1615] 1978    *Letter to a King: A Peruvian Chief's Account of Life under the Incas and under Spanish Rule.* Edited, arranged, and translated by Christopher Dilke. New York: E. P. Dutton.

Ponce Sanginés, Carlos
    1959a    "Investigaciones arqueológicas en Salla." *Notas de Arqueología Boliviana* 1(1): 1–29.
    1959b    "Las tumbas de adobe de Totora." *Khana* 33–34: 1–23.
    1962    "Fechas radiocarbónicas." Unpublished manuscript. La Paz: Centro de Investigaciones Arqueológicos en Tiwanaku.

Portugal Ortiz, Max
1985 "Informe de la prospección arqueologíca efectuada en la provincia Camacho del departamento de La Paz (primera parte)." *Arqueología Boliviana* 2: 17–28.
1988 "Informe de la prospección a Pacajes." *Arqueología Boliviana* 3: 109–117.

Protzen, Jean-Pierre
1993 *Inca Architecture and Construction at Ollantaytambo*. Oxford: Oxford University Press.

Quilter, Jeffrey
1989 *Life and Death at Paloma: Society and Mortuary Practices in a Preceramic Peruvian Village*. Iowa City: University of Iowa Press.

Rabinow, Paul
1977 *Reflections on Fieldwork in Morocco*. Los Angeles: University of California Press.

Raimondi, Antonio
1873 *El departamento de Ancachs y sus riquezas minerales*. Lima: Imprenta de "El Nación" por Pedro Lira.
1874 *El Perú*, vol. 1, *Parte preliminar*. Lima: Imprenta del Estado.

Rappaport, Joanne
1988 "History and Everyday Life in the Colombian Andes." *Man* 23(4): 718–739.
1990 *The Politics of Memory: Native Historical Interpretation in the Colombian Andes*. Cambridge: Cambridge University Press.
1992 "Reinterpreted Traditions: The Heraldry of Ethnic Militancy in the Colombian Andes." In *Andean Cosmologies through Time: Persistence and Emergence*, edited by Robert Dover, Katherine Seibold, and John McDowell, pp. 202–228. Bloomington: Indiana University Press.
1994 *Cumbe Reborn: An Andean Ethnography of History*. Chicago: University of Chicago Press.

Rasnake, Roger N.
1988 *Domination and Cultural Resistance: Authority and Power among an Andean People*. Durham and London: Duke University Press.

Reichert, Raphael X.
1977 "The Recuay Ceramic Style—A Re-evaluation." Ph.D. dissertation, University of California, Los Angeles. Ann Arbor: University Microfilms.

Reichlen, Henry, and Paule Reichlen
[1947] 1985 "Reconocimientos arqueológicos en los Andes de Caja-

marca." In *Historia de Cajamarca: I Arqueología*, edited by Fernando Silva Santisteban, Waldemar Espinoza Soriano, and Rogger Ravines, pp. 29–65. Cajamarca: Instituto Nacional de Cultura, Perú.

Relph, Edward
1976  *Place and Placelessness*. London: Pion.

Reyna, Stephen P.
1994  "Literary Anthropology and the Case against Science." *Man* 29: 555–581.

Riddell, Francis A., and Dorothy Menzel
1954  "Archaeological Investigations at Quebrada de la Vaca, Chala, Peru." Unpublished report. Sacramento: California Institute of Peruvian Studies.

Rivera, Mario A.
1991  "The Prehistory of Northern Chile: A Synthesis." *Journal of World Prehistory* 5(1): 1–47.
1995  "The Preceramic Chinchorro Mummy Complex of Northern Chile: Context, Style and Purpose." In *Tombs for the Living: Andean Mortuary Practices*, edited by Tom D. Dillehay, pp. 43–77. Washington, D.C.: Dumbarton Oaks.

Rivera Casanova, Claudia
1989  "Las torres funerarias de Viscachani." *Textos Antropológicos: Revista de la Carrera de Antropología-Arqueología* (Universidad Mayor San Andrés) 1(1): 79–92.

Rodman, Margaret C.
1985  "Contemporary Custom: Redefining Domestic Space in Longana, Vanuata." *Ethnology* 24(4): 269–279.
1992  "Empowering Place: Multilocality and Multivocality." *American Anthropologist* 94(3): 640–656.

Rosaldo, Renato
1989  *Culture and Truth: The Remaking of Social Analysis*. Boston: Beacon Press.

Roscoe, Paul B.
1995  "The Perils of 'Positivism' in Cultural Anthropology." *American Anthropologist* 97(3): 492–504.

Roseberry, William
1989  *Anthropologies and Histories*. New Brunswick and London: Rutgers University Press.

Roseberry, William, and Jay O'Brien
1991  "Introduction." In *Golden Ages, Dark Ages: Imagining the Past in Anthropology and History*, edited by Jay O'Brien and William Roseberry, pp. 1–18. Berkeley, Los Angeles, Oxford: University of California Press.

Rostworowski de Diez Canseco, María
1970a    "El Repartimiento de doña Beatriz Coya en el valle de Yucay." *Revista Historia y Cultura* 4: 153–267.
1970b    "Mercaderes del valle de Chincha en la época prehispánica: Un documento y unos comentarios." *Revista Española de Antropología Americana* (Madrid) 5: 135–177.
1975     "Pescadores, artesanos y mercaderes costeños en el Perú prehispánico." *Revista del Museo Nacional* (Lima) 41: 311–349.
1977     *Etnia y sociedad: Costa peruana prehispánica.* Lima: Instituto de Estudios Peruanos.
1978     *Señoríos indígenas de Lima y Canta.* Lima: Instituto de Estudios Peruanos.
1981a    "La voz 'Parcialidad' en su contexto en los siglos XVI y XVII." In *Etnohistoria y antropología andina,* edited by Amalia Casenelli, Marcia Koth de Paredes, and Mariana Mould de Pease, pp. 35–45. Lima: Museo Nacional de Historia.
1981b    *Recursos naturales renovables y pesca: Siglos XVI y XVII.* Lima: Instituto de Estudios Peruanos.
1988     *Conflicts over Coca Fields in XVIth-Century Peru.* Memoirs of the Museum of Anthropology, no. 21. Ann Arbor: University of Michigan.

Rowe, John H.
1945     "Absolute Chronology in the Andean Area." *American Antiquity* 10: 135–151.
1946     "Inca Culture at the Time of the Spanish Conquest." In *Handbook of South American Indians,* vol. 2, *The Andean Civilizations,* edited by Julian Steward, pp. 183–330. Washington, D.C.: Smithsonian Institution.
1948     "The Kingdom of Chimor." *Acta Americana* 6(1–2): 26–59.
1953     "Inference and Analogy in Archaeology." In *An Appraisal of Anthropology Today,* edited by Sol Tax, L. C. Eiseley, Irving Rouse, and C. F. Voegelin, pp. 252–253. Chicago: University of Chicago Press.
1957     "The Incas under Spanish Colonial Institutions." *Hispanic American Historical Review* 35: 155–199.
1960     "The Origin of Creator Worship among the Incas." In *Culture in History,* edited by Stanley Diamond, pp. 408–429. New York: Columbia University Press.
1962     "Stages and Periods in Archaeological Interpretation." *Southwestern Journal of Anthropology* 18(1): 1–27.
1967     "What Kind of a Settlement Was Inca Cuzco?" *Ñawpa Pacha* 5: 59–76.

| | |
|---|---|
| 1979 | "An Account of the Shrines of Ancient Cuzco." *Ñawpa Pacha* 17: 1–80. |
| 1985a | "La constitutión Inca del Cuzco." *Histórica* (Lima) 9(1): 35–73. |
| 1985b | "Probanza de los Incas nietos de conquistadores." *Histórica* (Lima) 9(2): 193–245. |
| 1987 | "Machu Pijchu a la luz de documentos de siglo XVI." *Kuntur* 4 (March–April): 12–20. |
| 1990 | "Machu Picchu a la luz de documentos de siglo XVI." *Histórica* (Lima) 14(1): 139–154. |
| 1995 | "Behavior and Belief in Ancient Peruvian Mortuary Practice." In *Tombs for the Living: Andean Mortuary Practices*, edited by Tom D. Dillehay, pp. 27–41. Washington, D.C.: Dumbarton Oaks. |

Rowe, John H., and Dorothy Menzel
| | |
|---|---|
| 1967 | "Introduction." In *Peruvian Archaeology*, edited by John H. Rowe and Dorothy Menzel, pp. v–x. Palo Alto: Peek Publications. |

Ruiz Estrada, Arturo
| | |
|---|---|
| 1978 | "Exploraciones arqueológicas en Cabanillas: Puno." In *El hombre y la cultura andina: III Congreso Peruano*, vol. 2, edited by Ramiro Matos, pp. 791–806. Lima: JERM. |
| 1983 | "Reconocimientos arqueológicos en Huiñaj, Huancavelica." *Boletín del Museo Nacional de Antropología y Arqueología* (Lima) 8: 37–39. |

Rydén, Stig
| | |
|---|---|
| 1947 | *Archaeological Researches in the Highlands of Bolivia*. Göteborg: Elanders Boktryckeri Akiebolag. |
| 1957 | *Andean Excavations I: The Tiahuanaco Era East of Lake Titicaca*. Monograph series no. 4. Stockholm: Ethnographical Museum of Sweden. |
| 1959 | *Andean Excavations I: Tupuraya and Cayhuasi: Two Tiahuanaco Sites*. Monograph series no. 6. Stockholm: Ethnographical Museum of Sweden. |

Sahlins, Marshall
| | |
|---|---|
| 1958 | *Social Stratification in Polynesia*. Seattle: University of Washington Press. |
| 1972 | *Stone Age Economics*. Chicago: Aldine. |
| 1981 | *Historical Metaphors and Mythical Realities: Structure in the Early History of the Sandwich Islands Kingdom*. Ann Arbor: University of Michigan Press. |
| 1985 | *Islands of History*. Chicago: University of Chicago Press. |

Salmon, Merrilee H.
| | |
|---|---|
| 1982 | *Philosophy and Archaeology*. New York: Academic Press. |

Salomon, Frank
 1982 "Andean Ethnology in the 1970's: A Retrospective." *Latin American Research Review* 17(1): 75–128.
 1987 "Ancestor Cults and Resistance to the State in Arequipa, ca. 1748–1754." In *Resistance, Rebellion, and Consciousness in the Andean Peasant World: Eighteenth to Twentieth Centuries*, edited by Steve J. Stern, pp. 148–165. Madison: University of Wisconsin.
 1991 "Introductory Essay: The Huarochirí Manuscript." In *The Huarochirí Manuscript*, edited by Frank Salomon and George L. Urioste, pp. 1–38. Austin: University of Texas Press.
 1995 "The Beautiful Grandparents: Andean Ancestor Shrines and Mortuary Ritual as Seen through Colonial Records." In *Tombs for the Living: Andean Mortuary Practices*, edited by Tom Dillehay, pp. 315–353. Washington, D.C.: Dumbarton Oaks.

Salomon, Frank, and George L. Urioste, eds.
 1991 *The Huarochirí Manuscript*. Austin: University of Texas Press.

Sánchez, Rodrigo
 1982 "The Andean Economic System and Capitalism." In *Ecology and Exchange in the Andes*, edited by David Lehmann, pp. 157–190. Cambridge: Cambridge University Press.

Sanderson, Stephen K.
 1990 *Social Evolutionism: A Critical History*. Cambridge, Mass.: Basil Blackwell.

Santacruz Pachacuti Yamqui Salcamaygua, Joan de
 [1613] 1950 "Relación de antigüedades de Este Reyno del Perú." In *Tres relaciones de antigüedades peruanas* (reproduction edition), edited by Marcos Jimenes de la Espada, pp. 207–281. Asunción: Guaranía.

Sarmiento de Gamboa, Pedro
 [1572] 1907 *History of the Incas*. Cambridge: Hakluyt Society.
 [1572] 1965 *Historia Indica*. Edited by C. Saenz de Santa María. Vol. 135, 189–279. Madrid: Biblioteca de Autores Españoles.

Savoy, Gene
 1970 *Antisuyo: The Search for the Lost Cities of the Amazon*. New York: Simon and Schuster.

Schaedel, Richard
 1948 "Stone Sculpture in the Callejón de Huaylas." In *A Reappraisal of Peruvian Archaeology*, edited by Wendell C. Bennett, pp. 66–79. Memoirs, no. 4. Menasha, Wisc.: Society for American Archaeology.

| | |
|---|---|
| 1952 | "An Analysis of Central Andean Stone Sculpture." Ph.D. dissertation. Yale University. |

Schreiber, Katharina J.
| | |
|---|---|
| 1992 | *Wari Imperialism in Middle Horizon Peru.* Anthropological Papers of the Museum of Anthropology no. 87. Ann Arbor: University of Michigan. |
| 1993 | "The Inca Occupation of the Province of Andamarca Lucanas, Peru." In *Provincial Inca: Archaeological and Ethnohistorical Assessment of the Impact of the Inca State,* edited by Michael A. Malpass, pp. 77–116. Iowa City: University of Iowa Press. |

Schrire, Carmel
| | |
|---|---|
| 1980 | "An Inquiry into the Evolutionary Status and Apparent Identity of San Hunter-Gatherers." *Human Ecology* 8: 9–32. |
| 1984 | "Wild Surmises on Savage Thoughts." In *Past and Present in Hunter-Gatherer Studies,* edited by Carmel Schrire, pp. 1–25. New York: Academic Press. |

Schuster, Angela
| | |
|---|---|
| 1992 | "Inside the Royal Tombs of the Moche." *Archaeology* 45(6): 30–37. |

Service, Elman R.
| | |
|---|---|
| 1962 | *Primitive Social Organization.* New York: Random House. |
| 1975 | *Origins of the State and Civilization.* New York: Norton and Co. |

Shady, Ruth, and Hermilio Rosas
| | |
|---|---|
| 1976 | *Enterramientos en chullpas de Chota (Cajamarca).* Investigaciones de campo no. 1. Lima: Museo Nacional de Antropología y Arqueología. |

Shanks, Michael
| | |
|---|---|
| 1994 | "Archaeology: Theories, Themes and Experience (a Dialogue between Iain Mackenzie and Michael Shanks)." In *Archaeological Theory: Progress or Posture,* edited by Iain M. Mackenzie, pp. 19–40. Aldershot: Avebury. |

Shanks, Michael, and Christopher Tilley
| | |
|---|---|
| 1982 | "Ideology, Symbolic Power, and Ritual Communication: A Reinterpretation of Neolithic Mortuary Practices." In *Symbolic and Structural Archaeology,* edited by Ian Hodder, pp. 129–154. Cambridge: Cambridge University Press. |
| 1987a | *Re-constructing Archaeology.* Cambridge: Cambridge University Press. |
| 1987b | *Social Theory and Archaeology.* Albuquerque: University of New Mexico Press. |
| 1989 | "Archaeology into the 1990s" and "Questions Rather than |

Answers: Reply to Comments on Archaeology into the 1990s." *Norwegian Archaeological Review* 22(1): 1–14 and 42–54.

Sherbondy, Jeanette E.
1982    "The Canal System of Hanan Cuzco." Ph.D. dissertation. University of Illinois.
1992    "Water Ideology in Inca Ethnogenesis." In *Andean Cosmologies through Time: Persistence and Emergence*, edited by Robert V. H. Dover, Katherine E. Seibold, and John H. McDowell, pp. 46–66. Bloomington: Indiana University Press.

Silverblatt, Irene
1987    *Moon, Sun, and Witches*. Princeton: Princeton University Press.

Silverman, Helaine
1993    *Cahuachi in the Ancient Nasca World*. Iowa City: University of Iowa Press.

Smith, John W.
1978    "The Recuay Culture: A Reconstruction Based on Artistic Motifs." Ph.D. dissertation. University of Texas at Austin. Ann Arbor: University Microfilms.

Solway, Jacqueline S., and Richard B. Lee
1990    "Foragers: Genuine or Spurious? Situating the Kalahari San in History." *Current Anthropology* 31(2): 109–146.

Soriano Infante, Augusto
1939    "Algo sobre la arqueología de Ancash." *Actas y trabajos científicos del 27 Congreso Internacional de Americanistas* (Lima, 1939) 1: 473–483.

Spaulding, Karen
1984    *Huarochirí: An Andean Society under Inca and Spanish Rule*. Stanford: Stanford University Press.

Spector, Janet D.
1993    *What the Awl Means: Feminist Archaeology at a Wahpenton Dakota Village*. St. Paul: Minnesota Historical Society Press.

Squier, E. George
1877    *Peru: Incidents of Travel and Explorations in the Land of the Incas*. New York: Harper and Brothers.

Stahl, Ann B.
1993    "Concepts of Time and Approaches to Analogical Reasoning in Historical Perspective." *American Antiquity* 58(2): 235–260.
1994    "Change and Continuity in the Banda Area, Ghana: The Direct Historical Approach." *Journal of Field Archaeology* 21(2): 181–203.

Stanish, Charles
1989a         "An Archaeological Evaluation of an Ethnohistoric Model in Moquegua." In *Ecology, Settlement and History in the Osmore Drainage, Peru*, edited by Don S. Rice, Charles Stanish, and Philip Scarr, pp. 303–320. International Series 545 (II). Oxford: British Archaeological Reports.
1989b         "Household Archaeology: Testing Models of Zonal Complementarity in the South-Central Andes." *American Anthropologist* 91(1): 7–24.
1992          *Ancient Andean Political Economy*. Austin: University of Texas Press.

Stanish, Charles, Edmundo de la Vega, and Kirk L. Frye
1993          "Domestic Architecture on Lupaqa Area Sites in the Department of Puno." In *Domestic Architecture, Ethnicity, and Complementarity in the South-Central Andes*, edited by Mark S. Aldenderfer, pp. 83–93. Iowa City: University of Iowa Press.

Starn, Orin
1991          "Missing the Revolution: Anthropology and the War in Peru." *Cultural Anthropology* 6(1): 63–91.
1994          "Rethinking the Politics of Anthropology: The Case of the Andes." *Current Anthropology* 35(1): 13–38.

Stern, Steve J.
1982          *Peru's Indian Peoples and the Challenge of Spanish Conquest: Huamanga to 1640*. Madison: University of Wisconsin Press.

Steward, Julian H.
1942          "The Direct Historical Approach to Archaeology." *American Antiquity* 7(4): 337–343.
1946          *Handbook of South American Indians*, vol. 2, *The Andean Civilizations*. Bureau of American Ethnology, Bulletin 143. Washington, D.C.: Smithsonian Institution.
1955          *Theory of Culture Change*. Urbana: University of Illinois Press.

Stocking, George W.
1968          *Race, Culture and Evolution*. New York: Free Press.
1974          "Introduction: The Basic Assumptions of Boasian Anthropology." In *A Franz Boas Reader: The Shaping of American Anthropology 1883–1911*, edited by George W. Stocking, pp. 1–20. Chicago: University of Chicago Press.

Strong, William Duncan
1933          "The Plains Culture Area in Light of Archaeology." *American Anthropologist* 35(2): 271–287.
1935          "An Introduction to Nebraska Archaeology." *Miscella-

*neous Collection*, vol. 93, no. 10. Washington, D.C.: Smithsonian.

1936     "Anthropological Theory and Archaeological Fact." In *Essays in Anthropology*, edited by Robert H. Lowie, pp. 359–369. Berkeley: University of California Press.

Strong, William Duncan, and John M. Corbett

1943     "A Ceramic Sequence at Pachacamac." In *Archeological Studies in Peru 1941–1942*, edited by William Duncan Strong, Gordon R. Willey, and J. M. Corbett, pp. 27–121. New York: Columbia University Press.

Tello, Julio C.

1929     *Antiguo Perú: Primera época*. Lima: Comisión Organizadora del Segundo Congreso Sudamericano de Turismo.

1940     "Actas de sesiones del Comité Regional de Lima." *Revista Chasqui* 1(2): 65.

1985     "Los sepulcros de Yanakancha." In *Historia de Cajamarca: I Arqueología*, edited by Fernando Silva Santisteban, Waldemar Espinoza Soriano, and Rogger Ravines, pp. 177–178. Cajamarca: Instituto Nacional de Cultura, Perú.

Terada, Kazuo

1979     *Excavations at La Pampa in the North Highlands of Peru*. Tokyo: University of Tokyo Press.

Terada, Kazuo, and Ryozo Matsumoto

1985     "Sobre la cronología de la tradición Cajamarca." In *Historia de Cajamarca: I Arqueología*, edited by Fernando Silva Santisteban, Waldemar Espinoza Soriano, and Rogger Ravines, pp. 67–92. Cajamarca: Instituto Nacional de Cultura, Perú.

Thomas, Nicholas

1992     "The Inversion of Tradition." *American Ethnologist* 19(2): 213–232.

Thompson, Donald E.

1968     "Huanuco, Peru: A Survey of a Province of the Inca Empire." *Archaeology* 21(3): 174–181.

1973a     "Archaeological Investigations in the Eastern Andes of Northern Peru." *Proceedings of the 40th International Congress of Americanists* (Rome, 1972) 1: 363–369.

1973b     "Investigaciones arqueológicas en los Andes orientales del norte del Perú." *Revista del Museo Nacional* 39: 117–125.

Thompson, Donald E., and Rogger Ravines

1973     "Tinyash: A Prehispanic Village in the Andean Puna." *Archaeology* 26(3): 94–100.

Thompson, John B.

1990     *Ideology and Modern Culture*. Stanford: Stanford University Press.

Tilley, Christopher
    1989            "Archaeology as Socio-political Action in the Present." In *Critical Traditions in Contemporary Archaeology*, edited by Valerie Pinsky and Alison Wylie, pp. 104–116. Cambridge: Cambridge University Press.
    1993            *Interpretative Archaeology*. Oxford: Berg.
    1994            *A Phenomenology of Landscape*. Oxford: Berg.
Titu Cusi Yupanqui, Inca Diego de Castro
    [1570] 1973    *Relación de la conquista del Perú*. Lima: La Biblioteca Universitaria.
Topic, John R.
    1986            "A Sequence of Monumental Architecture from Huamachuco." In *Perspectives on Andean Prehistory and Protohistory*, edited by Daniel H. Sandweiss and D. Peter Kvietok, pp. 63–83. Ithaca: Latin American Studies Program, Cornell University.
    1991            "Huari and Huamachuco." In *Huari Administrative Structure: Prehistoric Monumental Architecture and State Government*, edited by William H. Isbell and Gordon E. McEwan, pp. 141–164. Washington, D.C.: Dumbarton Oaks.
Topic, John R., and Theresa L. Topic
    1983a           "Coast-Highland Relations in Northern Peru: Some Observations on Routes, Networks, and Scales of Interaction." In *Civilization in the Ancient Americas*, edited by Richard M. Leventhal and Alan L. Kolata, pp. 237–260. Albuquerque: University of New Mexico Press.
    1983b           *Huamachuco Archaeological Project: Preliminary Report on the Second Season, June–August 1982*. Peterborough, Ontario: Trent University Department of Anthropology.
    1985            "El Horizonte Medio en Huamachuco." *Revista del Museo Nacional* (Lima) 47: 13–52.
Topic, Theresa L.
    1991            "The Middle Horizon in Northern Peru." In *Huari Administrative Structure: Prehistoric Monumental Architecture and State Government*, edited by William H. Isbell and Gordon E. McEwan, pp. 233–246. Washington, D.C.: Dumbarton Oaks.
Topic, Theresa L., and John R. Topic
    1984            *Huamachuco Archaeological Project: Preliminary Report on the Third Season, June–August 1983*. Occasional Papers in Anthropology no. 1. Peterborough, Ontario: Trent University.
    1987            *Huamachuco Archaeological Project: Preliminary Report*

Trigger, Bruce G.
                                    on the 1986 Field Season. Occasional Papers in Anthropology no. 4. Peterborough, Ontario: Trent University.

1982     "Ethnoarchaeology: Some Cautionary Considerations." In *Ethnography by Archaeologists*, edited by E. Tooker, pp. 1–9. Washington, D.C.: American Ethnological Society.

1985     *Natives and Newcomers: Canada's "Heroic Age" Reconsidered*. Kingston, Ontario: McGill-Queen's University Press.

1989     *A History of Archaeological Thought*. Cambridge: Cambridge University Press.

1991     "Distinguished Lecture in Archaeology: Constraint and Freedom—A New Synthesis for Archaeological Explanation." *American Anthropologist* 93(3): 551–569.

Trimborn, Hermann

1988     *Quebrada de la Vaca: Investigaciones arqueológicas en el sur medio del Perú*. Lima: Pontificia Universidad Católica del Perú, Fondo Editorial.

Tringham, Ruth

1978     "Experimentation, Ethnoarchaeology and the Leapfrogs in Archaeological Methodology." In *Explorations in Ethnoarchaeology*, edited by Richard A. Gould, pp. 169–199. Albuquerque: University of New Mexico Press.

Tschopik, Marion H.

1946     *Some Notes on the Archaeology of the Department of Puno, Peru*. Papers of the Peabody Museum of American Archaeology and Ethnology, 27. Cambridge, Mass.: Harvard University.

Tschudi, Johann Jakob von

1847     *Travels in Peru during the Years 1838–1842*. Translated by Thomasina Ross. New York: Wiley and Putnam.

Tyler, Stephen A.

1986     "Post-modern Ethnography: From Document of the Occult to Occult Document." In *Writing Culture: The Poetics and Politics of Ethnography*, edited by James Clifford and George E. Marcus, pp. 122–140. Los Angeles: University of California Press.

Uhle, Max

[1903] 1991     *Pachacamac: A Reprint of the 1903 Edition by Max Uhle, and Pachacamac Archaeology: Retrospect and Prospect: an Introduction by Izumi Shimada*. Philadelphia: University Museum of Archaeology and Anthropology, University of Pennsylvania.

Upham, Steadman
1987 "The Tyranny of Ethnographic Analogy in Southwestern Archaeology." In *Coasts, Plains, and Deserts: Essays in Honor of Reynold J. Ruppé*, edited by Sylvia W. Gaines, pp. 265–279. Anthropological Research Papers no. 38. Tempe: Arizona State University.

Urton, Gary
1981 *At the Crossroads of the Earth and the Sky: An Andean Cosmology*. Austin: University of Texas Press.
1984 "Chutas: El espacio de la práctica social en Pacariqtampo, Perú." *Revista Andina* 3: 7–56.
1988 "La arquitectura pública como texto social: La historia de un muro de adobe en Pacariqtampo, Perú (1915–1985)." *Revista Andina* 6(1): 225–263.
1990 *The History of a Myth: Pacariqtambo and the Origin of the Inkas*. Austin: University of Texas Press.
1992 "Communalism and Differentiation in an Andean Community." In *Andean Cosmologies through Time: Persistence and Emergence*, edited by Robert V. H. Dover, Katherine E. Seibold, and John H. McDowell, pp. 229–266. Bloomington: Indiana University Press.

Valcárcel, Luis E.
1925 *Del ayllu al imperio*. Lima: Garcilaso.
1964 *Historia del Perú antiguo*. 3 vols. Buenos Aires: Eudeba.

Vansina, Jan
1989 "Deep-down Time: Political Tradition in Central Africa." *History in Africa* 16: 341–362.

Varón Gabai, Rafael
1990 "El Taki Onqoy: Las raíces andinas de un fenómeno colonial." In *El retorno de las huacas: Estudios y documentos sobre el Taki Onqoy, siglo XVI*, edited by Luis Millones, pp. 331–405. Lima: Instituto de Estudios Peruanos.

Vásquez, Emilio
1937a "Las ruinas de Kachakacha." *Revista del Museo Nacional* 6(1): 52–57.
1937b "Sillustani: Una metrópoli pre-incáica." *Revista del Museo Nacional* 6(2): 278–290.
1939 "Ruinas arqueológicas de Puno, Quitimpu." *Revista del Museo Nacional* 8(1): 117–123.
1940 "Itinerario arqueológico del Kollao." *Revista del Museo Nacional* 9(1): 143–150.

Vásquez, Emilio, Alfredo Carpio, and Daniel E. Velasco
1935 "Informe sobre las ruinas de Tankatanka." *Revista del Museo Nacional* 4(2): 240–244.

Villar Córdova, Pedro E.
1923 "Las ruinas de la provincia de Canta." *Inca* 1(1): 1–23.
1930 "Arqueología del departamento de Lima: Caracteres fundamentales de la arquitectura andina costeña." In *Proceedings of the 23rd International Congress of Americanists, New York, 1928*, pp. 351–382.
[1935] 1982 *Las culturas pre-hispánicas del departamento de Lima.* Lima: Atusparia.

Wachtel, Nathan
1977 *The Vision of the Vanquished: The Spanish Conquest of Peru through Indian Eyes, 1530–1570.* New York: Harper and Row.

Wachtel, Nathan, ed.
1973 *Sociedad e ideología: Ensayos de historia y antropología andinas.* Lima: Instituto de Estudios Peruanos.

Wallerstein, Immanuel
1974 *The Modern World System*, vol. 1. New York: Academic Press.

Watson, Patty Jo
1978a *Archaeological Ethnography in Western Iran.* Viking Fund Publication in Anthropology 57. Tucson: University of Arizona Press.
1978b "The Idea of Ethnoarchaeology: Notes and Comments." In *Ethnoarchaeology*, edited by Carol Kramer, pp. 277–287. New York: Columbia University Press.
1982 "Review of R. Gould's Living Archaeology." *American Antiquity* 47: 445–448.
1986 "Archaeological Interpretation." In *American Archaeology Past and Future*, edited by David J. Meltzer, Don D. Fowler, and Jeremy A. Sabloff, pp. 439–457. Washington, D.C.: Smithsonian Institution Press.

Watson, Patty Jo, Stephen A. LeBlanc, and Charles Redman
1971 *Explanation in Archaeology: An Explicitly Scientific Approach.* New York: Columbia University Press.

Wegner, Steven A.
1988 "Cultura Recuay." Huaráz: Museo Arqueológico de Ancash.

Wheatley, Paul
1971 *The Pivot of the Four Quarters: A Preliminary Enquiry into the Origins and Character of the Ancient Chinese City.* Chicago: Aldine.

Wiener, Charles
1880 *Pérou et Bolivie: Récit de voyage suivi d'études archéologiques et ethnographiques et de notes sur l'écriture et*

*les langues des populations indiennes.* Paris: Librairie Hachette et Cie.

Wightman, Ann M.
1981 "Diego Vasicuio: Native Priest." In *Struggle and Survival in Colonial America,* edited by David G. Sweet and Gary B. Nash, pp. 38–48. Berkeley: University of California Press.

Willey, Gordon R.
1971 *An Introduction to American Archaeology,* vol. 2: *South America.* Englewood Cliffs, N.J.: Prentice-Hall.

Wilmsen, Edward N., and James B. Denbow
1990 "Paradigmatic History of San-Speaking Peoples and Current Attempts at Revision." *Current Anthropology* 31(5): 489–524.

Wilson, Peter J.
1988 *The Domestication of the Human Species.* New Haven: Yale University Press.

Wolf, Eric
1982 *Europe and the People without History.* Berkeley: University of California Press.

Wylie, Alison
1981 "Positivism and the New Archaeology." Ph.D. dissertation. State University of New York at Binghamton.
1985 "The Reaction against Analogy." In *Advances in Archaeological Method and Theory,* 8, edited by Michael Schiffer, pp. 63–111. New York: Academic Press.
1988 "'Simple' Analogy and the Role of Relevance Assumptions: Implications of Archaeological Practice." *International Studies in the Philosophy of Science* 2: 134–150.
1989 "The Interpretive Dilemma." In *Critical Traditions in Contemporary Archaeology: Essays in the Philosophy, History and Socio-Politics of Archaeology,* edited by Valerie Pinsky and Alison Wylie, pp. 18–27. Cambridge: Cambridge University Press.
1991 "Gender Theory and the Archaeological Record: Why Is There No Archaeology of Gender?" In *Engendering Archaeology: Women in Prehistory,* edited by Joan M. Gero and Margaret W. Conkey, pp. 31–54. Cambridge, Mass.: Basil Blackwell.
1992a "The Interplay of Evidential Constraints and Political Interests: Recent Archaeological Work on Gender." *American Antiquity* 57(1): 15–34.
1992b "On 'Heavily Decomposing Red Herrings': Scientific Method in Archaeology and the Ladening of Evidence

with Theory." In *Metaarchaeology: Reflections by Archaeologists and Philosophers*, edited by Lester Embree, pp. 269–288. Boston: Kluwer Academic Publishers.

Zaki, Andrzej
1978     "El mausoleo de piedra con decoración plástica in Santa Cruz: Callejón de Huaylas." In *El hombre y la cultura andina: III Congreso Peruano*, vol. 2, edited by Ramiro Matos, pp. 443–448. Lima: JERM.

Zuidema, R. Tom
1964     *The Ceque System of Cuzco: The Social Organization of the Capital of the Inca*. Leiden: Brill.
1973     "Kinship and Ancestor Cult in Three Peruvian Communities: Hernández Principe's Account of 1622." *Boletín del Instituto Francés de Estudios Andinos* 2(1): 16–33.
1974–1976     "La imagen del sol y la huaca de Susupuquio en el sistema astronómico de los Incas en el Cuzco." *Journal de la Société des Américanistes* 63: 199–230.
1977     "The Inca Kinship System: A New Theoretical View." In *Andean Kinship and Marriage*, edited by Ralph Bolton and Enrique Mayer, pp. 248–292. Special Publication no. 7. Washington, D.C.: American Anthropological Association.
1981     "Inca Observations of the Solar and Lunar Passages through Zenith and Anti-Zenith at Cuzco." In *Archaeoastronomy in the Americas*, edited by Ray A. Williamson, pp. 319–342. Los Altos: Ballena Press.
1982a     "Catachillay: The Role of the Pleiades and of the Southern Cross and Alpha and Beta Centauri in the Calendar of the Incas." In *Ethnoastronomy and Archaeoastronomy in the American Tropics*, edited by Anthony F. Aveni and Gary Urton, pp. 204–229. Annals 385. New York: New York Academy of Sciences.
1982b     "The Sidereal-Lunar Calendar of the Incas." In *New World Archaeoastronomy*, edited by Anthony F. Aveni, pp. 59–107. Cambridge: Cambridge University Press.
1986     "Inka Dynasty and Irrigation: Another Look at Andean Concepts of History." In *Anthropological History of Andean Polities*, edited by John V. Murra, Nathan Wachtel, and Jacques Revel, pp. 177–200. Cambridge: Cambridge University Press.
1989a     "At the King's Table: Inca Concepts of Sacred Kingship in Cuzco." *History and Anthropology* 4: 249–274.
1989b     "The Moieties of Cuzco." In *The Attraction of Opposites: Thought and Society in the Dualistic Mode*, edited by David Maybury-Lewis and Uri Almagor, pp. 255–275. Ann Arbor: University of Michigan Press.

1989c  "What Does the Equation 'Mother's Brother = Wife's Father' Mean in Inca Social Organization?" In *Variant Views: Five Lectures from the Perspective of the "Leiden Tradition" in Cultural Anthropology*, edited by Henri J. M. Claessen, pp. 132–156. Vakgroep Culturele Antropologie en Sociologie der Niet-Westerse Samenlevingen (ICA Publicatie: no. 84). Leiden: Universiteit van Leiden, Faculteit der Sociale Wetenschappen.

1990a  "Ceques and Chapas: An Andean Pattern of Land Partition in the Modern Valley of Cuzco." In *Circumpacifica: Festschrift für Thomas S. Barthel*, edited by Bruno Illius and Matthias Laubscher, pp. 627–643. Bern: Sonderdruck.

1990b  "Dynastic Structures in Andean Culture." In *The Northern Dynasties: Kingship and Statecraft in Chimor*, edited by Michael E. Moseley and Alana Cordy-Collins, pp. 489–537. Washington, D.C.: Dumbarton Oaks Research Library and Collection.

1990c  *Inca Civilization in Cuzco*. Austin: University of Texas Press.

1992  "Inca Cosmos in Andean Context: From the Perspective of the Capac Raymi Camay Quilla Feast Celebrating the December Solstice in Cuzco." In *Andean Cosmologies through Time: Persistence and Emergence*, edited by Robert V. H. Dover, Katherine E. Seibold, and John H. McDowell, pp. 17–45. Bloomington: Indiana University Press.

Zuidema, R. Tom, and Ulpiano Quispe

1968  "A Visit to God: The Account and Interpretation of a Religious Experience in the Peruvian Community of Choque-Huarkaya." *Bijdragen* 124(1): 22–39.

# AUTHOR INDEX

Agnew, John A., 14, 138, 219
Albarracin-Jordan, Juan V., 300
Alberti, Giorgio, 23, 117
Albó, Javier, 12, 27, 133
Aldenderfer, Mark S., 315
Aldunate del Solar, Carlos, 155, 169
Allen, Catherine J., 12, 13, 23
Alva, Walter, 35, 144, 239, 240, 242, 272, 293, 295
Amat Olazábal, Hernán, 191, 201, 203
Appaduri, Arjun, 14
Arellano López, Jorge, 168, 171
Arnold, Dean E., 24
Arriaga, Father Pablo José de, 33, 80, 81, 84, 92, 148
Ascher, Robert, 5, 10, 107, 305, 308
Avila, Francisco de, 74, 79, 80, 81–85, 90
Ayca Gallegos, Oscar, 161, 165, 166

Balboa, Miguel Cabello de, 59
Banco Popular del Perú, 233, 240, 251, 255
Bandelier, Aldoph F., 162
Barrett, John C., 11, 108
Bastien, Joseph, 12, 107
Bauer, Brian S., 68
Benavides C., Mario, 28, 184
Bengtsson, Lisbet, 174, 175, 178, 180
Bennett, Wendell C., 18, 163, 198, 201
Bermann, Mark, 166
Bertonio, P. Ludvico, 132, 162
Binford, Lewis R., 5, 7, 104, 305
Bloch, Maurice, 138
Bonavia, Duccio, 182
Bonnier, Elisabeth, 190, 202
Bradby, Barbara, 119, 120
Brewster-Wray, Christine, 28, 185
Bruhns, Karen O., 233
Brumfiel, Elisabeth M., 103, 108
Brush, Stephen B., 23, 95, 98, 117
Burger, Richard, 20, 217

Carmichael, Patrick H., 122, 146
Carneiro, Robert, 11, 104, 105, 107
Casnelli, Amalia, 12
Castillo, Luis Jaime, 35, 144, 293
Castro-Klarén, Sara, 72
Castro Rojas, Victoria, 155, 169
Chayanov, Aleksandr V., 118
Cieza de León, Pedro, 139–142, 146, 163
Clark, John Grahame D., 305
Clifford, James, 6, 306
Cobo, Father Bernabé, 32, 42, 47, 48, 49, 50, 52, 53, 56, 67, 83, 84, 112, 141–143, 151–152, 155, 161, 162, 163
Collins, Jane L., 26, 131
Colvin, Howard, 15, 16
Combs-Schilling, M. Elaine, 219
Conkey, Margaret W., 3, 4
Cook, Anita G., 187
Corbett, John M., 146
Cordy-Collins, Alana, 241–242
Crapanzano, Vincent, 6

D'Altroy, Terence N., 112, 189–190
D'Andrade, Roy, 6
Denbow, James B., 12
Diez de San Miguel, Garci, 117
di Leonardo, Michaela, 3
Dillehay, Tom D., 15, 107, 315
Donnan, Christopher B., 35, 144, 234, 239, 240, 242, 272, 293, 295
Doyle, Mary E., 80, 85, 88, 92, 93
Duncan, James S., 14, 15, 138, 219
Dunnell, R., 104, 308
Duviols, Pierre, 48, 57, 75, 80, 84, 93, 118

Earle, Timothy, 190
Engels, Frederick, 9
Espinoza Soriano, Waldemar, 13, 97, 99

Fabian, Johannes, 22, 105
Feld, Stephen, 15
Ferguson, James, 14, 15
Figueroa, Adolfo, 119, 120

Fischer, Michael, 6
Fleming, Stuart, 146
Flornoy, Bertrand, 190, 202
Fonseca Martel, César, 23, 95, 117, 119, 123
Fried, Morton H., 105, 120, 309
Friedrich, Paul, 106
Fritz, John, 7
Fuenzalida, Fernando, 82

Gad, G., 15
Gailey, Christine Ward, 291–293, 296
Gasparini, Graziano, 165
Geertz, Clifford, 4, 6
Gell, Alfred, 15, 22
Gero, Joan M., 109, 122, 310, 312
Giddens, Anthony, 11, 108
Gillet, David W., 12, 97
Godelier, Maurice, 106
Gould, Richard A., 305
Grieder, Terence, 147, 232–234, 251
Guaman Poma de Ayala, Felipe, 41–45, 47, 139–140, 142, 148, 163
Guillén Guillén, Eduardo, 55, 56
Gupta, Akhil, 14, 15

Hanson, Allan, 12
Harris, Olivia, 12, 27, 133
Hastings, Charles M., 189, 294
Hastorf, Christine A., 109
Hemming, John, 58, 272
Heredia Zavala, María de los Angeles, 169, 171
Hernández Príncipe, R., 80, 86
Herzfeld, Michael, 27, 124
Hobsbawm, Eric, 12
Hodder, Ian, 7, 8, 12, 108, 305
Holdsworth, D., 15
Holguín, Diego G., 95, 131
Holland, Thomas D., 308
Howell, Carol J., 152–154
Hrdlička, Ales, 150, 192, 193, 194, 268
Huertas V., Lorenzo, 85, 91
Huffman, Thomas N., 306

Hyslop, John, 152, 164, 165, 166, 168, 174, 214

Isbell, Billie Jean, 12, 13, 22, 23, 118, 119
Isbell, William H., 23, 28, 110, 150, 163, 182, 185, 187, 202, 215, 220, 223, 228, 230, 232, 233, 238, 241, 244, 249, 252, 256, 259, 264, 266, 267, 268, 277, 278, 280, 299

Jakobsen, Jan, 210
Jiménez de la Espada, D. Marcos, 162
Julien, Catherine J., 128
Julien, Daniel, 205

Karp, Ivan, 15
Kato, Yasutake, 147, 198, 290
Kauffman Doig, Federico, 210, 212
King, Anthony, 14, 138
Klein, Herbert S., 12, 98
Kleindienst, Maxine R., 305
Kolata, Alan L., 113, 122, 137, 289, 300, 310, 313
Kosso, Peter, 8
Kuljis Meruvia, Danilo, 168, 171
Kuper, Adam, 6

Lagos, Maria L., 98
Lapiner, Alan, 233, 239, 242, 251, 255
Larson, Brooke, 128, 130
Lavallée, Danièle, 232, 233, 242, 272
Leacock, Eleanor, 9
LeBlanc, Stephen A., 7
Lee, Richard, 11
Leone, Mark P., 7
Long, Norman, 108
Lothrop, Samuel K., 254
Lounsbury, Floyd G., 273
Lumbreras, Luis G., 18, 181, 182, 187, 232
Lyon, Patricia, 242

MacCormack, Sabine, 46, 47
MacGaffey, Wyatt, 12
Mackey, Carol J., 35, 144, 293

Marcus, George, 6
Marcus, Joyce, 13, 95, 306
Margolies, Luise, 165
Markus, Thomas A., 15, 138, 219
Marx, Karl, 22
Masuda, Shozo, 18
Mathews, James E., 300
Matos, Ramiro M., 189
Matsumoto, Ryozo, 258
Mayer, Enrique, 23, 95, 117
McClelland, Donna, 35, 144, 234
McCown, Theodore D., 205
Meddens, Frank M., 183, 300
Mena, Cristóbal de, 40
Menzel, Dorthy, 18, 21, 152, 153, 154
Millones, Luis, 72
Molinié-Fioravanti, Antoinette, 12, 129
Moore, Henrietta, 4
Morales, Luis de, 54
Morales Chocano, Daniel, 211, 215, 218, 226
Morris, Craig, 18, 112, 314
Moseley, Michael E., 2, 34, 106, 113, 121, 122, 137, 289, 294, 300, 310, 312, 313
Muñoz Ovalle, Ivan, 23, 315
Murra, John V., 13, 22, 95, 106, 113, 114, 115, 116, 127, 129, 303–304, 310–311

Navarro del Aguila, Victor, 181
Netherly, Patricia, 126, 306
Niles, Susan, 175, 178
Norconk, Marilyn A., 190
Nordenskiöld, Erland, 165
Noriega, Carlos G., 189

O'Brien, Jay, 108, 109, 124, 125, 308
Orgóñez, Rodrigo, 54
Orlove, Benjamin, 23, 95, 117, 118, 119, 120
Ortiz de Zuñiga, Iñigo, 114, 117
Ortloff, Charles, 310
Owen, Bruce D., 190

Painter, Michael, 26, 131
Parsons, Jeffrey R., 189
Patterson, Thomas C., 109, 113, 114, 146, 291–294, 314
Pease, Franklin, 67, 98
Pérez Bocanegra, Juan, 273, 274, 275, 276, 279
Pizarro, Francisco, 38, 62, 272
Pizarro, Hernando, 146
Pizarro, Pedro, 38, 40, 41, 42, 45
Platt, Tristan, 13, 133
Plog, Fred, 7
Polanyi, Karl, 22, 105, 117, 119
Poma de Ayala, Felipe Guaman. *See* Guaman Poma de Ayala, Felipe
Ponce Sanginés, Carlos, 169, 170, 171, 173
Portugal Ortiz, Max, 169, 171
Protzen, Jean-Pierre, 179

Quilter, Jeffrey, 138
Quispe, Ulpiano, 118

Rabinow, Paul, 6
Raimondi, Antonio, 162, 195–197
Ranger, Terence O., 12
Rappaport, Joanne, 97
Rasnake, Roger N., 13, 27, 133
Ravines, Rogger, 190, 191, 202
Redman, Charles, 7
Reichlen, Henry and Paule, 258
Relph, Edward, 15
Reyna, Stephen P., 6, 8
Riddell, Francis A., 152, 153, 154
Rivera, Mario A., 138
Rivera Casanova, Claudia, 169, 171
Rodman, Margaret C., 15
Rosaldo, Renato, 6
Rosas, Hermilio, 28, 215, 218, 226, 229, 234, 235, 239, 242, 243, 245, 259, 272
Roscoe, Paul B., 6
Roseberry, William, 108, 109, 124–126, 290, 308
Rostworowski de Diez Canseco, María, 13, 89, 95, 99, 118
Rowe, John H., 13, 18, 20, 32, 40,

47, 52, 58, 59, 62, 63, 67, 68, 69, 96, 97, 114, 147, 160, 178, 273, 305
Ruiz Estrada, Arturo, 182
Rydén, Stig, 160, 162, 165, 166, 169, 171

Sahlins, Marshall, 105, 119
Salomon, Frank, 13, 28, 75, 78, 79, 80, 85, 88, 89, 90, 93–97, 100, 137, 192, 194, 272, 273
Sánchez, Rodrigo, 119, 120
Sanderson, Stephen K., 5, 104, 105
Santo Tomás, Domingo de, 99
Sarmiento de Gamboa, Pedro, 55, 57
Savoy, Gene, 210
Schaedel, Richard, 158, 226, 250
Scheper-Hughes, Nancy, 6
Schjellerup, Inge, 209
Schreiber, Katharina J., 181, 187
Schrire, Carmel, 12, 305
Schuster, Angela, 144
Segovia, Bartolmé de, 46
Service, Elman R., 105
Sevillano, el (Mena, Cristóbal de), 40
Shady, Ruth, 28, 215, 218, 226, 229, 234, 235, 239, 242, 243, 245, 259, 272
Shanks, Michael, 7, 8
Sherbondy, Jeanette E., 13, 23, 65, 70, 99, 128
Shimada, Izumi, 18
Silva, Jorge, 13, 95
Silverblatt, Irene, 32, 49
Silverman, Helaine, 122, 137, 146
Solway, Jacqueline S., 11
Soriano Infante, Augusto, 202
Spaulding, Karen, 13, 75–76, 90, 93, 94, 100, 129, 130
Spector, Janet D., 3
Squier, E. George, 161, 162, 169, 171, 174, 179, 180, 206, 288
Stahl, Ann B., 11, 110, 304, 305, 306, 307, 308, 314, 315
Stanish, Charles, 122–123, 166, 315
Starn, Orin, 108, 126
Stern, Steve J., 128

Steward, Julian H., 11, 16, 104, 305
Stocking, George W., 5, 104
Strong, William Duncan, 5, 10, 146, 305

Tello, Julio C., 150, 206, 226, 258, 259
Terada, Kazuo, 197, 198, 258, 299
Thomas, Nicholas, 12
Thompson, Donald E., 113, 190, 191, 202, 209, 314
Thompson, John B., 106
Tilley, Christopher, 4, 7, 8
Toledo, Francisco, 56, 57, 75, 88, 128, 129, 148, 192
Topic, John R., 28, 201, 204, 205, 209, 216, 268, 270, 286, 294, 299
Topic, Theresa L., 28, 204, 205, 216, 268, 270, 286, 294
Trigger, Bruce G., 12, 305
Trimborn, Hermann, 152, 153
Tringham, Ruth, 305
Tschopik, Marion H., 162, 165
Tschudi, Johann Jakob von, 161, 188–189
Tyler, Stephen A., 6

Uhle, Max, 146
Upham, Steadman, 306, 314
Urioste, George L., 75, 78, 88, 90, 93, 192, 272, 273
Urton, Gary, 13, 23, 67, 109, 132

Valcárcel, Luis E., 13, 118
Vansina, Jan, 306
Varón Gabai, Rafael, 72
Villar Córdova, Pedro E., 162, 194, 195, 268

Wachtel, Nathan, 23, 129, 303–304, 307, 310–311
Watson, Patty Jo, 7, 12, 305
Wheatley, Paul, 313
Wiener, Charles, 207
Wightman, Ann M., 78
Willey, Gordon R., 18
Wilmsen, Edward N., 12

Wilson, Peter J., 15
Wolf, Eric, 126
Wylie, Alison, 3, 5, 7, 8, 12, 137, 304, 314

Zaki, Andrzej, 202
Zuidema, R. Tom, 13, 22, 23, 32, 52, 53, 62, 63, 65, 66, 67, 68, 69, 86, 97, 116, 117, 118, 272, 273, 275, 276, 279, 302, 306

GEOGRAPHICAL INDEX
(Boldface page numbers indicate references to maps, figures, or photos.)

Amazonia, 5, 10, 215
Anantoko, **164**, 168–169, 171
Ancash, 202
Andahuaylas, 72
Andamarca, 181
Andamayo, 235
Andes, 1–3, 10, 12, 14, 16, **17**, 18, 20, 127, 129, 132, 134, 307
Antisuyu, **39**, 44–45, 53, 65
Apacara, 181
Apurímac, 96, **178**, 182
Arequipa, **39**, 73, 174
Argentina, 1, 16, 18, **19**, 21, 160
Atoccpampa, 26
Ayacucho, 24–27, 36, 72, 150, **178**, 181–189, 185, 213, 214, 215, 287, 199, 300

Bambamarca, 205, 234
Bolivia, 1, 16, **19**, 20, 21, 27, 36, 122, 132, 133, 160, 161

Cahuachi, 137, **145**, 146, 147
Cajamarca, **39**, 40, 46, 62, 73, 198, 205, 206, 208, 209, **210**, 213, 215, 217, 218, 258, 287, 290, 294, 295
Cajatambo, 72, **73**, 86, 90, 192
Calca, 60
Callejón de Huaylas, 26, 28, 36, **39**, 73, 158, 195, 196, **197**, 198, 199,
202, 203, 204, 205, 208, 215, 240, 252, 268, 283, 287, 294, 295, 299
Cañete Valley, 117
Canta, **178**, 194, **206**, 216
Cara, 198
Caráz, **178**, 196, **206**, 216
Carhuarazo Mountains, 74
Carhuarazo Valley, **178**, 181, 187
Casma Valley, 293
Celendín, **206**, 209, **216**
Cerro Amaru, 204, 205, **206**, 207, **216**, 268, 286
Cerro Wallio de Cachicadan, 205
Chachapoyas, 209
Chaco, 61
Chamaya Basin, 215, 217
Chancas, **39**, 50, 72
Chancay River, 194, 195
Charcas, 72, **73**
Chetilla, 217, 218, 221, 225, 226, 228, 229, 242–243, 244, 245, **246**, 247, 260, 264, 267
Chiar Jakke, **164**, 171, **172**
Chicha Soras Valley, **178**, 183
Chile, 1, 16, 20, 21, 35, 36, 61, 138
Chillón River, 194, 195
Chimborazo Mountain, 74
Chinchaysuyu, **39**, 43–44
Chota-Cutervo, 28, 36, 37, **206**, 213, 214, **216**, 217, 218, 219, **220**, 221, 222, 224, 226, 227, 229, 230, 232, 234, 238, 239, 242, 252, 257, 258–263, 267–271, 275, 279, 281, 282, 286, 287, 294, 295
Chotano River, 213, 215, 217, 218, 234
Chucuito, **164**
Chupachu region, **178**, **206**, 216
Chupacoto, **178**, 196, 198, **206**, 216
Churucancha, 229
Chuschi, 22, 26, 118
Cinco Cerros, **178**, 193
Cochabamba, 129–130, 166, 310
Colla, 140, 152
Collasuyu, **39**, 43, **44**, 65, 162, 288
ColoColo, **175**, **176**
Colombia, 18, 61, 233

Combayo, 205
Concha, 93
Condesuyu, **39, 45**
Condorcaga, **217**, 218, **223, 224,** 227, 229, **230–233, 235–237,** 242, 264, 267, 271
Cordillera Blanca, 195, 202
Coricancha, 48, 49, 50
Coro Coro, **164,** 171, **172**
Coyor, **206, 208, 216**
Cutervo River, 213, **217,** 218, 242, 245
Cutimbo, **164, 170, 171**
Cuzco, 31, 32, 34, 36, 38, 40, 45, 46, 48, 49, 52, 54, 55, 57–63, 65–70, 72, 73, 79, 80, 84, 86, 94, 98, 99, 100, 101, 113, 117, 134, 137, 140, 152, 174, 177, **178,** 179, 197, 206, 214, 264, 279, 285, 287, 300, 302, 312

Ecuador, 1, 18, 21, 133, 217

Guancos, 87

Haucaypata, 31, 38, 40, 46, 48
Honcopampa, 26, 28, **178, 202, 203, 206,** 208, 215, **216,** 298
Huachoc, 94
Huallaga Chulpas, **206, 216**
Huallaga River, 190, 212, 287
Huallanay, **145,** 150, **151, 178,** 181, 182
Huamachuco, 36, 204, 205, **207, 208,** 213, 217, 218, 268, 282, 286, 287
Huamanga, **73**
Huanacauri, 74, 84
Huancabamba River, 217
Huanca Sancos, **178,** 183
Huancavelica, 129, 182, 188
Huánuco, 22, 114
Huaráz, 196, 198, 202, 212, 250
Huari, 24, 28, **178,** 184, 185, 187, 188, 196, 215, 269, 287, 298, 299, 300; Chequ Wasi sector, 28, **185, 186,** 299; Moraduchayuq, 28

Huarochirí, 14, 30, 32–33, 36, **73,** 74, 75, 78, 79, 80, 81, 83, 88, 94, 98, 101, 134, 137–139, 143, **145,** 149, **178,** 192, **193,** 194, 195, 271–273, 285
Huaylas, 196
Huayllabamba, **178,** 202, **206, 216**

Ica Valley, 18, 20, 21

Jargampata, **178,** 187, 189, 302
Jatun Malka, **178,** 189, **216**
Jauja, 72, 90, 140, 188, 189
Jesús de Machaca, 160
Junín: Department, 188, 192, 195, 268, 269; Lake, **178,** 189, **206, 216**

Kanasa, **164,** 173
Kolketín, 206, **211**
Kotosh, 191
Kuntur Wasi, **145,** 147, 290, 291

La Pampa, 198
La Torre, **217,** 218, 229, 245–247, **248, 249, 251–253, 255–267,** 271, 272
Lima, 25, 69, 72, 74, 75, 78, 80, 82, 162, 163, 165
Llacsa Tambo, 88
Lucanas Region, 181
Lucre Basin, **178**
Lupaca Region, 166

Malcoamayo, **164, 167**
Mangas, 87
Mantaro River, **178,** 181, 192, 214
Mantaro Valley, 36, 189
Marañon River Valley, 36, 190, 191, 192, 202, **206,** 209, 212, 215, **216,** 217, 218, 222, 268, 269, 281, 287, 298, 299
Marcahuamachuco, 205, **208, 209**
Marca Putacum, 88

Negropampa, **217,** 218, 234–236,

238–241, 242, 250, 252, 253, 260, 271
Nuñoa, 175

Ocros, 86
Ollantaytambo, 39, 54, 175, 177, 178, 180, 197
Otuco, 87

Pacariqtambo, 132
Pachacamac, 74, 145, 146, 147
Pacopampa, 217, 257
Pajatén, 212
Pallasca, 204, 206
Paloma, 138, 139
Pampas River, 24, 178, 181–183
Paria Caca, 73, 83, 84, 88
Paruro, 68
Pashash, 145, 147
Paucartambo, 175, 177, 178, 179, 197
Peru, 1, 16, 18, 19, 20, 24, 27, 34, 35, 36, 78, 118, 122, 131, 132, 133, 140, 149, 150, 152, 161, 162, 204, 284, 287, 290, 293, 300, 312
Pirka Pirka, 206, 209, 216
Pisac, 178, 179
Piscobamba, 178, 195, 206, 216
Pomabamba, 178, 196, 206, 216
Poopó, Lake, 21, 39, 73, 145, 164, 169
Potosí, 129, 130
Pumacayan, 178, 196, 198, 206, 216
Puno, 27, 28

Quebrada de la Vaca, 35, 145, 152, 154, 155, 156, 159, 161, 164, 261, 262
Quinua, 24–26
Quiquijana, 60
Quito, 61

Rapayan, 178, 202, 206, 216, 268, 287
Río de la Plata, 61

Río Mauri, 168
Río Pampas, 24, 178, 181–183

Salla, 173
Salsipuedes, 206, 210, 212, 216
San Damián de Checa, 79, 88, 90
Sandia, 164, 174, 178
San José de Moro, 144, 145, 146, 213
San Pedro de Atacama, 39, 73, 169
Saqsamarca, 184
Sara-Sara, 74
Sarhua, 183
Shillacoto, 191
Shimbe, Lake, 217
Sihuas, 178, 195, 206, 216
Sillustani, 163, 164, 167, 168, 169
Sipán, 144, 145, 146, 213, 240, 242

Tablachaca Valley, 204
Tantamayo, 178, 190, 191, 202, 216, 268, 287
Tawantinsuyu, 58, 69, 163
Tinyash, 178, 190–191, 202, 206, 216, 268, 269, 287
Titicaca, Lake, 21, 39, 73, 74, 96, 145, 161, 163, 164, 166
Tiwanaku, 20, 74, 145, 147–148, 177, 300, 314
Toconce Site, 155, 164, 169, 175
Tornapampa, 178, 197–198, 202, 206, 216, 269, 299
Totocache, 42
Tumibamba, 67, 98

Uchumarca Valley, 209, 210, 268, 287
Urubamba, 59
Utcubamba, 206, 209, 212, 216, 268, 287

Ventanillas de Otusco, 205, 210
Vilcabamba River Valley, 56
Vilcanota-Cuzco drainage, 162
Viracochapampa, 299
Vitcos, 32, 39, 54, 56, 57, 72, 73

Wilkawain, 178, 198, **199**, **200**, 201, **206**, **216**

Yanacancha, **206**, 207, **216**
Yauyos, 73, 83, 88, 192, 195, 285
Yuncas, 73, 89, 90, 93

TOPICAL INDEX
(Boldface page numbers indicate references to maps, figures, or photos.)

actors as agents, 11–12, 34, 102, 108, 109, 124, 134, 301, 315
adaptation, 102, 126
adaptive addition of institutions, 37, 104, 106–107, 288
adobe, 169, 171–173, **172**
age area hypothesis, 284
*aguaciles,* 76
*alcaldes,* 76
*altiplano,* 21, 27, 152, 161, 162, 163–168, 173–174, 213, 288, 300
Altiplano Phase, 166, **167**
*amayata,* 162
ancestor mummies, 30, 31, 34–35, 56, 57–58, 67, 69, 70–71, 74, 77, 78, 83–84, 85, 90, 93, 134, 142, 148, 160, 191, 205, 214, 270, 285, 297
ancestors, 272; as *ayllu* founders, 33, 36, 64–65, 70, 81, 85, 86, 139; importance of, 45, 82, 99, 292; of the Inca, 48, 54–56, 63–64, 68, 69–70; mythical, 57, 60, 83, 86, 271–272; worship of, 28–29, 36, 56, 59, 136, 219
ancient *ayllu* hypothesis, 3, 10, 30, 34, 102, 108, 110–124, 134, 158, 288–289, 300, 301
Andean culture, 22, 34, 106, 312; and *ayllus,* 136; deep structure of, 110, 124, 290; defined, 17–18, 21; as ideal construct, 108, 113, 116–117, 126, 307, 313; and the Inca, 23–24; survival of, 23, 107

Andean cultures chronology, 18–20
Andean past, 103–104, 126, 306, 308
Andean religion, 29, 49–50, 74, 77–78, 80, 82, 83; and divination, 33, 51, 81
anthropological theory, 5–6
Antisuyu, 44–45, 53
archaeological record as text, 4, 219, 273
archaeological theory, 7–10; remains as support of, 1, 2, 3
Atahualpa, 46, 55, 59, 62, 67, 149, 272
*aya,* 41, 80. *See also* dead; mummies
*ayap llactan,* 44. *See also* mortuary monuments
*ayllu,* 22, 29, 62, 66, 76, 88, 119, 120–121, 125, 299, 309, 310; absence of, 146, 147, 148; and ancestor mummies, 30, 56, 84–85, 90, 91–92, 93, 218, 285, 286; antiquity of, 3, 30, 37, 101, 103, 121–122, 188, 191–192, 219, 282–283, 289, 294, 311, 315; archaeological correlates of, 136–139, 286; in Bolivia, 27, 132–133; contingent history of, 132, 136; defined, 98–99, 134–135, 136; development of, 117, 297, 298–299, 301; features of, 36–37, 99, 159, 218, 285, 297; and mortuary monuments, 14, 37, 108, 143, 158–159; nature of, 12–14, 30, 36, 83, 86–88, 94–95, 97, 99–100, 101, 116, 122, 128, 275–281, 290, 296–297; in Peru, 132, 133; ritual requirements, 139; source of change, 126–128, 128–131; universality of, 2–3, 115, 136, 289, 307
*ayni,* 24, 118–120, 122–123, 125, 131–132, 289, 308, 309, 310

Bolivian lowlands, 21
built environment, 14–16, 33, 54, 219

burial practices, 141; Andean coast, 159–160; Huari, 184–187; Kuntur Wasi, 147; Moche, 144–146; Pachacamac, 146
burial vaults, 43, 184–187, **185, 186.** See also mortuary monuments; open sepulcher

*cabildo,* 76
*capac hucha,* 86. See also ancestors; women
Capac Yupanqui, 55, 59
*cayan,* 96, 139, 148, 156, 192, 285
central coast, 21, 140–141
central highlands, 21, 188–191, 192
*ceques,* 48, 52, 53–54, 67–68
*chacpa,* 82. See also huaca
chambered shaft grave, 206, **211.** See also mortuary monuments; open sepulcher
*chanca,* 81, 84
Chancas, 60, 72
Chavín, **19,** 20, 234, 290
*chicha,* 41, 42, 92, 293–294, 314
Chimú, 312
Chinchaysuyu, 43, 53
*chullpa,* 27–29, 36, 195, 201, **203–205,** 208–210, 212, 213, 215, 273; and ancestor mummies, 30; dates for, 173–174; defined, 160–161, 286; distribution, 35–36, 163, 174–176, **178,** 180, **206, 217,** 218; origin of and other terms for, 160–163; possible architectural influences, 28, 215–216; proto-, 166; variations, 160–161, 163–174, **174,** 188, 192–195. See also mortuary monuments; open sepulcher
Chupachu, 117, 190
Chuquito-Inca, **165,** 166, **167, 168, 169, 170**
Collasuyu, 43–44, 162
Colonial Period, 21, 183
Condesuyu, 44
*conopas,* 81. See also huaca
construction of society, 138

contingent history, 34, 109, 126, 132, 134, 136, 158, 289–290, 296, 299, 301, 311, 315
Coricancha, 40, 48, 49, 60, 74
*corregidor de Indios,* 76
*corregimientos,* 128
critical archaeology, 7, 103
cultural adaptation, 110, 124
cultural continuity, 108, 124, 126
cultural evolution, 1, 11
cultural uniformitarianism, 10
culture change, 24, 25, 26
*cunchur,* 81, 84
*curi,* 81–82. See also huaca

Day of the Dead, 43
dead, 15–16, 40–45, 139; eating of, 44; historiographic model, 32, 58–62, 68, 70; structural model, 32, 62–67, 68, 70; worship of, 51, 80, 259
doorways, 155, 164, 170, 173, 175, 182, 183, 188, 190, 191, 195, 198, 222, 227, **228,** 231, 248, **250,** 261–263
*duhos,* 140

Early Horizon, **19,** 20, 137, 147, 290
Early Intermediate Period, **19,** 20, 28, 122, 137, 187, 198, 201, 204, 213, 232, 233–234, 254, 258, 269–270, 281, 283, 284, 287, 290, 293, 294, 295–296, 301, 314
ecological complementarity. See vertical ecological complementarity
economic specialization, 116, 118
ecosystems approach, 103
ethnicity, 43, 83, 87–88, 115, 127, 282, 292–293, 295, 310
ethnic kingdoms, 115, 117, 128, 129, 152, 166, 169, 171, 302
ethnographic analogy, 4–5, 10–11, 107–108, 303–308, 312
ethnographic present, 34, 132
ethnography, 23, 27, 34, 111–112, 116–117, 125

ethnohistory, 23, 34, 116, 125; Huarochirí, 30, 69–100; Inca Cuzco, 30, 38–68, 117
evolution, cultural, 1, 11
extirpation of idolatries, 33, 71–72, 74–75, 77, 78–80, 81, 83, 86, 90, 127, 142, 143, 148–149, 179, 271, 272, 285

*forasteros,* 130

gender bias, 32, 41. *See also* women
*guaugues,* 50, 51, 53, 55, 56–57, 64

*Handbook of South American Indians,* 16
*huaca,* 47, 52, 53–54, 67, 72, 74, 79, 81, 84–85, 271, 273, 298; capture of, 149
*huaca* cemetery, 35, 140–141, 143–148, 196, 213, 291, 298; at Cahuachi, 146–147; at Conchopata, 187
*huaca* pyramid, 294
Huallallo Caruincho, 89, 271, 272
Huanacauri, 54, 57, 84
Huaráz, 250
Huari, 19, 20–21, 22, 183–187, 269, 287, 298, 299–300, 301
Huarochirí Manuscript, 78–79, 80, 83, 84, 86, 88, 89–90, 93, 94, 97, 98, 111, 271
Huarpa, 187
Huascar, 55, 59, 61, 62, 67, 149
Huayna Capac, 40, 46, 54, 55, 56, 58, 59, 61, 62, 67, 69, 98
hypothesis testing, 31, 34, 103, 133–135, 215–216, 284, 288, 312

identity, 43, 83, 87–88, 93–94
Inca Paullu, 54, 55
Inca Raymi Quilla. *See* Inti Raimi
Inca Roca, 53, 55, 59
Incas, 13, 16, 19, 21, 23, 27, 30, 38–68, 69–71, 106, 219, 302, 310, 312; and Andean culture, 23–24; economy, 22, 106–107, 111, 112–113, 113–114, 153; funerary practices, 143; history, 59–62, 271; kings, 23, 31–32, 58, 113, 178, 292; kinship, 23, 31, 58, 63, 70, 279; political institutions, 111, 113–115; religion, 31–32, 46–54, 67, 84, 94, 113; use of the *ayllu,* 13, 61, 66, 115, 127–128, 159, 311–312
Initial Period, 19, 20, 120
Inti Raimi, 46–47, 54

kinship, 33, 36, 52, 57–58, 63, 97, 99, 101, 119, 213, 219, 273–281, **274, 277, 278, 280,** 282, 285–286, 291–292, 296–298
*kullpi,* 162–163, 165, 173, 187, 195, 258–259
*kuraka,* 86, 97, 115, 120–121, 122–123, 128, 129, 130–131, 272

landscape, 97–98, 138, 270–271
Late Horizon, 19, 21, 180, 182, 183, 188, 189–190, 209, 210, 288
Late Intermediate Period, 19, 20–21, 177, 178, 181, 182, 188, 189–190, 191, 198, 209, 210, 213, 287–288, 301, 314
*llacta,* 95–96, 97, 98, 192, 285
*llautos,* 42
Lloque Yupanqui, 55, 59
Lupaca, 117, 128, 152, 166

*machay,* 80, 93, 143, 178–179, 182, 188, 193. *See also* mortuary monuments; open sepulcher
*malquis,* 80, 84–85, 87, 90–91, 92, 96, 97, 98, 149. *See also* ancestor mummies; mummies
Manco Capac, 56, 57, 58, 59, 60, 68, 84
Manco Inca, 46, 54, 55, 59
Marxism, 106, 114
masonry, 153, 163–164, 169, 171–173, 179–180, 191, 194, 219–222, 227–228, 231, 236–

238, 243, 267–268
Mayta Capac, 55, 59
megalithic chambers, 28, **186,** 215–216, 269, 299. *See also* mortuary monuments; open sepulcher
mesothermal valleys, 21
Middle Horizon, **19,** 20–21, 177, 178, 183, 184, 187–188, 191, 198, 201, 204, 210, 213, 214–215, 270, 287, 294, 299–300, 301, 314
middle range theory, 123–124
migration, 24, 25, 88–89
*minka,* 24, 118–121, 122–123, 125, 131–132, 133, 289, 308, 309, 310
*mita,* 77, 129, 130, 310
Moche, **19,** 232, 233, 234, 239, 240, 241–242, 250, 254, 269–270, 271, 293–294, 310, 312
moieties, 61, 62, 65, 66
moon, 49, 54, 83, 233, 251
mortuary house, 28, 153–154, 155, 156, 161, 162, 169, 182, 188–189, 194, 209, 299
mortuary monuments, 22, 27, 28, 32, 33, 90–91, 142, 281; and *ayllus,* 14, 30, 34–35, 37, 77, 91–92, 134, 139, 148; in construction of culture, 14–15; destruction of, 196, 224–225, 229, 237–238, 259–261; distribution of, 30, 158, 206, 214; location on landscape, 141–142, 169–170; and spatial organization, 96–97. *See also cayan;* chambered shaft grave; *chullpa; huaca* cemetery; mortuary house; mortuary tower; niche tombs; open sepulcher; *pucullos;* open sepulcher
mortuary practices, 43–45, 80, 143
mortuary tower, 28, 142, 173, 190, 205, 243
mummies, 28–29, 187, 268; appearance of, 42, 46; collection and looting of, 149–150, 150–151, 183; in Cuzco, 38, 40, 45–46;

destruction of, 149, 259–261; feeding of, 40–41, 89, 138; Inca, 51, 54–56, 60, 62, 65, 67, 70, 71, 178; at Inti Raimi, 46–47; in non-*ayllu* societies, 138–139; political function of, 56, 60–61; treatment of, 38–40, 43, 49–50, 80, 82; worship of, 71–72, 74. *See also* ancestors; ancestor mummies

narrative, 8–9, 290, 312
niche tombs, 205–206, **210.** *See also* mortuary monuments; open sepulcher
non-Inca social organization, 71, 78, 93
north coast, 21
northern Andes, 21
north highlands, 21, 204–213

offerings, 41, 42, 43, 47, 48, 49, 52, 84, 85, 92, 101, 140, 141, 154, 180–181, 183, 188–189, 196, 204, 212, 299
open sepulcher, 30, 35, 93, 138, 156–157, 281, 299; architecture of, 22, 77, 153, 154, 156–157, **232,** 243–245, **244,** 247–248, **249;** auxiliary buildings, 153–154, 229; and *ayllus,* 143, 158–159, 191–192, 195, 204, 205, 210, 212–213, 214, 270, 281, 297; colonial descriptions of, 139–142; construction materials, 163, 169, 173, 182, 230, 235; courtyards of, 154, 180–181; described, 192–201, **193, 194, 197, 199, 200, 202,** 204–206, **207, 208,** 210, **212;** distribution of, 284, 287; formal attributes of, 35, 142, 148, 151–156; ideal, 219, **220, 221,** 227–229, **228,** 259–268, 279–281; interior treatment of, 153, 164, 165, 170, 173, 187, 188, 189, 191, 195, 201, 205, 209; number of bodies in, 153, 164, 169, 173, **177,**

181–182, 183, 189, 192–193, 204; shape of, 153, 163–164, 166–168, 169, 170, 173, 175–176, 181, 182, 188, 190, 191, 197–198; spatial organization, 169–170, 173, 174–175, **176**, 179–180, 181, 188–189, 190, 206, 209, 230–231, 234–235, 242–243, 264–267, 282; radiocarbon dates, 173, 176–178, 198, 204, 210, 270; relative dates, 181, 182–183, 187–192, 195, 204, 232–234, 258, 269–270, 287–288; variation in, 170, 175, 189, 190, 191, 193–195, 201, 202, 205–206, 209–210, 268–269, 284, 286–287

Pacajes, 171–173
*pachaca,* 128
Pachacuti, 54, 55, 56, 60, 61, 68
Pachamama, 49
paint, 171, 173, **175**, 179–180, 182, 183, 198, 229, 248–249
*panaca,* 31–32, 56, 61, 62, 65, 66, 67, 68, 70, 99, 100, 101, 128, 137, 178, 285, 292, 302
Paria Caca, 83, 90, 96, 271, 272
past, 3–6, 15, 21–29, 33, 60–61, 102
platforms, 153, 164, 171, 198, 229–230, 245, 263–265
postprocessualism, 34, 37, 103, 108–110; and contingent history, 136; and culture change, 109, 132, 291–292, 301
processualism, 1, 11, 34, 102, 103, 104–106, 158, 288–289, 296, 299, 308–311, 315; and the *ayllu,* 37, 121–122, 136, 300, 302; and social institutions, 11, 37, 106, 107, 121–122
psychic unity of humanity, 105, 109
*pucullos,* 41, **42**, 43, 45, 148
*pururaucas,* 50

Quishuarcancha, 48

ranked social institutions, 106
recent *ayllu* hypothesis, 3, 10, 30, 34, 102, 124–133, 134, 158, 301
*Reciprocidad e intercambio en los Andes peruanos,* 117
reciprocity, 119–120, 122–123
Recuay, 201, 232, 233, 251, 255, 269–270, 271
redistribution, 119–120, 122–123
*reducciones,* 75–76, 77, 78, 84, 88, 98, 128–129, 130, 192
*regidores,* 76
relative correspondence, 6, 8, 102
ritual, 31, 194, 205, 212, 219, 259, 273, 285, 293; calendars, 52, 65, 138; concentration of power, 5, 302; role of mummies in, 36, 43, 46, 92, 138–139, 182, 291, 296; secrecy of, 142–143
roofs, 153, 163, 169, 170–171, 173, 175, 181, 189, 190, 191, 195, 197, 201, 228–229

sarcophagi, 196, 284. *See also* mortuary monuments; open sepulcher
sculpture, 122, 156, 191, 196, 201, 202, 210, 212, 222–224, **223**, **224**, 226–227, 229, 231, 232–234, **233**, **237**, 238–242, **239**, **240**, **241**, 243, 248–257, **252**, **253**, **255**, **257**–265, 267–268, 271–273, 282, 286
sea, 49
Sendero Luminoso (Shining Path), 25
sequence of evolutionary stages, 105, 308, 309–310
Sinchi Roca, 56, 59
social institutions, 11, 106, 123
social organization, 101, 270, 284
social relations, 118
sources of error, 1, 32, 303–314
south coast, 21
south highlands, 21, 168–188

stars, 49, 83
stele, 256, **264**, **265**
*sucancas*, 48
sun, 46–47, 48, 57, 60, 83, 94, 96, 178
*suyu*, 115

Taki Onqoy, 72–74, 78, 298
Tembladera, 255
temple mausoleums, 32, **206–208**, 259. *See also* mortuary monuments; open sepulcher
temple tombs, 138, 139, 196, 201. *See also* mortuary monuments; open sepulcher
temporal inversion, 110, 112, 125–126
thunder, 49, 83
*Time and the Other*, 105
Titi Cusi Yupanqui, 54, 57
Tiwanaku culture, **19**, **20–21**, 22, 113–114, 147–148, 165–166, 173–174, 177, 214, 298, 300, 301, 302, 310, 312–313, 314
Topa Inca Yupanqui, 54, 59, 60, 61, 62, 149
tradition, 24–25, 74, 77, 109–110, 124–125, 219
Tupac Huallpa, 46

uniformitarianism, 10
universal stages of evolution, 123

*verquis*, 42
vertical ecological complementarity, 22–23, 95, 116, 117, 118, 309–310, 311, 314–315
Vicús, 233, 239, 240, 242, 251, 255, 269–270, 271
Viracocha, 47–48, 51, 89–90, 96
Viracocha Inca, 54, 55, 59

Wankarani, 122, 137
women, 32, 40, 41, 45, 46, 47, 53, 56, 63, 64, 65, 71, 79, 81, 86, 90, 97, 140, 141, 147, 169, 255

Yauyos culture, 32–33, 34, 51, 83–84, 88–89, 98, 192, 219, 285
Yawar Huaca, 55, 59
*yllapa*, 41

*zaramama*, 81

www.ingramcontent.com/pod-product-compliance
Lightning Source LLC
Chambersburg PA
CBHW030332240426
43661CB00052B/1603